THE ENLARGED
EUROPEAN UNION

IAN BARNES

AND

PAMELA M. BARNES

LONGMAN

LONDON AND NEW YORK

Longman Group UK Limited
Longman House, Burnt Mill,
Harlow, Essex CM20 2JE, England
and Associated Companies throughout the world

Published in the United States of America
by Longman Publishing, New York

First published 1995

ISBN 0 582 081157 PPR

British Library Cataloguing-in-Publication Data

A catalogue record for this book is
available from the British Library

Library of Congress Cataloging-in-Publication Data

Set by 7 in 10/12.5 Times
Produced through Longman Malaysia, PP

CONTENTS

CHAPTER 1

Introduction: towards the new Europe?

Table 1.1 From six to fifteen – the development of the European Union

Date	Steps on the road
April 1951	France, Germany, Italy, BENELUX sign the Treaty of Paris, which founds the European Coal and Steel Community
1952	European Coal and Steel Community begins to operate
March 1957	France, Germany, Italy, BENELUX sign the Treaties of Rome forming the European Economic Community and EURATOM
1958	The EEC and EURATOM come into being
1973	UK, Ireland and Denmark join
1981	Greece joins
1986	Spain and Portugal join
July 1987	The Single European Act is ratified
1991	Intergovernmental Conferences begin which lead to the signing and ratification of the Treaty on European Union
November 1993	The Treaty on European Union is ratified
1995	Austria, Sweden, Finland join the European Union
1996	Intergovernmental Conference begins to revise the Treaty on European Union

The European Union (EU) is not, nor has it ever been, a static organisation (see Table 1.1). Its history has been one of change and development, apart from a brief period of so-called Eurosclerosis in the 1980s. The pressure for change in the mid and late 1990s had its origin in the disintegration of the Soviet Empire in the late 1980s. The scale and nature of the impact of that disintegration was to a great extent unexpected by the governments of the EU states. It carried with it the potential for unprecedented change. As a result, both the practice and the theory of political and economic integration within the European Union have changed in the period since 1989.

For the European Union the first indication of how momentous the changes were to be was the opening of the Berlin Wall in November 1989. This enabled the EU to fulfil its commitment (made by the original six Member States) that it would support the unification of the two Germanies, if this ever became a possibility. The unification of Germany was instrumental in derailing the progress towards economic and monetary union. It forced the German government's economic policy to focus on national events, because of the massive transfer of resources needed to support the economic development of the new Eastern Lander. However, in political terms, Germany was released from many of the constraints imposed on it by the peace settlement at the end of World War II.

The process of integration within the EU is taking place against a background of pressure for enlargement. This may create a European Union of at least 20 states by the early part of the twenty-first century. The EU has Member States whose combined borders reach from the Arctic Circle to the Northern shores of the Mediterranean. Following the unification of Germany and the accession of Austria, the EU now encompasses areas of Central Europe.

Much of the political controversy and lack of clarity about what the future of the European Union will be has come about as a result of the EU having to 'react' to the rapidly changing geopolitical environment. This formed the background to the Intergovernmental Conferences of 1991 which led to the Treaty on European Union (TEU).

The TEU left unresolved a number of questions. The continued pressures on the EU from the applicant and potential applicant states of the former Soviet Empire have made more urgent a resolution of the most fundamental question. What sort of European Union is envisaged in the phrase used in the TEU, '...an ever closer Union...' (TEU Art. A)? This ongoing debate will form the background to the Intergovernmental Conference (IGC) of 1996 which may revise the Treaty on European Union.

The process of European integration

The European Union is a system of government which does not fit neatly into the recognised theories of integration. It is therefore difficult to predict what the future European Union will be without a model from which to work. The authors of this text have taken a pragmatic view of the process of integration within the EU. The framework that proves the most useful against which to measure European integration is that given by Andrew Moravcsik (1994)

'...the EC can be analysed as a successful intergovernmental regime, designed to manage economic interdependence through negotiated policy coordination.'[1]

Moravcsik has brought together the main features of the different bodies of theory into a definition that enables an understanding of the way in which the EU functions. It gives the opportunity for an effective analysis of the different policy areas of the European Union, which is the main purpose of this text.

Limitations of the traditional theories of integration

Economic integration

The traditional view of economic integration is based on the differentiation of a number of different levels of cooperation between states. They may exist independently; there is no automatic progression from one level of cooperation to another.

The loosest form is that which exists among a group of states in a Free Trade Area. Tariffs and quotas are eliminated on trade amongst the members of the Free Trade Area, but maintained on trade with third countries. In a Customs Union, the barriers to trade are removed and a Common External Tariff is adopted for third-country trade. The introduction of a Common Market brings with it free movement of the factors of production – labour, capital, goods and services. Following from the Common Market, Economic and Monetary Union between the Member States carries with it the harmonisation of some national economic policies. In the final stage of full economic integration there is integration of Member States' economic polices and either a single currency or irrevocably fixed exchange rates.

Economic integration of all levels requires an accompanying level of political integration. The process of political integration is therefore inseparable from the process of economic integration. The speed at which the German state proceeded from Economic and Monetary Union in July 1990 to Political Union in October 1990 is an example of the recognition of this fact.

The European Union is a group of independent states that have agreed to a considerable pooling of their national sovereignty for the economic integration to succeed. It is in the interests of the Member States of the European Union to cooperate in this way. They are a group of small and medium-sized states. Table 1.2 gives the area of each state and its population. By becoming Member States of the European Union, they have been able to maintain a global position. They have benefited from the increased level of economic integration by becoming, as a group, among the world's richest states. Per capita GDP within the EU is given in Table 1.2.

Table 1.2 Basic statistics of the European Union (1993 figures)

	Area (1000 km²)	Population (millions)	GDP at market prices (1000 million PPS)	Per Capita GDP (PPS)
Belgium	31	10.0	180.0	17 849
Denmark	43	5.1	115.5	22 253
Germany	357	80.2	1 631.5	20 097
Greece	132	10.3	76.7	7 406
Spain	505	39.1	408.4	10 434
France	544	57.2	1 068.6	18 640
Ireland	70	3.5	40.4	11 334
Italy	301	57.8	847.3	14 584
Luxembourg	3	0.4	10.7	26 859
Netherlands	41	15.1	264.0	17 268
Portugal	92	9.8	72.3	7 323
UK	244	57.6	807.8	13 887
Austria	84	7.9	155.5	19 453
Sweden	450	8.7	159.2	18 256
Finland	338	5.1	71.5	14 110
EU 12	2362	3461	5523.2	
EU 15	3337	3700	5909.3	

Note : PPS = Purchasing power standard. A common unit representing an identical volume of goods and services for each country.
Source : Commission, 1995.

The Member States of the EU, however, remain independent nation states which are protective of their national interests. The result has been to leave the process of political integration within the EU lagging behind the process of economic integration. A common theme emerging from the analysis of each area of EU policy is the tension that exists because of the lack of political integration which is needed to enable the economic to function.

Political integration

Political integration was defined by Karl Deutsch as the creation, within a given geographical territory, of a sense of community, based on shared values. It was also essential to political integration to have established the necessary institutions to ensure a peaceful existence for the members of the community.[2]

The theories of political integration that have emerged to try to explain the integration process within the European Union fall into a number of categories.

1.   Those that look to the establishment of the European Union on the basis of a federalist model.

2.   Those that use the functionalist or neo-functionalist literature to explain the EU.

3.   The intergovernmentalist approach or, as Brigid Laffan explains it '...the realist or traditional school of international relations...'[3].

4.   The interdependency model.

None of the bodies of theory on its own satisfactorily explains the nature of the European Union or presents a model from which to predict what the European Union of the future will be.

Federalist approach

This is the oldest of the bodies of theory. Unions have existed with federal characteristics since the ancient Greek Leagues of city states. Other examples include the Dutch Federal Republic in 1579 and the Swiss Federation, established in the fourteenth century. John Pinder places the origins of present ideas of a federal Europe in Britain in the period between 1935 and 1940. He points out that these ideas are built, perhaps surprisingly,

'...on a long tradition of thought with its roots in British political philosophy.'[4]

The drafters of the early American federal constitution owed a great deal to the writings of the seventeenth century British political philosopher John Locke.

Federalism is a way of forming a political union among separate states which gives a number of advantages to the states over their continued existence in a unitary system. Central to the theory is the method used to divide the powers of government, so that the tasks being performed by the central and the regional governments are coordinated but remain independent. The allocation of the powers of government are to be divided in such a way as to limit the power of the central government. These limits are to be exerted by the control of the elected representatives of the citizens of the Union, in the Parliament and supported by the existence of a federal court.

For the proponents of federalism the establishment of a constitution that allocates the roles of the government is a crucial initial stage in the integration process. This is in direct contrast to the functionalist approach to integration, which avoids a formal constitution-drafting procedure.

Functionalism

The functionalist approach to integration theory was based on the work of David Mitrany, who put forward the thesis in the mid-1960s. In his thesis the traditional linkage between authority and a territorial area was to be broken in response to the need to link authority to a specific activity. The primary objective was to ensure that a peaceful and stable international regime would be established. This, in Mitrany's theory was

'...more likely to grow through doing things together in workshop and market place than by signing pacts in Chancelleries.'[5]

The origins of the International Monetary System (IMF) provide an example of this theory in practice. The IMF fitted with other attempts at integration, based in the establishment of an international economic system rather than a political regime, which were seen as the route to peace after World War II.

The IMF was set up as a result of the Bretton Woods Conference which was held in 1944 in the USA. At the conference a new monetary system to replace the pre-war system was established. It was based on fixed exchange rates and backed by the dollar and sterling as reserve currencies. The International Bank for Reconstruction and Development was set up at the same time to lend money to the European states affected by World War II. The main aims of this new system were to be backed by the IMF. Member States were to make contributions which could then be issued in the form of loans to other states with severe balance of payments difficulties.

The main problem with the functionalist explanation of the process of integration was that the approach had a very narrow focus, neglecting the influence of the context in which integration was taking place. This was certainly true of the IMF. The basic assumption had been that the economic difficulties which the IMF was set up to help to overcome would be short-lived and that the support would not be needed for longer than an initial transition period. This was an underestimation of the scale of the problem of post-war reconstruction.

Neo-functionalism

The neo-functionalist approach, developed in the early 1970s, appeared to offer a more accurate model of the integrative process. It seemed to provide the opportunity to predict events. In the neo-functionalist approach the context in which integration is taking place is taken into account. When the sectors of activity that the nation states are to put under joint control are identified, the political parties and the relevant interest groups become involved in the process.

While the integration process is essentially non-political, the political actors with responsibility for the activities in question are part of and not alienated by the process. It is important, however, that the sectors of activity chosen for integration are not controversial, that no vital interest of any state is threatened. Also, to be successful, the joint activity being undertaken must have a benefit that is greater than if the nations involved continued with the activity in isolation. Haas[6] and Lindberg[7] both analysed the European Coal and Steel Community in these terms.

The establishment of the European Coal and Steel Community brought together the coal and steel industries of the six Member States (see Table 1.1). The operation of these industrial sectors was be overseen by the creation of a High Authority with supranational powers. The intention was that, over time, the regulatory powers given to the High Authority would make it the focus of attention from the business and industrial communities. Within the institutional structure of the European Economic Community established in 1958, the Commission was to have the equivalent role to that of the High Authority of the ECSC.

Neo-functionalism assumes that there will be a gradual spillover from one area of activity to another as the integrative process in one area puts strains on other activities and the benefits of integration are seen to outweigh the disadvantages of non-cooperation. This is the fundamental problem with the neo-functionalist view of the integration process within the European Union. There has not been a gradual move from one policy activity to another. The same level of integration does not exist in all areas of the EU's activity. The commitment of the Member States of the European Union has not been equally made to all issues, so that the operation of the spillover effect cannot be seen to have successfully occurred.

Intergovernmentalism

Intergovernmentalism concentrates on the authority of the nation state. Groups of states agree to cooperate for a variety of purposes, but without loosing their independence and control of policies. The distinction normally made between the European Union and other international intergovernmental organisations is based on the degree of integration that has been achieved. There have, however, been periods of time when the intergovernmentalist approach has provided the most appropriate means to describe the EU, as national interests have been more evident than at others. The period of the mid-1960s and de Gaulle's dominance of the EU is one such example.

The scope of the activity of the EU was enhanced by the Treaty on European Union. However, two aspects of the TEU concentrated on the provision of increased opportunity for the states to cooperate in an intergovernmental framework, rather than that of the supranational framework of the European Community. The Treaty on European Union established an intergovernmental approach to the creation of the Common Foreign and Security Policy (CFSP) and Justice and Home Affairs. A commitment was made in the TEU to

'...the implementation of a common foreign and security policy, including the eventual framing of a common defence policy, which might in time lead to a common defence...'
(TEU Art. B)

and

'...to develop close co-operation on justice and home affairs' (TEU Art. B).

This is an extension of the cooperation between the Member States of the EU in these areas, but the framework in which it is set allows for different groupings of the Member States to emerge on some issues.

Interdependency

William Wallace[8] describes the interaction between the Member States of the European Union as a far more intensive relationship, both economically and socially, than existed 20 or 30 years ago. However, as he points out, this is not a unique aspect of relations between the Member States of the European Union. It is present in many groupings of states. For Wallace the distinction lies in the fact that the EU is a grouping of wealthy states in a small geographical area, which have established a number of supranational institutions to enable their cooperation to function, including acceptance of the supremacy of the European Court of Justice.

This returns the focus of attention to Andrew Moravcsik's definition. The EU is a successful grouping of states, which have established institutions to enable international cooperation to function. There is clearly a commitment to continued cooperation and pooling of sovereignty to allow the EU to operate. The system of government that has emerged has been and continues to be attractive to other states within the European region. In order to manage the economic interdependence, the system of government has some of the characteristics of a federal structure, but as long as the nation states continue to protect their vested national interests a federal state of Europe will not emerge from the European Union. The following brief review of the history of the EU demonstrates the way in which the federal ambition has been thwarted by the Member States.

The history of the European Union

The origins of the present European Union lie in the immediate aftermath of World War II. It formed as a result of a search for stability in Western Europe. A similar search for stability was taking place at the same time in the states of Central and Eastern Europe, but the outcome was very different from the attempts at integration in Western Europe. The EU was not the first attempt at integration, nor was it the only attempt during the first 15 years after World War II. A number of international organisations were established in the period from the mid-1940s to the end of the 1950s.

Globally, the United Nations and some of its agencies began their work. In the international economic sphere the GATT was established, along with the International Monetary Fund, the World Bank and the Organisation for Economic Co-operation and Development.

Within Europe, the European Union was one of a group of organisations of small and medium-sized states that emerged, with differing objectives. These included the Western European Union (an alliance of states with a defence objective). Many of the states of the EU belong to this organisation and, following the TEU, it has been seen as the European replacement for NATO. The Nordic Council was not established by a Treaty. It was a loosely based organisation established by the agreement of the Parliaments of the Scandinavian states. The greater part of the cooperation within this framework has been in the areas of social and welfare policies. The European Free Trade Association was established in 1960 with the objective of facilitating trade in industrial products between its Members. While some organisations were based on political integration, the majority, and the ones that have proved to be the most successful and enduring, were based on forms of economic cooperation.

The underlying pressure for these independent states to agree to cooperate was the need to create stability in Europe so that the process of reconstruction following World War II could begin. The means by which this cooperation was to take effect, however, differed for the different organisations that were established. In the case of the European Union the means to create stability was economic. This was a result of the recognition that political means to bring states together had failed during the period between World War I and World War II. The political redrawing of the boundaries of the states following World War I had unleashed a large number of divisive forces and enabled nationalism to take hold, and the result had been World War II.

The European Coal and Steel Community (ECSC), which was the forerunner of the European Economic Community, was established with an avowedly federalist framework (see Table 1.1). It was '...a first step in the federation of Europe...'.[9] The institutions that were established were to impose limits on the governments of all the states. It was not the intention of either Jean Monnet or Robert Schuman,[10] when they put forward the plan for the ECSC, that the nation states should be able to preserve their own national interests over those of another state.

The European Coal and Steel Community was therefore a group of states that had agreed to a pooling of sovereignty over a relatively limited area of economic activity. Supranational institutions were established to ensure that the ECSC functioned. The main purpose of the ECSC was to anchor the state of Germany so firmly into an organisation with the state of France that the benefits from continuing with the integrative process would outweigh any other motivations.

The institutional framework established by Monnet to run the ECSC formed the basis of the institutional framework of the European Union when the ECSC was incorporated into the Treaties of Rome in 1957. Two other Communities were formed in 1958 by the Treaties signed in Rome: the European Economic Community and EURATOM. The purpose of EURATOM was to enable peaceful use to be made of nuclear power. By 1967 the three communities had come together with a single bureaucracy. The more usual title then became the European Communities, which, before the TEU, had become commonly known as the European Community.

In deference to the fact that the signatories of the Treaty of Rome were independent nation states, the Treaty had provided for the major decisions being made by the Member States to be subject to unanimous decision. Minor matters, on the other hand, could be decided by a majority vote in the Council of Ministers which represented the national interests. It was envisaged that by 1966 all decisions would be taken by the weighted majority decision. This would have signified a massive transfer of allegiance from the Member States to the supranational organisation of the European Economic Community.

The French government led by de Gaulle objected in 1965 to the increased use of majority voting, seeing it as a move towards the creation of a more federal Europe, and an undermining of the role of the nation states of the EU. The following months of 1965 were the 'empty chair' period of European Union history, when the French Ministers were not allowed by their own government to take part in the deliberations of the Council of Ministers.

No EU business was possible, so agreement was reached in Luxembourg in early 1966, known as the Luxembourg Compromise. If an issue was considered to be of vital national interest for one of the Members of the EU, the decisions would be based on unanimous agreement. Following the death of de Gaulle a different approach was adopted by the French, but the use of majority voting remained a rare occurrence within the EU until 1987.

Under de Gaulle the French government had undermined the transfer of power from the nation states to the supranational authority of the European Union. The Member States of the EU were reminded of national interests which it was felt had to be preserved in order to protect a nation's sovereignty.

It was not until the Single European Act was signed and came into effect in 1987 that greater use was made of the majority voting system in the Council of Ministers. This was in order to achieve the legislative programme necessary for the operation of the Single Market. The use of the majority vote has been extended to a number of areas since the TEU. However the two intergovernmental areas of CFSP and Interior Affairs remain subject to unanimous vote (see Table 1.3). A more detailed analysis of the voting procedures is given in chapter 2.

Table 1.3 How the decisions are made in the Council of Ministers

	European Community	Common foreign and security policy	Interior affairs
National veto	Industrial policy	Joint action agreed in common areas	Conditions of stay for foreigners
	Culture		Fight against illegal immigration
	Research and development technology		Political asylum
	Environment (enlarged competence)		War against drugs
Majority vote	Economic and Monetary Union	Minor operational measures	Minor measures
	Entry visas to EU		
	Education and training		
	Trans-European networks		
	Preventive health		
	Consumer protection		
	Development aid		

A further French-led initiative, which has emphasised the intergovernmental aspects of the European Union, was the launch of the meetings of the European Council in 1974. This was the beginning of the series of regular meetings of the heads of state of the Members of the EU. It has taken on a policy agenda setting and guidance role for the Member States which is contrary to the original intention of the institutional framework of the EU. In the Single European Act of 1987 the informal status of the European Council was altered and it became included in the institutions of the European Union. A number of important events in the history of the EU have been at the instigation of the European Council. For example the preparations for the Intergovernmental Conferences (IGCs) in Maastricht in 1991 and the acceptance of the German Democratic Republic into the EU were a result of the work of the European Council.

The early draft Treaty on European Union presented for discussion in preparation for the 1991 Intergovernmental Conferences had included the phrase 'union with a federal goal'. This phrase was altered in the TEU to read

'...ever closer union among the peoples of Europe, in which decisions are taken as closely as possible to the citizen' (TEU Art A).

The TEU included a commitment to hold another IGC in 1996 to revise the Treaty. This is to begin in the Irish Presidency of 1996. There was, however, no requirement that the 1996 IGC return to the use of the word 'federal'.

The hope of Monnet and Schuman that they were beginning to create a federation of Europe remains to be fulfilled. The EU has some of the features of a federation, but it lacks two fundamental features.

The institutional framework of the European Union is described in detail in chapter 2. It has developed in such a way as to allow the institution that represents the national interests to dominate. The second feature is that there is no clear mechanism of distribution of power between the different levels of government. The principle of subsidiarity incorporated into the Single European Act in the chapter on the environment and extended, in the TEU, to all areas of policy is an attempt to identify the tasks of the different tiers of government, but it lacks clarity.

Table 1.4 Results of the 1994 referenda held in the Nordic States and Austria

Country	Turnout	Yes	No	Member
Austria	81	66.5	33.4	Yes
Finland	74	57	43	Yes
Sweden	83.3	52	46	Yes
Norway	88.8	47.7	52.3	No

Despite the continued debate about its nature among its Member States, the EU has attracted more Members since it began in 1958. It has grown as is shown in Tables 1.1 and 1.4 from six states to 16 in 1995. However, the European Union is at a break-point. In 1992 Hans Dietrich Genscher, then the German Foreign Minister, predicted a European Union of 35

Member States in the twenty-first century. While this is nothing more than a speculative figure based on the total number of Members in Western Europe and potential Members, going so far as to include the former Soviet states of Latvia, Estonia, Lithuania and even the Ukraine, 20 or even 24 states by the end of the first quarter of the twenty-first century is not impossible. The questions now being raised revolve around not just the nature of the EU of the future, but its suitability as an organisation for the newly emerging states of the former Soviet Empire.

The stability of the divided Europe

The desire to ensure that the state of Germany was firmly locked into an organisation of international states, in such a way as to prevent it becoming a threat to the states of Western Europe again, was not the only force for integration in Western Europe following World War II. By the mid-1950s, the states of Europe had become firmly divided into two groupings. One group, including the Federal Republic of Germany, was under the influence of the USA. The North Atlantic Treaty Organisation (NATO) emerged from the linkage of the USA and the European states in an organisation with security as its primary objective.

Another group was those under Soviet domination, including the German Democratic Republic. These states included Bulgaria, Romania, Hungary, Poland, and Czechoslovakia. The domination of these states by the Soviet Union led to repressive military control to maintain the relationship between the states.

The pressure for integration between the states of Western Europe was heightened as a defence against any possibility of an extension of the Soviet threat. At the same time the clear demarcation of the two groupings of states gave the Western European states a readily identifiable and coherent region within which to cooperate. The Treaty of Rome included the requirement that to be a Member of the European Union the applicant state had to be 'European'. The clear distinction between the states under Soviet domination – the existence of the so-called Iron Curtain – gave a certainty to that definition. The current 15 states of the EU, plus Switzerland, Iceland, Norway and a group of tiny states such as Andorra and Liechtenstein, were European. The rest were part of the Soviet Empire.

Any applicant state of the EU has still to be 'European', but the demise of the Soviet Empire has meant that the term must be redefined.

The fragmentation of the Soviet Empire and the introduction of a new uncertainty to Europe

Before 1989 most commentators on contemporary European integration took the view that the focus of attention within Western Europe was on the development of an integrated market economy. This was even the case when the former right-wing regimes of Southern Europe were being considered for membership of the European Union. The breaking down of the political divide between East and West has introduced a new situation. States that in the recent past have been neither market-oriented nor liberal democracies are attempting to move closer to the EU.

Although it was possible to track the changes that took place to a period well before 1989, the differences were then so marked that it was still possible to make a clear distinction and divide Europe into two parts. In the East there were the Socialist command economies, dominated by the Soviet Union. The Soviet Union had formed these states into the Council for

Mutual Economic Assistance (CMEA) or, as it was more commonly known, Comecon. They were also part of a military alliance known as the Warsaw Pact. The result was that pre-1989 Europe had:

- two economic systems with two trading blocs

- two major military alliances

- two Germanies.

The existence of the states of the Federal Republic of Germany and the German Democratic Republic had been recognised by the rest of the international community. The separate existence of the two states was a concrete and tangible acknowledgement of the separate nature of the two systems.

The Warsaw Pact ceased to exist in 1990, but it was not until 1991 that Comecon was finally wound up. In the West the EU was the major trading bloc and NATO acted as the military alliance for most states. Both these two organisations have survived the changes, although the role of NATO has become less central to European security as the Soviet threat appears to have retreated.

The European Union has become actively involved in the transformation process taking place in the states of Central and Eastern Europe, for a number of reasons.

- A sense of 'responsibility' for the states of Central and Eastern Europe which occupy the same small geographical region. Like the states of Western Europe, they are a group of small and medium-sized states which will benefit from cooperation with others.

- A desire to ensure that changes towards liberal democracy become permanent in these states to avoid any danger of a spilling over of other forces that remain from the communist and repressive era.

- A desire to give a permanence to the developments towards the market economy in the Central and Eastern European states. The development of these economies will be of more general economic benefit to the whole of Europe as trade becomes more liberal between the states.

The speed at which this situation changed was dramatic and surprised many seasoned observers, who might have expected the collapse of the Socialist states, but only over a much longer time-span: it has created for the European Union an opportunity to spread its ideals of individual freedom and liberal democracy, but it has also posed a major problem: it has created elements of instability. In particular there is the threat of mass economic migration to the West and the break-up of states that appeared to be permanent structures. Both of these elements can be seen in the context of the unification of Germany, but the problems go deeper in the states that lie to the east and south in Europe.

Once the rival Soviet-dominated system had been removed, there was no simple alternative left. There was no benchmark to measure capitalism against, so success could not be seen in terms of doing better than the rival system. The market economy was expected to resolve many problems that could not be resolved under the command economy. This in turn has prompted the question of what can be done if capitalism fails to provide the answers for the East.

There are many who saw the collapse of the Eastern bloc as inevitable, but there are few easy answers as to what is the correct strategy to follow now that victory has been won. It is easy to allow a political and economic system that is failing to fall apart, but it is difficult to create a new economic order. This is particularly so when the model that has been chosen, that of the market economy, has been refined and improved. The point had been reached where simply transplanting it in a crude way into the East could not work in the way that many of its advocates expected it to.

The demise of the Soviet Empire has left a vacuum and a great deal of concern about the way in which it will be filled. There is pressure on the European Union to develop a political role to match its economic strength. So far the strength of the Member States' national interests has prevented it from doing so.

Notes and references

1. **Bulmer S and Scott A** (1994) *Economic and Political Integration in Europe*, Blackwell, Oxford, p. 30.
2. **Deutsch K** *et al.* (1957) *Political Community and the North Atlantic Area*, Princeton University Press, Princeton, NJ.
3. **Laffan B** (1992) *Integration and Co-operation in Europe*, Routledge, London, p. 11.
4. **Pinder J** (1992) The Community after Maastricht: How Federal? *The New European*, Vol. 5, No. 3, 5.
5. **Mitrany D** (1966) *A Working Peace System*, RIIA, p. 25
6. **Haas E** (1968) *The Uniting of Europe*, Stanford University Press, Stanford, CT.
7. **Lindberg L** (1963) *The Political Dynamics of European Economic Integration*, Stanford University Press, Stanford, CT.
8. **Wallace W** (1992) *The Dynamics of European Integration*, RIIA, p. 19.
9. **Schuman R** (1950) *Declaration 9 May 1950.*
10. **Jean Monnet and Robert Schuman**, the 'founding fathers' of the European Union. Monnet was the director of the French Modernisation Plan and Robert Schuman the French Foreign Minister in 1950, when they presented the plan for the European Coal and Steel Community.

Further reading

Archer C (1990) *Organising Western Europe*, Edward Arnold, Sevenoaks, Kent.
Commission of the European Community, *Treaty on European Union.*
Dinan D (1994) *Ever Closer Union?*, Macmillan, London.
Hodges M (ed.) (1972) *European Integration*, Penguin, London.
House of Lords Select Committee on EC (1993) 28th Report: *Scrutiny of the Inter-Governmental Pillars of the European Union.*
Pinder J (1991) *European Community – the Building of a Union*, Oxford University Press, Oxford.
Urwin D (1989) *Western Europe since 1945* (4th edition) Longman, London.
Urwin D (1991) *The Community of Europe*, Longman, London.
Weigall D and Stirk P (1992) *The Origins and Development of the European Community*, Leicester.

CHAPTER 2

Making the European Union work?

The role of the institutions in the decision-making process of the European Union

Introduction

The European Union is an organisation with extensive powers and a special legal status. It has a unique political and judicial system within which decisions are made that enable it to function. The Member States are independent sovereign states which have agreed to a level of cooperation and joint actions that is not present in any other international organisation. Many decisions are made by the Member States on the basis of intergovernmental action. The European Union's decision-making procedures also have features normally associated with a federal system of government.

In a federal system of government, clearly defined tasks are usually allocated to the central government and the states that make up the federation. A United States of Europe that is similar to the USA may emerge in the long term. But within the EU there is currently no clear separation between central and state governments nor a recognised process by which power may be allocated between the tiers of government. This prevents the EU's system of government from being categorised as a federal system.

The European Union's unique institutional framework

The European Union is like any other democratic organisation of government with three separate branches of government – the legislature, the executive and the judiciary. These roles are split between a number of institutions – the Commission, the Council of Ministers, the European Parliament, the European Court of Justice and the Court of Auditors, the Economic and Social Committee (ECOSOC) and the Committee of the Regions (CoR). These institutions will be joined by the European System of Central Banks (to become the European Central Bank following the establishment of Economic and Monetary Union). There are also a number of specialist agencies, that are not part of the decision-making process of the EU but whose work is nevertheless important in the day-to-day running of the EU.

The objective of this chapter is to identify the features that are unique to the European Union's institutions and the relative importance of the roles of each institution within the institutional framework. The chapter will concentrate on the four institutions that are the main partners in the decision-making process – the Commission, the Council of Ministers, the European Parliament and the European Court of Justice.

The Commission is responsible for tabling the proposals, the Council has the decision-making power and in the dialogue between the two the European Parliament is taking an increasingly important role. The European Court of Justice is there primarily to ensure that the legislation is in keeping with what is set out in the Treaties (see Figure 2.1). This has led to what Jacques Delors, during his time as the President of the Commission, described as '...a complex system which required simplification'.[1]

The other institutions will be mentioned briefly. As the review of the role of each institution will show, a blurring of the roles of legislature and executive is taking place, with the European Parliament acquiring some of the powers of a legislature.

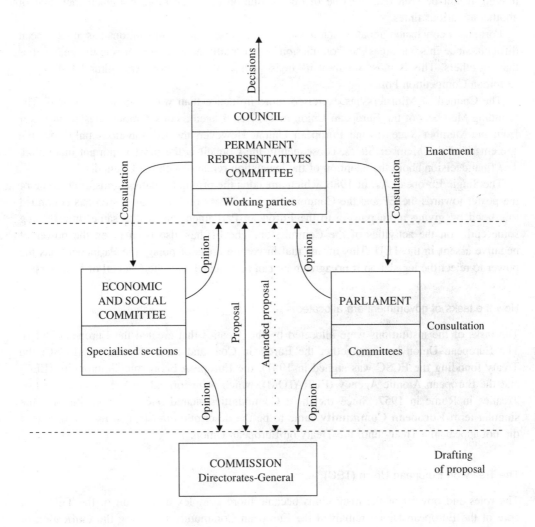

Figure 2.1 The decision-making process of the European Union
Source : European Commission (1993)

Where is the balance of power between the institutions?

It was never the intention that one institution should be more important than any of the others. The main aim of the system was to ensure that all the interests of all the Member States were taken equally into account in the decision-making process. This is why the tasks of the three branches of democratic government were shared. The Council of Ministers was established to ensure that the vital interests of the nation states were protected; the European Parliament was to be the counterweight representing the interests of the individual citizens in a direct way.

The role of the institutions, as set out in the Treaty of Rome, has changed as the EU has grown and more policy areas have been developed. This has altered the originally intended balance of power between the institutions. The overall pattern of each institution being needed for the European Union to function remains clear. However, within the framework of decision-making it can be seen that the role of one institution has been more dominant than that of another at various times.

Forming a conclusion about which is the most important of the institutions has always been difficult, since in some areas the Commission was formally given a greater role by the Treaties than in others. This is most apparent in areas such as the Common Agricultural Policy and Common Competition Policy.

The Council of Ministers has exercised more influence than was originally intended. The founding Members of the European Union in 1957 envisaged a considerable transfer of power from the Member States to the European Union. However, the EU functions only with the agreement of the Member States, consequently the Council is the most important institution. The final decision about the adoption of the legislation remains with the Council.

The Single European Act of 1986, which amended the original Treaties, transferred some of the power towards the EP and the Commission. The Treaty on European Union has continued this trend by giving more powers to the European Parliament but at the same time placing some curbs on the activities of the Commission. The EP has also been given the power of negative assent in the TEU. This means that in certain areas of policy the Parliament has the power to reject the legislation if no agreement can be reached with the Council of Ministers.

How the tasks of government are allocated

The tasks of the institutions were allocated by the Treaties that created the European Union. The European Union brings together the European Coal and Steel Community (ECSC; the Treaty founding the ECSC was signed in 1951), the European Economic Community (EEC) and the European Atomic Agency (EURATOM), which were formed with the signing of two Treaties in Rome in 1957. Since the three Communities shared one set of institutions, the singular term **European Community** came to be the description most often used, although it did not appear in a Treaty until the Treaty on European Union.

The Treaty on European Union (TEU)

The roles and powers of the institutions became more complex as a result of the TEU. The core of the European Union remained the European Community following the ratification of the TEU. However two other elements were included in the Treaty which led to the phrase 'the three pillars of the EU'. These were as follows.

- The European Economic Community, continuing the work of economic integration begun under the Treaty of Rome, ultimately leading to the Single Market supported by the Single Currency. The term European Community was formally incorporated into the Treaties, as it is to replace the term European Economic Community in the TEU.

- Common Foreign and Security Policy.

- Judicial and Home Affairs.

The last two were the intergovernmental pillars of the 'European Union'. This meant that in the strict legal sense the institutions became the institutions of the European Community when dealing with matters relating to the internal market, and the institutions of the European Union when dealing with issues relating to areas such as immigration, defence, and a definition of citizenship of the EU.

Although the TEU comprised changes to the Treaties establishing the European Community and the intergovernmental agreements establishing the European Union, the institutions still worked jointly for all parts of the Treaties. The officials were employed by the EC and not by the European Union. The institutions work for both the EC and the EU. The broad outline of the role of the institutions was the same. However, the voting procedures and the relative strengths of the institutions in each area were different. As two of the three pillars of action were based on intergovernmental agreement, the importance of the Council of Ministers was maintained.

While there are changes to the power of both the Commission and the European Parliament in the EC Treaty, they remain integral to the decision-making process, whereas in the European Union they are reduced to a consultative level. The powers of the European Court of Justice do not extend to the areas of intergovernmental cooperation. The result of the TEU, therefore, was to leave the roles and powers of the institutions less clear-cut. This is true for all the institutions, apart from the Council of Ministers.

The impact of the fourth enlargement

The EU is not a static organisation. The mid-1990s were dominated by the negotiations for entry to the EU of a number of states from the European Free Trade Association (EFTA). The timetable was set in 1992 for the applicants to be members of the EU by 1995/1996. At that time the applicants from EFTA were Austria, Sweden, Finland, Switzerland and Norway. As the Swiss government did not ratify the European Economic Area Agreement, its application was not considered with the other states. The 'no' vote in the 1994 referendum held in Norway led to the Norwegian government's withdrawl of its application (see Table 1.4). Following the 1995 enlargement the EU became a 15 Member State organisation. The proposals for institutional changes to allow for this increasing number of states were of major concern to the Member States of the EU for a number of reasons.

1. The larger states – Germany, France, the UK, Spain and Italy – were concerned that the changes would bring more smaller states into the EU which would be able to block proposals. It was the view of these governments that the small states, which together would represent a minority of the population of the EU, would have too much influence in the decision-making process.

2.   The smaller states of the EU were very concerned that unless a way was found to maintain a balance of power between the large and the small states their influence would be eroded.

3.   The governments of the applicant states were concerned that proposals to change the institutions should not make entry to the EU unacceptable to their electorates.

There was, however, no major overhaul of the roles and work of the institutions to meet the increased number of Member States. Instead the concentration was on merely increasing the numbers in each institution and addressing some issues relating to the work of the European Parliament. The 1996 Treaty amendments introduced more radical measures. These were necessary as the institutional framework of the EU had remained broadly that of the six Member State European Union established in 1958.

Recognition of the authority of the European Court of Justice (ECJ)

Although it is outside the decision-making process, the ECJ's existence and its role and powers separate the EU from other international groupings of states. The presence of the Treaties and the legal framework, including the European Court of Justice, means that the EU does not fit into a recognisable picture of other agreements between national governments. The Court is the supreme judicial authority of the EU. Its function is to act in an independent and impartial way to ensure that the legal framework given in the Treaties is observed in both its interpretation and its application in the Member States.

Legal instruments

The EU has the power to make decisions and turn these into legally binding instruments which will affect the population of the individual states that are members of the European Union. The Community uses four legal instruments.

- **Regulations.** If the legislation is adopted as a regulation, it is directly applicable throughout the whole of the EU.

- **Directives.** This form of legal instrument lays down compulsory objectives, but leaves it to the individual Member States how they transfer them into national legislation. This sometimes means that a country that is not committed to a particular directive will try to find ways to circumvent the legislation.

- **Decisions.** These are binding only on the Member State, the firms or individuals to whom they are directed.

- **Recommendations or opinions.** These are not binding unless they are concerned with measures in the coal or the steel sectors, when they become more like directives.

If a piece of legislation is not put into operation, the Court may take action. There are two areas of compliance that the Court may question: legal compliance and practical compliance.

Legal compliance

This simply means that each of the countries of the EU must make sure that it has in place a law that can be used to put the EU law into operation. If it does not have the necessary law, new national legislation must be introduced.

Sometimes countries may be slow in doing this. This has been true for example in the Netherlands with EU environmental laws. The Netherlands, with its great interest in environmental standards, tends to spend a long time in its own Parliament debating environmental laws. The consultation process may sometimes take as long as eight years. This may be contrary to the agreed timetable for a particular EU law.[2]

Practical compliance

This means that the countries have to make sure that they have the necessary administrative departments or personnel appointed so that the measures in the legislation are carried out.

The ECJ questioned the state of Luxembourg about its lack of measures to implement the Directive on the amount of waste from titanium dioxide production that should be allowed. Since titanium dioxide is not produced in Luxembourg, the Luxembourg government had seen no need to have personnel appointed to deal with the directive and the Court withdrew its question.

The principle of subsidiarity

The process for the allocation of powers to the EU and national levels of government

In any decision made by the European Union, the principle of subsidiarity has to be applied. The requirement to apply this principle became part of the Single European Act in 1987, when it was included in the environmental chapter (see chapter 14). Since the TEU this requirement has been extended to decisions made in all areas of European policy. The principle is designed to provide the means of deciding what policies should fall within the competence of the European Union for action, and what should be the role of the national governments.

This is not a new departure for the European Union. Decisions have been taken in this way since the European Union began. However, the pressures to clarify the nature of the relative roles of the supranational level of government and the national level had grown as the level of integration within the European Union had deepened. Some Member States, for example the UK and Denmark, were concerned that their national sovereignty was being undermined by the process of integration. Others felt that the process of integration was not proceeding quickly enough. The intention was that the Treaty on European Union would provide some of the clarity that was needed. It was necessary to identify the areas of policy in which the decisions would be taken at the supranational level and those to be left to the Member States.

The underlying debate surrounding the 1991 Intergovernmental Conferences (IGCs) that produced the TEU was therefore about the allocation of powers within the EU. The principle of subsidiarity was included in the Treaty as the way of deciding which areas belonged within the competence of the EU and which belonged to the Member States. This did not, however, provide the clarity that was being sought.

As it appears in the TEU, subsidiarity is the result of a compromise of views expressed by different Member States during the 1991 Intergovernmental Conferences. Much of the confusion comes from the origins of the concept itself and the different approaches to the application of the principle that have emerged over time. The TEU appears to have attempted a compromise by including all aspects of the interpretations of the principle of subsidiarity.

A centralising tendency

The first inclusion of the principle of subsidiarity in the Treaty came in the Environmental chapter of the Single European Act. The wording of the articles presupposed a centralisation of action, with the European Union responsible for the framework of environmental policy, setting its criteria and its content.

> Article 130r: 'The Community shall take action relating to the environment to the extent to which the objectives referred to in Paragraph 1 can be attained better at Community level than the level of the individual Member States.'

The objectives set in paragraph 1 were preceded by the statement that the

> '...Community ... shall have the following objectives: to preserve, protect and improve the quality of the environment ...'.

The language used here in the SEA sets the scene for a high level of environmental protection across the EU. The EU is given the responsibility to take over the role of environmental policy-maker, as the supranational level of government is the most capable of effective action.

A decentralising tendency

In the TEU the principle of subsidiarity was taken out of the chapter on the environment and applied through Article 3b to the entirety of European Union actions.

> With the addition of '...the Community shall take action, in accordance with the principle of subsidiarity, *only if and in so far as* [my italics] the objectives of the proposed action cannot be sufficiently achieved by the Member States ... and can therefore ... be better achieved by the Community' (Art. 3b. TEU).

The language of the article has become less clear. The presupposition now appears to be towards a decentralisation of power.

The German government view, put forward in the 1991 IGCs, was based on a definition of subsidiarity as the identification of the most effective way for actions to be taken within the EU. The German view upheld the emphasis on the centralising tendency of the principle of subsidiarity that was present in the SEA. This was seen in the phrase '... be better achieved by the Community...' included in Art. 3b of the TEU.

The prevailing wisdom in the UK was that the application of the subsidiarity principle meant a 'curb' to the power of the European Union. The UK government supported the presupposition that subsidiarity meant a decentralisation of power away from the EU, returning it to the Member States (see the above extract).

This view was prevalent not only in the UK. It was the way in which the TEU was made acceptable to the electorates of a number of other Member States, such as Denmark, and also to the EFTA applicant states. It reinforced the view that the Member States of the EU were able to maintain their own national standards in some areas of policy.

The wording of the TEU article on the principle of subsidiarity therefore represents a pragmatic response to the problems of trying to achieve agreement on the difficult questions surrounding the allocation of competence for actions within the EU. Article 3b of the TEU does not contain a clear definition of the policy areas and actions that come within the exclusive competence of the EU or the national governments. In a report by the Commission in November 1993 it was stated that

'...SUBSIDIARITY cannot be reduced to a set of procedural rules; it is primarily a state of mind, which to be given substance presupposes a political answer to the fundamental questions which the application of the principle will undoubtedly raise...'.[3]

The principle of subsidiarity is therefore a very general political statement, which may be interpreted in a number of different ways. It was included in the TEU. As such the European Court of Justice will be asked to make judgements on the basis of the principle. The ECJ may not be able to make any rulings on the basis of such a broad and ill-defined Treaty article. A clear definition of the subsidiarity principle will be part of the 1996 IGC debates.

The democratic deficit

A major concern for the EU is the apparent lack of interest among the electorate in the integration process within the EC (see Table 2.1).

Table 2.1 How do Europe's citizens view Europe?

	Strongly oppose	Oppose	No view	Favour	Strongly favour
Italy	2	8	7	52	31
Greece	5	6	8	39	43
Portugal	2	6	13	29	51
Luxembourg	5	11	5	50	30
Spain	3	9	11	47	31
Netherlands	6	13	5	52	24
Ireland	4	9	13	41	33
Belgium	3	13	9	53	21
France	6	14	7	49	24
Germany	7	15	6	45	26
Denmark	15	17	3	37	28
UK	13	19	11	40	17

Source: Commission, 1993

In some cases this is not just a passive lack of commitment to the EU, but may spill over into violent opposition. This has been seen on a number of occasions among the French farming community, and in disputes over the Common Fisheries Policy. The first Danish referendum on the TEU in 1992 showed the level of Danish feeling against integration. In the Euro-elections held in June 1994 the overall turnout was the lowest since direct elections began in 1979 – 56.5 per cent. The lowest national turnouts were in the Netherlands (35.6 per cent), Portugal (35.7 per cent) and the UK (36.2 per cent).

The Treaty on European Union gave the right to citizens of the Union to vote in the local elections in the area in which they were living if they fulfilled the local residence criteria. This was in addition to the right to vote in the European Parliamentary elections. The TEU gave more power to the elected EP in certain key areas of policy making. But merely increasing the opportunity to vote in elections and the powers of the European Parliament will not overcome the problem of the democratic deficit. The Members of the European Parliament represent very large constituencies, e.g. in the UK numbers reach almost 500 000. Only a tiny proportion of individual constituents will actually know the name of their MEP, let alone how to contact him/her.

The democratic deficit is more than a lack of interest in the EU. The issue is also one of concern about the openness and transparency of the work of the institutions and making the working of the institutions more accessible to the general public. Various measures to introduce this transparency to the decision-making process have been taken by the institutions; these will be referred to in the detailed review of their roles.

In particular, the TEU established a new institution to enable local people to have greater representation in the EU's decision-making process. This was the Committee of the Regions (CoR). The CoR is a 220 member committee with a consultative role, able to comment on the proposals being put forward by the European Commission. However, as the review of the CoR will show, a number of issues will leave the CoR in a relatively powerless position.

Other institutions

There are other institutions of the European Union, whose role in the decision-making process will be referred to briefly in this chapter. These include

- the European Investment Bank (EIB)

- the Economic and Social Committee (ECOSOC)

- the ECSC Consultative Committee

- the Court of First Instance, which helps with the workload of the ECJ – the Court of First Instance was established in 1987 by the Treaty amendment known as the Single European Act (SEA)

- the Court of Auditors, which monitors the EU's financial management – this was given the status of an EU institution in the Treaty on European Union

- the Committee of the Regions (CoR), which was established by the TEU.

The first three were established under the Treaty of Rome. The ECOSOC, the ECSC Consultative Committee and the CoR are advisory bodies rather than decision-makers, but according to the Treaties their advice has to be noted.

Other specialist agencies

As the work of the European Union has grown, other organisations have been formed to take on specific tasks to ensure that the EU is able to function. These offices and specialist agencies are sited in various parts of the EC rather than being concentrated in the three main centres of Brussels, Luxembourg and Strasbourg. The decisions about their locations were subject to lengthy political bargaining processes within the EU to ensure that all the states received a share of the Community agencies. These specialist agencies include:

- the European Environment Agency (Copenhagen)

- the Medicines Evaluation Agency (London)

- the European Bank for Reconstruction and Development (EBRD, London)

- the Trade Mark Office (Madrid)

- EUROPOL Drugs Agency (The Hague)

- the Foundation for Training (Turin)

- the European Monetary Institute (EMI), which is to be the forerunner to the European Central Bank (Frankfurt)

- the European Work Health and Safety Agency Bilboa

- the European Centre for the Development of Vocational Training (Salonika)

- Office for Veterinary and Plant Health Inspection and Control (Dublin).

Review of the roles of the EU institutions

The Commission of the European Community: 'initiator and executive'

The role of the Commission is to act as:

1. the initiator of legislation and rule-maker in its own right

2. the supervisor of the implementation of the legislation

3. the manager of the EU's financial resources

4. the external face of the European Union.

Organisation of the Commission

There are 20 members of the Commission, two from each of the larger states (France, Germany, Spain, Italy and the United Kingdom), and one from each of the other states (after the fourth enlargement of the EU in 1995). Each Commissioner is appointed by the mutual agreement of the 15 governments of the Member States. However, the Commissioners once appointed may not take instructions from their own national government. They are to act in the interests of the Community, and the European Parliament supervises their actions.

'The Commission shall consist of members who are chosen on the grounds of their general competence and whose independence is beyond doubt.' Article 16 TEU

Since the ratification of the TEU the Commissioners have served for a term of five years, to coincide with the term of the European Parliament. Under the arrangements before the TEU the Commission served for four years. This change was to ensure that the European Parliament was able to exercise supervisory powers over the Commission. All the Commissioners' appointments are renewable.

Each Commissioner is responsible for one area or portfolio, but that may be dealt with by more than one Directorate-General (D-G; see Table 2.2).

Table 2.2 Directorates-General of the Commission

DG I	External relations
DG II	Economic and financial
DG III	Internal Market and industrial
DG IV	Competition
DG V	Employment, social
DG VI	Agriculture
DG VII	Transport
DG VIII	Development
DG VIX	Personnel and administration
DG X	Information, communication, culture
DG XI	Environment
DG XII	Science, research, development
DG XIII	Telecommunications, information
DG XIV	Fisheries
DG XV	Financial institutions, company law
DG XVI	Regional policy
DG XVII	Energy
DG XVIII	Credit and investments
DG XIX	Budget
DG XX	Financial control
DG XXI	Customs union, indirect taxes
DG XXII	Coordination of structural policies
DG XXIII	Enterprise, SMEs, tourism

The President of the Commission is chosen from the list of nominated Commissioners. As the president is in office for five years, the role has a very high profile. The President of the Commission is more easily identifiable as the 'public face' of the European Union than the Head of State whose country holds the six-monthly rotating presidency. This was certainly true of Jacques Delors, who was first appointed as President of the Commission in 1985 and served until 1994 (see Table 2.3).

Table 2.3 Former Presidents of the Commission

Year		Year	
1958–1967	Walter Hallstein (Germany)	1977–1981	Roy Jenkins (UK)
1967–1970	Jean Rey (Belgium)	1981–1985	Gaston Thorn (Luxembourg)
1970–1972	Franco Maria Malfatti (Italy)	1985–1994	Jacques Delors (France)
1972–1973	Sicco Mansholt (Netherlands)	1995–	Jacques Santer (Luxembourg)
1973–1977	Francois-Xavier Ortoli (France)		

The work of the Cabinets

The work of the Commissioners is helped directly by teams of staff known as Cabinets. The Cabinets are small teams of officials who are close to the individual Commissioners and act as the Commissioners' personal advisors. They form a crucial link between the Commissioners and their officials and the interest groups and businesses outside Brussels who are concerned about the nature of Community policy. The Cabinets are closely involved in the formulation and refining of policy. They are direct points of contact with their Commissioners. It is possible to contact them directly and use the Cabinet members as a means of influencing the decision-making process.

Administrative staff of the Commission

The administrative staff of the Commission is smaller than that of many of the larger government departments of some states. The work is coordinated by the Secretariat General, which is headed by an influential and experienced bureaucrat. Further sub-division takes place into Directorate-Generals which deal with 23 different policy areas. In total there are about 16 700 officials, 15 per cent of whom are translators and interpreters in the bureaucracy.

The accession of the new states of Austria, Sweden and Finland increased the work of the Commission administrators. In 1994 it was decided to increase the number of Commission officials. It was estimated that new posts for 483 officials, 300 translators and 75 interpreters would be needed in the Commission Language Service. These new posts were the result of the adoption of the two new official working languages of the EU.

In addition to the numbers for the Language Service, 1500 other administrative posts were needed. Between 400 and 500 each were allocated for Austria and Sweden, and between 250 and 300 for Finland. The increased costs of the salaries and pensions for Commission officials was becoming a concern, and so the decision was made that of the 1500 required posts, only 500 would be new appointments. Staff would be appointed to the other 1000 as existing posts became vacant as a result of natural wastage.

A policy of gradual recruitment was adopted so that nationals of the new states would be appointed over time. Commission officials are normally appointed as the result of competitive examinations, although some national officials may be seconded to the Commission.

Coordination between the different Directorate-Generals to ensure the coherence of policy is difficult. The bureaucratic structure of the DGs is vertically organised and the horizontal linkages between the DGs may be difficult to establish to ensure that policy is coherent. For example, the Commission published a consultative Green Paper on Industrial Competitiveness and the Protection of the Environment in 1992.[4] The proposals made there required coordination of policy objectives being set by no fewer than five DGs.

It is the responsibility of the Secretariat General to ensure that coordination does take place, but it remains an area of concern. One method of overcoming these problems has been to establish Task Forces for specific issues, which are independent of the DGs and are able to work with officials dealing with more than one policy area.

How the Commissioners are appointed

All the potential Commissioners are nominees of national governments. It has been the practice in the UK to propose Commissioners from both the main parties. The UK Commissioners in 1994 were Sir Leon Brittan from the Conservative Party and Bruce Millan of the Labour Party. After 1994 Bruce Millan was replaced by the former Labour Party leader, Neil Kinnock (see Table 2.4).

The President

The nomination of the President of the Commission is by common agreement of the Member States after consultations have taken place with the European Parliament. The importance of the consultation with the EP was enhanced after the TEU. Jacques Delors was the first President of the Commission to be elected in his final term in 1993 by the procedures of the TEU. His appointment as the President of the Commission was approved by an overwhelming majority of 278 votes in the European Parliament.

His successor in 1994, Jacques Santer, did not meet with such general approval by the European Parliament. His appointment was confirmed by a majority of only 22 votes of the 521 MEPs present. The opposition to him stemmed from the fact that the EP considered that the Council of Ministers had not used the correct consultation procedures. Jacques Santer had been a compromise candidate, chosen by the Council of Ministers, when the UK government had vetoed the appointment of the former Belgian Prime Minister, Jean-Luc Dehaene, to the Presidency of the Commission.

It is possible for a President of the Commission to be compulsorily retired. This requires action by the European Court of Justice. It must be formally requested by the rest of the Commission or the Council of Ministers.

The rest of the Commission

The European Parliament has the power to dismiss the whole Commission by a vote of censure under Article 144 of the Treaty of Rome. Under the terms of the TEU it will also have the right to approve the list of proposed Commissioners. Each new Commission will need a vote of investiture from the Parliament before it can take office. It is also a requirement of acceptance that the new Commission present itself, and its programme, to the European Parliament for approval, before going to the Court of Justice for the formal oath taking ceremony accompanying investiture.

Table 2.4 Commissioners appointed in January 1995

	Portfolio
Jacques Santer, President (Luxembourg)	CFSP, monetary matters, institutional questions, IGCs
Manuel Marin (Spain)	External relations – Mediterranean, Middle and Near East, Latin America
Martin Bangemann (Germany)	Industrial affairs, information technologies, telecommunications
Sir Leon Brittan (UK)	External relations, common commercial policy
Karel van Miert (Belgium)	Competition
Hans van den Broek (Netherlands)	External affairs CE states, CFSP
Joao de Deus Pinheiro (Portugal)	External affairs ACP states
Padraig Flynn (Ireland)	Employment and social affairs
Marcelino Oreja (Spain)	Relations with EP, communications, audio-visual policy, publications office, institutional questions, IGC preparations
Edith Cresson (France)	Science, RTD, JRC, education
Ritt Bjerrgaard (Denmark)	Environment, nuclear safety
Monica Wulf-Mathies (Germany)	Regional policy, CoR, Cohesion Fund
Neil Kinnock (UK)	Transport including TENS
Mario Monti (Italy)	Internal market, taxation
Emma Bonino (Italy)	Consumer Policy, Fisheries
Yves-Thibault de Silguy (France)	Economic and financial affairs, monetary matters
Christos Papoutsis (Greece)	Energy, EURATOM, SMEs, tourism
Anita Gradin (Sweden)	Immigration, JHA
Franz Fischler (Austria)	Agriculture and rural development
Erkki Liikanen (Finland)	Budget

Source: Commission, 1994

The work of the Commission

The Commission meets in full session once a week in Brussels. All decisions are the result of a complex discussion, consultation and bargaining process. However, the final decision is a collective one achieved by consensus.

'The guardian of the Treaties'

The primary role of the Commission, given to it by the Treaties, is sometimes described as the 'guardian of the Treaties' and the 'motor of Integration'. This means that the Commission is required to perform a number of different tasks.

1. To initiate the legislation

In the Treaty of Rome this right of the Commission to initiate legislation is set out in Article 155, which is unchanged by the TEU. It means that the Commission has a great deal of power as the Council of Ministers is not responsible for the initiation and drafting of the legislation.

The Commission becomes the 'motor of integration' because it has control over the speed at which legislation can be introduced. Sometimes it is in fact necessary for the Commission to act to remove legislation from the list for consideration in order to speed up the decision-making process. However, in practice the process is not so clear-cut.

The Commission's proposals are the result of a number of influences. Some of the legislation is in direct response to the Commission's role within the EC and the need to establish means of carrying out its other functions. Often the legislation is the result of an issue being brought forward from discussion by the heads of state or national government officials; on other occasions it is the result of pressure from various interest groups or sometimes from the European Parliament.

In order for the legislation to be progressed the Commission must listen to a large number of opinions from the earliest stages of drafting the legislation. Because of the complicated procedures to have a piece of legislation that involves the other institutions adopted, the Commission is unlikely to introduce any legislation that does not have a high likelihood of success.

A complex network of advisory and consultative committees is consulted by the Commission in its drafting of legislation, ranging from the Union of Industries in Europe (UNICE) and the European Trade Union Confederation (ETUC) to specialised groups such as the Committee of Transport Unions in the Community (ITF-ICFTU). There are also more than 3000 special interest groups with more than 10 000 employees based in Brussels, who actively lobby on behalf of their particular interests. Brussels has been called 'the second lobbying capital of the world after Washington'.[5]

There are some areas where the Commission is able to act on its own to make legislation. These are where issues are mainly administrative and concern the effective operation of an area of policy. Most of this work is done in connection with the Common Agricultural Policy. Sometimes it is the result of a particular emergency that the Commission is able to act on its own. Once the agreement had been reached for the timetable to complete the Single Market, the Commission was left with a considerable degree of independence over the presentation of the legislation that was needed.

2. To ensure that the rules of the Treaties are followed

The Commission has powers of investigation and can impose fines on individuals or companies that breach rules on competition. It has the power to refer cases to the European Court of Justice.

The Commission is heavily dependent on information being given to it in many areas of its supervisory work. Increasingly, legislation requires a reporting-back procedure to the Commission on its implementation, but the frequent lack of commitment by a member state or an individual company to doing this is an ever-present problem for the Commission in its supervisory role.

3. Managing the Community's finances

The Commission manages the Community's finances. It is the Commission's responsibility to draft the Budget of the European Union, and it then has the direct responsibility for a number of areas of EU spending. The Budget has to be agreed by all the institutions and the

Commission has to ensure that it operates within what was agreed, as the EU is not legally permitted to have a budgetary deficit. This places considerable constraints on the Commission's ability to manage the Budget. The Council controls the upper limits of the budgetary expenditure, so that if problems emerge during any one financial year the Commission has to refer back to the Council for action.

The Commission takes the general management decisions in the two major spending areas of the Budget:

1. the price support mechanism of the Common Agricultural Policy in the Guarantee section of the European Agricultural Guidance and Guarantee Fund (EAGGF)

2. the Structural Funds, i.e. the European Regional Development Fund (ERDF), the European Social Fund (ESF) and the Guidance section of the EAGGF. In recognition of the continued disparities in standards of living across the EU, problems of poverty and unemployment these funds have been considerably increased in recent years, as has the role of the Commission in their management.

Finally, the Commission is also responsible for the management and coordination on behalf of the EU of a number of environmental and scientific programmes with non-EC states, especially the states of the European Free Trade Association (EFTA) and the assistance to the states of Central and Eastern Europe through PHARE. This is the programme being supported by 24 states of the Organisation for European Co-operation and Development (OECD) to help in the reconstruction of Poland, Hungary, the Czech Republic, Slovakia, Bulgaria and Romania.

4. Negotiator

The Commission has the responsibility for acting as the external face of the EU in a number of international fora, for example in the negotiations to achieve agreement in GATT (General Agreement on Tariffs and Trade). The Commission also acts on behalf of the European Union in negotiations for membership of the EU.

The Council of Ministers: 'the decision makers of the European Union'

The role of the Council of Ministers is to:

1. provide broad guidelines of policy

2. represent the interests of the Member States

3. make the decisions about the adoption of the legislation

4. perform the pre-eminent role in the context of the intergovernmental 'pillars' of the European Union.

The primary role of the Council of Ministers is to take the decisions about the proposals which then become European Union. In 1992 the Council adopted 383 regulations, 166 directives and 189 decisions. While it holds the balance of power amongst the institutions because of this, the roles of the institutions have been so allocated that it is not possible for the system to work without input to a greater or lesser extent from all the institutions.

The Council does not have the formal right to initiate legislation: that lies with the Commission. As has already been mentioned, the Council can bring pressure to bear on the Commission to propose legislation, but the Commission still holds the right to draft the legislation. The European Parliament then has the right of scrutiny of the legislation. As the powers of the EP have been enhanced, the EP may amend or reject certain legislation if agreement cannot be reached with the Council.

The organisation of the Council

The Council is made up of the representatives of the governments of the Member States. Each Member State of the EU has a seat on the Council of Ministers, but the number of votes allocated depends on the state's population. The actual representatives present at the meetings vary with the policy area under discussion. Depending on the subject, the Council may be composed of agriculture ministers, education ministers, ministers of the environment or ministers of transport, for example. These are the 'Technical Councils'. If the Meeting is of the Ministers for Foreign Affairs, it is called the General Council. For meetings of the Ministers of Finance the term ECOFIN is used.

The frequency of meetings of the Council varies. There are no set times, but the different groups usually meet once a month. However, it is possible to meet as often as is required. The meetings normally take place in Brussels, but sometimes meetings are called for Luxembourg. During a period of monetary crisis, for example, the ECOFIN meetings may occur very frequently. The Agricultural Council meets more often in the spring, when agricultural prices are fixed.

Table 2.5 Meetings of the Council 1992–1993

	1992	1993		1992	1993
Agriculture	14	11	General Council	12	19
ECOFIN	10	11	Internal Market	7	6
Fisheries	5	5	Environment	5	5
Transport	4	4	Research	3	5
Telecommunications	3	3	Social	3	4
Consumer protection	3	2	Health	2	2
Education	2	2	Culture	2	2
Energy	2	2	Industry	2	5
Development	2	2	Budget	2	2
Tourism	1	0	Justice	1	1
Joint (Environment/Energy, Environment/Development, General/Agriculture)	0	3			

Note : Only one meeting of the Council of Social Ministers was scheduled during the British Presidency of the second half of 1992. This followed the British 'opt-out' of the Social Chapter of the Maastricht Treaty.
Source : Compiled from (1) Corbett R, in Neill Nugent (ed) *Annual Review of the Activities of the EC*, 1992 p. 46; (2) Corbett R, *Annual Review*, 1993, Blackwell, Oxford, p. 41

The Council of Ministers always meets in closed session. This is because part of the time it is acting as the executive branch of government. It is not usual for the executive branch of any government to make public the way in which it reaches its decisions. There is, however, growing pressure for the Council to hold some of the meetings at which it is actually adopting the laws in public. This was done during the British Presidency in the second half of 1992, when some of the formal sessions of the Council were televised. At the end of 1993 an agreement was reached within the EC institutions, and following pressure from the EP, for the voting record of the Council of Ministers to be published. This, it is hoped, will remove any problems that come about because the votes are leaked sometimes incorrectly, either partly or by innuendo.

Rotating Presidency

Each of the Member States of the European Union holds the Presidency of the Council of Ministers in turn. The civil service of the state holding the Presidency takes on certain tasks during this period on behalf of the whole Community. The General Council Secretariat numbers only 2200 officials, and therefore this assistance from the member states is of vital importance. Providing this administrative support does, however, impose a financial burden on the smaller states of the EU during their presidencies.

There are considerable advantages for a state holding the Presidency, as it has greater control than the other states on the policy agenda. The legislation or other measures produced during a particular Presidency can frequently be seen to reflect national interests. It is the responsibility of the state holding the Presidency to chair the meetings of the Council.

A round of presidencies began in the first half of 1987 with the Belgian Presidency and finished in the second half of 1992 with the British. The order is decided alphabetically by the state's own spelling of its name (Table 2.6).

Table 2.6 Rotating Presidencies 1987–1992

Belgique	Ireland
Danmark	Italia
Deutschland	Luxembourg
Ellas (Greece)	Nederland
Espana	Portugal
France	United Kingdom

The round of presidencies beginning in 1993 followed the same pattern but because the work of the first half of the year differs from that of the second half, pairs of countries altered their alphabetical position, so that in 1993 Denmark held the presidency from January to June, Belgium from July to December. In 1994 Greece held the presidency before Germany.

The pattern of rotation was altered following enlargement of the Community to include the three EFTA states – Finland, Sweden and Austria. A new round and ordering were instituted which did not strictly follow the alphabetical convention. The French held the Presidency for the first six months of 1995, followed by Spain. The order is then Italy, Ireland, the Netherlands, Luxembourg, UK, Austria, Germany, Finland, Portugal, France, Sweden, Belgium, Spain, Denmark and Greece. This re-ordering was done to avoid the possibility of six small states, two of them new members, holding the Presidency between 1996 and 1999.

In order to ensure that the transition from one to another is smooth, the outgoing and the incoming presidencies work closely with the incumbent. This is the so-called 'Troika'. The work of an incoming Presidency may be hindered by unresolved issues from the previous one, and so the contact between the Presidencies is of vital importance.

Voting procedures within the Council

Originally votes taken in the Council of Ministers were on the basis of unanimity. This frequently led to long delays while legislation was debated in order to reach agreement. It also led to a curious 'horse trading' process of agreements taking place in order to have legislation accepted. When the Single Market White Paper was produced in 1985 with an outline of nearly 300 measures to be introduced by 1992, it was realised that the timetable could not be met as long as decisions continued to be taken by unanimity. The principle therefore was introduced that certain measures could be taken on the basis of a qualified majority of votes (QMV) in the Council of Ministers.

Although the European Union is a group of independent sovereign states, it is obvious that some of the states are larger and exercise more influence than others. Germany, France, the UK, Italy and Spain have much larger populations than, for example, Belgium, Denmark, the Netherlands and, the most extreme example, Luxembourg. Based on population, the larger states have more votes in the Council of Ministers than the smaller ones.

Prior to 1995, a total of 76 votes were allocated between the Member States (see Table 2.7). 54 votes were necessary to obtain the majority decision. Voting could be blocked by a coalition of states that carried 23 votes. This meant that the largest five states could not outvote the smaller states on a particular issue: they needed to have the support of at least two smaller states to be successful in a vote on legislation. Similarly, the seven smaller states could not form a blocking vote; they needed to have the support of three of the large states in the vote.

Table 2.7 Allocation of votes by Member State (population figures correct 1 January 1993)

Country	Population (millions)	Votes
Germany	80.6	10
France	57.5	10
Italy	56.9	10
UK	57.9	10
Spain	39.1	8
Belgium	10.0	5
Greece	10.3	5
Netherlands	15.2	5
Portugal	9.8	5
Austria*	7.9	4
Sweden*	8.6	4
Denmark	5.2	3
Ireland	3.5	3
Finland*	5.0	3
Luxembourg	0.4	2

* New members 1995
Source : *Europe,* 12 December 1993, 11

This balance was altered following enlargement of the EU. While there was agreement that the principle should be maintained of all the states of the EU having representation in all the institutions, there was clearly a need for further reform of the EU. The foundations for reform had been included in the TEU and certain proposals were made about the allocation of voting in the future if current population criteria were used. However, no major reform of the institutions was done in preparation for the entry of the EFTA states. Instead amendments were made to the existing framework.

The voting procedure in the Council of Ministers was based on a total number of votes of 87. This meant that in a vote of 87, the majority would be 61 and the blocking minority 27. The majority vote had to be cast by no fewer than 10 of the 15 states. Before enlargement the blocking minority could be reached by the votes of a combination of two large states and one small. Under the new proposals, this was altered.

The smaller states were concerned that this would mean an erosion of their influence within the EU. Other states such as Spain and the UK were concerned that the smaller states would acquire too much influence. In April 1994 the UK government had launched a vigorous campaign against an increase of the blocking minority from 23 votes to 27, whatever the size of the EU. A compromise was reached during the 1994 Greek Presidency of the Council of Ministers, which allowed for an extra consultation period about legislation, if the votes against were in the range between 23 and 27. This still applied following the 1995 enlargement. Even though Norway did not become a member of the European Union, the compromise agreement continued, with an extra consultation period if the minority vote was between 23 and 25 votes in the Council of Ministers.

The European Council

Following a French-led initiative in the mid-1970s, the meetings of the Heads of Government have taken on a separate identity, and normally take place twice a year. If a majority of the Heads of Government request it then additional meetings may be convened. The main role of the European Council is to direct policy-making by providing the broad guidelines for new policy developments.

The European Council was not included in the Treaties in 1958. It became part of the institutional framework in the Single European Act in 1987. The membership of the Council was outlined there as the Heads of State or Government of the Member States and the President of the Commission. Its work is assisted by the Ministers for Foreign Affairs and a member of the Commission. This gives a possible total of 32 individuals who have rights to be included in the deliberations of the European Council.

As the role of the European Union in the area of security and foreign affairs has evolved as one of the intergovernmental pillars of the Treaty on European Union, this has become the responsibility of the European Council. The Commission or any Member State of the EU may submit questions to the European Council for consideration. If a rapid decision is needed then it is possible for the European Council to be convened within 48 hours. Monitoring of the international situation in the areas covered by the Common Security and Foreign Policy is done by a Political Committee. Voting procedures are governed by the requirement for unanimous decisions.

COREPER and its functions

The work of the Council of Ministers is supported by the institution, established in the original Treaty of Rome, known as COREPER. This is the Committee of Permanent Representatives of the nation states. The members of this Committee act as ambassadors for the individual states to the Community and are based in Brussels. The brief of this Committee set out in the Treaty is that the members should be responsible for preparing the work of the Council of Ministers and carrying out any tasks that it is asked to do by the Council.

The Committee is sub-divided into COREPER 1 and COREPER 2. COREPER 2 comprises the more senior of the Permanent Representatives and deals with issues relating to the work of the European Council, the General Council of Ministers and ECOFIN. Often the work with which COREPER 2 is involved is the more politically sensitive.

COREPER 1 comprises the Deputy Permanent Representatives. Their main concerns are the environment, social affairs, transport and the internal market. The Common Agricultural Policy because of its complex and technical detail, is dealt with in a separate organisation known as the Special Committee on Agriculture (SCA). All the committees meet once a week.

The whole structure relies on the work done in various consultative committees and working groups which feed the views of interested groups and their advice to both the COREPER Committees. The administrative support is given by a secretariat, numbering more than 2000 staff, whose work involves providing the administrative support for all levels from the Council of Ministers itself to the various specialist working parties.

The European Parliament: 'the voice of democracy'

The role of the European Parliament is to:

1.   reject, amend or take steps to approve legislation

2.   approve the appointment of the Commission

3.   act with the Council of Ministers as the budgetary authority of the European Union

4.   approve agreements with non-EU states

5.   table questions to the Commission and the Council

6.   receive petitions from the citizens of Europe

7.   appoint an ombudsman.

The election of the Members of the European Parliament (MEPs)

The Members of the European Parliament have been elected by direct universal suffrage since 1979. Prior to that the Members were nominees from the Member States. The methods used by the Member States in the elections vary. All the states apart from the UK use some form of proportional representation (PR). In Northern Ireland proportional representation is used to ensure that the Nationalist minority is represented.

Arguments in favour of a common electoral system are clear. As long as the Parliament that represents the citizens of the EU is elected by different methods, the question of lack of democracy remains. The UK's adherence to the 'first past the post' system is not the only major difference. The states using proportional representation do not all use the same form. There are differences in the age limits for eligible candidates, which vary from 18 to 25. Voting is spread in some states across two days rather than one.

In the states using a party list system of PR, different means are used to identify the successful candidates. French and Greek list systems are based on a party list of candidates being presented to the electorate. The number of candidates returned depends on the proportion of the votes cast for the party. For example in Greece, 4 per cent of the vote equals one candidate. If the party achieves 40 per cent of the vote, then the first ten candidates whose names appear on the party list will be elected. Voters in Belgium are also presented with a party list, but have the right to identify an individual candidate from the list. In this case it may be that the first names on the list are not the candidates who are elected.

The number of seats in the EP is allocated to the Member States on the basis of population size. As can be seen in Table 2.8 this results in some anomalies, the most obvious being the representation for Luxembourg.

Table 2.8 Number of seats in the EP allocated to the Member States

	1989	1994	1999
Belgium	24	25	25
Denmark	16	16	16
Germany	81	99	99
Greece	24	25	25
Spain	60	64	64
France	81	87	87
Ireland	15	15	15
Italy	81	87	87
Luxembourg	6	6	6
Netherlands	25	31	31
Portugal	24	25	25
UK	81	87	87
Sweden			21
Austria			20
Finland			16
Total MEPs	518	567	624

The increase in the number of MEPs between the elections of 1989 and 1994 was agreed by the Member States during the British Presidency of the Council of Ministers in December 1992. This was the result of German unification and the increase in the population of Germany to over 80 million. The other larger states of the EU were also given the right to elect more MEPs. The figures for 1999 were proposed by the EP in 1993 for the first elections to follow the enlargement of the Community to include the EFTA states (see Figure 2.2).

In the United Kingdom the increase in 1994 was split so that five more seats were allocated to England and one to Wales. The sitting MEPs themselves were in favour of a system of proportional representation being used to elect the new MEPs. By using a party list form of PR, it would not have been necessary to redraw the constituency boundaries. However, their proposal was not accepted and in order to form the new constituencies a Bill had to be introduced into the UK Houses of Parliament. Nowhere in that Bill was the issue of PR mentioned. The new seats in the UK were based on population figures (see Table 2.9).

Figure 2.2   The allocation of seats for the 1994 European Parliamentary Elections

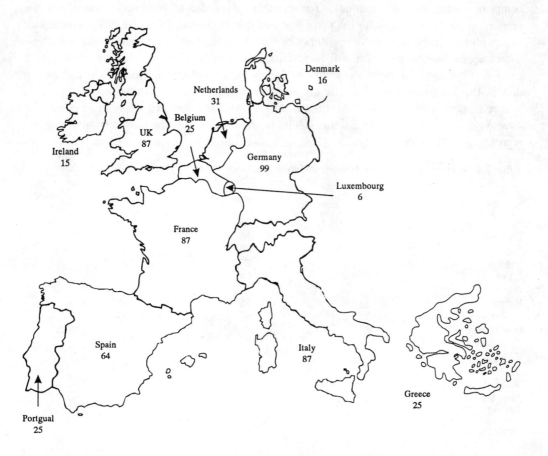

Table 2.9 Changes in the size of the European Parliamentary constituencies in the UK (based on population)

	1989	1994
England	531 686	512 835
Scotland	491 429	491 429
Wales	555 655	444 525
Northern Ireland	380 489	380 489

The Members of the European Parliament elect their own President (Table 2.10). The Presidents serve for terms of two and a half years.

Table 2.10 Presidents of the EP since the beginning of direct elections in 1979

1979	Simone Veil (French MEP)
1982	Piet Dankert (Dutch MEP)
1984	Pierre Pflimlin (French MEP)
1987	Sir Henry Plumb (UK MEP)
1989	Enrique Baron Crespo (Spanish MEP)
1992	Egon Klepsch (German MEP)
1994	Klaus Hansch (German MEP)

The elected MEPs do not sit in national groupings, but are grouped according to political affiliations (Table 2.11).

Table 2.11 Party groups in the European Parliament

	1994	1989
SPE	200	197
EPP	148	162
ELD	44	44
Green	22	27
EDA	24	20
ARC	8	16
ER	13	12
LU	12	13
IND	96	27
Total	567	518

Note : SPE, Group of the Party of European Socialists; EPP, European People's Party; ELD, Liberal and Democratic Reformist Group; Green, Green Parties; EDA, European Democratic Alliance; ARC, Rainbow Group; ER, Technical Group of the European Right; LU, Left Unity; IND Independents.

The largest groups returned in both the 1989 and 1994 elections were the SPE (including the British Labour MEPs), the EPP (the British Conservative MEPs have been part of this group since 1991) and the Liberal Democratic and Reformist Group. The two British Liberal Democratic MEPs elected to the EP for the first time in 1994 joined the ELD.

Parliamentary committees

The greater part of the EP's scrutiny of legislation is done in the 20 specialist committees to which the members belong (Table 2.12). Each of the MEPs belongs to at least one of these committees. The membership is organised in such a way as to broadly reflect the differing strengths of the political groupings in the EP. The role of chair of the committees is allocated on the basis of the largest political grouping being able to nominate the largest number of chairpersons.

Table 2.12 European Parliament's Permanent Committees

Foreign Affairs and Security
Agriculture, Fisheries and Rural Development
Transport and Tourism
Environment, Public Health and Consumer Protection
Budgets
Economic and Monetary Affairs and Industrial Policy
Culture, Youth and the Media
Energy, Research and Technology
Development and Co-operation
External Economic Relations
Civil Liberties and Internal Affairs
Legal Affairs and Citizens' Rights
Budgetary Affairs
Social Affairs, Employment and the Working Environment
Regional Policy and relations with regional and local authorities
Institutional Affairs
Women's Rights
Petitions

The MEPs are also members of 22 interparliamentary delegations which maintain contacts with other parliaments and international organisations. The MEPs meet representatives of the 70 African, Caribbean and Pacific states that are members of the Lome Convention twice a year. This is part of their supervisory role of the Community's actions.

The power of the European Parliament: a new legislature?

The powers of the EP were limited in the original founding Treaty of Rome. The Parliament was known as the General Assembly and consisted of the nominees of the Member States. They tended to be very committed to the ideal of European integration, but the Assembly was regarded as little more than a 'talking shop'.

Following the introduction of direct universal suffrage in 1979 the powers of what then became the Parliament were increased to give the MEPs a greater share in the decision-making process. The Single European Act of 1987, which amended the original Treaties, was influential in shifting some more of the power towards the EP and the Commission from the Council of Ministers. The TEU has continued this trend of giving more powers to the European Parliament but has placed some curbs on the activities of the Commission. The new EP powers included more involvement in the enactment of legislation, the right of 'prior approval' of the appointment of the Commission President and the Commissioners, and the power of assent for all major international agreements.

The procedures have become very complex as a result of the adoption of different forms of voting and differing involvement of the EP in the formation of legislation. In some areas of policy the EP may give its opinion on legislation, but the Council does not have to take it into account. This is the **consultation procedure.**

The SEA gave the EP the right to be more closely involved through a **co-operation procedure** in the formation of legislation based on just ten articles of the Treaty amendment (Figure 2.3). The EP has two readings of the proposed legislation under this procedure and may propose amendments. If these amendments are endorsed by the Commission, they can be rejected by the Council only if there is a unanimous decision of all the states. The result of the co-operation procedure was to strengthen the relationship between the EP and the Commission in the policy-making process.

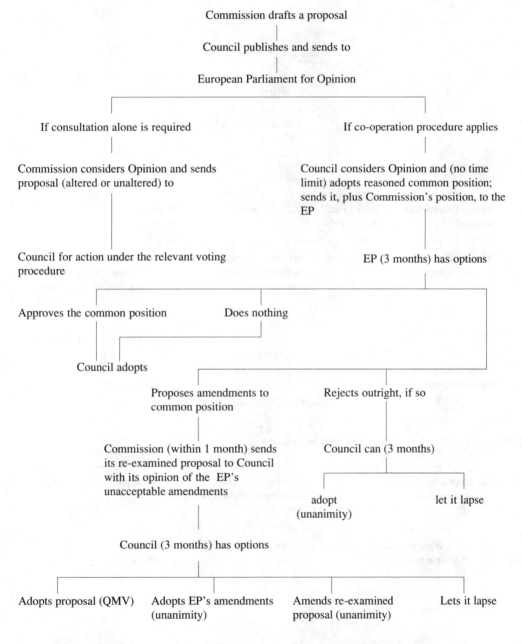

Figure 2.3 The legislative procedure of the European Community (the cooperation procedure)
Source : House of Commons, Session 1992–1993, Trade and Industry Committee, 2nd Report, *Trade with Europe*, 28 April 1993, HMSO, London, p. 19

In the TEU the powers of the Parliament were enhanced by the introduction of the **co-decision procedure**. The co-decision procedure is applied to areas of policy including the free movement of workers, the Single Market and consumer protection (see Figure 2.4). This extended the right to the EP to have a third reading of the legislation. Just as in the

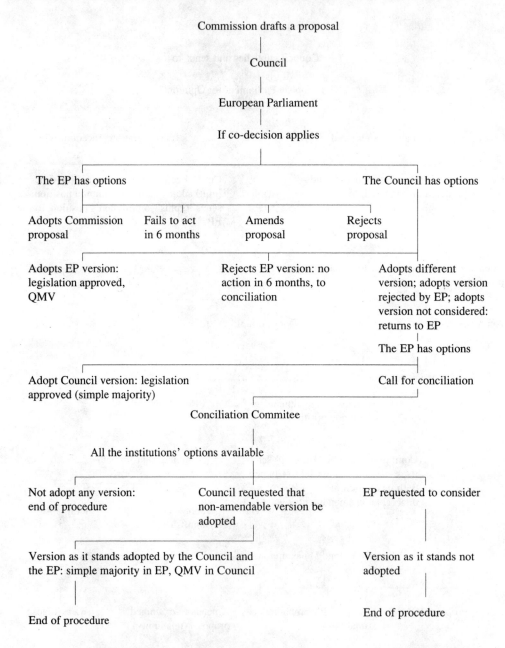

Figure 2.4 The legislative procedure of the European Community (the co-decision procedure)
Source : House of Commons, Session 1992–1993, Trade and Industry Committee, 2nd Report, *Trade with Europe*, 28 April 1993, HMSO, London, p. 20

co-operation procedure, the EP may propose amendments to the legislation that the Council intends to adopt. The new feature introduced by the co-decision procedure is the right of the EP of negative assent, i.e. if the Council does not accept the EP's amendments after the second reading, the two institutions meet in a Conciliation Committee. The Conciliation Committee was established at the end of 1993. Its primary role was to find a form of wording for proposed legislation that would lead to a settlement of any disputes.

If the Conciliation Committee is able to find an acceptable form of words, the legislation must be endorsed by both the EP and the Council of Ministers. If they fail to agree, the Council may approve the text of the legislation by itself. The EP has the right to reject legislative proposals at this stage, by an absolute majority of the MEPs. The legislation cannot then be adopted. This is seen as an important extension of the EP's powers within the legislative process.

However, it is subject to constraint. The EP does not have a right to amend legislation following the third final reading, and this means a great deal of the decision-making power still rests with the Council of Ministers. It may be that MEPs will feel obliged to accept legislation with which they are not in full agreement in order to have some legislation passed. Time limits have been placed on the procedures in an attempt to speed up what is often a lengthy process from the proposal of legislation to its adoption.

The EP's powers to amend the legislation have been increased to include the EU's polices on transport, social action, vocational training, research, environmental protection and overseas development. Treaties with non-EU states have become subject to the approval of the European Parliament before they are ratified. This power was used for the first time in 1994 when Austria, Sweden, and Finland joined the EU. There was some concern that the EP would not endorse the Accession Treaty so that the timetable for accession could be met.

There were further developments in the EP's powers of scrutiny and supervision in the TEU. The EP was given the right to set up a committee of inquiry to investigate contraventions or maladministration in the implementation of Community law. Alongside this was the right to appoint an ombudsman to receive complaints from the citizens of the EU about maladministration by the Community institutions. This was part of the ongoing attempt to make the working of the EU more open to its citizens. The EP was also granted the power to ask the Commission to initiate legislation.

In his opening address, Klaus Hansch, who was elected President of the EP following the 1994 Euro-elections, identified the growing power of the EP to act as the legislature.

'The Council of Ministers can no longer be the only legislature. There will be two – with the Parliament being on an equal basis. In future the President of the EP will be much more equal with the President of the Commission.'[6]

However the new powers of the EP are still subject to constraint and uncertainty.

Control over the Budget of the EU

This is an important part of the role of the EP. Along with the Council of Ministers the EP is the Budgetary Authority of the Community. It has scope to amend the spending plans proposed by the Commission. If no agreement can be reached with the Council about the EU's spending plans, then the EP can reject the whole Budget. Following the TEU, MEPs were also given a much greater influence in decisions about agricultural spending.

Working languages

The EU has 11 official working languages (since the 1995 enlargement), all of which are used within the EP. This causes many practical difficulties. With 11 official languages in the EP there are more than 150 possible combinations for translation, e.g. Danish to Greek, Spanish to German, Finnish to Irish. The EU is concerned that the democratic institution of the EP should not be undermined by attempts to cut back the number of working languages to a more manageable figure.

European Court of Justice: the most federal of all?

The role of the European Court of Justice is to:

1. declare void any legal instrument adopted by the Commission, the Council of Ministers or the national governments that is incompatible with EU law

2. pass judgement on the validity or interpretation of points of EU law

3. deliver an opinion on agreements with non-EU states.

The European Court of Justice is outside the decision-making process of the European Union. However, the presence of the Court gives the EU its uniqueness. The role of the ECJ in interpreting the European Union agreed law makes the decision-making process effective. The Member States have agreed to be bound by the rulings of the Court, based on the legislation to which they agreed in the Council of Ministers.

The terms of the founding Treaties of the EEC, the ECSC and EURATOM, which were reaffirmed in the TEU, give the ECJ the role of ensuring that the Member States comply with the terms of the Treaties. The Court is therefore obliged to put the European Union first in its interpretation and rulings on the EU's legislation. Because of its role in the interpretation of the Community's Treaties and legislation, the Court has been termed 'the most federal of the EC institutions'.[7]

In performing its two main functions:

1. to directly apply the law of the Community

2. to interpret the provisions of Community law

the ECJ must ensure that the application of the law by the Member States is consistent for the whole of the EC.

The organisation of the Court

The Court is based in Luxembourg. It has had 15 Judges since the fourth enlargement of the EU in 1995, appointed from the Member States. Prior to the Fourth Enlargement a thirteenth judge had been appointed, so that a majority decision could always be reached. The greater part of the work of the Court is done by groups or chambers of Judges. There are four chambers of three Judges and two chambers of five Judges. It is only for the most serious actions that all 15 Judges sit in plenary session.

The Judges are assisted in their work by eight Advocates-General. Both Judges and Advocates are appointed by the mutual agreement of the Member States to sit for a period of six years. The practice has been adopted of changing only half the Judges at any one time, because of the complexity of the matters with which they deal. This ensures that there is continuity, and more experienced Judges to work with those who have been members of the Court for only a short time.

All the 15 states of the EU appoint a judge. The eight Advocates-General are appointed one from each of Germany, France, Italy and the UK, with the other four coming in turn from the other Member States. The appointments are renewable.

Although they are appointed by a Member State, the work of the Judges and the Court is guaranteed to be independent. The guarantee comes from the Treaties themselves and is ensured by the Member States through their ratification of the Treaties. Their independence is further guaranteed by the fact that they hold their deliberations in secret. The appointment of a President of the Court is at the discretion of the Court itself.

The Court rulings

The different types of legislation that the European Union has at its disposal are outlined in the introduction to this chapter. Articles 169 and 170 of the Treaty of Rome, now incorporated into the TEU, give the Court the right to rule on infringements of the legislation. Actions may be brought by the Commission, individuals or other member states for failure to comply with the Treaty obligations. The usual procedure is to settle matters before they reach a full session of the Court.

Table 2.13 Infringements by Member State, 1993

	B	DK	D	EL	E	F	IRL	I	L	NL	UK	P	Total
1	25	38	22	29	26	23	21	23	25	21	46	34	333
2	73	28	96	96	81	82	70	84	66	53	50	92	871
3			1			1		1		1	2		6
4											1		1
5						1		1		1	1		4
6			1							1			2
7			1										1
Total													1209

Note : 1, Terminated after Article 169 letter; 2, On-going; 3, Reasoned Opinion; 4, Terminated after Reasoned Opinion; 5, On-going; 6, Referrals to the ECJ; 7, On-going
Source : Commission (1994), *11th Annual Report on Monitoring the Application of Community Law*, COM (94) 500, Final, p. 110

Initially, the infringement of the legislation is pointed out in a communication from the Court which gives the Member State concerned the necessary time to take action to comply with the legislation. This is known as an Article 169 letter. Following this, if no action is taken, the Court may issue its Reasoned Opinion identifying the problem. If the Member State does not implement the measures required, the case is referred to the Court for Judgement. Table 2.13 gives the established infringements of EU law and the ECJ's actions in 1994.

Probably the biggest change brought by the Treaty on European Union to the Court of Justice was the right of the Court to fine member states that did not comply with earlier judgements from the Court (Article 171 TEU). The Commission will recommend the size of the fine that the Court itself will decide is required as a penalty.

This article of the Treaty was based on a UK proposal and is intended both to strengthen the rule of law within the EC and to help British companies. Implementation of legislation is a concern. The record of some Member States on the implementation of the EU's regulations and directives is not as good as in others, as is shown in Tables 2.13 and 2.14. This additional penalty was seen as a way of ensuring that the level of infringements of EU legislation were brought under control.

Table 2.14 Implementation of Directives

Member State	Directives applicable on 31 December 1993	Directives for which measures notified	%
Belgium	1149	1042	90.7
Denmark	1149	1096	95.4
Germany	1153	1025	88.9
Greece	1148	1011	88.1
Spain	1147	1034	90.1
France	1150	1032	89.7
Ireland	1148	1019	88.7
Italy	1149	1022	88.9
Luxembourg	1149	1042	90.7
Netherlands	1149	1062	92.4
Portugal	1146	1022	89.2
UK	1148	1060	92.3

Source : Commission (1994) 11th Annual Report on Application of Law, p. 7

Ineffective or partial implementation of directives may undermine the operation of the Single Market. It is therefore very important that the Court has both the penalties to ensure the implementation of legislation and the information to take action. Not only did the Eleventh Report on the Application of EC Law identify the number of pieces of legislation implemented, but it also pointed to the fact that more cases of infringement of the legislation were being reported to the Commission by individuals. It was then possible for the Commission to initiate proceedings.

The ECJ is also available to be consulted by national courts for a ruling on the interpretation or applicability of European Union legislation. This must be done if there is no way in which the national legislation can be used to decide on a particular issue. This procedure is known as a preliminary ruling.

The ECJ is also asked to deliver its opinion on agreements made between the EU and non-member countries. These opinions are binding. During the period when the EU was negotiating with the EFTA states to form the European Economic Area (EEA) it was the ECJ's concerns about the way in which legislation would be dealt with that caused delays in the final signing of the agreement.

The Court of First Instance

As the workload of the Court grew at the end of the 1980s with the programme to complete the Single Market legislation, the Court of First Instance was established under the Single European Act. It began its work in 1989 and had 12 members appointed for renewable terms of six years, one judge coming from each Member State. From 1995 this number was increased to 15. As with the judges of the ECJ, these judges are appointed by mutual agreement of the governments of the Member States. The Court is partially replaced every three years in the same way.

The Court of First Instance rules on various types of case, including those concerning

1. private citizens of individual companies

2. competition and dumping measures

3. coal and steel

4. compensation proceedings

5. actions brought by European Union officials.

Its judgements may be submitted to the Court of Justice for appeal procedures.

Following the ratification of the TEU, it is possible for the Council of Ministers to extend the jurisdiction of the Court of First Instance by unanimous agreement. It is hoped that any future extension of the workload of the Court can be dealt with in this way without having to wait for major restructuring and amendment of the Treaty.

The Court of Auditors

The Court of Auditors was set up in 1977. It has the very specific role of checking on the financial management of the EU. Its remit covers all the revenue and expenditure of the EU and any agencies it may set up. All the Member States appoint a Member, whose independence of action is guaranteed. Among the increased powers of the EP is the right to consultation over the appointees to the Court. The TEU requires that the members of the Court of Auditors be people who have belonged to external audit bodies in their own state or who are specially qualified for the office.

The main responsibility of the Court of Auditors is to draw up an annual report on the implementation of the European Union's Budget. In order to maintain supervision of the work of the Court of Auditors, the Court has to submit a statement of assurance of the validity of the accounts to both the EP and the Council of Ministers. It may also be asked by any of the institutions of the EU to respond to specific questions about the EU's finances.

The European Investment Bank (EIB)

The EIB was established in 1958 by the Treaty of Rome. It is based in Luxembourg. Its primary role is to finance capital investment schemes that the EU has identified as being important for balanced growth within the EU. The projects the EIB supports are in the less favoured regions of the European Union. They are predominantly projects associated with improving the infrastructure of those regions.

The Bank is administered by a Board of Governors nominated from the Member States. However, the work of the EIB is autonomous. The Board of Governors appoints its own Board of Directors, which consists of 22 administrators and 12 deputies, serving for a renewable five year term. The Board of Directors takes the major decisions about the loans and the day-to-day operation of the EIB. The Management Committee deals with the operational side of the running of the Bank, being responsible for the drafting of the contracts and loan agreements.

The Bank can issue guarantees and loans up to a ceiling of 250 per cent of its capital holding. This has been increased several times. In 1993 it was decided that the scope of the then £6.2 billion holding should be extended. This was to include energy, environmental and inner city projects in addition to the transport-based projects supported previously.

The Economic and Social Committee (ECOSOC)

Established jointly in the EEC and EURATOM Treaties in 1958, ECOSOC is a consultative committee which brings together different economic and social interest groups. The membership numbers 220 appointees of the Member States (Table 2.15), who are based in Brussels and whose appointments are for four year renewable terms.

Table 2.15 Membership of the ECOSOC

State	Number of members	State	Number of members
Belgium	12	Luxembourg	6
Denmark	9	Netherlands	12
Germany	24	Austria	11
Greece	12	Portugal	12
Spain	21	Finland	9
France	24	Sweden	11
Ireland	9	UK	24
Italy	24	Total	220

Source: TEU Art. 194 and the Draft Accession Treaty

Three groups are represented on the Committee:

1. employers – representatives of both the public and the private sector

2. workers – predominantly trade union representatives

3. various other interests, including small and medium enterprises, consumer groups and environmental organisations.

The primary role of the ECOSOC is to advise all the main institutions in the decision-making process. It is organised into nine specialist groups which have the right to be consulted before certain decisions are made. It may also issue its opinion on all aspects of European Union legislation (Figure 2.5).

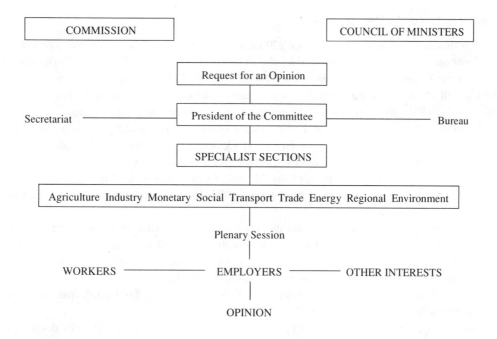

Figure 2.5 ECOSOC procedures for issuing an Opinion.
Source : Europe in Figures, 3rd edition, Eurostat, 1992, p. 35

The deliberations of ECOSOC are not influential in the decision-making process and are non-binding, but the Committee does provide a forum for the various interests to put forward their concerns. The members of the Committee serve only in a part-time capacity, and often the proposals they are being asked to comment on are not forwarded to them until a relatively late stage in the decision-making process.

ECSC Consultative Committee

In listing the institutions of the European Coal and Steel Community, the Treaty includes the provision that a consultative committee should be set up to assist the Commission (Art. 7 TEU Provisions amending the ECSC Treaty). This is merely repeating the original provisions of the ECSC Treaty of 1951.

The Commission of the European Community had considerable rule-making powers given by the 1951 Treaty over the coal and steel sectors, subject in a number of cases to consultation with the Consultative Committee. This has not been changed by the TEU. The Committee has the right to be consulted over the definition of what constitutes unfair practices or discriminatory practices. In consultation the Committee and the Commission may also set both the minimum and maximum steel prices during a crisis period. Quotas, on the other hand, are set by the Commission with the assent of the Council.

The Committee of the Regions

The Committee of the Regions (CoR) is a 220 member committee with a consultative role, able to comment on the proposals put forward by the European Commission. The same distribution of seats on the Committee is used as is used for the ECOSOC. The members are appointed by the Council of Ministers, based on proposals made by the national governments. However, the intention is that the members should act independently of the national governments.

Progress on the establishment of the Committee of the Regions was delayed initially by the slow ratification of the TEU. At the end of 1993, when the Treaty was ratified, problems remained for this new European Union institution. Some of the states were slow to name their nominees. Of the 12 Member States of the EU only Greece, Holland, Denmark and Belgium had nominated their representatives by the end of 1993. However, the first meeting of the CoR took place in January 1994.

In the UK the rules for choosing the members of the Committee of the Regions were the subject of the first defeat for the UK government during the TEU ratification debate. It was originally proposed that the government should pick the UK representatives, but the final decision was that they should come from elected local councillors.

The distribution of representatives from the UK is 14 seats from England, 5 from Scotland, 3 from Wales and 2 from Northern Ireland.

Proposals with a specific regional implication are referred to the Committee for discussion. The Committee has also to be consulted on all questions involving education, training, culture, public health and economic and social cohesion. Decisions about projects that are part of the £300 billion trans-European networks (TENS), i.e. investment in transport, telecommunications and energy links between the member states and with the rest of Europe, are referred to the CoR. Among the first projects the Commission put forward for consultation were the rail links between Heathrow and Paddington and between the Channel Tunnel and London, and an electricity cable from Italy to Greece.

The powers of the Committee of the Regions may be added to in the future as the European Union develops. This is entirely in keeping with Article A of the Treaty on European Union which talks about decisions being taken 'as closely as possible to the citizens', i.e. the principle of subsidiarity. Some view the Committee as an embryonic EC senate which would be able to complement the views of the EP with a strong regional and local flavour.

However, the placing of the CoR alongside the ECOSOC in the TEU is perhaps unfortunate if these are the future objectives of this Committee. The ECOSOC was also originally set up with much broader future objectives in mind. These developments for ECOSOC have not occurred. There is a danger that the same marginalisation may occur for the CoR.

Conclusions

A number of the EU's problems are the result of the unique nature of the decision-making process. Some of the problems, while they have a political significance, may be classed as more practical, affecting the routine operation of the institutions. These include the following:

1. The number of institutions involved.

2. The physical distance between the seats of the decision-making bodies. It was decided in the original Treaties which established the EU that a single geographical location would be identified for the institutions of the European Union. However, the allocation of the institutions agreed in 1965 has remained. The Commission is housed in Brussels, the Court in Luxembourg, and the European Parliament is probably the most itinerant of all, moving between Brussels and Strasbourg with its supporting secretariat in Luxembourg.

3. Working languages: the European Parliament operates in all 11 (post-1995) official working languages of the European Union. This carries with it an enormous routine administrative workload with the translation and distribution of documents. Anything else would undermine the democratic rights of all the citizens of Europe to be represented and to represent.

4. The existence of differing sets of rules that govern decision-making in the various policy areas. There are clearly, for example, operational problems that are yet to emerge because of the UK opt-out of the Social Chapter of the TEU (see chapter 15).

The pressures for institutional change and reform are continuing. Enlargement of the EU will bring an increase in the numbers involved in the decision-making process as more states become members of the EU. These states all have their own national concerns which will have to be dealt with.

The most important issues, however, relate to the allocation of powers of government between the institutions and the interests that each institution represents within the EU. The main objective of the system of sharing the power of government between the institutions was to ensure that a balance was maintained between the interests of the European Union and the interests of the Member States.

As the European Union has developed, the Council of Ministers has exercised more influence in the decision-making process than was originally intended. The strengthening of Qualified Majority Voting in the Single European Act in 1987 speeded the process of decision-making. It also resulted in the loss of the right of national veto over some areas of policy. But there was still a lack of clarity about the way in which power was to be allocated between the institutions. Introducing the principle of subsidiarity into the Treaty on European

Union was intended to overcome this problem, but failed. The decision-making process of the EU is still dominated by the Council of Ministers (the representatives of the national interests) rather than the European Parliament (the representatives of the citizens).

References

1. **Commission of the European Community** (1991) *Report to the European Parliament on the Maastricht European Council.*
2. **House of Lords (1992) Select Committee on the European Community**. *Implementation and Enforcement of Environmental Legislation*, p. 12.
3. **Commission of the European Community** (1993) Report *On the adaptation of Community legislation to the subsidiarity principle*, COM (93) 545 Final, p. 2.
4. **Commission of the European Community** (1992) *Industrial Competitiveness and Protection of the Environment*, COM (92), 1986.
5. **Thomson I**, Bibliographic Snapshot. *European Access*, No. 3, June 1993, 38.
6. **Hansch K**, *The European* 22/28 July 1994, 1.
7. **Lodge J** (ed.) (1993) *The European Community and the Challenge of the Future* 2nd edn, p. 33.

Further reading

Begg D *et. al.* (1993) *Making Sense of Subsidiarity,* CEPR.
Commission of the EC (1991) *Report to the European Parliament on the Maastricht European Council.*
Commission of the European Community (1992) *Maastricht Treaty on European Union.*
Commission of the European Community (1992) *Conclusions of the European Council in Edinburgh.*
Commission of the European Community (1992) *Europe in Figures*, 3rd edn, EUROSTAT.
Commission of the European Community (1992) *Industrial Competitiveness and the Protection of the Environment*, COM (92) 1986 Final.
Commission of the European Community (1994) *11th Annual Report on monitoring of the application of EC law,* COM (94) 500.
Duff A (ed.) (1993) *Subsidiarity within the European Community*, Federal Trust.
Foreign and Commonwealth Office (1993) *Europe After Maastricht*, Memorandum to the Foreign Affairs Committee.
Jacobs F *et al.* (1992) *The European Parliament*, 2nd edn, Longman, London.
Noel E (1993) *Working Together – the Institutions of the European Community*, Commission of the European Community.
Peterson J (1994) Subsidiarity a definition to suit any vision, *Parliamentary Affairs*, Vol. 47, No. 1, 116.
Nugent N (1994) *The Government and Politics of the European Community*, 3rd edn, Macmillan, London.
Nugent N (ed.) (1993) *Annual Review of the Activities of the EC 1992*, Blackwell, Oxford.
Nugent N (ed.) (1994) *Annual Review of the Activities of the EC 1993*, Blackwell, Oxford.

Appendix 1

The European Parliament

There were 20 Parliamentary Committees in the European Parliament elected in 1994 (Table 2A.1).

Table 2A.1 The Committees of the European Parliament 1994–1999

Committee	Chair	Party	State	Members (no.)
Foreign affairs/security	Matutes, A.	EPP	Sp	52
Agriculture/Fish/Rural	Jacob, C.	EDA	Fr	45
Budgets	Samland, D.	PES	Ger	33
Economic/Monetary, Industry	Wogau, K. von	EPP	Ger	50
Energy/Research/Technology	Desama, C.	PES	Bel	26
External Economic Relations	Clercq, W. de	LDR	Bel	25
Legal Affairs/Citizens' Rights	Casini, C.	EPP	It	25
Social Affairs/Working Environment	Hughes, S.	PES	UK	40
Regional Policy/Planning	Speciale, R.	PES	It	37
Transport/Tourism	Cornelissen, P.	EPP	Ne	28
Environment/Public Health/ Consumer Protection	Collins, K.	PES	UK	44
Culture/Youth Education/Media	Castellin, L.	EUL	It	36
Development/CoOperation	Kouchner, B.	PES	Fr	36
Civil Liberties/Internal Affairs	Vittorino, A.	PES	Port	31
Budgetary Control	Theato, D.	EPP	Ger	18
Institutional Affairs	Lopez Moran, F.	PES	Sp	40
Fisheries	Canete Arias, M.	EPP	Sp	22
Rules of Procedure	Fayot, B.	PES	Lux	23
Women's Rights	Dijk, N. van	Green	Ne	36
Petitions	Newman, E.	PES	UK	27
Employment (temporary)	Talero Villabos, D.	EPP	Sp	36
ACP/EU Assembly	Plumb, Lord	EPP	UK	70

Source : Kendall, V., Europe's new Parliament, *European Trends*, 3rd Quarter 1994, Economist Intelligence Unit, 66

Table 2A.2 The cost of running the European Parliament

Total cost 1994	$660 million
Each MEP	+$1 million
Cost to each voter	$3
Annual building rents	
Brussels	$37 million
Luxembourg	$13.6 million
Strasbourg	$12.9 million
New EP building in Brussels +$40 million per annum	

Source : Parliament's new powers, *Eurobusiness*, June 1994, 12

CHAPTER 3

What has the Single Market achieved?

Introduction

The Single Market (alternatively called the Internal Market) is an economic space without internal frontiers, where there is free circulation of goods, services, capital and people (these are generally known as the four freedoms). To achieve this there has to be a high degree of harmonisation of laws that affect business. Governments must not use regulations to interfere with the trade process. The Single Market was explicitly part of the Treaty of Rome, which came into force in 1958. However, while the EU quickly removed tariffs between the Member States, it was slow to remove other restrictions on trade. There remained a wide variety of barriers to the free circulation of goods and services across national boundaries, which would not normally be tolerated within a national economy.

The purpose of this chapter is to analyse critically the achievements of the Single Market programme. It asks if the EU has really managed to achieve a revolution with its strategy to remove the economic barriers between the Member States. The chapter begins with an analysis of the theory of economic integration, looking at the possible gains from the creation of a customs union. It then discusses the dynamic effects of integration, and in particular the impact of economies of scale on industrial structures. Finally, the chapter considers the task of implementing existing legislation and developing further initiatives to ensure that the Single Market is fully completed.

Economic integration in the EU

Economic integration means, within the context of the EU, the combining of the economies of the Member States to form a much larger European economy. The purpose of the exercise is firstly to achieve an improvement in the economic welfare of the members. Secondly, it is hoped that this process will also promote political integration. In the absence of free trade, the degree of economic integration will depend, in part, on the political will of like-minded states to form agreements. Some of the possible types of agreements are listed below in order of the degree of commitment they require from participants.

1. Trade Agreements

These give specific trade preference to certain countries. They may in some cases have a political motive, or be simply designed to assist in trade links.

2. Free trade areas (FTA)

These are agreements to remove tariffs and quotas and some other restrictions that stop the flow of goods between members. Britain was a member of such an organisation, called the European Free Trade Area (EFTA), from 1960 to 1973. EFTA was designed to promote trade mainly in industrial goods. No tariffs are imposed on fellow members of an FTA, and individual members are free to set their own tariff levels against non-member states. In order to avoid trade being deflected via the country with the lowest tariff wall, rules of origin have to be used. Rules of origin help to distinguish between domestically produced products and those that are imported. However, definitions can be complex where components are purchased from outside the FTA to be used in products assembled within it.

3. Customs unions

Customs unions have been used in the past to promote political as well as economic integration. The best known example was the Zollverein, which was established in 1834, and contributed greatly to the unification of Germany. The main features of a customs union are as follows:

I.   Tariff barriers are eliminated between member states.

II.   A common external tariff (CET) is established. Within the EU, this is known as the Common Customs Tariff (CCT). This ensures that import duties are charged at the same rate regardless of the point of entry.

III. The customs revenues are distributed among the members according to an agreed formula.

Features II and III help to overcome some of the problems of trade deflection.

4. Common Markets

This is a further step along the road towards greater economic integration. It incorporates the existence of a customs union with features such as free movement of capital and labour. The harmonisation of business laws and some agreement as to non-tariff barriers is required. Finally, there should be common policies to deal with areas such as transport, energy, industry and taxation.

5. Economic union

This implies a complete abolition of differences in economic policy based on the individual nation state. The economies of the economic union should be managed collectively as if the organisation were a completely integrated economic unit. In an economic union, there must inevitably be a considerable loss of economic sovereignty, so for example there would be just one currency with one central bank, and the basis of fiscal and monetary policy would have to be fully agreed. It is difficult to imagine this stage being reached without a high degree of political integration.

The theory of customs unions

The idea of a customs union is to create an area of free trade, so that once goods enter into it, or if they are produced within it, they are free to circulate without paying tariffs. Because goods may enter the union at any point, there are problems of distributing tariff receipts. The Netherlands, for example, receives a significant amount of cargo destined for Germany, and if it were allowed to keep the tariffs for its own use, it would benefit at the expense of the Germans. To overcome this problem the EU uses all customs receipts to finance its activities via the Budget (see chapter 7). Imports into the customs union pay the same level of tariff regardless of the point of entry. Because of this tariff, the customs union discriminates in favour of member states and against non-members. The degree of discrimination varies depending on individual trade agreements that the customs union has with external trading partners. The EU allows more generous terms to less developed countries than to Japan, for example.

Initially, economic theory was kind to customs unions, as they were regarded as a step towards free trade. Jacob Viner, however, suggested that they may not always increase economic welfare if trade diversion is greater than trade creation. Trade diversion is the switching of supply of a particular good from a cheaper source outside the customs union to a more expensive one within it. An example is agricultural products. The UK, prior to membership of the EU, was able to buy food at the cheapest prices on the world market, which was a significant benefit to a country that was a major food importer. As a result of EU membership, the price of imported food rose significantly. Trade creation, on the other hand, is said to be a benefit in that it indicates that comparative advantages are being exploited, and that the consumer has a greater choice of products at more competitive prices.

It is possible to illustrate the phenomenon of trade creation by using a simple numerical example. A is the home country, B joins with A in the customs union, and C is the rest of the world. The product is compact disc players (Table 3.1).

Table 3.1 Trade creation

	Price in ECU before the Customs Union			Price in ECU after the Customs Union		
Country	A	B	C	A	B	C
Cost of production	160	140	100	160	140	100
100% tariff imposed by A		140	100			100
Price in A	160	280	200	160	140	200

Before the customs union is formed, A's consumers buy their compact disc players from home suppliers at ECU 160 each, because of the effects of a 100% tariff. Once the customs union is formed, it is possible for A's consumers to buy their CD players at ECU 140 each from B. As a result of customs union membership trade is being created. It is interesting to note that if the tariff levels were different it might change the benefits of membership. If the tariff were set at 50%, A's consumers would be purchasing their CD players from C, because they would cost only ECU 150. Joining the union would be trade-diverting, because purchases would shift to B as a more expensive source.

The trade effects of forming a customs union are illustrated in Figure 3.1. Before the customs union came into existence, the country imposed a tariff that took prices up from P1 to P3. This meant that consumer demand was less than it might have been at q3.

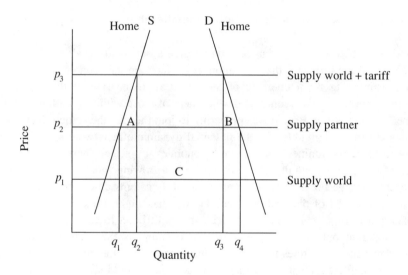

Figure 3.1 The trade effects of forming a Customs Union

If a customs union is formed with the partner country, supplies can be bought at P2, so that home production will fall from q2 to q1, but consumption will increase from q3 to q4. Because of the effects of the common external tariff, existing purchases from the rest of the world will cease. The model therefore contains a mixture of trade creation and trade diversion as follows:

- A is the production effect, in that it represents the saving gained by importing q1 to q2

- B is the consumption effect, i.e. the savings made by the consumer, who now consumes q3 to q4 at lower prices

- A and B are therefore the production and consumption effects of trade creation

- C is the adverse effect of trade diversion, which is the increase in the price of imports from P1 to P2 multiplied by the quantity of imports q2 to q3.

There have been many criticisms of the above analysis, not least from those who suggest that customs unions can only be a second-best solution. If trade creation is such a good thing, they argue, then why not go all the way and have free trade, which gives no trade diversion? Even if trade diversion helps the exporter of higher priced goods, the exporter is still an inefficient producer. While this argument holds true if all countries adopt free trade, this is not a practical suggestion. If a country moves towards free trade on a unilateral basis, there is no reason to think that others will follow. The advantage of forming a customs union is that it is one way of ensuring that those who participate will have certain tariff-free access to markets. Concessions are negotiated among a number of trading nations, and the union usually covers a wide range of products, so that for the union to work there must be general compliance with its rules.

The dynamic effects of Customs Union membership

The static effects of creating a customs union give a once-and-for-all gain or loss, but do not take account of the influence that the union might have on the economies that are members. It would be surprising if membership of an organisation the size of the EU did not have a long-term influence on the economic development of those within it, and indeed the states that remained outside. When Britain was preparing to join the EU, the static effects of membership were thought to be negligible, but the potential dynamic effects were said to be important. In particular, the opportunities for greater economies of scale, increased specialisation, the benefits of competition and the association with fast-growing economies were stressed.

In order to judge the impact of membership of a customs union, an attempt must be made to construct a model of the economy that shows what might have happened had membership not taken place. In an ever-changing world, this is difficult to calculate. Some of the impact may be apparent only in the long term. An example is the argument that a competitive environment helps economies to develop. This suggests that the presence of competition helps to get rid of inefficiency within business, and acts like a 'cold shower' stimulating industry to modernise and improve. It could also reasonably be pointed out that competition can kill off whole sectors of industry that deserve to survive for the social good. In fact, little can be proved in these kinds of debate, which is why they are popular with politicians who like to use them in order to rationalise political decisions.

A more promising area of investigation is the impact of economies of scale. N Owen in his study of trade in industrial goods within the EU from the 1960s onwards, regards competition between companies as something of a brawl.[1] There are many companies trading in very similar products within a mass market, and no one company can hope to produce the total range of products within a sector. Cost advantages are important, even though it may be the quality of the product that determines the success of sales in foreign markets. This is because the better the rate of profit, the more scope the firm has to develop non-price features.

Within a larger market, companies have the opportunity to increase production and enjoy falling costs. Some of these opportunities exist at the expense of other, less efficient, producers. This is illustrated in Figure 3.2. In this example, variable costs such as wages and raw materials are the same for everyone, but fixed costs per unit of output fall with increased scale of production.

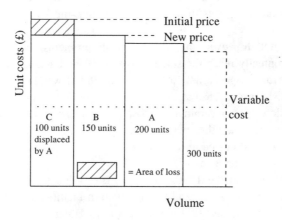

Figure 3.2 Economies of scale and competition
Source : Adapted from Ref. 1

In the case illustrated in Figure 3.2, there are three countries, A, B and C. If C's market is opened up to competition as a result of joining a customs union with A and B, then the lowest cost producer, A, can step into C's market. A's industry can as a result expand production from 200 to 300 units, and so reduce its costs. C's industry is no longer able to compete, and so must go out of business, as prices fall to the level of the next most efficient producer, B. As a result of falling prices, it is possible to envisage an increase in the overall size of the market, and if this process continues progress can be made towards the optimum size of plant. This increased specialisation may not be well regarded by C, which experiences the inevitable loss of jobs.

The production of refrigerators is an interesting example of this process. Italian firms were able to grow and dominate the market within the EU from having a very small-scale industry in the 1950s. This was done by exploiting economies of scale. Italian producers were able to fully exploit the expanding market for cheap family-sized refrigerators in the 1960s. By 1967 the average size of plant of the producers making up 50% of each country's output varied considerably. In Italy, the most efficient country, capacity of the largest producers averaged 850 000 per year, compared to 570 000 for Germany, 290 000 for France and 170 000 for Britain.

By 1967, Ignis (later Philips) and Zanussi were producing 1 million and 700 000 units respectively. They relied on automated plants producing a narrow range of standardised volume refrigerators. The 'cheap and cheerful' product penetrated both the French and German markets to such an extent that their competitors either went 'upmarket' or left the area of production. In some cases, firms imported Italian machines and resorted to vendor branding. Total Italian production rose from 500 000 units in 1958 to 5.4 million units in 1972.

Italian producers recognised early that the best size of plant to produce refrigerators with the level of technology available in the late 1960s and 1970s was probably one capable of producing about 800 000 units per year, while UK producers were thinking in terms of

200 000 units per year. As a consequence, Italian machines could be produced for something like 15 per cent less than similar UK models in the late 1960s. Italian machines were kept out of the UK market until EU membership by a combination of tariffs and transport costs. It was not until the late 1970s, after a series of amalgamations, that the UK producers could match the Italians for cost.

Mass production is not, however, the answer to all problems, because in the case of refrigerators markets eventually reach the stage where everyone has a machine. Zanussi found that its 'cheap and cheerful' image became a liability: in 1985 it was losing money, and had to be rescued by the Swedish firm Electrolux. Not only was it no longer efficient relative to other producers, but it was slow to move into upmarket replacement models, which were colour coordinated. At the same time, another major Italian producer, Indesit, was also in financial difficulties and had to ask to be placed into receivership.

The nature of competition changed, with the industry becoming much more subjected to global competition, especially in the 1990s. In 1994, Electrolux took over the white goods division of the German company AEG, and had production facilities based around the world. One of its major plants, employing 3000 workers, was in Hungary, which was designed to exploit the growing market in the Central and Eastern European states.[2] Electrolux also faced competition within the European market from other multinationals such as Whirlpool, which had bought the white goods division of Philips in 1991. The drive from these companies was to achieve market share on a global basis. This allowed them to develop strategies based on economies of scale in production, marketing and research, and technological development.

The completion of the Single Market

After many years of making little progress with the Single Market as an issue, it was revisited and became an important aspect of the EU's policy agenda in 1985. The Milan European Council decided to launch a campaign for its completion. A programme of important measures was set out in the White Paper *Completing the Internal Market*,[3] with a target date for completion of 31 December 1992. This suggested nearly 300 measures that were considered to be important in removing barriers to trade. However, the original list was reduced to 282 because some of the measures were not needed or were consolidated. (Other measures were included to support the programme, so that in total 500 Single Market measures were actually passed in the period to the end of 1992.) Approximately 95 per cent of the White Paper directives had been agreed at the Council of Minister level by 1 January 1993. However, many of the directives had still to be incorporated into national law by the mid-1990s, and there were still some areas of disagreement, for example animal health and fiscal harmonisation.

The Single Market was launched after many years of doubt concerning the direction of European economic integration. Prior to this time, European economies had experienced an era of slow economic growth, and there had been bitter disputes between the Member States about the structure of the EU budget. The Single Market Programme offered a solution to economic stagnation that was virtually free of any budgetary implication. It also reflected the belief in markets in general, and a support for deregulation. It therefore fitted the political realities of the time when it was launched in 1985. In order to gain general acceptance, many of the measures were agreed as a result of compromises. However, considerable progress was made in achieving the four freedoms, and the programme was closely linked to almost all EU policy areas. So, for example, the Common Agricultural Policy (CAP) was reshaped to take account of the need to remove the artificial price differences between the Member States (see chapter 8). Similarly, the EU attempted to move towards Economic and Monetary Union, which was seen as being an essential underpinning to a Single Market (see chapter 6).

The nature of the debate concerning the completion of the Single Market changed once 1993 had arrived. The White Paper became a reference point in the history of the development of the market rather than being the blueprint for action. The EU then needed to build on the success of the Single Market. In November 1992 the Sutherland Report was published, which proposed a strategy to ensure that the Single Market operated effectively after 1992.[4] This was followed in June 1993 by a communication from the Commission to the Council of Ministers and to the European Parliament entitled *Reinforcing the Effectiveness of the Internal Market*, and a strategic programme in December 1993 entitled *Making the Most of the Internal Market*.[5] These documents further developed the Sutherland Report's conclusions, and laid the foundation for the future. While the documents did not carry the authority of the White Paper of 1985, they set out a number of practical steps. They acknowledged the fact that there was still more to be done in order to complete the Single Market, and made it clear that the EU was not going to rest on its past achievements.

The basis of the Single Market

The Single Market campaign saw a return by the EU to its core economic role, as set out in the Treaty of Rome. This was reinforced by the Single European Act, and most recently by the Treaty on European Union. Article 3 of the TEU replaces a similar Article in the Treaty of Rome, and calls for

1. the elimination, as between Member States, of customs duties and quantitative restrictions on the import and export of goods, and all other measures having equivalent effect

2. an internal market characterised by the abolition, as between Member States, of obstacles to the free movement of goods, persons, services and capital

3. a system ensuring that competition in the internal market is not distorted

4. the approximation of the laws of Member States to the extent required for the functioning of the common market.

The Single Market campaign

The 1985 White Paper identified three broad types of barrier to the completion of the Single Market: physical barriers, technical barriers and fiscal barriers. These barriers were in place for a variety of reasons. In some cases they existed because of a need to regulate aspects of economic activity, often for the protection of the consumer. Many had been in existence for a very long time, and were part of a national tradition. These restrictions hampered trade between the Member States, and created a situation where there was economic stagnation and an inability to compete on a global basis. It was hoped that the completion of the Single Market would

1.   allow the full exploitation of an enlarged market

2.   encourage firms to become more efficient as they faced increased competition and had greater opportunities

3.   benefit the consumer by offering a wider choice of goods at lower prices

4.   speed up the process of political integration.

Physical barriers

Until their removal in 1993, significant physical barriers to trade existed at the customs posts throughout the EU. These posts existed as a convenient point to check the compliance with national rules on indirect taxation, and allowed the fixing of differing prices for agricultural products. Britain, Denmark and Ireland kept minimal border controls in place after 1992, for a variety of national reasons, including the wish to deter terrorism and to help the fight against drugs. The UK also wished check the spread of rabies to its territory.

The removal of the internal barriers created a need to ensure that the EU's external barriers were improved. This was especially the case with the conclusion of the Schengen Agreement. Although not all member states are party to the Agreement, it has virtually removed all evidence of border controls between its members (see chapter 5).

Throughout the EU millions of customs forms were abolished, although there was a need to maintain an adequate record-keeping system to collect taxes and to generate adequate trade statistics. The UK Customs and Excise surveyed 1000 firms and found that the removal of many of the procedures at ports, and the introduction of the EU statistical system Intrastat, had been a benefit. It was expected that savings for UK business would amount to £440 million over a five year period, despite the set-up costs involved.[6] Not surprisingly, there were a number of problems associated with the reliability of trade statistics in the initial stages, and many businesses felt that the procedure was bureaucratic.

Technical barriers

This is the problem of meeting the divergent national product standards and technical regulations, and closed markets in the public sector. An example of liberalisation of product standards concerned the general insurance industry. As of 1 July 1994, insurance companies could compete across borders on the same basis as in their home state, so adopting a single licence system. They were also allowed to set their own rates for policies without having to clear them with the state in which the policy was being sold. This meant that the industry had become deregulated, and it was possible to compare and buy insurance policies across the EU. The fact that rates of insurance are different in different states points to the possibility of intense competition. Table 3.2 gives the extent of variation in car insurance, and indicates that countries with an efficient industry might be able to gain business.

Table 3.2 The cost of car insurance

Country	Average insurance for an experienced driver of a Peugeot 405 (ECU)	Average premiums of a young driver of a Seat Ibiza 1.2 (ECU)
Greece	127	155
UK	134	687
Portugal	157	285
Netherlands	159	473
Denmark	192	446
Spain	212	718
Italy	219	375
France	237	806
Germany	304	957
Luxembourg	367	372
Belgium	394	480
Ireland	585	1 821

Source : Financial Times, 1 July 1994, 19, quoting Bureau Européen des Unions de Consommateurs

Some of the differences shown in Table 3.2 reflect differences in taxation or regulation concerning consumer protection. Even taking account of these factors, there are a number of reasons why the rates will often tend to vary, including

1. variations in road safety

2. the cost of compensating victims

3. the level of service offered

4. traditional methods of selling insurance products, including ownership of outlets

5. cultural factors, such as a distrust of foreign insurance products.

In some countries there are restrictions on the sale of certain kinds of insurance policy. For example, kidnap insurance is forbidden in Italy. This is because of a fear that it will encourage demands for ransoms. In other cases, there may be tax reasons for choosing some insurance policies from certain states, which suggests that further progress needs to be made on the process of fiscal harmonisation.[7]

There is a strong case for trying to ensure that technical standards are not a barrier to trade. Even the most mundane items can fall foul of the technical requirements written into legislation or regulations. The EU has been the subject of a great deal of ridicule when inappropriate attempts have been made to ensure that the technical regulations applying to products are exactly the same. However, the EU has been unjustly criticised on many occasions for its attempts to win agreement about technical standards. For example, the EU was wrongly accused of attempting to standardise coffins throughout the EU. Instead the Commission had been trying to harmonise the legislation for the transfer of corpses, and had simply suggested that coffins should be watertight and strongly built to withstand journeys.[8]

Attempts to win detailed agreement on technical standards has often been a failure. This is called the old approach to technical harmonisation. It failed in many areas because new products were being developed far faster than the EU's ability to generate standards for them. The old approach still applies in areas where important health and safety issues are concerned, and it is in these areas that progress has been slowest because of the detailed work involved.

In contrast, the 'new approach' calls for agreement only on essential technical requirements, and non-essential items are subject to the principle of mutual recognition. This was based on a principle established by the Cassis de Dijon case of 1979, when the European Court of Justice held that there must be mutual recognition of products. In this case, the German government tried to prevent the sale of French alcoholic blackcurrant juice on the grounds of its low alcohol content. As the product was as at least as safe as any other alcoholic beverage, the restriction was unreasonable. The case established the principle that products should be allowed to circulate freely throughout the EU unless they threatened the health or safety of the consumer, damaged the environment or threatened other aspects of the public interest. This was even to be the case if the technical or quality requirements differed from those imposed on domestic products.

At the European level, most standards are set by the European Standards Committee for Standardisation (CEN). However the standards for telecommunications and electrical products are set by ETSI and CENELEC. CEN was established in 1961, and has the EU states and the EFTA states as members, with seven states, mainly from Central Europe, as affiliates. In the UK the body dealing with standards is the British Standards Institution (BSI), while international standards are set by the International Standards Organisation (ISO). Electrical products are covered by the International Electrotechnical Commission. The more participants there are involved in standard-setting, the more time consuming it tends to be. Typically, it has taken on average 2 years to agree a UK standard and 4 years to agree an EU standard. It takes on average 6 years to agree an international standard, largely because over 130 countries are involved. While the EU was very slow in terms of standard-setting in the past, in the period after 1985 this speeded up because of the new approach adopted by the EU which meant that the legislative harmonisation was limited, and the supporting technical specifications were developed by the standards organisations.

Public procurement (purchases by government departments, local government and other public sector organisations) amounted to ECU 550 billion in 1991, which was 14.4 per cent of the EU12 GDP. In the past, these markets had been closed to non-national competition, with only 0.14 per cent of GDP going to non-national EU suppliers. While up to half of public purchases could not realistically be provided by non-nationals, this is still a major market. Cecchini[9] estimated savings of ECU 21 billion if these markets were opened to EU-wide competition. Many of the directives designed to liberalise procurement were slow to be adopted, or were persistently circumvented by national authorities. At the same time, surprisingly little use was made of the remedial measures that companies could have used to gain redress for being discriminated against. Even if companies are aggrieved, many take the view that undertaking legal action would harm their future commercial dealings.

A requirement of the EU directives related to public procurement was that larger contracts be advertised in the *Official Journal*. The number of contracts advertised in the *Official Journal* did increase from 19 000 in 1988 to 67 000 in 1993. However, the Commission recognised that there were shortcomings in the process, including the following:

1. Poor access to contracts for small and medium-sized companies, many of which lacked the capacity to operate across national borders.

2. Many national officials were ignorant of procedure and needed more training.

3. The spread of information was not adequate.

4. There was a need for greater clarity about technical standards.

5. Payments needed to be made more quickly.

6. The system for facilitating appeals needed to be improved.[10]

Fiscal barriers

The EU consists of a number of separate tax territories, each with its own system of taxation. The physical barriers that existed between the Member States of the EU prior to 1993 had an important role in the collection of taxes. If tax rates are significantly different between countries, this can have an impact on the location of businesses and where consumers choose to spend their money. The setting and collection of taxes is close to the heart of national sovereignty, and as a consequence of this the EU uses unanimous voting for taxation issues. As a result, progress towards fiscal harmonisation has been slow. The tax system is important to governments because

● it raises revenue

● it can be used as an incentive

● it affects the distribution of income

● it can promote efficiency

● it has a social impact.

Not only does a lack of sovereignty in taxation issues cause political problems concerning the right of sovereign states, but it can also make the conduct of domestic economic policy difficult. The more harmonised taxation policy is within the EU, the less flexibility individual Member States have to address problems such as budget deficits.

The case for harmonisation of taxes within the EU is that without it tax competition is likely to emerge, where the location of both business and private transactions is influenced by the tax system. If border controls exist, it is possible to isolate a country's taxation system to an extent, by not permitting certain transactions to take place. For example, cross-border shopping to take advantage of lower taxes in another state can be prevented by strict import controls. However, as soon as the EU decided to open its frontiers as part of the Single Market programme, tax competition was inevitable. The EU needs to move towards a harmonised system of taxation that does not distort market conditions. This implies that there must be a harmonisation of tax rates, the tax base and the enforcement of taxes.

At the very early stages of development, the EU was able to agree to the setting of common customs duties for goods entering the customs union. The use of value-added tax dates back to the first VAT directive of 1967, which required the Member States to introduce the tax by 1972. While VAT is a major source of revenue for the Member States, a portion of it is donated to the EU budget. The rates that applied throughout the EU varied considerably until 1993, when customs-based formalities at the borders relating to the documentation and payment of VAT were removed.

As of 1993 there was an agreed minimum standard rate for VAT of 15 per cent throughout the EU, with special lower rates and exemptions for particular countries, for example the UK retained a zero rate on children's clothes. The very high rates of luxury tax were also to be phased out. For the individual, once goods are purchased and VAT is paid, those goods can be moved around the EU without paying further VAT on entering another Member State. Table 3.3 shows the VAT rates in force in 1995. The fact that Member States are prepared to keep their standard rates of VAT largely within a range of 15 to 20 per cent means that they are unlikely to distort trade.

Table 3.3 Standard VAT rates in 1995

Country	% VAT	Country	% VAT
Austria	20	Italy	19
Belgium	20.5	Luxembourg	15
Denmark	25	Netherlands	17.5
Finland	22	Portugal	17
France	18.6	Spain	16
Germany	15	Sweden	25
Greece	18	UK	17.5
Ireland	21		

Value-added tax used to be refunded and collected at the borders between the Member States, but this was replaced on 1 January 1993. A temporary system was put in place in which VAT was collected within the Member State where the goods were being purchased. Border controls for VAT have gone, but their removal created a highly bureaucratic system of tax collection. In 1997 a definitive VAT regime should be in place, based on collecting VAT in the country of origin. The benefit of this system is that a business sending goods from London to Paris would charge the UK VAT, in the same way as if the goods were being sent to Manchester. The French company could then reclaim the VAT via its national VAT return. Although this system fits in well with the philosophy of the Single Market, it has been criticised. If VAT is collected in the country where the goods are produced, this will favour those countries with balance of payments surpluses within the EU. Deficit countries will lose out unless an adequate system of compensation can be found.

The existence of duty-free sales is an anomaly. These are to be retained at ports and airports until 1999, but there are limits to the extent of purchases. The agreement to retain duty-free sales was designed to help producers of luxury items such as perfumes and whisky. They feared that without these sales their businesses would suffer. Also, the sales are profitable for the owners of the shops and they are popular with travellers. This concession has been criticised: the sales need to be monitored, and they offer tax breaks to the travelling public, which is generally made up of the more affluent members of society.

There has been no effective harmonisation of excise duties on alcohol and tobacco products, and this has led to significant problems. Social attitudes vary greatly with respect to these kinds of products. In countries such as the UK, excise duties are set at higher rates in order to discourage smoking and drinking to excess. If taxes on these items were reduced, many would feel that public health was being threatened. While rates of taxes and therefore prices to consumers do differ, the free movement of people should ensure that the differences are not so significant that the trade becomes difficult to monitor.

The impact of a lack of harmonisation can be demonstrated in the case of cross-border trade between the UK and its continental neighbours. As of 1993, a very high limit was placed on the amount that individuals could import of duty-paid items from other member states. The basic condition was that whatever was imported had to be for the individual's own consumption, or for private gifts. This made it worth while for individuals to take shopping trips from the UK to France, and in many cases resell their purchases.

The price of beer in France is significantly lower than it is in the UK. Part of the reason for this is the fact that in 1994 the duty on beer in the UK was 30 pence per pint, compared with only 4 pence per pint in France (the EU recommended duty was 8 pence). In 1993, the duty-paid allowance for personal consumption into the UK was fixed at 110 litres per person. The UK Brewers Society (BLRA) claimed that 1.9 million hectolitres (330 million pints) was imported into the UK by individuals, which amounted to 15 per cent of the UK take-home market. To overcome this, the UK brewing industry suggested reducing the duty on beer in the home market, in order to

1. make personal imports less attractive

2. encourage consumption of the home-based product.

The case against reducing excise duty is that the long-term trend for beer consumption is downward. When Denmark reduced its duty on beer by 30 per cent between 1991 and 1993, the market remained flat. Also, doubts were expressed about the value of the survey carried out by the UK brewers, given that the decline in UK sales was not as marked as was estimated, and the sale of French beer also declined in that year. The brewers' estimate seemed to assume that nearly all passengers carried their allowance home. Alternative estimates suggest that the volume of beer crossing the North Sea might really be in the region of 800 000 hectolitres. Not every passenger carries their beer allowance home, because of the weight and inconvenience of carrying such a large volume of the beverage.[11] However, it is also clear that the higher allowances, and reduced supervision by the Customs and Excise, led to the growth of an illegal trade, which also took advantage of the even wider difference of duty on wines, spirits and tobacco products. On wine, for example, the duty was £0.2 per bottle in France, compared to £1.01 in the UK, and cigarettes cost about £1 per pack less in France. The illegal trade may be worth as much as £35 million per year, while the total loss of tax to the UK exchequer from all cross border import of alcoholic drinks and tobacco has been put at £250 million per year.[12]

The above example of cross-border shopping illustrates the dilemma facing policy-makers. If they propose that there be a harmonisation downwards, they risk losing revenue and sacrificing important social values. The way to resolve this is to try and agree much narrower differences in indirect tax rates, but this creates problems in terms of reconciling different social values.

Another area of fiscal harmonisation that has made disappointing progress is that of company taxation. In December 1990 a committee of eight independent experts, chaired by

Onno Ruding, a former Dutch Finance Minister, was asked to investigate the impact of differing systems of corporate taxation within the EU. The Ruding Committee reported to the Commission in March 1992.[13] It was asked to investigate three questions.

1. Do differences in the business taxes distort the Single Market?

2. Will the interplay of market forces (tax competition) sort the problem out?

3. What measures does the EU need to take?

There was also a recognition of the need to face up to the rights of Member States, and subsidiarity. The findings of the Committee came as no surprise. They were as follows.

1. Significant differences did exist between the company taxation systems of the Member States. These included differences in the tax rates and the tax base, as well as differences in the treatment of cross-border flows of corporate income and the way in which losses were offset.

2. The differences could influence where companies established themselves.

3. Tax competition would not get out of hand, because governments needed to maintain income, but Member States tended to use tax concessions to attract mobile international investment.

The Committee recommended that the EU encourage

1. the removal of discrimination in the company tax system

2. the setting of a minimum level of corporation tax

3. the maximum transparency in the taxation system.

A small number of directives have been agreed that should improve the situation, particularly with regard to double taxation. These include the Mergers Directive and the Parent Subsidiary Directive, both passed in 1990. The first aims to make taxation neutral in the case of a cross-border merger; the second tries to prevent double or triple taxation when companies operate in different states. However, progress has been slow and new legislation often takes years to win agreement.

The gains from completing the Single Market

It was fortunate that the launch of the Single Market campaign coincided with an upturn in the economic cycle. The period from 1984 to 1990 was one of economic success, with industrial output in the EU growing by 20 per cent and 8.5 million jobs being created. Intra-EU trade had also grown back to the levels it enjoyed in the early 1970s. This meant that the process of carrying through the legislative programme set out in the White Paper was conducted at a time when confidence in the economy was high. The campaign had an extra advantage in that it did not impose an additional cost on the EU budget.

It is difficult to calculate the benefits from the completion of the Single Market without knowing the cost to the EU economy of the restrictions. However, many non-tariff barriers come to the notice of the EU only if there are complaints. Despite these difficulties, the Commission attempted to quantify the known costs, via a series of surveys commissioned into the monetary value of the opportunities being missed by the Member States. The summary of these findings was published in a popular form in 1988, in Paolo Cecchini's *The European Challenge: 1992 The Benefits of a Single Market* (known as the Cecchini Report). This showed the cost of *not* completing the Single Market to be as high as £140 billion, therefore that was the size of the potential benefits to be gained from pushing ahead and removing the technical, physical and fiscal barriers to trade. The welfare gain from removing the barrier was estimated to be between 5 and 7 per cent of the EU's GDP, and there were benefits in terms of creating a large number of new jobs. The consumer would also gain from being able to buy goods and services at lower prices.

The Cecchini Report was a political document, designed to encourage progress towards the completion of the Single Market. As a consequence, the estimates of the benefits were not assured. The researchers employed by the EU produced the most favourable estimates that were likely to materialise if all barriers were removed. However, many of the reforms that were part of the programme reflected the need to win agreement rather than being ideal in terms of removing barriers to the Single Market. In addition, the survey was not able to take account of the ways in which producers were already able to overcome the barriers. That is, the potential nuisance value of many restrictions could well be far less for firms already well organised for trade.

It was hoped that the completion of the Single Market would create 1.8 million jobs in the long term, but more than 500 000 people were expected to lose their employment as a result of deregulation. Sectors such as telecommunications, mechanical engineering and pharmaceuticals were set to grow, even against the strong external pressures of Japan and the USA, while employment would decline in sectors such as the glass industry, textiles, railway equipment, clothing and furniture.

The benefits of the completion of the Single Market are unlikely to be evenly spread. There will be winners and losers unless measures are taken to compensate regions that have less efficient industrial structures. Low labour costs members such as Portugal were thought to have a competitive advantage in a Single Market. However, the availability of even cheaper labour in Central or Eastern Europe, or even outside Europe, may cast doubt on this, especially since the completion of the Uruguay GATT Round in 1994, which should improve the international trading environment. Also, in many cases success will be related to existing industrial competitiveness and the ability to attract future investment rather than lower labour costs. A further danger is the prospect of Member States' using state aids to protect key industries if the competition is from within the Single Market (see chapter 10).

The European Commission clarified its view of the Cecchini Report in 1994, when it emerged that the macroeconomic consequences of the programme to complete the Single Market would take several years to materialise.[14] This suggested that the following points were important.

1.   Timing issues – the legislation was still being brought into effect.

2.   Complementary measures still needed to be put into place.

3. The macroeconomic environment had changed considerably since the launch of the programme. Events such as the unification of Germany, the liberalisation of trade with the Central and Eastern European states and the move towards a recession after a period of economic growth changed the way in which the European economy operated.

Achievements of the Single Market

While there were difficulties in isolating the impact of the Single Market from other events, the Commission suggested that it might have added 0.4 per cent per annum to economic growth in the years 1988 to 1992. This was before the Single Market had achieved its full potential. Areas of particular success included the following:

1. Most of the restrictions on goods crossing borders within the EU were removed.

2. Intra-EU trade increased from 53.4 per cent of imports in 1985 to 59.3 per cent in 1992. Exports rose from 54.9 per cent to 61.3 per cent.

3. Individuals could move freely.

4. There was mutual recognition of professional and higher education qualifications, which made it easier for professionals to operate across frontiers.

5. There was freedom to provide many services across the EU, although some work needed to be done in areas such as financial services.

6. Road and air transport services were liberalised.

7. There was harmonisation of technical regulation.

8. Public sector contracts became more open to bidders from outside the home state.

9. Indirect taxes were sufficiently in line, that there was no need to restrict individuals from taking their purchases into another state.

10. Free movement of capital increased the extent of cross-border investments and mergers.

11. The EU became an attractive destination for foreign direct investment.

Foreign direct investment (FDI)

A feature of the Single Market has been increased foreign direct investment, particularly by US and Japanese companies. In part, this can be explained by the need to invest surpluses created by trade imbalances. Inward investment has been encouraged by the success of the Single Market, and perhaps a fear that attempts might be made to exclude foreign companies or restrict their activities. For some non-EU countries the creation of a 'fortress Europe' has appeared a significant threat, especially at times when trade wars threaten to break out. The trends in FDI flows are given in Table 3.4.

Table 3.4 Flows of direct investment between the EU and the principal economic areas (ECU millions)

Direct investments from:	1988	1989	1990	1991
EU to the USA	22.0	23.7	6.3	9.1
USA to EU	1.3	8.9	9.1	5.4
EU to Japan	0.2	0.7	0.9	0.4
Japan to EU	2.2	4.2	4.8	1.7
EU to EFTA	2.6	2.4	3.3	2.8
EFTA to EU	8.4	8.5	11.0	6.8
EU to former CMEA	0.1	0.1	0.3	1.3
Former CMEA to EU	0	0	0	0.4
EU to ACP[1]	0.3	0.3	0.2	1.4
ACP[1] to EU	0	0	0	0.4
EU to the world	31.6	33.3	19.3	26.8
The world to EU	16.1	27.9	33.2	21.2

[1]   Excluding ACP states that are also members of OPEC
Source: Eurostat, quoted by *Europe*, 21 April 1994, 17

Table 3.4 shows somewhat erratic progress, with a significant downturn of outward investment between 1989 and 1990. This caused the EU to be a net importer of capital. The main reason for this was the decline in investment from the UK, which moved from being a capital exporter to an importer of investment.

Foreign direct investment is a substitution of capital exports for goods exports. The two might be closely related, for example, if investment in a plant to assemble cars results in an increase in the export of components. The attractions of FDI to the member states of the EU are that it

● assists the balance of payments

● generates employment

● assists economic growth

● transfers valuable technology and production skills.

The challenge for the EU is to avoid excessive competition for FDI. This can result in many of its overall benefits being lost, as firms from outside the EU are offered incentives to move to a specific location.

The EU generally welcomes FDI that is related to the establishment of a manufacturing base, because it is a useful job-creation mechanism. This welcome is constrained to an extent by the fear that new producers within the EU will challenge those already in place. An example of this is the Japanese car manufacturers, who created new jobs in the UK but were a threat to the French and Italian producers. This created the threat that these would be treated as part of the Japanese external car quota, and would not be permitted free circulation within the Single Market. FDI in the services sector has often been associated with franchise operations such as McDonalds, the chain of fast food restaurants. While these activities do create jobs, they are often poorly paid. Finally, a great deal of the FDI is concerned with the financial services sector, which offers limited opportunities for job creation.

FDI means that the activity of foreign firms becomes internalised within the Single Market, which may assist relations with governments or consumer loyalty. It reduces the problems associated with technical barriers, and gives the prospect of enjoying economies of scale. There may also be savings because of lower wage and non-wage costs. Even within a market the foreign firm must make a choice of where to locate. The Japanese have consistently favoured the UK as a location within the EU, with about 45 per cent of their investment going there in 1991, and just over 30 per cent in 1992. This probably indicates that there may be other factors at work, such as political stability, cultural acceptability, quality of infrastructure and the availability of incentives.

Stage Two of the Single Market

In March 1992 a high-level group was formed under the former Commissioner Peter Sutherland with a brief to identify ways of securing the benefits of the Single Market on a long-term basis. The group presented its report to the European Council held in December 1992. The report, entitled *The Internal Market After 1992 – Meeting the Challenge*,[15] recognised the unprecedented legislative achievement of the initiative, which left only 18 proposals outstanding. The report called for the EU to make the rules have the same effect everywhere. This meant that there needed to be greater mutual confidence between the Member States. It would therefore be necessary to:

1. clarify the nature and extent of any remaining barriers within the Single Market

2. develop an effective communications strategy, so that people are aware of their rights concerning the Single Market and have an early warning of any new legislation

3. make every effort to ensure that all EU legislation is transposed into national law

4. ensure that any infringements are rapidly dealt with

5. explain to business the new laws and how they operate – consumers would also need to be satisfied that mutual recognition would not result in a reduction in the safety of the products they purchased, and that in the case of anything going wrong there would be adequate redress

6. ensure that business could participate fully in the market, and that the new trend towards subsidiarity did not lead to creation of new trade barriers

7. accelerate the development of practical cooperation between national and EU institutions.

The Commission's strategy for the second stage

The Commission built on many of the ideas in the Sutherland Report, when it set out its aspirations for the next stage of the Single Market in the publications, *Towards a Strategic Programme for the Internal Market* and *Making the Most of the Internal Market*.[16] The framing of the strategy reflected the sensitivity of the Commission that the measures adopted should not erode the rights of the Member States. However, legislation at all levels should be carried out in a coherent way that did not result in a refragmentation of the EU because of national initiatives.[17]

The EU had as a priority the completion of the measures remaining from the 1985 White Paper, and their transposition into national law. There was also a need to ensure that in the future the existing legislation is fully utilised and applied. This is important in order to prevent new barriers appearing, and to enable the existing barriers to be removed. In this respect the process of transposing EU legislation into national legislation in a clear and transparent way is of particular importance. There was also a need to ensure a common interpretation of regulations. In addition, the effect of regulation and directives needed to be monitored. The fact that the EU has legislated in a particular area is no guarantee that the legislation will be effective, and there may be a need to return to the issue at a later date.

What still needs to be done?

The free movement of goods within the Single Market was almost assured for most sectors in 1993, but there were significant gaps in a number of areas. These included the following.

Improving the environment for consumers

The Strategic Programme called for the consumer to gain from greater choice and competition. At the same time it was important to ensure that consumers' rights were protected. Consumer groups have constantly criticised the operation of the Single Market. For example, the Bureau of European Consumers (BUEC) declared that 'The Single Market will not exist for European consumers on 1 January 1993 and will not be implemented for many years yet.'[18] It listed a multitude of sectors where the situation was far from satisfactory. These included the fact that at that time lists of authorised food additives had not been approved, and rules for labelling were incomplete. There were no EU regulations banning furniture-filling materials that emitted toxic fumes when they burned. Television standards were still different. Consumers were not protected against aggressive sales of insurance policies, and air transport would not be fully liberalised until April 1997.

The issue of price differentials within the Single Market has proved controversial. With a wide geographical spread, differences in tastes and national taxation regimes, and variability in the national distribution systems, prices may vary. The situation is made worse by exchange rate movements and differences in wage rates and inflation rates. Some of these factors will become less important over time, but there are price differences that are significant and are maintained by state or EU support. An example commonly quoted is that of car prices, which have varied by as much as 30 per cent. While individuals can go to another EU state to buy a car to import into their own country, the automobile manufacturers were able to persuade the EU that the maintenance of an adequate service network meant that bulk imports by unauthorised dealers was not acceptable. An example of the variation in the price of cars came with the launch of the Ford Mondeo in March 1993. At the time of the launch, the variation in price was 22 per cent between the different member states for the same model and specification. A year later, the price of the Mondeo 1.6CLX was still 19 per cent higher in Germany than in Spain. Table 3.5 gives the selling price of the Mondeo after taking into account taxes and specifications.

Table 3.5 Price differences of cars (Ford Mondeo, 1.6 CLX, tax-excluded prices, adjusted for differing specifications)

	Price, cheapest = 100 in May 1994
Germany	118.7
UK	110.5
France	109.2
Netherlands	106.2
Portugal	100.4
Spain	100.0

Source : European Commission, quoted by *The Economist*, 27 August 1994, 31

Some of the above differences reflect the problems of pricing with variable exchange rates, and also domestic conditions within particular markets. However, consumer groups have consistently argued that such differences are not acceptable in a Single Market.

Improving the environment for business

The original purpose of the Single Market campaign was to improve the environment for business. With this in mind, it was felt that there needed to be a strong competition policy. This would be helped by the introduction of competition in previously excluded areas such as energy, telecommunications and postal services.

The system of cross-border payments

The virtual collapse of the European Monetary System's (EMS) Exchange Rate Mechanism (ERM) in August 1993 meant that payment for goods and services became more subject to the whims of the foreign exchange markets. It made worse a problem that had already been seen as a significant disincentive to trade. In an ideal world the solution to many of the problems of cross-border payments would have been the adoption of a single currency. This was a pillar of the Treaty on European Union, but few seemed to believe that it was a realistic possibility within the time span proposed in the Treaty.

In the absence of European Monetary Union (EMU), the Commission has sought to pressurise banks within the EU to stop profiteering at the expense of the consumer and small business. There are only 200 million retail cross-border payments every year within the EU, which is small in relation to domestic transactions. Cross-border payments are only 0.8 per cent of domestic business in the UK, and even in an open economy like Belgium's they amount to only 4 per cent. The Commission blames this on the high level of charges, which can be 20 times the equivalent national rates.[19]

The Commission wished to ensure that such payments were as rapid, reliable and inexpensive as payments made within the domestic economy. It proposed that there be closer cooperation between the banks and their customers. The Commission proposes the first European-wide 'Users' Charter', which would set out customer service targets. This would give customers the right to have full information about the cost of services in advance, a breakdown of charges and the right to legal protection. A survey in 1993 showed that the quality of service offered to business had improved, although charges were still significantly higher for cross-border payments. The average time for payments was found to be 4.6 working days, with 87 per cent of all transactions within the EU being completed within 6 working days. There were, however, cases where payments had taken 70 days to complete.[20]

Technical standards

It was felt that there were still important issues to be addressed related to technical standards. Not only was there a need to maximise the benefits to be gained from existing standards, but, where appropriate, new standards needed to be developed. There are some significant gaps in the range of EU standards. To tourists, the most significant failure is the absence of a European standard for electrical plugs, although attempts have been made to agree one. In 1994 there were over 20 plug configurations, with a number of differing types of socket. The EU has attempted to create a standard for plugs, but it would be expensive to introduce it. A report commissioned by the UK government analysed the costs and benefits of introducing a Europlug.[21] This found that the cost to the consumer of a change to the new standard might be as high as £78 million per year in the UK if the government tried to accelerate the change by imposing stringent wiring regulations. However, just allowing the free market to operate with no legislation would cost the consumer £19 million per year. There would be benefits to European firms of eventually being able to produce for just one type of plug, but this would also be an advantage for producers from outside the EU.

Europe has gained internationally from its move towards the adoption of common standards, because of the size and importance of the market in which they operate. However, as we have seen from the example of the Europlug, new standards impose costs. Some of these costs fall on the manufacturers of products. Where companies have products that fail to match up to standards, they may have to consider whether the cost of complying with the new standards is really worth while. For example, the European Toy Directive put a number of small toy manufacturers out of business.

The move to complete the Single Market led to a rush to agree EU standards. There were complaints that some of the standards had been poorly drafted and were subject to misinterpretation, especially between the differing national certification and testing bodies which confirm that a standard has been met. To try to overcome some of these problems, the European Organisation for Testing and Certification (EOTC) was set up in January 1993, to ensure that the differing national bodies recognise each other's work. There are in the region of 10 000 independent testing laboratories and a large number of certification organisations within the EU. The mutual recognition of test certificates will mean that many of these will go, which should cut costs for industry over a period of time.

Intellectual and industrial property

Following the completion of the GATT Round and the establishment of the World Trade Organisation, the EU has had to take greater note of its international responsibilities with respect to intellectual and industrial property. In 1993, the EU agreed that books and films should benefit from copyright protection for 70 years after the author's death, while musical recordings could receive royalties for 50 years from the date of recording. This measure was agreed by a majority vote, and meant that it was not possible to exploit the position where certain states had lax rules. Therefore, the Beatles' early recordings, which were not due royalties in Germany because of a 25 year copyright rule, will be entitled to payment from July 1997. The owners of the Beatles' copyright will then be able to receive royalties because a 50 year rule will come into effect.[22]

Implementation of the Single Market

As the Single Market has become a legislative reality, the need has arisen to make the legislation work. The first stage was to ensure that when directives were passed they were transposed into the law of the nation states. This was more difficult than might be imagined, because of the need to frame appropriate national legislation. In addition, the national parliaments had to have their say. The Commission has the task of ensuring that each of the 2 000 pieces of legislation passed, in each of the EU's official languages, is monitored to ensure that it complies with the original directives.

The Commission is responsible under Article 155 of the EEC Treaty for ensuring that the legislation is then enforced, and in this respect it has relied not only on its own resources but also on those of a number of pressure groups, and the complaints from business and the general public. The Commission has tended to receive a large number of complaints about aspects of the Single Market, most commonly about the free movement of goods.

It is the national administration that usually has the task of administering the legislation concerning the Single Market. This decentralisation means that there has to be a degree of control over the activities of national administrations, because without such a system distortions can creep into the mechanisms. In this respect, there needs to be a regular audit of the activities of those who are responsible for implementing the legislation. If there is a failure, the first point of access for complaint must be to the national administration. In the UK, the Single Market Compliance Unit was set up to

1. advise those who have evidence of a breach of EU law

2. research and verify cases where breaches have occurred

3. act as a focus for complaints from outside the UK.

The normal practice is for Member States to deal with complaints on a bilateral basis. After this there are national courts, and finally there is the European Court of Justice. Generally, legal action is very time-consuming and expensive. It can take up to three years to bring a case to the European Court of Justice. The only case where the EU takes a specific view as to the remedies available to complainants is the case of public procurement. In other areas there is a provision for judicial review, for example with regard to the Customs Code or the mutual recognition of qualifications.

Changing the structure of the EU market to permit free movement means that there has had to be an improvement in the control over goods entering into the market from outside the EU. This also applies to areas such as migration, because individual nations' borders are also in place to protect the whole of the EU. The following points must be recognised.

1. National authorities are now acting on behalf of the whole EU. This means that they need to be aware of a wide range of EU rules.

2. National laws need to be transparent (to be easily understood and have a clear meaning), especially as the EU has adopted subsidiarity. Devolving governmental tasks downwards to the most appropriate level is desirable, in the sense that the citizen can feel closer to the instruments of government. However, it means that there are opportunities for national law-makers to diverge in the way that rules are set, and so they may create new barriers within the market.

The Commission has a range of tools it can employ to promote mutual recognition and ensure that barriers to trade do not reappear. The prospect of the EU regressing to the point where a range of new and significant barriers could be a significant new obstacle to trade led to the EU taking positive action in the form of Directive 83/189/EEC, which has applied to goods since 1988. Member states are required to inform the Commission of any planned rules or regulations. Once the Commission has been informed, a process of vetting takes place. Action can be taken against Member States that refuse to recognise the technical standards of other Member States. However, the process needs to be more transparent than at present, with the onus on Member States to declare which products they refuse to accept and the basis on which this is done. Animal health is a good example of this, where it is possible to create a major public reaction against certain products. However, these kinds of problem could be best resolved by joint EU action taken to resolve the overall problem rather than discrimination against the products of a particular Member State.

Conclusions

By the mid-1990s there were clear signs that the investment in the Single Market was starting to show some return, despite a period of recession and slow economic growth. The programme did not impose any financial costs on the EU budget, but was able to achieve a major change in the way that business was conducted across the national borders of Europe.

The Single Market was slow to come about, and needed a combination of the right political and economic climate to achieve the current situation. Any further progress may be perceived as being harmful to national sovereignty, especially as it challenges national tradition. However, some loss of sovereignty is a price the Member States must be prepared to pay to achieve progress. It is not realistic to expect the Single Market to move forward without a high degree of integration across a wide range of policy areas. Moving onwards to the next stage where the achievements could be consolidated and built on, is inevitably a lower profile task. However, if the process of economic integration is allowed to stagnate as it did in the 1970s, it is easy to envisage a situation where new barriers come into place and the achievements of the 1992 campaign are eroded.

Notes and references

1. **Owen N** (1983) *Economies of Scale, Competitiveness, and Trade Patterns Within the European Community*, Oxford University Press.
2. *The European*, 1 July 1994, 32.
3. **Commission** (1985) *Completing the Internal Market*, COM (85) 310 final.
4. **Sutherland P** *et al*. (1992) *The Internal Market After 1992 – Meeting the Challenge*, Commission of the EU.
5. **Commission** (1993) *Reinforcing the Effectiveness of the Internal Market*, COM (93) 256 final, and *Making the Most of the Internal Market*, COM 632 final.
6. *Financial Times*, 11 May 1994, 10.
7. **Lapper R** (1994) Hard Work to be Free and Single, *Financial Times*, 1 July 1994, 19.
8. **Commission** (1994) *Do You Believe all You Read in the Newspapers?* London Office, p. 10.
9. **Cecchini P** (1998) *The European Challenge 1992*, Gower, Aldershot.
10. *Europe*, 15 January 1994, 9.
11. *Financial Times*, 9 June 1994, 22.
12. *Financial Times*, 6 June 1994, 5.
13. See *Fiscal Studies* (1992), Vol 13, No. 2 for a series of commentaries on the Report.
14. **Commission** (1994) *The Community Internal Market – 1993 Report*, COM (94) 55 final, p. 17.
15. **Sutherland P** *et al*. (1992), op. cit.
16. **Commission** (1993) COM (93) 256 final and COM (93) 632 final, op. cit.
17. Ibid., 4.
18. *Europe*, No. 5891, 6 January 1993, 15.
19. *Europe*, 26 March 1992, 8.
20. *Europe*, 2 October 1993, 7.
21. **Department of Trade and Industry** (1994) *Costs and Benefits in the UK of Plug Harmonisation in Europe*, HMSO, London.
22. *Financial Times*, 15 June 1993, 2.

Further reading

Baldwin R (1994) *Towards an Integrated Europe*, CEPR.
Commission (1993) *Growth, Competitiveness and Employment in the European Community*, COM (93) 700.
Commission (1994) *The Community Internal Market – 1993 Report*, COM (94) 55 final, p. 17.
Cutler T *et al*. (1989) *1992 – The Struggle for Europe*, Berg.
Jacquemin A and Sapir A (Eds) (1990) *The European Internal Market*, Oxford University Press.
Oxford Review of Economic Policy (1993) European Internal Market, Vol. 9, No. 1.
Robson P (1987) *The Economics of International Integration*, Allen and Unwin, London.
Swann D (1992) *The Single European Market and Beyond*, Routledge, London.

Appendix 1

Update on the Single Market

By 1995, the Council of Ministers had adopted over 95 per cent of the 282 measures which made up the 1985 Single Market White Paper. The issue of completion of the Single Market is complicated by the fact that some of the legislation is in the form of Regulations, which have a direct impact on the Member States, and Directives which have to be transposed into national legislation. By February 1995 the EU average for implementation of Single Market measures by the Member States had reached over 90 per cent for the first time.

There were problem areas, such as intellectual property (67 per cent of legislation had been transposed), and public procurement (70 per cent of legislation had been transposed). As can be seen from the table below, the state which had the best record for transposition of legislation was Denmark which had a record of scepticism about the extent to which integration should go.

Table 3A.1 Implementation of the Single Market White Paper measures, February 1995

	Measures notified	Not applicable	Derogations	Measures not notified	Partial Notification
Denmark	209	2	0	5	2
France	205	0	0	9	4
Luxembourg	204	4	0	11	0
Netherlands	204	1	0	11	2
UK	202	1	0	12	3
Belgium	196	1	0	14	6
Spain	191	1	3	20	1
Ireland	190	4	0	22	1
Italy	190	4	0	22	1
Portugal	188	4	3	18	2
Germany	184	3	0	23	5
Greece	169	4	3	39	1

Source: *Europe*, 27/28 February 1995, 9

Note: At that time 219 measures had been adopted, but agreement had not been reached on the implementation of all measures in the Member States. This accounts for the totals not being uniform.

CHAPTER 4

A common and integrated Transport Policy

Introduction

The EU's Common Transport Policy (CTP) was slow to develop, but since the mid-1980s progress has been made in the completion of the Single Market for transport services. However, many of the liberalisation measures agreed will not come into effect until nearly the end of the century, and they must be accompanied by the harmonisation of a number of measures, such as taxation and social conditions. This chapter analyses some of these measures, and argues that if the CTP is to be a success, the process of integrating the EU's transport system must make further progress, in particular with the completion of Trans-European Networks (TENs). The chapter examines the two modes of transport that have grown most rapidly, and been the subject of the greatest degree of controversy. In the case of road transport the very different national practices have been of particular importance, while the effectiveness of the liberalisation of civil aviation has been questioned.

For nearly 30 years the CTP made very little progress, despite many documents being produced, which gave the appearance of a common policy. In 1985, the European Court of Justice ruled that the Council of Ministers had infringed article 75 of the Treaty of Rome by failing to ensure freedom to provide services in the sphere of international transport, and to lay down the conditions under which non-resident carriers could operate transport services in a Member State. Then, after a slow start, there was progress towards liberalising the market in transport services, despite many disappointments. However, it is unlikely that the main restrictions on the market for transport services will be fully removed until the end of the century.

Like many other policies, the transport area is one where there is shared responsibility between the Member States. Many of these also have extensive bilateral relations with third countries, for example in the area of air transport. With the spreading of the EU across Europe, the relationships with other states and their land links is also of importance. The insistence of the Member States in protecting their individual national interest has helped to keep the transport system fragmented. National governments are frequently the target of vested interests, who gain from the fragmented provision despite the overall losses in welfare.

Transport developments cannot be left entirely to the free market. With the enlarging of the EU and the removal of many of the barriers between East and West, the task of developing a Europe-wide transport system has become more urgent. Also, it is clear that the issue of how to maintain the rights of individual states is still important, especially where environmental issues are concerned. Also, given the limits of the EU's budget, there must be an equitable system of paying for infrastructure.

The basis of policy

The basis of the CTP is set out in Articles 74 to 84 of the Treaty of Rome. These call for:

1. a common set of rules governing transport, with equality of treatment

2. state aids to be permitted in order to promote public service

3. a progressive reduction in costs

4. the provisions to apply to road, rail and inland waterways, with the addition of sea and air transport at a later date.

The Treaty on European Union (TEU) did not alter the basic provisions of the Treaty of Rome significantly, except by references to transport safety and the addition of Article 129 b,c,d and Article 130 d covering the development of Trans-European Networks and their role in promoting economic and social cohesion.

Article 129 b of the TEU states that

1. '...the Community shall contribute to the establishment and development of Trans-European networks in the areas of transport, telecommunications and energy infrastructures'

2. 'within a framework system of open and competitive markets, the Community shall aim at promoting the interconnection and interoperability of national networks as well as access to such networks.'

The TEU stresses the importance of islands and peripheral regions, harmonisation of technical standards, support via loans, feasibility studies, and the new Cohesion Fund. The Commission is given the role of coordinating the activities of the Member States, and also relations with third countries.

The rationale for a Common Transport Policy

One of the reasons for having a CTP is that the industry is of great importance to the European economy. The transport industry represents about 4 per cent of the EU GDP, but this increases to between 7 and 8 per cent of GDP if private transport is included. In 1991, it employed an estimated 5.6 million people. The importance of the sector is of course increased considerably if the equipment sector is included, the most important element of this being the construction of motor cars.

Transport is a growth industry, which tends to be linked to the overall growth of economies. From 1970 to 1990 the average annual growth of the EU economies was 2.6 per cent. In that time the growth of goods transport was 2.3 per cent and that of passenger transport was 3.1 per cent. The systems have been characterised by a considerable emphasis on development, but very little attempt has been made to plan for the long term or to integrate the different national transport systems.

An effective transport system is an essential element of efforts to create an integrated and prosperous European economy. The development of trade within Europe has resulted in a dense, relatively efficient network of transportation routes. It is a complex system made up of several different modes of transport: waterway, air, road, rail, pipelines. The transport system's development has been hampered by the division between East and West in Europe, and by the insistence of each state that it needed to consider its own transport priorities first. There are problems associated with the density of the networks, and the need to respond to changes in the economy and technological change. Social factors and working conditions are important. Finally, it should be remembered that political changes have been influential in terms of transport networks. The most dramatic example of this is the need to accommodate the transportation needs of the economies of Central and Eastern Europe, which are undergoing transition.

The basis of the CTP therefore involves action to

● reinforce the functioning of the Single Market

● promote sustainable development

● remove artificial constraints to the development of an integrated transport system

● strengthen economic and social cohesion by developing infrastructure to reduce the disparity between the regions

● improve safety

● take measures in the social field, for example drivers' hours

● conduct relations with third countries.

The growth in transport has generally been welcomed, in that it assists the meeting of people and the more efficient trading of goods. Each of the different modes of transport has increased its operating efficiency, but the environmental effects of the increase in activity are less welcome. Transport is one of society's great consumers of non-renewable energy sources. It also helps to generate a considerable amount of pollutants, which are not only damaging to individual health, but may also be contributing to global warming. This means there is an argument for not allowing the market full reign. Individuals' demands for greater car ownership may move traffic away from the more energy efficient and environmentally friendly means of carrying people, such as the trains.

External relations

The European Commission has competence over external relations with respect to transport under Article 113, which relates to the Common Commercial Policy. As a consequence it covers bilateral and multilateral agreements concerning market access and capacity and tariffs.

This is an increasingly pressing issue on the mainland, given the likely further expansion of the EU. The European transport system does not stop at the borders of the EU. If the former Soviet Union is to be helped, it needs good links with the West, as do the Central European states, which may join the EU in the future.

A number of Member States still wish to preserve their own bilateral powers with regard to access to their individual markets, especially with regard to civil aviation. This weakens the coherence of EU commercial relations, as well as leading to other EU operators being disadvantaged within the Single Market.

There are also problems to be solved with regard to states that share borders with the EU, in particular with respect to transit states. An example of this is the disruption caused by the war in the former Yugoslavia, which made the land route with Greece go via Hungary. Similarly, there are problems with the Swiss, who limit the size of trucks that pass through their country and, as a result of a referendum held in February 1994, intend to ban road transit through their territory in 2004 for environmental reasons.

Changed patterns of demand

The pattern of demand for transport services has changed significantly over time. Factors that have influenced the change in demand include the following:

- A movement of manufacturing away from many of its traditional urban sites.

- A reduction in the level of stocks that business wishes to hold, and a movement towards the adoption of just-in-time (JIT). Under this system, the level of stocks in the manufacturing sector is kept at the very minimum by manufacturers. It relies on a very good distribution system to maintain production.

- The rise in the service sector and its multi-site operations.

- Greater mobility among professional people.

- The increase in disposable incomes, which means that more use is made of transport.

The volume of freight transport increased by more than 50 per cent over the 20 year period 1970–1990 (Table 4.1). Most of this was accounted for by the increase of traffic on the roads. Despite the growth in traffic, investment in inland transport infrastructure has declined from 1.5 per cent of GDP to 1.3 per cent of GDP between 1975 and 1980. In the 1980s it was in the region of 1 per cent. About 66 per cent of investment went on roads, while 23 per cent went to rail. Investment in airports increased from 2.9 per cent of the total to 5.6 per cent. The distribution of traffic that benefits from this investment is given in Table 4.1.

The early industrialisation process depended a great deal on the use of waterways for bulk transport, and they are still important for the carriage of some bulk goods where time is not important, such as coal and iron ore. The process of integrating the waterways system has continued. Pipelines have developed as a means of carrying large volumes of oil and gas in the period after World War II. The volume of transport by pipeline and inland waterways increased slightly in 1970–1990, but their percentage share declined. Marine transport, not

Table 4.1 Distribution of EU freight transport by modes

	1970 %	1980 %	1990 %
Road	50.6	60.6	69.9
Rail	27.8	20.2	15.4
Inland water	13.6	10.8	9.2
Pipeline	8.0	8.4	5.5

Source : Commission of the EC (1993), The future development of the Common Transport Policy, *Bulletin of the EC*, Supplement 3/93, p. 7

shown in Table 4.1, is of greatest importance between states. It experienced a 35 per cent growth between 1975 and 1985, after which there was little growth.

Railways replaced the waterways as the carriers of bulky goods. By the beginning of the twentieth century, a basic network had been established in Western Europe, with all countries apart from Spain using the same gauge. Networks tended to be focused very much on the transportation needs within the individual states. The railway system has faced a long period of decline because of its general inflexibility and high fixed costs. It has faced very severe competition from road haulage and the trend towards ever greater car ownership. On longer passenger routes air travel is competitive, while manufacturing has less need to move heavy bulk items. There has, however, been a resurgence of interest in high-speed passenger routes, which are directly competitive with air travel. Table 4.2 indicates that for travel between some of the major European cities the train is not only cheaper, but faster.

Table 4.2 High-speed trains compared with air transport

Route served by high-speed trains	Rail journey time (city centre to city centre)	Fare (first class one-way ticket, US$)	Air journey time (city centre to city centre)	Air (lowest one-way ticket, US$)
Dusseldorf–Amsterdam	2 h 10 min	48	2 h 55 min	147
Geneva–Milan	2 h 30 min	76	2 h 55 min	225
Frankfurt–Munich	3 h 30 min	106	2 h 55 min	165
Frankfurt–Zurich	4 h 05 min	134	3 h	254
Stockholm–Gothenburg	3 h 10 min	130	3 h	254
Milan–Rome	3 h 50 min	76	3 h 5 min	122
Munich–Vienna	4 h 40 min	93	3 h 5 min	231

Note : For air travel, one hour has been added to include the time of city centre transfers
Source : *The European*, 1 February 1994, 22

Table 4.2 illustrates that on the shorter journeys rail is not only cheaper, but saves time. On the longer journeys there are money savings, but not time savings. There is also a strong belief that rail is environmentally more friendly. In contrast to the growth of road transport, the volume carried by rail decreased by 15 per cent, in the period 1970–1990, while its share of the market dropped from 27.8 per cent to 15.4 per cent.

There has been a massive growth in road transport since the end of the 1950s. This has resulted in a new mobility throughout Europe. It has been caused by the spread of industrial concerns, and a rise of the private car ownership. Road transport has been seen as having significant disadvantages, such as congestion, pollution, more accidents and a lack of coherent planning. This has been used to justify a general policy of favouring rail.

While air freight is relatively unimportant in volume terms, its importance is underlined by the fact that Heathrow is the busiest 'port' in Britain in terms of the value of freight passing through it.

Passenger traffic increased by over 85 per cent in 1970–1990. The fastest growth was by air. Changes in aircraft design have enabled larger numbers of people and cargoes to be carried at ever-lower costs. Within Europe, air transport has mainly been concerned with the movement of people and predominantly across national borders. However, travel by air within countries has increased with the opening of regional airports. Air transport is not as influential as in the USA, because the population is clustered close to the European core. Also the system is less developed, and generally more expensive.

Road transport has retained its overall dominance. Bus passengers increased by 45 per cent and rail passengers by 25 per cent but their share of the market fell (Table 4.3).

Table 4.3 Distribution of EU passenger transport by modes

| | 1970 | 1980 | 1990 |
	%	%	%
Private car	76.1	77.8	79.0
Rail	10.0	8.0	6.6
Bus and Coach	11.7	10.6	8.9
Air	2.2	3.5	4.6

Source: Commission of the EC (1993), The future development of the Common Transport Policy, *Bulletin of the EC*, Supplement 3/93, 8

The completion of the Single Market

The great spur to advancing the CTP was the need to complete the Single Market. The EU initially opted for a policy of liberalising transport as a way of ensuring progress toward a CTP, but this could not be achieved by simply removing restrictions. There was a need to agree EU-wide rules and create an environment where competition could be constructively encouraged. There were real efficiency gains to be made in the distribution system if domestic providers changed their operations to meet the competitive challenge. The problems of completing the Single Market are as follows.

● Where a single network is involved, there is a tendency towards monopoly.

● National subsidies given to transport providers can create problems, for example with competing international airlines operating on the same routes. However, subsidy may be welcome for the maintenance of domestic rail networks. Generally, state aids should be for restructuring and be transparent.

● Opening up national markets can lead to resistance. There are fears of lower safety and social security standards.

● Structural changes need to be managed, they cannot be left to unrestricted market forces.

● It is difficult to ensure that all transport modes cover their full costs, including those for the environmental damage they cause.

Without the above points being addressed, there is a danger that the competitive process is distorted. This in its turn either affects the pattern of development or offers a justifiable cause to those who oppose the process.

Two sectors of the industry have been at the centre of debate about the impact of the Single Market. The first is road haulage, because of its importance as the main method of carrying goods throughout the EU. The second is civil aviation, which is growing fast, and is the most important means of long-distance passenger movement within the EU. In both sectors liberalisation has proved difficult because of entrenched vested interests. In addition, there have been a number of problems associated with harmonisation and infrastructure provision that have required new solutions.

Liberalising road haulage

Transport is basically a competitive industry, but there has been a long tradition of restrictions placed on the sector. Restrictions on the road sector have been introduced as a way of protecting rail from what is seen as unfair competition. Also, there is a fear that if the process of competition gets out of hand it could be a destructive force, either by eliminating competitive elements or by forcing safety standards to be compromised. For passengers there is a need to retain a basic service also, which often means trying to maintain whole networks.

The road haulage industry has been a central concern for the CTP because

1.   it is the most important mode of transport

2.   both international and domestic freight transport have been subjected to a variety of controls and restrictions in terms of prices and entry into markets.

The extent of regulation has varied from country to country. At one extreme Germany has operated restrictions on capacity and fixed price bands; at the other the UK has operated a relatively liberal regime. The UK allowed open access to its domestic market from 1968, when the Transport Act removed all controls on road haulage capacity. In Germany, environmental considerations, the desire to promote the national rail network and the political leverage of the road haulage industry ensured the continuation of strict controls on road haulage capacity. Not only did this protect established firms from the impact of new competition, but also a compulsory tariff ensured that German hauliers enjoyed healthy profit margins by avoiding damaging price wars.

There was a wide diversity in the way the twelve domestic transport markets operated. This lack of standardisation proved to be a major hurdle for the Commission in its attempts to liberalise national and international road haulage. The operation of international road haulage is characterised by the use of the quota system. This means that hauliers need to obtain a permit to undertake international journeys. There are two types of permit.

The bilateral permit

From 1965, a series of bilateral agreements were negotiated annually between individual Member States to determine the number of road haulage licences to be granted to non-domestic carriers. If the journey involves transit through a third country, then a permit will be required for that country too e.g. UK–France–Spain. Permits are not required by all EU members, for example a British haulier can freely enter any of the Benelux countries. Indeed, the operation of a permit system does not automatically mean that competition will be impeded, providing the number of permits made available to hauliers can satisfy the demand. However, some Member States, notably the UK's three main European trading partners, France, Italy and Germany, have imposed highly restrictive quotas.

The multilateral or Community permit

In an attempt to overcome some of the effect of these restrictions, the EU introduced the multilateral permit in 1977. This allowed unlimited international journeys within the EU. This type of permit became increasingly important. In 1983 it accounted for 5 per cent of total intra-EU road haulage, and by 1988 this had risen to 16 per cent. The EU then followed a policy of making this type of permit even more widely available. The idea was that multilateral permits would gradually replace the bilateral system until 1 January 1993, at which time all quotas were to be removed.

The 1993 deadline came and went, and it was not until the Transport Council of 28 September 1993 that a firm date for the complete liberalisation of cabotage (i.e. the right to conduct haulage operations in another Member State) was agreed as 1 July 1998 (30 years after the initial proposal by the Commission). The previous arrangements of multilateral and bilateral quotas were therefore to remain in place for a further five years and six months, even though they contravened Article 75 of the Treaty of Rome.

Paying for infrastructure

The reasons for the delay in the completion of the CTP were largely concerned with the problem of funding the transport infrastructure, and reconciling the needs of the Member States and those of the larger EU market. Resident hauliers have the benefit of a better understanding of their home market conditions, but this advantage could be unfairly eroded if non-resident hauliers enjoyed access to markets without paying for their share of costs. Indeed, hauliers that operated from lower wage countries might also enjoy advantages in competing in certain markets.

Traditionally within the Member States, the cost of transport infrastructure has been met by taxation which is related to usage of roads. Excise duty is at a relatively high level in most EU states compared to the USA. In states where there are toll roads, payment is made on the basis of direct usage. In June 1993, the Transport Council came to a political agreement that mainland states without toll roads could introduce a Euro-regional tax disc. The maximum would be ECU 1250 per year, but there was provision for daily and weekly rates. The receipts would be divided between the states from third-country hauliers on the basis of Germany 73 per cent, Belgium 13 per cent, Netherlands 9 per cent, Denmark 4 per cent and Luxembourg 1 per cent. There were special arrangements for other non-toll states, and to take account of border regions (some vehicles move across borders on a daily basis, for example).

Harmonisation issues

There were other issues that divided the Member States. These included the weight that trucks might carry, which can vary by as much as 30 per cent depending on the EU Member State. Table 4.4 gives the position in April 1994.

Table 4.4 Lorry weight limits (tonnes) for articulated vehicles and drawbar combinations in EU member states

Country	Number of axles		
	4	5	6
Netherlands	38	44	50
Italy	36	44	48
Belgium	40	44	44
Luxembourg	39	44	44
France	38	40[1]	44
Spain	38	40	40[1]
Portugal	38	40	40
Germany	36	40	40
Greece	38	40	40[1]
Ireland	35	40	40
United Kingdom	35	38	38[2]
EU limits for international transport	38	40[1]	40[1]

[1]   44 tonnes for combined transport – the movement of goods by more than one mode of transport in a single journey

[2]   44 tonnes for combined road/rail transport

The UK moved from a maximum of 32 tonnes to 38 tonnes in 1982, but gained a derogation which meant that the 40 tonne maximum for international journeys did not need to be introduced until 1999 (although from April 1994, 44 tonne lorries could be used to take containers to and from railheads). The delay in implementing EU rules was justified by a need to strengthen the load-bearing capacity of road bridges. (No details as to the location of the unsafe bridges were ever published.) Larger vehicles are permitted within some states, for example the Netherlands permits up to 50 tonnes. The argument in favour of greater lorry weights was that it would help to reduce costs and to reduce the numbers of lorries carrying freight. However, the vibration caused by large vehicles is a concern.

Finally, the social legislation covering the way that industry operates was subject to considerable variation, particularly at the operational level, where drivers' rest periods are not enforced uniformly. However, underlying all the technical problems was the power of vested interests which wished to keep the markets separate, for example domestic road haulage contractors, the rail interests, and trade unions that feared an open market for road haulage would mean a reduction in social conditions.

The costs and benefits of liberalisation

The experience of the road haulage industry within the USA seems to prove that liberalisation results in substantial economic benefits. In 1980 the Motor Carrier Act passed in the USA effectively removed restrictions on road haulage between the various states. The effect was to encourage an expansion in the industry, and the competition from new entrants helped to reduce costs. The real cost of haulage fell, although the number of bankruptcies increased.

Within the EU, the importance of the new arrangements was that they offered real competition in many domestic markets for the first time. Not only should this encourage the search for efficiencies, but trucks could more easily obtain loads for return journeys, so they would more often be fully loaded. While the Commission has made a great deal of the argument, trucks generally run empty on return journeys even within Member States, largely because of a lack of knowledge of other opportunities.

Doubts have been cast on the impact of these reforms by Whitelegg,[1] who suggests that the most important factor influencing the growth of road freight is the growth of GDP (Table 4.5).

Table 4.5 Proportionate contribution to increased road freight activity in Germany 1987–2000

Source of growth	% of total growth
Increase in GDP	54.2
Spatial restructuring	26.3
Loss of rail freight	6.9
Impact of logistics	6.9
Impact of cabotage	5.7

Source : Whitelegg J (1993), *Transport for a Sustainable Future*,
Bellhaven Press, London, p. 153

The growth in freight traffic going by road has not been universally welcomed, because of the potential impact it has on the environment. This has led to calls from the EU and a number of other sources for a growth in combined transport, using rail for longer journeys and road transport for the collection and delivery stages of journeys only. However, road transport offers greater flexibility and convenience. The International Road Haulage Social Union suggested that the benefits of long-distance transport might be as follows:

1. That it is cheaper, given that transferring to rail imposes significant costs and may even double the costs. Only a proportion of this could be set against the reduced social cost.

2. That 80 per cent of haulage is for less than 100 kilometres, and not suitable for rail. Probably only 10 per cent of road traffic could be easily transferred to rail.

3. External costs may be reduced by new technologies, i.e. more environmentally friendly vehicle design.

Maritime cabotage

Maritime transport is the other area in which market forces have been consistently undermined. Coastal trade is not important in many states, but has some significance where there are long coastlines, or numerous islands that form part of the state. Full liberalisation started on 1 January 1993, but derogations were permitted, and the process of liberalisation will not be complete until 1 January 2004, when smaller vessels serving the Greek islands will be subject to competition.

Airline deregulation

The features of airline deregulation that make it different to liberalisation of road transport are the speed at which it is expected to take place, and the fundamental changes that it might bring to the industry if it is a success. While road transport will always have a large number of operators and offers opportunity to states that have low labour costs, the costs of entry into civil aviation are higher. However, given the ease with which aircraft can be relocated within the market, the opportunities for non-national carriers to dominate a market are far greater.

In 1993, the EU launched its third package of reforms designed to liberalise the industry by the end of the century. Many expected that significant changes would come immediately, and that there would be immediate benefits to travellers in the form of lower fares. These failed to materialise, in part because a crisis of profitability was facing parts of the industry. More fundamental than this in terms of holding back the pace of change was the link between the Member States and their civil aviation industries. It appeared that the states were not prepared to gamble on market forces, at least until their national players were in a condition to survive the intense competition that complete liberalisation would bring.

The development of civil aviation

Until the 1990s the EU civil aviation industry was organised in a way not dissimilar to that in the rest of the world, i.e. it was highly regulated and mostly state-owned. The ownership of national airlines had in the past been concerned with imperial or military needs, but was also an issue of national pride. Before World War II, a major problem was the generation of sufficient business to make routes profitable, hence the need was felt to restrict competition. In the period from the 1950s onwards, air travel became increasingly accessible. Regulation was retained, and the profitability of airlines depended on their ownership of licences to provide services on the routes with high traffic densities. The operation of international services was usually shared on a bilateral basis between the national flag carriers, such as British Airways and Air France.

In contrast to the scheduled airlines[2] fares were highly competitive holiday charter businesses. From the 1960s onwards, large numbers of people experienced new, value-for-money holidays by air. These often made it possible to have a two-week holiday, which included full accommodation and flight, for the same cost as the scheduled airfare. As air travel grew, there was growing public dissatisfaction with this state of affairs, with increasing attempts by individuals and organisations to overcome some of the more extreme conditions.

The civil aviation industry has moved from being an infant industry to being a provider of a mass service, where technological progress is driving down costs and global competition is of increasing importance. Civil aviation employs about 400 000 people in the EU, and European airports an additional 500 000 people. On top of this, there are jobs related to the provision of services to the industry away from the airports, and there are many jobs associated with manufacture of aircraft. In all, the Committee of Wise Men's report to the European Commission, *Expanding Horizons*[3] estimated that '10 million jobs in the European Community alone are related to the availability of an efficient air transport industry'. However, despite its importance, the European industry is highly fragmented, which has made change difficult. The major catalyst for change to the industry has come with liberalisation at the EU level.

Civil aviation reform

The European Commission was committed at an early stage to liberalising civil aviation. However, the major breakthrough came with the 1986 Nouvelles Frontieres judgement of the ECJ, which confirmed that competition rules did apply to the air transport sector. Competition rules applied under Article 85 of the Treaty of Rome, which prohibits anti-competitive agreements and actions, and Article 86, which concerns the abuse of a dominant market position. Merger Control legislation also applied to the sector from its coming into force in 1990.

The first steps towards the liberalisation of civil aviation within the EU came with the first package of reforms in 1987. This was followed by a second package, which came into effect in 1990. A final package of reforms came into operation on 1 January 1993. This was very radical, for the following reasons.

1. It introduced free pricing for scheduled airfares. Carriers were permitted to set fares with only 24 hours' notice, and these could have immediate effect. This was in contrast to the situation in the past where fares were the subject of a lengthy approvals process, and were set at a level that permitted even inefficient airlines to make a profit. Safeguards were introduced to prevent the downward spiralling of fares.

2. It strengthened the rules against predatory pricing.

3. It made entry into the industry easier. Companies were expected to be registered in the EU, to be financially viable and capable of offering a safe service to customers. Once a company was licensed it did not require permission to offer a service.

4.   It allowed duly licensed air carriers to operate on virtually all routes between airports in
     the EU. Bilateral capacity-sharing agreements and discretionary route licensing were to
     disappear. This opened up the domestic markets to airlines from any Member State.
     However, there will not be full cabotage rights until 1 April 1997.

Liberalisation of civil aviation is part of the process of completing the Single Market in the
services sector. The advantages that should come about as a result of the market becoming
more contestable are that

1.   the threat of oligopoly will be reduced

2.   there will be a greater incentive to become more efficient

3.   the price of air travel will fall

4.   a greater variety of flights will be available.

The hope is that a new spirit of competition will emerge based on rivalry between existing
carriers. They will seize opportunities to take advantage of the access they will have to
previously closed markets. In addition to this, there might be additional small carriers prepared
to enter the market, as well as the charter airlines which will wish to develop further. Finally,
there will be competition from the new high-speed trains and the Channel tunnel.

The new competitive environment could be difficult to realise, because a number of the
scheduled airlines are inefficient and cannot compete with the industry's best operators. Most
small carriers prefer a secure niche in the market, where they are going to be free of predators.
Also, new entrants in the market can be highly vulnerable and can go out of business as Air
Europe did in the early 1990s. There is uncertainty as to whether liberalisation will lead to a
greater number of airlines or create a new generation of mega-carriers that will swallow up
their competitors. The example that has been most closely followed is that of the USA.

The US experience

The EU has tended to follow the USA in its attempts to deregulate its transport provision. In
the case of the EU, the reasons for adopting this strategy probably have more to do with
finding common ground for minimal agreement than with a belief in the joys of the free
market economy. If, however, deregulation is to be a success, there are important lessons to be
learnt. The first is to avoid the financial chaos that has been associated with the US
experience. The deregulation of US civil aviation took place in 1978, but even in the
mid-1990s the industry was in a state of almost permanent upheaval. In the early stages of
deregulation, many new providers entered the US market and there was considerable
undercutting of fares. Fares fell by an average of 20 per cent in the short term, because of the
impact of competition. However, in the longer term many of these benefits to the consumer
would have come about anyway, because of improved efficiency. The combined effect of
excess capacity and aggressive fare-cutting meant that the industry lost money. The losses
made by civil aviation, in the late 1980s and early 1990s, were greater than the whole of the
industry's profits since the origins of powered flight. By 1992, 117 carriers, including some

well known names such as Pan American, had gone into bankruptcy. However, a curiosity of US company law is that companies frequently re-emerge from the process to trade again. While small profits were earned by the most efficient operators, the industry managed to lose $1.2 billion in 1993. Globally, there was a trend towards excess capacity in the 1990s, due to airlines taking an excessively optimistic view of future growth trends. Even in 1993, a year in which there was an increase in passenger demand, carrying capacity grew faster than the number of passengers. European airlines have generally tended to have smaller losses

The result of the losses in the USA was that airlines restructured, cut expenditure, and deferred or cancelled aircraft orders.

The consumer appeared to be far more cost conscious, which led to the growth of no-frills basic services in the USA. Merger activity and strategic alliances increased among the larger world airlines. In the USA, instead of a fragmented market structure emerging, the industry started a process of consolidation. This resulted in the dominance of eight major airlines which took about 95 per cent of the market. Instead of there being a variety of services organised between a wide range of destinations, major carriers flew into hub airports and passengers transferred to smaller airports. This 'hub and spoke' provision caused considerable inconvenience to passengers. Following the creation of mega-carriers within the USA, there was considerable debate as to whether such a development was appropriate in Europe. It was argued that without European mega-carriers, European airlines would lose out in the global battle for dominance in civil aviation.

If the US experience were replicated within the EU, there could be only four major carriers operating, with perhaps a limited number of smaller ones feeding flights into the major hub airports such as London Heathrow. However, the European experience should be different, for the following reasons.

1. Chapter 11 of the US bankruptcy code permits companies to survive and emerge to compete again. European countries do not generally have such a provision.

2. The European airlines are not so burdened with debt, largely because of the effects of state ownership.

3. In many countries of the EU, the state is unlikely to permit the national carrier to go under.

4. There is little enthusiasm for the creation of a US-type system.

Cross-border mergers of European airlines were not a significant feature of the way that the market developed in the early 1990s. The major obstacle was that Member States typically had a financial stake in the national flag carriers. Mergers may come about if a significant number of these businesses are privatised, and the scale of some of the losses made by carriers is reduced. The tendency within Europe was to try and reach operating agreements with other airlines, as an alternative. At the same time there were a series of agreements with US airlines. This was to ensure that there was mutual use of booking systems, that route-sharing could take place, and that difficulties about access to the rival continental markets were reduced. Examples of this trend included the agreements between Air France and Continental, Sabena (33 per cent owned by Air France) and Delta, and British Airways and US Air.

The airline industry in financial crisis

The financial crisis that faced the US civil aviation industry in the 1990s was reflected in a similar situation within the EU. In 1993, EU airlines lost in the region of $2 billion (£1.3 billion); in 1992 they lost $1.35 billion; and in 1991 $1.1 billion. This was despite an increased passenger load. Most state-owned airlines appeared to be losing money, although the non-state sector was profitable. Table 4.6 indicates the gap between the two sectors.

Table 4.6 Europe's scheduled airlines 1993

Airline	Country	Profit/loss (US$ million)	Employees	Aircraft	Aircraft orders
Aer Lingus	Ireland	−272	5 373	29	3
Alitalia	Italy	−10	18 034	97	63
Air France	France	−1 479	42 092	147	23
British Airways	UK	147	49 584	250	61
Iberia	Spain	−502	23 000	120	33
KLM	Netherlands	−299	24 615	95	13
Lufthansa	Germany	−66	44 194	218	12
Olympic	Greece	−180	10 754	57	0
Sabena	Belgium	−130	9 698	45	0
SAS	Scandinavia	−63	21 000	160	11
Swissair	Switzerland	−5	17 367	61	30
TAP	Portugal	−211	9 500	37	4

Source : *The European*, 22 July 1994, 23

Given the above situation, it is hardly surprising that financially strong airlines such as British Airways favoured open competition, with uncompetitive carriers being allowed to go out of business. However, because many airlines in Europe are state-owned or state-assisted, national governments took an active interest in the restructuring process. They were unwilling to sacrifice their national carriers, and looked for a European solution that would permit the continued existence of their national airlines. The European Commission proposed that there should be an orderly restructuring in the industry. States such as Belgium would have liked to reintroduce capacity-sharing arrangements, but this kind of strategy would have been contrary to the EU's decision to liberalise the industry.

The reasons for this financial crisis were investigated by a Committee of Wise Men, who reported to the European Commission in December 1993. They suggested that the reasons for the financial crisis were as follows.

1. Europe's airlines combined below-average growth with below-average profitability, a phenomenon that was possibly unique.

2. The major flag carriers in the European industry had a cost disadvantage of up to 45 per cent against their international competitors. A significant part of this was due to low productivity.

3. European airlines paid more for air traffic control, and congestion added significantly to their costs.

4. European airlines had added financial costs due to less favourable leasing arrangements and exchange rate risks.[4]

A major difficulty was that the European civil aviation industry was not as efficient as that of the USA. While efficiency does not guarantee profitability, it does mean that prices can be lower, and more customers may be attracted as a result. Table 4.7 compares the productivity and labour costs of the US and EU industries.

Table 4.7 Analysis of European versus US labour costs and productivity in 1992 (Financial Measures, US$)

	US industry	European industry	Percentage difference
Gross salaries per employee	40 534	44 493	10.26
Social charges per employee	11 722	10 573	−9.80
Total labour costs per employee	52 256	55 066	5.38
Total labour costs per ATK[1]	15.55 [2]	21.27 [2]	36.76
Social costs as a percentage of the total	22.43%	19.20%	−14.40
Physical productivity (ATKs per employee)	336 019	258 908	−22.95
Departures per employee	13.24	6.28	−52.57

[1] ATK = available tonne kilometres: the number of tonnes of capacity available for the carriage of revenue load (passengers and cargo) multiplied by the distance flown
[2] In US cents

Source: Committee chaired by Herman De Croo, *Expanding Horizons*, Report to European Commission, 1994, p. 14

What Table 4.7 indicates is that the major differences in costs are due to problems of physical productivity, although the cost of employing labour is also greater in Europe. Other factors assist carriers in the USA, including lower fuel costs and journey distances which advantage air transport.

Given the above situation it is not surprising that Karl Heinz Neumeister, the Secretary General of the Association of European Airlines, commented that it was ironic that liberalisation measures had occurred 'at a time when the industry was too weak to take full advantage of them, and doubly ironic that they are aimed at bringing new market entrants into competition'.[5]

A free market for civil aviation

The liberalisation process can work only if the basis of competition is the same for all participants in the market. It would have been unrealistic to suggest an immediate move to the free market, simply because it would have been politically unacceptable. However, consumers are unlikely to accept that they should be denied access to the benefits that a fully efficient civil aviation industry is able to provide. In the spring of 1994, the cost of an economy return fare between Brussels and Lisbon was £800, which was about three times the price of a similar internal flight in the USA. Despite some setbacks, liberalisation did have some beneficial effects, and many fares did fall in the EU. They also tended to be up to 30 per cent cheaper when the flight started in the UK, which had the most liberalised market. Also, the competitive pressures meant that the scale of losses increased, which meant that something had to be done to restructure the industry. The tendency was for national governments to try to maintain the structure of the industry, but the consequences were that the scale of the problem became even worse.

State aid was given that might well have resulted in viable businesses being pushed out of existence if they could not attract similar funding. Table 4.8 indicates one of the main problems of subsidies. While the industry was sustaining record losses, it was still expanding capacity. The reasons for this were that national airlines wished to hold on to market share, and were reluctant to surrender valuable landing rights at major airports. At the same time, a number of companies were locked into investments in aircraft because of decisions made when the industry was doing well in the late 1980s.

Table 4.8 Increase in the number of seats offered on scheduled intra-EU services

	Annual capacity increase
1988	11.6
1989	14.5
1990	9.7
1991	9.2
1992	7.8
1993	3.5

Source : Commission (1994), *The Way Forward for Civil Aviation in Europe*, COM (94) 218, final, p. 2

The only way that seats could be filled was to engage in competition for the limited market. In order to overcome the fixed fare structures that operated, there was a shift towards more promotional fares. However, as Table 4.9 indicates, this was not entirely successful.

Table 4.9 Intra-European scheduled air traffic

Passengers travelling at	1990	1991	1992	1993
full fare (%)	39	37	33	29
promotional fare (%)	61	63	67	71
load factor (%)	62.5	56.8	56.8	58

Source : Commission (1994), *The Way Forward for Civil Aviation in Europe*, COM (94) 218, final, p. 4

As can be seen from Table 4.9, load factors (percentage of seats occupied) actually fell. If the market had been allowed to operate, it might be reasonable to assume that capacity would have been reduced, and load factors would have increased. This in turn might well have moved the industry into an overall profit.

The problem of state aid

Give the crisis facing civil aviation, it was inevitable that the states would take action to protect what they regarded as valuable national assets. There was a need to restructure an industry, and to ensure that the state aids did not waste taxpayers' money by simply maintaining an inefficient industrial structure. In an industry such as civil aviation, which is cyclical, there is a danger that subsidies are used to prop up an inefficient business, so that it is only just viable at the peak of a boom and returns to crisis in the next slump.

Between 1991 and 1994 huge amounts of state aid were given to European airlines (Table 4.10). This required the permission of the European Commission, which granted permission for the help with some reluctance.

Table 4.10 State aid to EU airlines (ECU million)

	Subsidies	Loan guarantees	EU approval	Period
Sabena	1650	None	Dec. 1991	3 years
Iberia	760	None	July 1992	1 year
Aer Lingus	220	None	Dec. 1993	3 years
TAP Air Portugal	910	900	June 1994	4 years
Air France	3000	None	July 1994	3 years
Olympic	1880	300	July 1994	3 years

Source : *The European*, 28 July 1994, 18

Air France proved to be a major test for the EU. Following the reported loss of Ff. 3.8 billion (£440 million) in the first half of 1993, a radical plan to restructure Air France was proposed. The total loss of Air France for 1993 actually turned out to be Ff. 8.48 billion (£1 billion). This was about a third of all losses by airlines globally for that year. The first restructure plan was rejected by the workforce, and following a wave of discontent it was withdrawn by the government. A substitute was accepted in 1994, which involved Ff. 20 billion of state aid over a period of three years, and would result in 5000 job losses. The job losses were accepted only with some reluctance, but there was a limit to the extent that the French government could fund Air France losses, under EU competition rules. State aids in the EU are normally permitted only for restructuring purposes.

Profitable airlines such as British Airways argued that the supporting of loss-making airlines meant that they were unable to take advantage of opportunities in the French market. With a workforce of 40 000 and national unemployment at over 11 per cent of the workforce, it is easy to appreciate why the French government would wish to restructure the company in a gradual way, although the level of funding given could well have established a totally new airline. In contrast, British Airways, when it was restructured between 1980 and 1986, reduced its workforce from 50 000 to 39 000. It also abandoned a number of international routes, and disposed of property, in the build-up to privatisation.

The Committee of Wise Men recommended that the European Commission should attempt to limit state aids in line with the Treaty. That is, they should only be sufficient to sort out the problems of the industry, and not distort the competitive process. They suggested that

● aid should be given on a 'one last time' basis

● restructuring plans should be submitted that would ensure viability

● the airlines should be privatised

● governments should refrain from interfering in the commercial decisions of the airlines

● public money should not be used either to buy other airlines or to expand capacity beyond the limits of the market

● restructuring should be carefully monitored.

While the European Commission accepted these recommendations, it is difficult to see that they will be carried out fully, given the different philosophies with regard to industrial policy within the EU. Indeed, it could be reasonably argued, given the evidence of the past, that 'one last time' state aid had been given to a number of airlines already.

New competition is limited by congestion in the major airports

In November 1993, a report from the UK's Civil Aviation Authority suggested that the third package of reforms showed few signs of working. This was because of difficulties of gaining landing rights at key airports. Only 38 of 636 scheduled international air routes in the EU had more than two carriers, while 411 were monopolies.[6] The open skies policy was in effect closed to new airlines, because they could not gain access to the key airports. The rights to land were 'grandfathered', i.e. they were owned by, and passed on by, particular companies. This gives a competitive advantage to airlines such as British Airways, which took 38.5 per cent of slots at Heathrow in 1992. The pressure for slots is unlikely to be reduced, because expansion of the major airports has generally been resisted, frequently by local residents. In other cases, there is a lack of physical space to accommodate the expansion.

National governments continue to negotiate on a bilateral basis

This is particularly true on the issue of access to landing slots at key hub airports. In the 1990s the US government still felt that there was a need to negotiate its access to key airports such as Heathrow.

No unified system of air traffic control

Although this has been recognised as a problem, it is difficult to envisage the full exploitation of air travel until Europe's airspace is fully utilised. Military considerations may prevent this development from being completed. However, in 1993 the EU agreed to a small step: a move towards compatibility of equipment for air traffic control.

Variations in social costs

This had come about because of the legacy of state ownership, and the differing requirements of the Member States. It prevents some airlines from being fully competitive even though huge numbers of jobs have been lost in the industry due to restructuring.

The EU was slow to move towards a Single Market for civil aviation. If the CTP is to work in this sector, a great deal more effort needs to be put into coordination of the infrastructure of the industry. The EU could contribute more to this process by increased funding. As it is a service sector industry, which has a rising demand for its product, there should be no reason why liberalisation should not work, provided there are adequate safeguards against destructive competition and abuse of monopoly powers.

It seems unlikely that the benefits of liberalisation will become apparent until the late 1990s. This is because of the scale of the task of reorganising the industry. To achieve this, there must be a willingness by the national governments to encourage the competitive process. This has not always been apparent. For example, in April 1994 the European Commission had to order the French government to give access to Orly airport for non-national airlines. Appeals to economic nationalism do not often carry a full price tag, and until there is a full realisation that the cost of inefficiency has to be born by either the consumer or the tax payer there will not be further progress. Without this progress, many European airlines will lose out in the battle for shares in the global market.

Trans-European networks

If the European economy is to operate as a Single Market, the transport infrastructure must be in place. The EU states have tended to consider their own domestic transport needs rather than those of the overall European economy. This has led to areas of the European economy being left remote from the main stream of economic development. At the same time, a mismatch within the transport provision has led to inefficiencies in the system. Greater integration of transport provision should ensure that competition is maintained throughout the European Union, that transport times are faster, and that capacity is more fully utilised. Also, it should help to avoid significant bottlenecks like those in the road network.

It has been estimated that the lack of an appropriate transport network costs the EU in the region of ECU 3.75 billion to ECU 6 billion a year, and that the figure could rise to ECU 13.6 billion by 2010. The European system is fragmented, which has led to inefficiency. If air transport is taken as an example, in the USA the air traffic control system deals with three times the number of flights with only 22 air traffic control centres (the EU12 has 42). Similar inefficiencies are to be found in other sectors.[7]

The establishment of Trans-European networks in the fields of energy, transport and telecommunications requires the Member States to combine with the EU in order to achieve an overall coherence. This should promote economic growth, cohesion and integration within the European area, reaching well beyond the geographical limits of the present European Union. Not only should the volume passing through the networks increase, but there will be efficiency gains via interoperability and interconnectability of the networks. The Commission's White Paper *Growth, Competitiveness, Employment – the Challenges and the Ways Forward into the 21st Century* identified a number of reasons why Trans-European infrastructure (the basis of TENs) was important. These included:

- better, safer travel at lower cost

- effective planning in Europe in order to avoid a concentration of population

- bridge building towards Eastern Europe in order to step up investment and promote trade.

This was to be achieved by:

- removing regulatory and financial obstacles

- getting private investors involved in projects of European interest

- identifying projects on the basis of master plans.[8]

Originally TENs were seen as separate networks, but the EU began to see benefits from adopting an intermodal strategy. This would lead to the modes of transport being interconnected, with the hope that this would lead to the creation of an integrated transport network. The most important aspect of this would be the linking of road and rail, so that long-distance haulage would be by inland waterway or by rail, with shorter distances by road.

The network within the EU12 would be based on

1. roads – 58 000 kilometres

2. railways – 70 000 kilometres of track, of which 23 000 kilometres would be for high-speed trains capable of travelling at 200 kilometres per hour

3. inland waterways – 12 000 kilometres

4. intermodal platforms, which would assist the movement of goods between the modes of transport, for example road to rail

5. air traffic management and control systems for the 250 most important airports

6. improved port infrastructure.[9]

The development of network will be a medium- to long-term task. The European Commission has helped the process along by drafting plans for key sectors. These plans should, if they are fully accepted, offer a degree of certainty to potential investors including the private sector. The hope is that the TENs will assist in promoting economic social cohesion by meeting regional needs, sustaining economic activity, assisting the balance between urban and regional centres, and promoting tourist activity. There is also firm belief that the creation of the network should embrace the whole continent.

A successful strategy for the completion of TENs could assist the process of economic and social cohesion. Inadequate links with remote regions are associated with poor regional economic performance. However, it is difficult to say whether inadequate infrastructure is the result of poor economic performance or causes the poor economic performance. Infrastructure needs vary according to the industry involved. Simply linking the core with the periphery does not always help, because the overall system may not be coherent. Also, transport infrastructure can create a corridor effect, which can cause environmental damage but offer little benefit to the region it goes through. Finally, improving one kind of transport mechanism may simply divert traffic away from other modes. So, for example, a better road system can often add to the competitive pressures on the rail network. The way to counter this is to develop further the network of high-speed trains. However, this involves a huge investment to lessen the railways' dependence on infrastructure that dates back to the last century.

Associated with the provision of adequate networks is the problem of financing. The provision of road networks will not provide many benefits for states that use transport corridors to other markets. To some extent this has been resolved by the use of the Euro-regional tax disc within the EU. Even more pressing is the problem of the Central European states, which simply lack the resources to provide adequate links. Private sector consortiums have provided some of the solutions, for example in the construction of motorways. In 1994, the Hungarian government chose to use a consortium led by Bouygues, the French construction group, to upgrade, extend and operate its M5 motorway.[10]

Prior to its expansion to 15 Member States, the level of funding required within the EU was estimated by the European Commission to be ECU 220 billion for the period 1994 to 1999 for transport TENs (ECU 400 billion over 15 years). Additional to this, will be the cost of ensuring that the network provides adequately for the new Member States. Austria is generally well served within planning documents because of its status as a major transit state. However, the addition of Finland and Sweden poses new problems which will require significant additional resources from the EU.

Funding should come from a variety of sources, and would involve partnership arrangements between the public and private sectors, the differing levels of government and the EU. Sources from the EU include the Cohesion Fund (available to the four poorest EU states), the European Investment Bank (EIB), guarantees from the European Investment Fund and contributions from the EU budget.[11] The problem for the EU and the Member States was where to find such large amounts of funds, given the need to constrain both national and EU budgets. The use of a special European Union bond was proposed by the Commission.

The need to embrace an all-European strategy, and to integrate the provision within the Member States, implies that new routes need to be established and action taken on badly integrated modes of transport. At the same time there need to be arrangements to make border crossing with non-EU countries easier. All this should be within the framework of a pan-European regulatory framework, taking further and wider some of the progress made with the creation of the European Economic Area.

Conclusions

The 1980s were an important period in laying the foundations for the Common Transport Policy. In the early 1990s, there were important agreements which should liberalise the two key sectors of road haulage and civil aviation. While there may be scope for further liberalisation of other modes of transport, it may be difficult to liberalise the international rail sector, given that it is normally a state-owned sector. Liberalisation, in any case, only takes the process so far, and represents the minimum that needs to be done. It does not address the difficulty of ensuring an adequate regulatory framework, although some significant progress has been made in harmonisation of the national laws and agreeing the basis of competition.

Liberalisation of road haulage proved to be more difficult than was once imagined, and the missing of the 1993 deadline for liberalisation demonstrated the need to link the process with harmonisation of regulation, and the all-important issue of funding of the provision of infrastructure. What has yet to be fully addressed is the need to ensure that road haulage does not totally dominate the provision of surface transport. The need to come to terms with the Swiss ban on lorries may well ensure that the EU promotes, even more actively, the cause of intermodal provision. However, its ability to do so is limited by the fact that the Member States control and fund the provision of infrastructure.

Air transport seems destined to grow, although the cost of fares and its unsuitability for bulk cargo will place limits on its total size, given current technology. While the industry is subject to significant changes due to the liberalisation process, it cannot achieve its full potential without a loosening of state control and a pooling of national sovereignty in air traffic control. It may be that public pressure, brought about by the failure to deliver lower cost air fares, or dissatisfaction with the quality of service, will ensure the changes take place. However, as with reform of road haulage, strong vested interests are holding back the process.

For the future, there also needs to be a significantly higher level of support for research and development related to transport systems. This is needed to promote the efficiency of the industry, and to reduce its environmental impact. It is also related to the effective use of investment, which is the essential feature of the creation of TENs.

References

1. **Whitelegg J** (1993) *Transport for a Sustainable Future*, Belhaven Press, London, p. 153.
2. *Europe*, 2 October 1993, 16.
3. **Committee chaired by Herman De Croo** (1994) *Expanding Horizons*, Report to the European Commission, p. 5.
4. Ibid.
5. *Europe*, 17/18 May 1993, 15.
6. *The Guardian*, 4 November 1993, 15.
7. *Europe*, 6/7 April 1992, 13.
8. **Commission of the EC** (1993) *Growth, Competitiveness, Employment – the Challenges and the Ways Forward into the 21st Century*, COM (93) 700 final, p. 11.
9. *Europe*, 31 March 1994, No. 6202, 10.
10. *Financial Times*, 3 May 1994, 3.
11. *Europe*, 31 March 1994, 10.

Further reading

Commission (1992) Commission Communication on the Future Development of the Common Transport Policy – a Global Approach to the Construction of a Community Framework for Sustainable Mobility, COM (92) 494.

Commission (1993) *The Future Development of the Common Transport Policy*, Bulletin of the EU, Supplement 3/93.

Commission (1993) *Trans-European Networks; towards a Master Plan for the Road Network and Road Traffic*.

Commission (1994) *The Way Forward for Civil Aviation in Europe*, COM (94) 218 final.

House of Lords (1994) *Growth, Competitiveness And Employment In The European Community*, Select Committee on the European Communities, 7th Report Session 1993–94, HL paper 43.

House of Lords (1994) *Common Transport Policy – Sustainable Mobility*, Select Committee on the European Communities, 8th Report Session 1993–94, HL paper 50.

House of Lords *Maximum Weights and Dimensions of Road Vehicles*, Select Committee on the European Communities, 17th Report Session 1993–94, HL paper 84.

OECD (1990) *Competition Policy and the Deregulation of Road Transport*.

CHAPTER 5

Free movement of people?

Introduction

This chapter concentrates on the issues that relate to the free movement of people. The first part of the chapter focuses on the free movement of people 'within' the European Union. The essential rationale for the free movement of people within the EU was that of removing the barriers to the transfer of a factor of production – the human resource. It was seen as the most direct way to solve any problems that might exist of matching the work force to the vacant jobs. This result has not been achieved. Large numbers of EU nationals do not move around the EU easily and frequently in search of employment. Although free movement of people was one of the four freedoms of the Treaty of Rome, and has therefore been an objective of the EU since the 1950s, in the mid-1990s barriers still existed to the movement of people.

The second part of the chapter deals with the increasingly difficult issues that surround the development of an EU Common Policy on Migration. The Completion of the Internal Market and the creation of an area without internal frontiers has provided the impetus for the states of the EU to try to reach a Common Policy on Migration into the EU. The major source of difficulty in the creation of such a policy is the lack of acceptance that the EU is the competent body to deal with the movement of third-country nationals. This has been dealt with in the past by a series of intergovernmental agreements between states of the EU, and bilateral agreements between EU states and the states of origin of the migrants.

Migration by Europeans

Movement pre-World War II

Movement by people is a complex matter, but can broadly be divided into two categories: that which is politically motivated and that which is economically motivated. The distinction between the politically motivated mover and the economically motivated is that the economic migrant has made a voluntary decision; the politically motivated had no choice. In individual cases a move may be prompted by a political motivation, but the decision about where to settle becomes an economic one. The history of Western Europe during the past two centuries has been characterised by massive movements of people. Migration out of the European region to the USA during the late nineteenth and early twentieth centuries provided a valuable 'safety valve' during a period of rapid population growth in Europe.

These waves of movement to the USA were inspired primarily by economic motives, although some people moved away from persecution because of either political or religious beliefs. Estimates suggest that by the beginning of World War I more than 55 million Europeans, from both the Western and the Eastern parts of the continent, had moved to the USA.

Movement post-World War II

Later in the twentieth century, particularly associated with World War II, movements were politically motivated. The tremendous upheaval of World War II sent more than 26 million people moving around Europe in its immediate aftermath. Later examples of political movers came as a result of the repatriation of French citizens from North Africa and the Portuguese from Angola and Mozambique in the 1970s. More recently, in the 1990s, there has been the ethnic cleansing of the former Yugoslavia.

Within a few years of the ending of World War II, economic reconstruction had led to a clear distinction within the states occupying the Western part of the continent. The use of migrant labour played an important part in that reconstruction. Some states were clearly demanders of additions to their labour forces to assist with the economic recovery. They included Germany, Belgium and France. Others, such as Italy, Spain, Portugal and Ireland, were exporters of labour. Of the EU 6, only Italy was an exporter of labour to the other states. By 1960, more than half of the intra-EU movement was being made by Italian workers from the poverty-stricken southern Mezzogiorno region. It was apparent, however, that Italy could not meet the demands of the other EU states on its own.

Free movement of labour was established to encourage workers to move. But apart from Italian workers the number of EU nationals moving was small, because of the opportunities that existed for workers in their home states. The other EU states became part of an ever-growing and increasingly complex arrangement of bilateral international agreements with states such as Turkey, the former Yugoslavia and those in North Africa. This situation continued until the oil crisis of 1973 and the economic recession that followed. The demand for workers then fell and rising levels of unemployment among home populations meant that migration was no longer encouraged from the third countries.

These groups of workers who were recruited in the 1960s were usually young, unmarried and unskilled labour. The intention was that they should not become permanent members of the receiving country, but should return home at the end of their fixed-term contracts. The term 'guest workers' came to be used for these groups. This was true not only for the majority of workers who were recruited from the third countries, but also of the Italian workers who had moved into the northern European states.

The oil crisis of 1973 and the economic recession of the early 1970s halted the flow of migrants into the Union, and stemmed the flow of Italian workers to the northern states within the EU. For example, the number of Turkish workers recruited to work in Germany fell from 103 793 in 1973 to merely 1228 in 1974. Within the EU the number of nationals in states other than their own fell from a high of 7 per cent, prior to the oil crisis, to 2 per cent by 1984. Between 1987 and 1991 1.5 million people moved from one Member State to another, a movement of about 300 000 people per annum. By 1991, of the 13 million foreigners resident in the EU, 8 million were non-EU nationals, more than 50 per cent of whom were nationals from North Africa or Turkey (Tables 5.1 and 5.2). Table 5.3 identifies the actual numbers of EU nationals who are resident in states other than their own home state.

Table 5.1 Presence of North Africans in the principal host countries of the EU (thousands, end of 1992)

Nationality	Belgium	France	Germany	Netherlands	Italy	Spain
Algerian	10.7	619.9	7.4	0.6	4.0	1.1
Moroccan	141.7	584.7	69.6	156.9	78.0	28.2
Tunisian	6.4	207.5	26.1	2.6	41.2	0.4

Source : Council of Europe (1993), Political and demographic aspects of migration flows to Europe, *Population Studies* No. 25, 37

Table 5.2 Turkish immigration in Western Europe (1991)

Host country	Thousands	Percentage
Germany	1694.6	70.65
Netherlands	204.3	8.52
France	201.5	8.40
Belgium	84.9	3.54
Switzerland	64.9	2.70
Austria	59.9	2.50
Denmark	29.7	1.24
Sweden	25.5	1.06
UK	19.0	0.79
Norway	5.5	0.23
Italy	4.7	0.20
Greece	3.2	0.13
Others	1.0	0.04
Total	2398.7	100

Source : As Table 5.1

Luxembourg is a special case, with more than 30 per cent of its labour force coming from other EU nations. However, as Table 5.3 shows, almost 40 per cent of the migrants to Luxembourg are non-EU nationals. Apart from Belgium, where the percentage is 5, there is no other state of the EU where the number of EU nationals in the labour force exceeds 3 per cent of the working population. There is nothing in the continuing EU strategy of encouraging the movement of people which suggests that the overall figures will alter significantly in the future. The tendency remains for EU nationals to form small proportions of the migrant populations within the EU states.

Table 5.3 Distribution of the population of the Member States of the EU by nationality (1990)

Origin	Bel	Den	Fra	Ger (w)	Ger (e)	Gre	Ire	Ita	Lux	Net	Por	Spa	UK
						Country of residence							
Bel		328	59 705	18 697		1382	700	4107	10 688	23 554	960	11 979	5000
Den	2558		3460	13 429		1277	900	1408	1531	1579	391	6716	12 000
Fra	94 266	2048		77 602	246	6811	1300	20 044	14 564	8935	3019	28 881	37 000
Ger	28 071	8437	51 483	293 649		12 286	3200	28 784	9672	44 331	4484	45 576	42 000
Gre	20 908	544	6735	31 627	482		1000	13 459	852	4878	54	655	15 000
Ire	2401	956	3326	8872	337	583		1219	551	3438	212	2426	639 000
Ita	241 175	1990	253 679	519 548		6725	1400		19 999	16 925	1137	15 765	84 000
Lux	4691	9	2792	4764		45		235		286	29	214	1000
Net	65 278	2036	16 009	101 238	201	3000	2000	5322	3642		1670	17 033	23 000
Por	16 538	328	645 578	74 890		364		2373	38 477	8278		613	32 000
Spa	52 246	859	216 015	126 963		971	800	7864	2200	17 192	7294		28 000
UK	23 345	10 226	50 106	85 748	140	17 321	52 800	19 511	3205	39 044	7761	78 210	
Total, non resident EU national	549 076	27 761	1305 562	1357 027	1406	50 765	60 900	104 326	105 381	167 900	27 011	208 068	890 000
%[1]	61	17	36	28	0.7	29	76	19	90	24	27	51	35

[1]   Non-resident EU nationals as percentage of total migrants.
Source: Adapted from Table 5.1 source, p. 74–76

It may be that the type of mover may alter, but not the numbers of EU nationals who are prepared to move. A number of changes in the economies of Western Europe have resulted in a change in the type of employment opportunity available. The restructuring of industry, following technological developments, and the concentration of employment in the tertiary sector of economic activity since 1984 has led to the tendency for those who move to be in search of skilled employment. There are fewer unskilled jobs available, and the opportunities for low-income unskilled migrants have fallen.

The EU was not concerned in the past with agreements made by the individual states with third countries. The removal of the internal borders will make it easier for migrants from third countries to move within the Union. The issue of control of the external borders and a unified EU stance on the movement of people from outside the EU into the EU has become a source of controversy. The potential for politically motivated movement is greater than the actual numbers who moved at the end of World War II. All these political refugees would require a home and the possibility of employment, and this would result in numerous pressures on the states of the European Union. The Yugoslavian disintegration alone had sent more then 2.5 million people to other states by the end of 1993. The temporary emergency arrangements made to deal with this influx of refugees cannot be maintained indefinitely in a hope that the conflict will be resolved and people allowed to resume their former lives.

The right of access and residence to the German state is given to groups of ethnic Germans resident outside the state of Germany. These migrants, in combination with the numbers of asylum seekers shown in Table 5.4, pose a large number of problems of integration for the German state.

Table 5.4 Applications for asylum in selected EU states 1983–1991 (thousands)

Country	Number
Belgium	67.0
Denmark	45.1
France	298.3
Germany	959.2
Greece	29.8
Italy	70.3
Netherlands	94.0
Portugal	2.9
Spain	33.6
UK	126.5

Source : Adapted from Salt, J. (1993), p. 76 (see Further Reading)

Future patterns of migration

It is probable that in the future a number of trends will dominate the pattern of movement of people within the European Union.

1. The movement that traditionally took place from the poorer Southern states will continue, but at a slower rate than in the 1960s and 1970s. Portugal, Greece, Italy, Spain and, in the north, Ireland have been countries of traditional out-migration. Host states have in the past been predominantly Luxembourg, France, the former Federal Republic of Germany, Belgium and the United Kingdom. The Netherlands and Denmark have been characterised by a balance between out-migration and the movement of people into the state. Major curbs to movement will be the high costs involved, especially of housing in the more expensive areas, and the barrier within the EU because of lack of language competence.

2. The numbers of highly skilled, qualified and professional workers will grow. This is particularly the case as an increasing number of qualifications are recognised generally throughout the Union and students who have spent time in European institutions, outside their home country, graduate. The pattern of such movements will be to direct the flow of people towards the key urban and technological centres, e.g. London, Paris, Munich, Lisbon and Athens.

3. Third-country migration is expected to grow, but not at the rate of the 1950s and 1960s, after 1995. The situation of migrants from third countries is very complex. A major problem is that of illegal movement into the EU, which presents different problems from that of the legitimately recruited workers. In 1991 approximately 8 million nationals of non-Union countries were resident in the EU, mainly in France and Germany. The market for the relatively unskilled worker has fallen, although the pressure still exists in countries to the south of the Mediterranean to move into the European Union. There is in fact an increase in the number of non-EU nationals migrating to Italy, Spain, Portugal and Greece.

This presents the Union with a series of new problems.

- The number of illegal movers, which is difficult to assess accurately.

- The impact on the Southern states of the Union with problems of high levels of unemployment. The increase in numbers of migrants adds to the competition for employment within the receiving countries.

- A problem for the Union as a whole when these migrants move further north into the traditional receiving States of the EU. Countries such as the UK, France and Germany have since the 1970s placed restrictions on the numbers they are prepared to accept.

Within the northern states of the European Union since the 1970s, the priority has been to settle the migrants who were already there and restrict the numbers entering. For the second generation of migrants who are seeking to move throughout the EU for employment there will be the same problems of language and housing constraints as for EU national groups. However, their problems may be worsened because of racial discrimination.

4. The disintegration of the Soviet Empire and the freeing of the countries of Eastern Europe has created a potential for massive movement into the Union. In comparison with other third-country migrants these workers have a higher level of skills. The numbers who move from Central and Eastern Europe will depend on how quickly the many economic difficulties of these states are overcome.

5. Increases in the number of people who make short-term moves within the Union. Many of these will be students who take part in exchanges through the European Action Scheme for the Mobility of University Students, with its apt acronym ERASMUS. The ERASMUS programme was established in 1987, with two objectives:

- to bring about greater mutual recognition of qualifications

- to encourage greater mobility of staff and students in educational institutions across the EU. The target was set of 10 per cent of students participating in exchanges.

A measure of its success was given in 1992 when the programme was extended to include institutions in the EFTA states. ERASMUS was included in the SOCRATES programme from 1994.

Why free movement of people?

The right of nationals of the European Union states to move freely around the EU and reside in states other than their state of origin was established in the Treaty of Rome. This was not, however, a general right of residence; the movement referred to was of the economically active. In 1957 the majority of migrant workers within the EU were Italians who were employed on short-term or·fixed-term contracts. At a time of high demand for labour and limited surplus in the other states of the EU, encouraging the movement of workers to fill this demand was important for the effective functioning of the integrated market. The priority for these workers was to ensure that they were not subject to discrimination in the labour market of the host country. It was therefore important to establish a legal basis within the EU for the implementation of measures to protect migrant workers.

The European Union has retained this priority, seeing the free movement of workers as the most direct means by which to spread the benefits of the Single Market. However from the evidence, movements of labour do not play a *major role* in reducing inter-country differences in unemployment across the Union.[1] The reasons why this is the tendency, despite the legal basis for freedom of movement, are complex. Within the EU there is an acknowledgement that there has to be additional support for measures in the future that will encourage more people to move.

Originally the flow of workers from one state to another was limited because of the large number of opportunities within the home states for employment. More recently the flow of workers has been limited because of the lack of opportunities in the receiving states. Increasingly, policies adopted by the EU are designed to provide support for regional and local economic development and job creation (see chapters 14 and 15). However, the objective remains of removing the barriers to opportunities for individuals to move to find employment anywhere within the EU.

The legal basis on which the free movement of workers is built is in Article 3 of the Treaty of Rome, which states that one of the activities of the Union is to ensure that any obstacles to the freedom of movement of people are removed. This principle was given further legitimacy in the SEA article 8 which described the internal market as an area without internal frontiers. Articles 48 to 51 of the Treaty of Rome dealt in more detail with the principle of freedom of movement, and these articles are backed by the Articles 52 to 58 on the freedom of establishment.

The right of freedom of movement was given for the purpose of employment. Under current regulations, the migrant worker has the right to be accompanied by his or her immediate family. Regulation 1612/68 entitled a worker to be joined by his or her spouse and descendants under the age of 21 who are dependent, and also dependent relatives in the ascending line of the worker or spouse. Following the publication of the White Paper on the Single Market in 1985, the Commission proposed that the 1968 Regulation should be extended to include any other dependent member of the family living under the roof of the migrant in the country of origin. This proposal was not accepted by the Member States.

Movement of people was seen as a necessary prerequisite of economic growth. The emphasis was accordingly placed on those who were moving for employment, i.e. the economically active, which included the self-employed. The right of residency was also given to those who became unemployed following such a move. In the case of the self-employed the right of residency covered the right to take up and pursue activities as well as setting up and managing businesses.

In EU law the right of entry and residence did not exist independently of the economic motivation. The ECJ ruled that the internal market equated with the operation of a Community-wide market under conditions equivalent to those of a national market. As such, the barriers to the movement of people had to be abolished: both the physical barriers at the borders and any national practices that constrained movement.

More recently a wider objective has been given to this section of the Treaty of Rome. The basic right to free movement has been given to all EU nationals, whether they are economically active or not, and irrespective of nationality. The determining factor is whether or not they are accepted as the national of one of the Member States.

'Every citizen of the Union shall have the right to move and reside freely within the territory of the Member States, subject to the limitations and conditions laid down in this Treaty and by the measures adopted to give it effect.' Article 8a, TEU

In addition, migrants have to provide evidence of health insurance and that they have sufficient means to live.

Obstacles to free movement of people

The commitment to the social dimension and the furthering of social cohesion in the EU has broadened the opportunity for people to move within the EU. The groups now being included are those who wish to study and those who wish to live in another Member State for private reasons. The easing of restrictions on the groups that can move is necessary if progress on the social dimension is to be made. The EU is politically committed to this concept, although many obstacles remain.

The basic cause of many of the problems for those who move lie in the different laws on social provisions within the Member States. The problems of achieving harmonisation of social security benefits carry major difficulties for the individual states. From the beginning, the role of the states as the collectors and distributors of social benefits could not be interfered with by the European Union. The expectation was that over time, with increased economic integration, the policies of the individual states would naturally come into line. The possibility for joint action between the European Union and the Member States was present, but the EU did not take over the role of the individual states because of the political implications. If a worker became unemployed in one Member State the amount of unemployment benefit to which he or she was eligible might be smaller than in his or her home state. For the mover the goal of harmonisation of social benefits across the Union is desirable, but remains a distant prospect.

The European Union has adopted a number of regulations to ensure that the principle of equality of treatment is applied to those who move and that discrimination of all types is abolished. The objectives of these regulations are not to harmonise the national systems. Instead they are regularly updated to ensure that people who move are protected against the adverse effects of national legislation.

Any benefits received are paid under the conditions that apply in the state of employment and these conditions may differ from those of the home state. These regulations also establish the right for families of migrant workers to be covered by the host state's provisions in the same way as anyone considered to be a family member in that state. Other groups that receive the same protection as a consequence of the regulations include the survivors of migrant workers, stateless persons and refugees.

The benefits covered include the range of benefits paid in cash or kind for sickness, maternity benefits, invalidity benefits, old age benefits, survivors benefits, accident at work benefits, occupational injuries compensation, death grants, unemployment benefits and family benefits. The EU and the nation states must ensure that in their interpretation of the regulations, the emphasis is placed on not removing the ability to move. There are some excluded categories, including benefits for the victims of war and special schemes for civil servants. As the process of integration within the Union moves forward, the likelihood of national civil servants' wanting to move increases. The right of access to employment in public service has been supported by rulings of the Court of Justice. In late 1993 the Commission proposed a regulation for discussion by the Council of Ministers which would have ensured that increased access was possible to employment in the public service of any state.

There is very limited protection for unemployed people who wish to move within the EU. The 1995 Social Action Programme introduced measures to help with the mobility of this group. If movement is to be the most direct means by which the problem of unemployment may be solved, then clearly this group needs to be specially targeted for help.

The right to receive unemployment benefit is given for a period of only three months. Further claims are not possible in the same period of unemployment. One concern expressed is that free movement of people will result in the formation of a group who migrate around Europe in search of the best social benefits and health care. This is unlikely to happen in large numbers because of numerous other obstacles to movement of people – language, housing, lack of knowledge of the different states. The current regulations remain as a barrier to movement of those who would benefit most from being able to move. The same is true of the positions of those on low incomes or receiving other forms of benefit.

Obstacles to the movement of the retired population

The right of movement and the right of residence for the retired population is accepted within the EU. However, a number of problems occur for pensioners who wish to move because of differences in

1.   the statutory age of retirement within the EU

2.   the growing tendency of individuals to retire early and the lack of portability of private pensions taken by individuals to provide for this opportunity

3.   the differences in the value of pensions from one state to another.

Table 5.5 gives the differences between the retirement ages within the EU and the actual retirement age as more people take the opportunity to retire early.

Within the EU the retired population were able to have their statutory pensions paid in another Member State. However, the differences in statutory retirement age may be a barrier to movement. If the example is taken of Belgium with its retirement age of 65, and France where it is 60, there is the possibility of difference in the amount of pension received. This difference means that if a worker has spent almost all his working life in Belgium, but finished in France, under EU law, if he wished to take early retirement he would be entitled to only a pension calculated on a pro rata basis to the period of activity in France, which would result in a smaller pension than that of other Belgian nationals.

For pensioners whose pensions were not transferable to another Member State, but part of a contractual scheme, the possibility of settling in any state other than the one in which the pension was paid was reduced. As a large number of people began to take part in occupational pension schemes, which were not covered by European Union regulations, free movement

Table 5.5 Actual and statutory retirement ages in the EU

Country	Retirement age Actual	Statutory
Belgium	59.3	65/60
Denmark	62.7	67
France	59.6	60
Germany	61.0	65
Greece	63.0	65/60
Ireland	63.7	66
Italy	61.2	65
Luxembourg	60.1	65
Netherlands	60.4	65
Portugal	63.9	65/62
Spain	62.3	65
UK	62.5	65/60
EU average	61.3	65

Source : Adapted from *Financial Times*, 17 February 1994, 18

became a less attractive option as it carried the possibility of lost benefits. The size of the state pension provision in the Northern states of the EU is lower than that of the Southern states, so supplementary private pension plans became more common in states such as Belgium than in Greece. Table 5.6 gives the spread of private and company schemes in the EU and a measure of the worth of the state provision.

Table 5.6 Pension rights and benefits within the EU

Country	What pensions are worth as a percentage of final income[1] Married couples	Single persons	Spread of private and company schemes
Belgium	73	80	Common
Denmark	60	77	Common (staff)
France	88	83	Common but organised for staff
Germany	77	69	Common (in the former FRG)
Greece	107	114	Rare
Ireland	42	62	Common
Italy	89	89	Rare
Luxembourg	78	77	Rare
Netherlands	49	67	Common
Portugal	94	98	Rare
Spain	97	98	Rare
UK	44	59	Common

[1]   For manual workers in the manufacturing sector
Source : Adapted from *The European* 8/11 April 1993, 41

The Commission raised the question of the portability of supplementary private pensions on a number of occasions. During 1994, a Draft Directive was prepared which would have ensured that migrant workers suffered no undue loss from private pension schemes as a result of their decision to move. The Draft Directive required a unanimous vote in the Council of Ministers. While it was supported by the UK national government, other states, including Germany, were not in favour of the proposals. Since the German government held the Presidency of the Council of Ministers in the second half of 1994, the progress on the Draft Directive was slowed.

A much easier issue to resolve was related to workers who were posted or seconded to other EU states. Agreement was reached that they should be able to continue to contribute to private pension schemes in their own home state, and to take advantage of any national tax concessions on payments that might exist.

Assessing the effectiveness of the protection given to migrant workers' social security benefits is difficult. The large number of cases referred to the ECJ would suggest that many problems remain with the implementation of existing legislation. In the mid 1990s it was apparent that additional measures were required, including measures

1. to ensure that provision was made for national civil servants to move

2. to overcome the complications of applying the pro rata principle, especially where workers lived in one state and worked in another

3. to resolve the difficulties of transferring private supplementary occupational benefits.

Will movement contribute to social cohesion?

Movement following total liberalisation in the mid 1990s is unlikely to achieve the aims of distributing the benefits of economic integration more widely within the EU. Nor is it likely to have a dramatic effect on the desire to establish the social dimension to the Union, for a number of reasons.

1. Despite actions taken at Union level to improve the ability of people to move, a number of obstacles to movement remain. Levels of movement of EU nationals within the Member States remain low, as shown in Table 5.3.

2. More critically, the trend identified as being the most likely to grow is that of the movement of skilled, professional, and managerial groups. The central objective of actions taken at Union level must be to ensure that the benefits of growth are evenly distributed, and that the most disadvantaged regions are those where the growth is higher than the Union average. The movement of these groups will exacerbate the existing regional divide.

3. There are two types of region where economic growth is slower than in the rest of the Union: the areas of rapidly declining traditional industries and the regions that have been late to develop. Movement from these regions of the most ambitious and enterprising and the more youthful members of the population will encourage further decline. Movement into the areas of development will bring additional benefits to the already more developed regions.

Towards a Common Migration Policy?

The legal basis for movement of third-country nationals into the European Union is given in the Treaty of Rome, the Single European Act and the Treaty of European Union. However, the European Union competence given in these articles of the Treaties is limited. The three most pressing concerns for the EU in its attempts to reach a Common Policy on Migration are the establishment of policies on visas, asylum seekers and immigration. The TEU did not draw together the existing framework into a coherent policy. Rather, it continued the fragmented response of the EU. Some questions relating to third-country Movers were left to be dealt with as part of EU competence, others on an intergovernmental basis.

The provision to adopt a common visa policy was added to the Treaty on European Union by the inclusion of a new Article 100c, and the EU is therefore the recognised competent body to deal with the issue. The existing visa requirements of each Member State will be replaced by a uniform format for visas from 1996. Agreement was reached in 1994 about the states for whom visas would still be required.

Aside from this, the issues of asylum and immigration are subject to intergovernmental agreements between the Member States and to the application of the principle of subsidiarity. A series of bilateral and intergovernmental agreements have been reached which are outside the remit of the European Parliament and the Commission. There is provision in Article K of the TEU to transfer questions about asylum and immigration to the full EU competence. However, there are divergent national interests and the necessary unanimity vote may prove impossible to achieve.

A decision was reached among the Member States at Maastricht, in December 1991, on a definition of who was to be regarded as a citizen of the European Union. Article 8 of the revised provisions of the European Community Treaty defined a citizen of the EU as 'every person holding the nationality of a Member State'. Citizens of the EU, defined in this way, have the right of free movement and residence in the EU. However, this right was not transferred to the citizens of third countries with residence in the EU. Freedom of movement and rights of residence for third-country nationals may be acquired by individuals, subject to EU secondary legislation.

The Member States have established a number of cooperative frameworks in which to discuss issues relating to the movement of people. As these are intergovernmental initiatives, the Commission may have observer status at the discussions, but does not have the right of initiation of legislation. In this capacity the Commission is therefore represented on the ad hoc Group on Immigration.

Other cooperative frameworks have been established to consider issues such as

- TREVI (terrorism)

- CELAD and GAM 92 (drugs trafficking)

- SCENT (fraud)

- EUROPOL (information for police authorities).

The integration of third-country nationals may be supported through measures with assistance from the European Social Fund.

The Dublin Convention

The Dublin Convention was signed in 1990. It proposed common ground rules for dealing with the question of asylum seekers. The basis of the proposals was that of 'first host country', i.e. the decision made by one state to admit an asylum seeker would be accepted by all. The UK government objected to this on the grounds of national safety, and since unanimity was required for the principle to be adopted, the Convention was still unratified in 1994. In presenting its communication on controls at the borders in early 1994, the Commission recommended that this Convention be ratified by the end of 1994.

The External Frontiers Convention

The External Frontiers Convention was established to provide a list of nationalities that would require visas for EU entry and also a common list of prohibited individuals. As with many of the above-listed conventions and fora, the provisions of the Schengen agreement formed the basis of this Convention. The list of nationalities that required visas for entry to the EU was accepted by the states who ratified the Schengen agreement. The list identified 129 states whose nationals would require visas, 20 whose nationals would not and about 30 states about which no clear decision had been made. Following its publication in the UK, this list led to many comments expressing concerns about its seeming to discriminate against nationals from countries in Africa and Asia.

The ratification process of the External Borders Convention was delayed because of the dispute between the UK and the Spanish governments over Gibraltars borders. The Commission view was that although the ratification procedure of the whole of the Convention was delayed, this issue was outside the EU competence and should be resolved by the national governments of Spain and the UK in a bilateral agreement.

The Schengen Agreement

The Agreement was signed in 1985 by

● France, Germany and the Benelux states.

By 1994

● Italy, Spain and Portugal had signed

● Greece, which had no land border with any other Member State had moved from observer to full status

● Denmark and Austria had been granted observer status

● Switzerland had increased its cooperation with the other states

● UK and Ireland continued to refuse to ratify the Agreement.

The Irish government, whose only land border is with the UK, was in a difficult position. Its opposition to Schengen was not very strong, but signing the agreement risked the free movement agreement that the Irish had with the UK. As the UK is the traditional receiving state of a large number of Irish migrants (see Table 5.3), for the Irish government to ratify the Schengen Agreement would have had a detrimental effect.

The Schengen Agreement provided a framework for the removal of all checks for travellers at internal land and sea borders of the Union. It also established the basis of the common procedures for customs and other controls at external borders and airports. Under its provisions it was also possible to decide on policies on immigration, asylum, policing and the necessary legal changes to implement them.

A computerised information system (Schengen Information System (SIS)) was developed to link the national governments through a central unit in Brussels. The Schengen Information System contained information on people wanted by the police forces of the states who were signatories to the Schengen Agreement. The computerised data banks held information on more than one million people, including details of false passports, car thefts and arms traffic. It had originally been planned to have the SIS in place for the beginning of 1993. However, because of technical difficulties it did not become operational until March 1995. Five Member States (Germany, France, the Netherlands, Belgium and Luxembourg) were able to establish the necessary computerised link, but Spain, Portugal, Italy and Greece had technical problems before meeting the deadline.

As the UK and Irish governments had not ratified the Schengen Agreement it was unclear whether their police forces would have access to the SIS. In mid-1994, it was agreed by the Schengen signatories that the SIS would be linked to the European Information System (EIS), which covered all the twelve EU states.

The opposition of the UK to the Schengen Agreement was based on

1.   the view that no legal Treaty obligation was established to remove the physical barriers of controls at the borders to the movement of people

2.   the view that the details of the Schengen Agreement were incompatible with the UK principle of maintaining its own frontier-based system of border control.

The Danish government had at first also refused to sign the Schengen Agreement, but in 1994 requested observer status to the Agreement, and so there was no difficulty in their access to the SIS.

Conclusions

Free movement of people involves a number of issues that have been the subject of much controversy within the Union. There was an assumption that within the Single Market free movement of labour would equalise the differences in unemployment. The wide disparities in employment opportunities within the EU suggested that there would be a strong force pulling people out of the worst-affected regions. However, labour is not perfectly mobile within the EU. There are a number of issues relating to the physical obstacles to free movement within the EU that remain to be resolved for EU nationals. There is evidence that cultural and linguistic differences are also barriers to free movement.

In the mid-1990s, there is no evidence to suggest that the Single Market has had an impact on the pattern of migration within the EU. The number of EU nationals moving within the EU is unlikely to increase. However, it is important for the integration of the EU as a whole that people feel that there are opportunities available to them if they wish to move for employment. Overall, the inflows from outside the EU are likely to have a greater impact than the pattern of movement of European Union nationals around the EU.

There are a large number of conventions and agreements on the movement of people into the EU. However, many of the agreements have been concluded on the basis of intergovernmental action. Both political and practical difficulties have emerged to slow down the harmonisation of the national policies into one that is acceptable throughout the EU.

Consensus on how to deal with third-country nationals is urgently needed because of the new relationships of the EU with many groups of states. Agreements have been reached to liberalise trade with the states of Central and Eastern Europe and increased support has been agreed for some of the states of the former Soviet Union. These agreements will bring additional pressures to allow for easier access for third-country nationals to the European Union. As the state closest to the region of Central and Eastern Europe, the German government is particularly concerned to ensure a coordinated response from the EU.

The pressures on the EU to reach agreement on a Common Policy on Migration have resulted in an important step forward in establishing a political face for the EU. In its development of a concept of citizenship, along with the provisions entitling citizens of the EU to vote in European and national elections, the EU has made an important breakthrough. An opportunity has been provided for a transfer of allegiance from the national level, for the citizens of the EU, to the supranational. While many issues remain to be resolved about the movement of third-country nationals and their rights of residence and movement within the EU, this is an important consequence of the attempts at reaching a Common Policy on Migration. Movement of people will remain for some time as an intergovernmental concern. The Member States have not reached political agreement on the transfer of the protection of the external border of the EU to the competence of the European Union.

References

1.   **Commission of the EC** (1993) *Employment in Europe – 1993*, COM (93) 314, p. 14.

Further reading

Commission of the EC (1993) *Green Paper on European Social Policy*, COM (93) 551.
Commission of the EC (1994) *Communication on Immigration and the Right of Asylum*.
Council of Europe (1993) *Political and Demographic Aspects of Migration Flows to Europe*, Population Studies, No. 25, 1993.
European Parliament (1991) *Freedom of Movement for Persons and Problems Relating to National Security in the Community*, Malangre Report. July 1991.
House of Lords (1989) *Free Movement of People and Right of Residence in the EC*, HL 26, 6 February 1990.
House of Lords (1992) *Community Policy on Migration*, HL 35, 17 November 1992.
Salt J (1993) *Migration and Population Change in Europe*, UNIDR Research Paper No. 19, 1993.

CHAPTER 6

Monetary integration in the European Union

'...financial independence or sovereignty is a thing of the past.'[1]

Introduction

At the heart of the debate about the desirable speed of economic integration within the European Union is the issue of how far and how fast to take the process of monetary integration. There is now a high degree of integration between the exchange rate and financial systems of the EU Member States. By the early 1990s there seemed to be an inevitable link between the success of the European Monetary System (EMS) and the movement to Economic and European Monetary Union (EMU). However, the decision of the Intergovernmental Conference concluded at the Maastricht Summit of December 1991 to adopt a strategy of moving towards a single currency for the EU by 1999 proved to be highly controversial. Indeed, the British government made a point of distancing itself, as far as was decently possible, from the process. A period of extreme exchange rate instability followed the attempts to ratify the Treaty on European Union. This caused concerns about the survival of the EMS in a meaningful form, and doubts as to whether EMU would ever be achieved.

This chapter examines the progress towards greater monetary integration. It argues that by the early 1990s there was a case for claiming considerable success for the EMS in its task of creating a zone of monetary stability. However, the task of moving towards just one currency for the EU was one of far greater magnitude, which damaged the achievements of the EMS. There are considerable practical difficulties in moving to EMU, which may prove insurmountable unless there is considerable progress in terms of political integration. There must be willingness to see the EU in terms of being one economy, rather than just a Single Market. Within this context, EMU requires an acceptance of significant redistribution of resources between the Member States, and a shared responsibility for actions that goes far beyond that which has been apparent to date.

There is general support for the idea of stable currencies, and a recognition that they assist the process of international trade. Most EU states have achieved a reasonable degree of domestic price stability, largely through their own efforts. To achieve stability with regard to the exchange rate between currencies is regarded by many as being equally important. This is a policy objective that can only be realistically achieved by international coordination. This has been the role of the EMS within the EU. However, abandoning the national currency and adopting a European alternative is inevitably going to be controversial. In all stable economies, the notes and coinage are a recognisable symbol of nationhood. They are objects that most of us grow up with and identify with. In Germany, the very fact that the value of the currency was wiped out by inflation twice within many people's lifetime means that the stable domestic value of the mark is valued even more. Apart from the emotional issues, there are major practical considerations to take into account.

This chapter therefore considers two related themes:

1. the operation of the EMS, and why it proved difficult to maintain in the period of monetary instability in the early 1990s

2. the longer term process of moving the EU towards EMU.

It suggests that the real benefits that appeared to come from the stability of the EMS were sacrificed in an attempt to move towards EMU, and that there may now be a need to reconsider both strategies in the light of a very changed economic and political environment.

Monetary integration

Monetary integration can take place at a number of different levels. If national governments are able to maintain price stability within their economies, this should be reflected in a stability of exchange rates. Any adjustment to exchange rates would simply reflect the changes taking place within the real economy, such as differing levels of productivity or innovation. This leads to a system of freely floating exchange rates, where market forces coordinate transactions. Because the free market model does not work, there have been a number of attempts at international coordination. These include the following.

1. *The International Monetary Fund (IMF) system* – this existed between 1945 and 1973, and was often described as a fixed exchange rate system, although it did permit devaluation. The degree of policy coordination involved was limited, in part because it operated as a global system.

2. *A pegged but adjustable system* – this involves limited day-to-day variations in the value of one currency against another, with some acceptance that rates may change more substantially on occasions. There is a degree of policy coordination within the system. The best example of this was the Exchange Rate Mechanism of the European Monetary System, as it operated until August 1993.

3. *Monetary union* – this involves currencies being held at fixed values against one another. Examples of this are the gold standard, the link between the Irish and British pounds until 1979, and the current link between the Belgian and Luxembourg francs. It should be noted, therefore, that monetary union can take place without economic union.

4. *Economic and monetary union (EMU)* – this involves currencies being held at fixed values against one another, or operating with a common currency. In addition, the autonomy that Member States enjoy with regard to monetary and fiscal policy is severely

limited. This step takes members a long way towards complete economic integration. In the early 1970s, the attempt at EMU involved little in the way of coordination of economic policy. The move to EMU in the 1990s still appeared to lack the required commitment to policy coordination, and as a consequence faltered in 1992 and 1993.

The exchange problem

For the benefits of international trade to be fully realised, it is important to have an efficient exchange rate system. In an ideal world, competitors should face no costs other than those associated with transporting goods, in their attempts to penetrate markets. The problem for the EU is that the current exchange rate system does impose costs, which means that the operation of the Single Market is threatened.

Exchange rates are the price of one currency in terms of another. That is, if we wish to purchase an item such as a car from Germany which costs Deutschmark (DM) 24 000, and the exchange rate is DM3 = £1, the price will be £8000 in the UK. If the value of the pound goes up, so that we now get DM4 = £1, then the price of the car will fall in the UK market to £6000. This revaluation of the pound (devaluation of the DM) means that it becomes much easier to sell German cars in the UK. However, the UK exporters will have a much tougher time selling their products to Germany.

Wide fluctuations in currency values were rare in the period from 1949 to 1971, because of the dominant role of the IMF and the central role of the US dollar. This was the era of what were called fixed exchange rates. That is, most of the major trading currencies were tied in a fixed relationship to the US dollar, for example £1 = $2.80 for the period from 1949 to 1967. This fixed relationship meant that it was possible to predict the price of goods in international trade with a great deal of certainty. Exporters could fix a price well in advance and be certain that their profit levels would not be harmed by random changes in the values of a currency. For exchange rate stability, participating currencies must be backed by high levels of gold and foreign exchange reserve, and there must be confidence in the system and those participating in it.

The disadvantage of the IMF system, especially for the UK, was that the value of the foreign currency reserves was never fully adequate. In extreme cases of difficulty, the IMF might be approached for a loan or the value of the currency might be devalued. This happened in 1967, when the value of the pound sterling fell from $2.80 to $2.40. The devaluation took place after three years of trying to defend the pound by slowing down domestic UK economic growth. This was to cause future UK governments to look with caution at the option of sacrificing domestic economic objectives for the sake of the international value of the currency.

The failure of floating exchange rates

In an ideal world, the value of a currency should reflect purchasing power parity. That is, after taking account of the effect of different levels of indirect taxation, a basket of items should cost the same amount regardless of the country of purchase. However, this is far from the case.

In the late 1960s there was some support for the view that a collapse of the international system of fixed exchange rates would be a good thing. The UK in particular had suffered from speculative attacks on the pound, which many thought had set back economic growth. The need was felt always to respond to external pressure on the value of the pound. If the pound became a target for speculators interest rates had to be raised in order to attract short-term monetary deposits into the UK. This had the effect of raising the costs to industry of borrowing money and dampened consumer demand, often at times when these were contrary to the needs of the domestic economy. The effect was one of stop/go economic management, which was harmful to long-term investment. If the pound was to float freely, the argument went, then the economy would be isolated from the whims of speculators. Added to this, there was a belief that in the event of a balance of payments deficit, the currency would simply float down in value. This would cause imports to become more expensive and exports to be cheaper. In a reasonable period of time, there was a belief that the system would simply resolve the problem by promoting exports and discouraging imports. This belief in free market forces was to be tested in the 1970s.

The reality of floating exchange rates was that the market mechanism for currencies was found not to give the desired results. World trade under the IMF system grew by 7.5 per cent per annum, while under floating rates it grew by only 3.3 per cent per annum. This does not mean that floating rates caused the slowdown in trade growth, but clearly fixed rates were associated with better times. The slowdown in an immediate sense was largely due to the effects of the two oil crises in the 1970s, but there were also deeper structural causes.

With floating rates the value of currencies has moved up and down spectacularly, with currencies appearing to be overvalued and undervalued for significant periods of time. While this has offered considerable opportunities to dealers and speculators in the currency markets to profit from the movements, it has not been easy for business to judge the price of its exports. This has been particularly the case in the UK, where a failure to join the ERM of the EMS in 1990 meant that the pound has fluctuated widely against the DM, the key currency in the EU (Table 6.1).

Table 6.1 German marks to the British pound

Year	Rate
1968	8.00
1978	3.85
1981	5.07
1984	3.80
1987	2.74
1989	3.25
1992	2.84
1994	2.60
1995	2.42

Note : January figures with the exception of 1981 (February)

While large national companies have had the resources to cope, small and medium sized enterprises (SMEs) have found it more difficult to involve themselves fully in trade. The risk of making exchange rate losses, or the cost of buying adequate forward cover, has acted as a deterrent to the SME sector. The costs of exchange rate dealings can be as much as ten times higher for the SME sector compared with the multinationals. The large multinational corporations such as Ford and General Motors have exploited the movements in currency values by shifting production away from high-cost centres to low-cost ones. So, for example, they both moved production from the UK in the late 1970s and early 1980s to such an extent that the Ford and Vauxhall were predominantly foreign-produced vehicles. When the value of the pound fell, they started to show some interest in increasing UK production again.

The causes of exchange rate instability

The cause of much of exchange rate instability can be seen, in part, as a lack of information on which to base decisions as to the true value of a currency. The value of a currency should be determined to some extent by the state of balance of payments of a country and yet, despite ever more sophisticated collection and processing techniques, it takes many years to get an accurate indication of what is going on. Globally, there has been a tendency to underestimate the value of exports and imports. This has led to the creation of what is known as the black hole. In the late 1980s there appeared to be a world trade deficit of $74 billion, which is of course a logical impossibility, unless there was trade with Mars. This inconsistency has been ironed out to a certain extent, but other sources of confusion have arisen. An example is the problem of creating adequate trade statistics within the EU following the removal of border controls in 1993 (see chapter 3).

The uncertainty that poor trade statistics create, plus the differing views taken as to the long-term prospects for particular economies, leads to a situation where the value of a currency depends very much on market sentiment. Indeed, if an economy is growing rapidly, the extent to which foreign investors see this as a favourable tendency may cause a currency to rise despite balance of payments deficits.

The development of the international money markets in the late 1960s and early 1970s was to be affected by two major trends.

1. The US dollar was no longer a force for stability at the centre of the international monetary system. This was because of the effects of substantial balance of payments deficits caused by the war in Vietnam. There were too many dollars in the system, and some states started to insist on holding a proportion of alternative currencies, or gold. Up to 1973 there was a link between the dollar and gold, but this disappeared as the currency floated.

2. The liberalisation of capital movements on a global basis meant that the opportunities for speculative attacks became far greater. This situation accelerated in the 1980s. The amount of money going through the major financial centres is now so large that it is difficult to hold off a concerted speculative attack.

The extent to which massive flows of foreign exchanges had become a reality was demonstrated by the Bank of England three year survey of foreign exchange markets dealing up to April 1992. This showed that in 1992, London was still the major centre with $303 billion (£177 billion) per day of spot and forward dealings going through it, a rise of 62 per cent on 1989. London also had 30 per cent of the global trading of $1000 billion per day. The relative positions are given in Table 6.2.

Table 6.2 Foreign exchange dealings – daily turnover of the three main financial centres (in $ billion)

	March 1986	April 1989	April 1992
London	90	187	303
New York	50	129	192
Tokyo	48	115	128
Total	188	431	623

Source : Bank of England Press Notice, 24 September 1992

The survey also showed that the proportion of activity in London devoted to spot trading had fallen by 14 percentage points to 50 per cent, reflecting a growth to 50 per cent of forward trading. Forward trading is the buying and selling of currency in the future. It is normally done by firms that wish to avoid the risk of sharp currency movements affecting the viability of commercial transactions. Forward trading grew by 125 per cent from $65 million to $146 million, while spot trading grew by 24 per cent from $119 billion to $147 billion.

A government normally intervenes in a foreign exchange market using its central bank, which uses either interest rates or foreign exchange reserves to maintain a stable value for its currency. In order to keep the value of its currency down, a central bank must either lower interest rates or sell its own currency and buy up other currencies. This risks creating domestic inflation, if money supply has to be increased. A much more serious problem arises if the value of a currency looks like falling. The central bank then needs to buy up any quantity of its own currency needed to prevent the value from falling. This means raising interest rates to abnormally high levels or using its own foreign exchange reserves to buy up surplus currency in the market. The extent of this action is limited by the size of reserves available to the countries defending a currency. If reserves are not adequate they simply run out, and the value of the currency falls.

Speculators work in the market by taking a view on the movements of currencies. In 1992, prior to the UK pound's exit from the ERM, speculators sold sterling when it was at the floor of the market. Their intention was to buy it back at a lower rate once the currency was devalued. At the height of the speculation against the pound, the turnover in London money markets rose to around £300 billion in the day. It is estimated that between £15 billion and £20 billion was spent defending sterling, which following a 15 per cent devaluation means that the losses were in the region of £2.25–£3 billion. The huge sums of money lost caused considerable resentment. The magazine *Central Banking* was to comment that the loss was 'just as if Norman Lamont (the Chancellor of the Exchequer) had personally thrown entire hospitals and schools into the sea all afternoon'.[2]

It is, however, possible to overrate the impact of speculators in the interbank market. In 1985 the markets were dominated by commercial bank dealers taking short-term positions. By the early 1990s, the situation had changed because

1. the growth in forward markets meant that corporate treasurers of large corporations tended to be involved, to the extent of about 20 per cent of the market

2. pension fund managers moved funds in order to protect their assets

3. a number of investors are attracted by high interest rates and many invest on a short-term basis. About £50 billion moved into London between 1985 and 1992. Many of these short-term investors were the real gainers from devaluation, because they enjoyed a long period of high interest rates but were able to leave sterling by selling their pounds as the Bank of England supported the currency.[3]

The first attempt at EMU

The link between achieving monetary integration and successful economic integration has long been recognised. As early as 1960, Robert Triffin was proposing a plan to achieve European Monetary Union (EMU) by stages. At an official level, attitudes were influenced by the 5 per cent revaluation of the German Mark and Dutch Guilder in 1961. In 1962 the Commission produced a plan which proposed concrete stages leading to monetary union with irrevocably fixed exchange rates and a European reserve currency. In 1968 the Werner Plan also called for the permanent fixing of exchange rates, along with the introduction of a European unit of account and a European Monetary Fund. While the proposals of the early 1960s were quickly lost in the mists of time, the Werner Report was influential and is still seen as a source of inspiration in the current attempts to achieve monetary union.

The issue of EMU was first raised seriously in 1969, when the stability of the dollar-based system was first put into serious doubt. The Treaty of Rome had not seriously considered macroeconomic coordination, because it offered a threat to national sovereignty. In the case of the monetary system, there was no need for concern as long as the IMF system worked. Indeed, the EU's currency for the purpose of its own transactions was the Unit of Account (UA) which was valued at exactly the same level as the US dollar.

As soon as the dollar-based system started to come apart, however, there was a need for the EU to consider alternative arrangements, not only for the purposes of payments made by the EU, but also because of the central role played by the Common Agricultural Policy (CAP). The devaluation of the French franc and revaluation of the German mark in 1969 led to the creation of artificial Green currencies (officially known as representative rates) to be used in agricultural trade. Prices for the CAP were fixed in UAs on an EU-wide basis, which meant that devaluation of the French franc would have caused the price of food to rise in France. In order to prevent the French consumer paying more, the Green rates were introduced (see chapter 8).

The first attempt at EMU followed the Smithsonian Agreement in November 1971 which devalued the US dollar, so that its new rate became £1 = $2.60. The dollar was at the centre of the new system, and the EU currencies plus those of the new members were expected to keep within a band that was no more than 2.25 per cent from the highest to the lowest point. This was called the snake, and it was expected to keep within a wider band of 2.25 per cent either side of the US dollar (called the tunnel). The hope was that the currencies would converge, so that EMU would be achieved by 1980, perhaps with a new currency with the suggested name of the Europa.

The new system was launched in April 1972 but it was soon in trouble, with the Bank of England spending $2.6 billion defending the pound in one week in June. This situation could not be sustained, and the British decided that it would be better to float the pound downwards than to sacrifice the growth of the economy.

The failure of EMU was due to the lack of any attempt to provide a meaningful support mechanism for the member currencies. In addition, there was no attempt to coordinate national economic policies. The whole project might in any case have been to no avail, given that the US dollar, the centre of the EMU, was to devalue in February 1973. This was followed by the destabilising effects of the oil crisis. By the mid-1970s the snake was nothing more than a collection of the stronger EU currencies, plus the Swiss franc.

The first moves to resurrect the idea of EMU came in 1977, with an initiative proposed by the then President of the Commission, Roy Jenkins. His proposal proved to be premature, but in 1978 the French and German governments were able to agree on a more limited proposal, i.e. the creation of the EMS. This was designed to create a zone of monetary stability within the EU. No target date was set for EMU, and indeed for most commentators this was simply not on the agenda, given the failure of the first attempt. By 1979, when the EMS was first introduced, the problems of trying to cope with monetary instability had convinced the majority of EU states that free floating rates did not work well. A degree of stability had started to return to the exchange rate system, which offered a good opportunity for the initiative to be introduced. Also there were problems associated with speculative pressures on the German mark, which was under constant upward pressure as the value of the US dollar weakened. There was also a fear that the EU, as an organisation, could not function effectively without an agreed unit of account. In the absence of the dollar-based UA, several artificial currencies were in use.

The European Monetary System

The EMS came into existence in 1979 as an attempt to replace wildly fluctuating floating exchange rates, which were a feature of the international monetary system after the first oil crisis with an area of monetary stability, with a degree of stability between the price of one currency and another. All the Member States of the EU participate in the EMS, although it was not until 1984 that Greece became a member, and Spain and Portugal did not join until September 1989. Despite difficulties in the early years, caused by the second oil crisis and the French Socialist government pursuing divergent national policies, the EMS survived to become part of the Treaties (via the Single European Act). Its further development came to be regarded as central to the process of completing the Single Market, because exchange rate instability was seen as a significant barrier to trade.

There are three main features of the EMS, although the system offers the prospect of both partial and full membership. These are the ECU, the ERM and the EMI.

The European Currency Unit (ECU)

This is a composite of the EMS currencies weighted according to their importance in trade. Article 109g of the Treaty on European Union states that 'The currency composition of the

ECU shall not be changed'. On 1 November 1993 the weightings of the basket of currencies making up the ECU were as given in Table 6.3.

Table 6.3 Weights for the ECU as of 1 November 1993

Currency	Amount in national currency	Weights in percentages
Deutschmark	0.6242	32.63
French franc	1.332	19.89
Dutch guilder	0.2198	10.23
Belgian/Luxembourg franc	3.431	8.29
Danish krone	0.1976	2.56
Irish punt	0.00852	1.06
Subtotal 1		74.66
Italian lira	151.8	8.18
UK pound	0.08784	11.45
Greek drachma	1.44	0.53
Spanish peseta	6.885	4.50
Portuguese escudo	1.393	0.71
Subtotal 2		25.34
Total		100.00

These weightings had changed in the past. The last time they were fixed was in 1989. In the period to 1993, the stronger currencies had increased their weighting from 70.8 to 74.66 per cent, as shown in subtotal 1. In 1995 the weightings did not change as a consequence of enlargement.

The ECU replaced the Unit of Account which had ceased to be useful in the 1970s era of floating exchange rates. It has four functions.

1. It acts as the central rate of the exchange rate mechanism of the EMS.

2. It is the basis of the divergence indicator (see below).

3. It is the nominal currency that the EU uses to conduct its transactions. This means for example, that prices for agricultural products within the CAP are denominated in ECUs.

4. It is used as a means of settlement between monetary authorities in the EU.

The Exchange Rate Mechanism (ERM)

This was a system of fixing exchange rates within a narrow band of 2.25 per cent either side of the ECU. There were exceptions to this as the system operated until September 1992, where new entrants to the ERM operated with a wider 6 per cent margin. The only Member State currency not to be part of the ERM was the Greek drachma.

Member States could devalue their currency if there were problems of maintaining its value, but this was not to be done to gain an unfair competitive advantage.

From August 1993, the ERM became a much looser system, with the bands set at 15 per cent either side of the ECU. This meant that currencies could diverge from one another at the top and bottom of the range by 30 per cent. (Note: The actual bands are not +15 per cent and −15 per cent, they are +16.12 per cent and −13.88 per cent. This reflects the fact that if the mark appreciates by 15 per cent, for example, the French franc will have depreciated by only 13.4 per cent.)

A novel feature of the system was the use of the ECU base divergence indicator. When a currency reached 75 per cent of its maximum spread within the mechanism – the divergence threshold – there was a presumption that action would be taken to correct this situation. Corrective action was not compulsory until the actual maximum spread was reached. It is not clear whether this mechanism has any real meaning in the wider band system.

The European Monetary Institute (EMI)

This was established on 1 January 1994, and its location was chosen to be Frankfurt. It replaced the European Monetary Cooperation Fund (EMCF).

Article 100f of the Treaty on European Union sets out the functions of the EMI with respect to the operation of the EMS. These are to

- strengthen cooperation between national central banks

- strengthen the coordination of the monetary policies of the Member States with the aim of ensuring price stability

- monitor the functioning of the European Monetary System

- hold consultations concerning issues falling within the competence of the national central banks and affecting the stability of financial institutions and markets

- take over the tasks of the European Monetary Cooperation Fund (which has now been dissolved)

- facilitate the use of the ECU and oversee its development.

The EMI retained the funding arrangements of the EMCF, which were designed to assist Member States whose currencies were under speculative pressure or that were facing problems with their balance of payments situation. These arrangements include the following.

1. *Very Short Term credit facility* – This is the funding arrangement designed to keep currencies within the ERM. The facility was strengthened as a result of the Basle-Nyborg Agreement, which meant that credit was virtually automatic and unlimited. Loans must be repaid on average after three months, but limited amounts may be carried forward.

2. *Short-term monetary support* – This allows central banks to borrow in order to finance temporary balance of payments difficulties. Loans are initially for three months, but may be renewed once. This facility has been used very infrequently.

3. *Medium-term finance* – These are loans with conditions attached. Finance is granted for between two and five years. Once again, it has rarely been used.

4. *EU Loan Mechanism* – This enables the EU to borrow on the world markets up to ECU 6 billion, which can be re-lent to Member States on the same terms. However, conditions are normally attached to these medium-term loans, although their severity may vary. In 1983, the French government borrowed ECU 4 billion with only a vague commitment to impose austerity measures. In contrast, the ECU 1.75 billion loan granted to the Greek government in 1985 contained more detailed conditions.

The developing European currency unit

The ECU's increasing use for official transactions between Member States and between central banks was inevitable. However, as a parallel to this there has been a developing use of the ECU for private purposes. The private ECU is simply a basket of currencies concocted in the same way as the official ECU. There is no connection between the two, but it is now the case that individuals and companies can hold bank accounts that are denominated in private ECUs throughout the EU. Even Germany, where such accounts were not permitted in the early years on the grounds that they were potentially inflationary, has agreed to permit them.

It is possible for sophisticated private borrowers to raise ECU mortgages, and for UK borrowers these have often offered substantially lower rates of interest than those offered domestically. Companies can now use the ECU for invoicing, and for raising funds. This way, some of the exchange rate risk can be avoided. The rapid growth of ECU denominated assets in the 1980s indicates the dissatisfaction that the business sector feels with continued exchange rate instability. However, it often makes sense to borrow using the ECU only if the income generated from an investment comes from the whole of the EU. Although it is possible to buy exchange rate cover, this can be expensive and can take away the benefits of lower interest rates available on ECU loans.

The growth of the private ECU is seen by some as the start of a new European currency, but some caution should be shown with regard to this claim. First, some exchange rate risk remains, especially in an era of +/– 15 per cent bands within the Exchange Rate Mechanism. Second, it could be argued that if monetary integration were fully developed there would be no need to hold accounts in an artificial currency. Third, some of the currencies that form part of the ECU are of doubtful quality. Finally, despite greater attempts at European awareness, most of the general public do not know what an ECU is. In an attempt to improve the lot of European travellers, American Express and Thomas Cook started to issue travellers' cheques denominated in ECUs. The response to these has been poor. In 1989, American Express pulled out of the market and Thomas Cook had to admit that there was little market for them.

The market for ECU-denominated bonds showed a substantial expansion in the period when EMU looked to be a growing possibility.[4] However, after the exchange rate crisis of September 1992, there was a decline in enthusiasm for the currency. Until the third stage of EMU is reached, there is no domestic authority responsible for the maintenance of orderly and efficient markets in the ECU. The Commission suggested that some of the problems could be overcome by giving the ECU full foreign currency status in the Member States, and that the definition of the ECU should defined in law within the Member States.[5]

The EMS in operation

There have been five distinct phases in the EMS's development.

1. 1979 to March 1981 – only minor changes in the ERM central rates, in part due to the impact of oil price rises.

2. March 1981 to March 1983 – significant changes in the ERM due to the French pursuing an expansionary economic policy.

3. March 1983 to August 1992 – only five realignments in the ERM with the system showing far greater stability. The EMS is seen as the basis of EMU, and becomes less flexible.

4. September 1992 to 1993 – significant monetary turbulence, with sterling and the lira suspending their membership of the ERM, the peseta and the escudo devaluing, and the Finnish markka and Swedish krona breaking their informal link with the ERM. This was followed by further turbulence in 1993, and a forced movement to wider bands of +/–15 per cent.

5. 1994 – from the start of the year, the focus of the foreign exchange markets moves to the US$/Japanese yen relationship. The remaining members of the ERM start to operate informally within narrow bands.

6. March 1995 – Spanish domestic political pressures result in devaluations of peseta and escudo.

Table 6.4 gives the overall picture.

The above situation shows that the EMS was a pegged, but adjustable, exchange rate system. It needed exchange rate adjustments to make it work, but they had not to take place too often, otherwise a floating system would have emerged. If a currency came under pressure, action was expected to defend its value. Domestically, this meant that monetary authorities had to raise interest rates, while they used their foreign exchange reserves to prop up the value of the currency. Until the end of 1992, some countries could use capital controls to stave off speculative attacks, but this weapon disappeared with the end of the first stage of EMU and completion of the Single Market. Assistance was available from stronger currencies, and indeed there was an assumption that the strongest currencies would be sold in order to bring the markets into line. Assistance from the strongest currencies was not unlimited, however, as became apparent in the currency instability of 1992 and 1993.

While the tendency was to see the EMS as a collective effort on the part of the EU, there is no doubt about the dominant influence of the German Bundesbank. All the realignments of the ERM were to revalue the Deutschmark cumulatively by 41.8 per cent by 1990. The cumulative effect of the post-September 1992 devaluations was probably to revalue the mark by a further 6 per cent.

German inflation rates were consistently lower than the EU average until the problems associated with reunification started to emerge. This led to the credibility of the ERM depending increasingly on the mark, its strongest element. Membership of the ERM meant that economies could not realign their currencies easily, and the tendency was not to allow devaluation in order to compensate fully for differing domestic inflation rates. Participation in the ERM indicated a commitment to tackling problems without being driven by domestic political expedients, as the maintenance of exchange rates became the primary objective of

Table 6.4 The ERM in action

Year	Date	Currency	% realignment
1979	13 March	Start of EMS with +/– 2.25% bands except Italy with +/– 6%	
	24 September	DM	+2
		DKR	–2.9
	30 November	DKR	–4.76
1981	23 March	ITL	–6
	5 October	DM, DG	+5.5
		FF, ITL	–3
1982	22 February	BF	–8.5
		DKR	–3
	14 June	DM, DG	+4.25
		ITL	–2.75
		FF	–5.75
1983	21 March	DM	+5.5
		DG	+3.5
		DKR	+2.5
		BF	+1.5
		FF, ITL	–2.5
		IR£	–3.5
1985	22 July	BF, DKR, DM, FF, DG, IR£	+2
		ITL	–6
1986	7 April	DM, DG	+3
		BF, DKR	+1
		FF	–3
	4 August	IR£	–8
1987	12 January	DM, DG	+3
		BF	+2
1989	19 June	Spanish peseta enters with 6% bands	
1990	8 January	Italian lira adopts narrow bands	–3.7
	8 October	UK joins with +/– 6% bands	
1992	6 April	Escudo enters +/– 6% band	
	14 September	BF, DM, DG, DKR, ESC, FF,	+3.5
		IR£, PTA, UK£, ITL	–3.5
	17 September	UK£, ITL suspend ERM membership	
		PTA	–5
	23 November	ESC, PTA	–6
1993	1 February	IR£	–10
	14 May	PTA	–8
		ESC	–6.5
	2 August	Widening of ERM bands to +/– 15% for all members of the ERM	
1995	1 January	Austria joins ERM	
		Finland and Sweden elect to stay out	
	5 March	PTA	–7
		ESC	–3.5

economic policy. The view was therefore that ERM had an effect on domestic inflationary expectations. It was felt that it was possible to achieve disinflation at a lower cost in terms of unemployment, because there was an overall belief that the system was anti-inflationary.

Within the ERM the problem of interdependence between economies became even more serious. The fact that devaluation could take place only in specific circumstances meant that any state wishing to improve its competitive situation could do so in the long term by improved efficiency. In the short to medium term, the way to gain an advantage was to have a lower rate of inflation than one's partners. This led to a situation of competitive deflations. In a period of recession, this inevitably causes the general situation to deteriorate.

Even in its most successful phase, the ERM was criticised. The ERM currencies often appeared no more stable than other currencies, and the inflation rates within Europe were similar to those found worldwide. Added to this, the rates of economic growth of the ERM states were not particularly good in the 1980s. The domination of the system by the German central bank, and the German obsession with controlling inflation, may have been deflationary. Also the stability displayed by the ERM was achieved with the assistance of capital controls. Once these went, the ERM was subject to increased pressure. Finally, the stability of the ERM currencies in the late 1980s was of nominal rates, (those quoted in the money markets), but changes in consumer prices in Member States meant that real exchange rates moved considerably (the exchange rate after the effects of inflation has been taken into account). This is illustrated in Table 6.5.

Table 6.5 Real effective exchange rates 1988–1993 (1987 = 100)

	1988	1989	1990	1991	1992	1993
Austria	95.3	92.4	92.5	90.3	91.8	95.4
Belgium	97.4	96.1	100.5	100.2	101.3	101.2
Denmark	99.6	97.3	103.0	100.0	101.4	103.9
Finland	103.4	107.9	112.5	104.8	85.5	75.7
France	97.6	95.2	97.5	93.4	94.6	97.1
Germany	100.5	98.3	104.1	102.6	106.1	112.5
Ireland	94.7	86.8	88.4	82.7	81.4	76.0
Italy	97.8	102.3	109.0	109.8	108.0	88.6
Netherlands	97.3	91.9	93.2	92.7	96.4	101.0
Spain	105.0	113.2	122.3	126.5	128.9	117.0
Sweden	103.7	110.4	112.2	110.7	111.2	84.8
UK	105.7	110.0	105.4	109.2	106.7	96.9

Note : A fall in the index is equivalent to an increase in price competitiveness
Source : Economic Commission for Europe, (1994) *Economic Survey of Europe in 1993–94*,
United Nations, p. 49

Table 6.5 shows that the majority of economies experienced periods of deteriorating competitiveness, caused by domestic inflation in economies such as Italy's, and by revaluation of nominal exchange rates as in the case of Germany. Periods of improved competitiveness were a result of devaluations of nominal rates, which impacted on real rates as in the case of the UK, or by achieving low rates of inflation as in the case of the Netherlands.

On the positive side, the ERM had a great deal of credibility, and there were strong arguments for building on this. Suggestions that the instability of the exchange rate would be replaced by instability in interest rates (which would also have been damaging to business) appeared to have been disproved. It was accepted that there will need to be greater coordination of monetary policy in the future, especially after the removal of capital controls. The currencies of the ERM were not perfect substitutes for each other. However, in 1989 Taylor and Artis found that there was 'unequivocal evidence that the ERM has brought about a reduction in both conditional and unconditional variance of exchange rate changes'.[6]

The EMS in crisis

As a consequence of the Maastricht Intergovernmental Conference in 1991, the EMS became the centre of the EU's plans to further economic integration with the move towards EMU. This caused the system to take on a new dimension, with adjustments in exchange rates being phased out in preparation for the adoption of a single currency. However, the EU did little after the decision had been made to make EMU a reality, despite conducting a rigorous policy debate about the merits of moving towards EMU, and adopting a radical set of proposals in the TEU. As a consequence, the defences were not adequate to cope with the massive wave of currency speculation that hit the EMS currencies in 1992 and 1993. A number of devaluations took place. The UK and Italy suspended membership of the ERM, Scandinavian countries shadowing the ERM had to abandon their strategy, and there was an enforced movement towards the wider +/– 15 per cent bands in August 1993.

The reasons behind the speculative pressures were complex. A major contributory factor was that no real effort was made to implement EMU, despite the Maastricht Summit's adoption of the policy. Although a timetable was agreed, no plan of action was put into place that would deliver the economic strategy to move towards EMU. Difficult decisions about the realignment of currencies ready for stage 2 of EMU were avoided. Member States remained free to pursue their own national economic policy agendas. In particular, Germany faced a series of problems associated with unification.

It was decided that unification required German economic and monetary union (GEMU) to make the process work. It was recognised that GEMU would benefit the citizens of the former German Democratic Republic in the sense of ensuring that the value of small savings would be protected, and that workers would receive a living wage. After unification, all wages were paid at parity, i.e. one Ostmark for one Deutschmark. Up to 4000 Ostmarks worth of saving could also be converted at parity, except for pensioners, where the limit was 6000 Ostmarks. Above these amounts, the going rate was two Ostmarks for one Deutschmark. This was clearly an overvaluation of the Ostmark, perhaps by as high as a factor of three. It was based on political expedients rather than the economic needs of the region. Its macroeconomic impact was inflationary, because it gave the cash-rich East German population a substantial increase in real purchasing power. In the past, many had extensive savings but because goods of quality were in short supply they were not able to use them. Once GEMU had taken place, a massive tide of consumer demand followed.

The German solution was to try and squeeze inflation out of its economy by high interest rates and a general tightening of monetary conditions. This led to upward pressure on the Deutschmark. In a free-floating system the mark would have been considerably revalued, but membership of the ERM prevented this. However, all other ERM members had to try to match German interest rates, in order to prevent their own currencies' devaluation. European interest rates were therefore determined by German domestic policy. In retrospect, either a significant revaluation of the mark or its suspension from the ERM might have forestalled the problems facing other members. However, the Deutschemark was the pivotal currency within the ERM, and the reason for its credibility up to that time.

The crisis facing the ERM emerged against a background of severe problems in ratifying the TEU, and a slide towards recession. Not only did the Danes falter in their attempts to ratify the Treaty at the first attempt, but there were concerns that the French might also fail. The President of the Bundesbank fuelled the instability by making politically inappropriate statements about the operation of the ERM. The British monetary authorities also contributed by not acting early enough to protect the pound, so that there were doubts about the UK's commitment. The devaluation of the Italian lira also shook confidence in the system.

Once there were doubts about the Member States' commitment to the ERM, longer term factors came into play. The massive wave of speculation that was unleashed was caused by a realisation that parities would have to change to take account of the overvaluation of currencies. There was also a perception that there was a limit to the extent that the deflationary aspects of the ERM might be politically unacceptable to Member States facing recession.

Faults with the EMS

In addition to the tendency towards competitive deflation, the following criticisms have been made concerning the operation of the EMS, all of which have implications for the exchange rate crisis of 1992 and 1993.

1. Member States considered only their national self-interest when trying to set monetary policy. Germany, for example, was distracted by the effects of monetary growth caused by reunification.

2. The ultimate cost of defending a currency was not shared. All adjustment of monetary policy fell on the weaker states.

3. The actual costs of exchange rate intervention fell on the country devaluing. When the Bundesbank bought currency to defend the pound, and sterling devalued, the Bank of England had to pay for the losses the Bundesbank sustained.

4. It was wrong to move to EMU from the base of EMS without significant real convergence in the European economies.

5. The EMS was designed to assist monetary stability, not to deliver EMU. It was about nominal as against real integration.

At no stage was there a commitment that the members of the ERM would have unlimited support for their currencies if they were placed under pressure. However, there were suggestions that more support might have been available for the currencies facing pressures to devalue.

It could be argued that many of the above problems of the ERM could have been resolved by moving quickly towards European Monetary Union. However, there was little enthusiasm for such a strategy once the crisis overtook the ERM. The UK, for example, started to distance itself from the ERM once membership had been suspended. It was felt that the cost of membership had been far too high. This had implications for the progress towards EMU. If the monetary integration could not withstand a crisis in its more flexible form, EMU looked a distant prospect. The convergence criteria could not be achieved if there were major realignments within the system. These were made worse by the enforced devaluation of the French franc in August 1993.

Moving towards EMU

The success of the EMS in the 1980s produced demands that further progress be made towards monetary integration in the EU. This was centred around the threat that financial liberalisation presented to the EU. There was evidence to suggest that liberalisation would lead to greater financial innovation and increased difficulties in keeping control of money supply. Added to this, the abolition of capital controls resulted in even greater movements within the EU, and so placed pressure on the ERM. In the past capital controls shielded weak currencies from speculative attacks and isolated domestic interest rates from fluctuations in international markets. While these arguments for greater integration were based in part on perceived threats, there were positive reasons for moving the system forward towards EMU. These were that EMU would:

1. enhance the process of political and economic integration

2. make the EU a more powerful player in the world economy, and reduce the influence of the US dollar on the EU

3. aid the creation of the Single European Market, and lead to Member States' comparative advantage being fully exploited

4. reduce the transaction costs of changing from one currency to another – at present, if an individual started with £100 and changed into each Member State's currency in turn, the individual would end up with only £60 by the time the money was back into pounds again

5. eliminate the cost of currency fluctuations – at present any advantages gained by businesses from being efficient can easily be wiped out by currency movements.

At a meeting in Hanover on 27 and 28 June 1988, the European Council set up a working party under the chairmanship of Jaques Delors, President of the European Commission, to develop proposals for the progressive realisation of EMU. The report that was produced is generally known as the Delors Report.[7] It laid down a series of proposals for moving towards EMU, and created an active political and economic debate surrounding the contribution of the monetary system within Europe to economic and political integration. In effect the report created a situation where the EMS was no longer a mere device for cooperation between Member States to promote exchange rate stability. The Delors Report suggests that there be three stages towards monetary union, similar to those later adopted by the Maastricht Summit in 1991.

At the Maastricht Summit, the EU agreed to the text of the Treaty on European Union. The implications of EMU were far-reaching, in that the EU started to involve itself far more in the conduct of national economic policy than ever before. The Treaty declared that EMU should be compatible with the general economic principles on which the EU is founded. At a more practical level, the importance of maintaining a timetable for the adoption of economic policies based on coordination of Member States' economies was stressed. These should lead to the introduction of irrevocably fixed exchange rates, and the eventual introduction of a single currency, the ECU. This ECU will not of course be the basket of currencies which makes up the present ECU, but will be the name of a new currency representing the irrevocably fixed values of national currencies.

Moving towards the adoption of a single currency

The Treaty envisaged that there will be three stages in the move towards the introduction of the single currency. The use of a timetable for implementation reflects the experience gained with implementing the Single Market. It was designed to ensure that progress is made, and that no individual Member State can delay the process for its own political purposes. The requirement that states meet the convergence criteria before adopting the single currency satisfies the states that wish to see that the quality of the new currency meets the highest standards with regard to stability.

Stage 1

The first stage has taken place, and involved the completion of the Single Market with freedom to move goods and capital by 1 January 1993.

Stage 2

The second stage commenced on 1 January 1994. This stage is designed to prepare the ground for the establishment of the single currency. Member States are expected to have their currencies within the normal bands of the ERM at this stage. The European Monetary Institution was founded, but will be liquidated once the European Central Bank has been created at the start of the third stage of EMU. It is designed to be an institution independent of the Member States. The EMI was put into place to coordinate the transition to the third stage of EMU. In particular, its purpose will be to coordinate monetary policies with a view to ensuring price stability and to oversee the development of the ECU. It will prepare the establishment of the European System of Central Banks (ESCB) It has already assumed the role of the European Monetary Cooperation Fund, which no longer exists. As a consequence it has taken over the short-term holdings of gold and foreign exchange reserves that were pooled on a temporary basis as part of the EMS. It will also be able to hold and manage foreign exchange reserves as an agent for and on behalf of national central banks.

The convergence criteria

The adoption of a set of convergence criteria was designed to ensure the transition to EMU would not cause a sudden monetary shock to the participating currencies. They were also meant to be a reassurance to Germany that the EMU would not be inflationary. As a consequence, the real convergence of economies was not part of the calculation, and unemployment, national income levels and growth were not among the criteria. The move to stage three of EMU depends on the progress of the Member States towards achieving strict convergence criteria. These are set out in the two protocols attached to the Treaty. They have the same legal status as the Treaty itself, but are placed there because they are only temporary arrangements. The criteria are as follows.

1. Reference values are placed on planned or actual government deficits of 3 per cent of GDP at market prices and on the ratio of government debt of 60 per cent of GDP at market prices.

2. For one year inflation rates must be within 1.5 per cent of the three best-performing economies.

3. For one year long-term interest rates must be within 2 per cent of the three best-performing economies.

4. The currency should have remained within the ERM for the two previous years without devaluation. This was thought to mean the 2.25 per cent band, which was in existence at the time when the TEU was negotiated. However, Article 3 of the protocol on Convergence Criteria states that Member States shall have 'respected the normal fluctuation margins provided by the exchange rate mechanism for at least two years'. No mention is made of the width of the margins, so the 15 per cent margins agreed in August 1993 may well apply. The EU has the flexibility to choose which bands it wishes.

Achieving convergence

The fact that only France and Luxembourg appeared to meet all the criteria for convergence at the time of the Maastricht Summit was an indication that there was a great deal to be done. As Table 6.6 demonstrates, even after the TEU had been ratified and stage 2 of EMU had been launched, there had been no progress towards achieving the convergence criteria.

Government deficits

Article 104c of the TEU sees it as the Commission's role to monitor the development of the budgetary situation and the stock of government debt. Budget deficits tend to rise as a consequence of economies going into recession. While tax revenues fall, the cost of welfare payments increases as more people seek help because of unemployment. As economies start to grow, the deficit should fall if public expenditure is kept under control. The major hurdle is achieving a ratio of 60 per cent of government debt to GDP. For countries such as Italy and Belgium, with a ratio of over 100 per cent, it is difficult to envisage that sufficient debt will be paid off unless privatisation can generate the funds. Reducing the value of the debt significantly by inflation within the economy is an option that is contrary to the spirit of the exercise.

Table 6.6 Convergence criteria for EMU (1994)

	Inflation rate (%)	Budget deficit(% GDP)	Long-term interest rates (%)	Public debt ratio	Number of criteria fulfilled
Austria	2.8[1]	4.6	6.5[1]	62.6	2
Belgium	2.7[1]	5.3	7.2[1]	138.4	2
Denmark	2.1[1]	4.4	6.9[1]	79.9	2
France	1.7[1]	5.4	6.4[1]	44.1[1/2]	3
Finland	1.2[1]	4.7	7.9[1]	72.5[1]	2
Germany	3.0[1]	3.1	6.2[1]	48.6[1]	3
Greece	10.8	16.0	19.6	120.4	0
Ireland	2.4[1]	2.5[1]	7.3[1]	92.9	3
Italy	3.8	9.2	8.3[1]	118.6	1
Luxembourg	2.8	2.2[1]	7.8[1]	10.0[1]	4
Netherlands	2.6[1]	3.0[1]	6.2[1]	80.8	3
Portugal	5.8	6.5	7.7[1]	66.7	1
Spain	4.8	6.1	9.0[1]	55.6[1]	1
Sweden	2.5[1]	11.0	8.1[1]	83.0	2
UK	2.5[1]	5.3	7.3[1]	48.8[1]	3

[1]   Achieved convergence criteria
Source: *The Guardian*, 10 October 1994, p. 19, quoting Deutsche Bank

However, the Treaty offers the possibility of progression even if government deficits exceed the 60 per cent if

● the ratio has declined substantially and continuously and reached a level close to the reference value, or

● the excess over the reference value is only exceptional and temporary and the ratio remains close to the reference value.

In September 1994, it was suggested that Ireland would qualify for inclusion in the list of states eligible to join EMU by virtue of a much reduced public sector debt. Over the seven years from 1987, the national debt had fallen from 116 per cent of GDP to around 90 per cent. This was achieved with the assistance of generous EU structural funds. However, help on this scale is unlikely to be available to the larger, more prosperous states that have substantial deficits.

Inflation

Member States' rates of inflation must converge for the achievement of EMU, but this requirement can lead to competitive deflation. As states try to achieve inflation targets, they may need either to increase taxation or to raise interest rates. This can have a significant effect on the level of unemployment in an economy.

Interest rates

The criterion with respect to interest rates appears to be strange, given that a 2 per cent difference is a very considerable margin in a low-inflationary environment. If interest rate differentials were of that order of magnitude, it would indicate that financial markets felt that there was considerable economic divergence.

ERM Membership

The moving of the goalposts with respect to the permitted margins means that it is not clear whether membership of the ERM has any meaning at all. This requirement suggests that there needs to be a period when nominal exchange rates of potential EMU members are stable. It is difficult to see the system being viable if it is highly volatile. This suggests that there may be an attempt to return to the old 2.25 per cent margins prior to EMU. Indeed, the Netherlands and Germany kept with the narrow band after the August 1993 decision to widen the bands to 15 per cent either side of the ECU.

Stage 3 option 1

This can commence as early as 31 December 1996. In this case the Council will decide by a qualified majority that a critical mass of at least seven states have met the convergence terms. If this is achieved these states can move to a single currency. This looked unlikely even before the currency crisis of 1992.

Stage 3 option 2

A failure to achieve this target will mean that option 2 comes into effect. There is no need for a critical mass of states to meet the convergence terms. All that is required is that the European Council confirm in mid-1998 those that have met the criteria for adoption of the single currency. This means that EMU can commence on 1 January 1999. In practice it is likely that at least three states will achieve the convergence criteria – the three states forming part of the benchmark for inflation and interest rates. Indeed, at least two of the potential new members of the EU may be well placed to join EMU.

Once stage 3 has been introduced, the European System of Central Banks will come into existence. The ESCB is to be composed of the European Central Bank and central banks of the Member States. The primary objective of the ESCB is to maintain price stability. The function of the ECB is to ensure that the tasks imposed on the ESCB are implemented either by the ECB's activities or through the national central banks.

Article 105 of the TEU sets out the basic tasks of the ESCB as follows.

● To define and implement the monetary policy of the EU.

● To conduct foreign exchange operations.

● To hold and manage the foreign exchange reserves of the Member States.

● To promote the smooth operation of the payments system.

- To contribute to a smooth conduct of the policies relating to the prudent supervision of credit institutions and the stability of the financial system.

- The ECB will have the exclusive right to *authorise* the issue of notes within the Member States. However, the actual *issue* of notes will be carried out by the ECB and the national central banks. These are the only notes that will have legal tender status within the Member States.

The UK position

If EMU goes ahead, the UK government will need to make a decision as to the future of the pound. The UK government made it clear at the time of the Maastricht Summit that it had great doubts about the wisdom of entering into the third stage of EMU. The Protocol relating to the UK recognises that

'the United Kingdom shall not be committed to move to the third stage of economic and monetary union without a separate decision to do so by its government and Parliament.'

The UK has to inform the Council if it wishes to move towards the third stage of EMU. If it does not, the UK will be excluded from key aspects of the process, such as the appointment of the Board of the ECB. If EMU is a success, it is unlikely that the UK will want to disadvantage its financial services industry by excluding itself. In any case, while the Conservative government fought hard to establish the UK veto within the protocols of the TEU, in practice no state is ever likely to accept the third stage of EMU if it is believed to be against its national interest.

Making EMU work

At the micro level, the move to a single currency would involve significant technical changes in the retail sector, where new cash registers would need to be installed. In the financial sector all debts would need to be converted to ECU. The foreign exchange markets for EMU Member States' currencies would be replaced by a major new market in ECU, which would rival that of the US dollar and the yen. In the event of a gradual transition, the costs would be higher if countries were operating in dual currencies.

To make EMU work, the process of economic and political integration will have to develop further than it has today. All states will need to accept that there are going to be severe limits to their national sovereignty, in that the responsibility for a great many decisions taken by national institutions will move to the EU level. Inflation rates will have to be harmonised so that the process of adjustment will be minimised. If inflationary expectations among the workforce do differ it will be politically difficult to impose wage restraints. Finally, all Member States will join the EMU arrangements at an exchange rate that reflects their levels of productivity and competitiveness. The exchange rate on membership may prove to be the ultimate stumbling block, because it will be easy for workers to judge their relative position in the wages league. This may provide the stimulus for inflationary wage settlements in regions where productivity is relatively low. An example of this was the problems that arose as a consequence of the unification of Germany. Wage rates in the East rose quickly after unification, to the point where they were often comparable with those in the West. However, productivity was nowhere near as high, and as a consequence jobs were lost.

Two of the major issues relating to EMU are discussed in detail below.

Sovereignty

The transfer of decision-making power in key economic areas from the Member States to the EU has led to a number of concerns, including

1. a lack of democratic control

2. integration being taken further than is desirable

3. it being difficult to leave the system once in it

4. a loss of national control over fiscal and monetary policy.

The reduced role for national parliaments in controlling economic affairs concerns many who might actually see technical merits in the EMU proposals. EMU would lead to a more important role for the European Parliament in overall economic affairs. Those who support EMU point to the fact that in practice there is very little sovereignty for the nation state in the current system. The reality is that the powerful German central bank dominates the European scene to such an extent that German interests dominate the EU's monetary policy. For Britain and the weaker economies that seem to face one crisis after another, there is often no policy option other than to follow the international money markets. So although the proposed ESCB will have a high degree of operational independence, it will at least be accountable in an overall sense to the Council of Ministers, and to the European Parliament.

The suggested limits on national control of fiscal monetary policy are hotly contested. Those against them suggest that there is no need for budgetary control in order to achieve the internal market. If Member States overspend and get into financial difficulties, there is no reason why they should be bailed out by the rest; if they were, the safety valve of devaluation of a currency would disappear, and this would reduce national sovereignty even further.

Finally, it has been pointed out that the whole notion of EMU is fundamentally flawed, in that most of the objectives of the plan could be achieved by monetary union alone. There are many examples of monetary union that have worked well, for example the sterling area, the French franc area and the nineteenth century gold standard. All these were operated for a long period of time without any substantial loss of political sovereignty.

Regional problems

A major problem for EMU is that of regional disparity. The gap between the rich and poor regions of the EU is considerable, and it is suggested that EMU might make things worse. The question in economic terms is, is the EU an optimum currency area? That is, are the benefits to the smooth organisation of trade sufficient to offset the costs of being unable to devalue? It is important when creating EMU that exchange rates are initially set at the right rate. If they are set too high, especially in a backward regional economy where productivity is low, the region will be unable to compete in trade. With an independent state, one solution to a balance of payments deficit would be devaluation. Where there is monetary union this is not an option, and so there is a danger that money will flow out of the region, making the crisis for the region worse. Without interference there is a possibility that there will be some automatic adjustment, because the surplus area will have an increased money supply which may cause inflation. However, this may not be tolerated by the central bank which may tighten monetary controls. The other automatic mechanism that should exist in a market economy is wage flexibility. If unemployment starts to rise, workers should be prepared to accept lower wages. In reality, wages do not tend to be flexible downwards in Europe, so a long-term problem will exist. Indeed, most of the current areas of high unemployment were also problem areas over 30 years ago when the EU was first launched.

To make EMU work for the EU, there will need to be a much more active regional policy. The structural funds have increased in size, but they are still only a part of the EU budget, and that budget is small relative to that of the Member States. In an economy such as the USA, not only is there greater labour mobility, but the federal budget compensates for some of the decline in income. It has been estimated that for every dollar that income declines, federal tax payments are 30 cents lower, and at the same time 10 cents is transferred to the region by the federal government. It is unlikely that the EU will be able to create a comparable mechanism within the foreseeable future.[8]

The multi-speed Europe

The greatest threat to the integration process will come if a significant number of states fail to achieve the EU convergence criteria. With relatively few states adopting the single currency, there would be a danger of a two- or three-speed Europe. There would be the inner core of low-inflation economies. Beyond this would be a bloc of states waiting to join EMU, and perhaps states such as the UK wishing not to be members under any circumstances. It would be politically damaging if the core of highly integrated economies were seen as being superior to the other Member States. Overall, there is a prospect that the Single Market will suffer as a result of fragmentation, caused by differing exchange rate regimes within the EU. The problem that faces high-quality currencies of the EMU is that they may be seen as a refuge in times of monetary turbulence. This was the fate of the Deutschmark float in the 1970s, which often faced problems of overvaluation. For those that remain outside EMU, there will be higher transactions costs to pay in their dealings with other states. Also, there may be an interest rate premium to pay. The higher interest rates may come about because of the greater risk of dealing in non-EMU currencies.

Conclusions

It is highly unlikely that the EU will achieve EMU before the end of the century, unless there is concerted action on the part of the Member States to see it happen. Indeed, it would take up to three years to print the currency and change the slot machines to accept the new currency.

The crisis that befell the ERM was inevitable, given that there was little attempt to implement the TEU. However, there is a need to move back to monetary integration, for no other reason than it assists trade. It is clear that certain actions are required to move the process back to where it was at the start of the decade. While the use of +/–15 per cent bands was a useful short-term device, it is not the basis for a permanent system. Indeed this was recognised by many states, which did not change their monetary policy after August 1993. The result was that key currencies such as the French franc returned to where they had been prior to the crisis.

For the EMS to be fully restored, economic growth needs to be fully embedded in Europe. Once this has been achieved, the institutions of monetary integration need to be examined. The EU needs to build up confidence in the system again, before there is progress either towards narrow bands or towards achieving EMU. This means that the process of promoting convergence is important. If the EU attempts to return to semi-fixed rates too early, it runs the risk of setting up targets for speculators.

To achieve EMU, the EU needs to move either very quickly, as in the case of German Economic and Monetary Union, or very slowly, with detailed planning of the process. Both strategies require a political will to tackle problems collectively rather than ignoring them. If realignments of currencies come about because of speculative pressures, it will be difficult to restore credibility. If the process of restoring confidence takes place, it will be because the major states of the EU still wish to advance political integration. There will also have to be sustained pressure on the part of business, which generally appears to favour currency stability. For the public's confidence to be restored, there must be no repetition of the transfer of huge sums of public money to the speculators and away from important social uses.

References

1. **Peter Leslie**, Deputy Chairman of Barclays Bank at the Financial Times Conference 'Europe after Delors', 30 November 1989. Quoted in the *Financial Times*, 1 December 1989, 4.
2. *Financial Times*, 30 November 1992, 14.
3. *Financial Times*, 25 September 1992, 2.
4. **European Parliament** (1993) *Removing the Legal Obstacles to the Use of the ECU*, A3-0296/93.
5. *European Economy* (1994) Supplement A, No. 6, June.
6. **Taylor M P and Artis M J** (1989) *What has the European Monetary System Achieved?* Bank of England Discussion Paper No. 31, March.
7. **Committee for the Study of Economic and Monetary Union** (1989) *Report on Economic and Monetary Union*, Office for Official Publications of the European Communities, Luxembourg.
8. **Eichengreen B** (1993) European Monetary Unification and Regional Unemployment, in Ulman L, Eichengreen B, Dickens T (Eds) (1993) *Labor and an Integrated Europe*, Brookings Institute, p. 195.

Further reading

Barrell R (Ed.) (1992) *Economic Convergence and Monetary Union in Europe*, Sage, London.
De Grauwe P (1992) *The Economics of Monetary Integration*, Oxford University Press.
Emerson M and Humne C (1991) *The ECU Report*, Pan, London.
European Economy (1990) One Market, One Money, No. 44, October.

Fitoussi J P *et al* (1993) *Competitive Disinflation*, Oxford University Press.
De Grauwe P and Papademos L (Eds.) (1990) *The European Monetary System in the 1990s*, Longman, London.
Gros D and Thygesen N (1992) *European Monetary Integration*, Longman, London.
Journal of Common Market Studies (1989) The European Monetary System, Special Edition, March, Vol. 27, No. 3.
Minkin R (1993) *The ERM Explained*, Kogan Page, London.

CHAPTER 7

Paying for integration: the budget of the European Union

Introduction

If the European Union is to develop further, it is important that it develops a budgetary strategy that enables it to realise its ambitions. This is because the EU's budgetary contribution is at the heart of many innovative programmes. It is the budget that helps to move the EU beyond the status of just a single market. However, it is difficult to gain a consensus among the Member States as to the long-term shape of the budget. Attempts to change the size and improve the balance and operation of the budget have often resulted in prolonged bouts of hostile debate among the Member States. Settlements tend to reflect compromises rather than a fundamental consensus. This chapter argues that this situation reflects the deeper and more fundamental doubt about the direction in which the EU should be moving.

An increase in the real size of the EU budget transfers power away from the nation state, which is welcomed by those who wish to take the integration process further. It follows that, for those who oppose integration, any level of expenditure may be seen as undesirable. However, many critics point to the inefficient way in which money is currently spent, and see the first step as being one of managing the current level of resources better. The issues of the overall size of the budget and the effectiveness of spending are therefore linked.

The EU's budget came into being for four main reasons, i.e. to

1. distribute the income from the collection of tariffs

2. support agriculture as a key economic sector

3. provide funds for administration

4. resource the Social Fund.

The budget has grown in size and importance as the EU has developed, but not always in a coherent manner. This was because of the need to reconcile the conflicting objectives of promoting economic efficiency and the political requirement that there should be a greater element of redistribution in the budgetary process. The redistributing elements came into greater prominence as new member states sought to offset the gains that France and other states had made via the Common Agricultural Policy (CAP).

Following the Maastricht Agreement in December 1991, it took a year to agree changes in the budget that were designed to assist with its implementation. While the Treaty on European Union envisaged the bold step of achieving Economic and Monetary Union (EMU) by 1999, the budgetary arrangements that followed did not reflect this. The budgetary agreement reached at Edinburgh in December 1992 was essentially a minimalist framework for EU finances for the period up to the end of 1999. The framework was adjusted to accommodate new members that were join the EU before that date. Additionally, other pressures may cause the basis of the budget to be rethought, not least the need to control CAP expenditure.

The arrangements for the EU's finances for the period to the end of 1999 were agreed at Edinburgh and contain the following elements.

1. *Own resources* – these are the four major sources of income allocated to the EU. There are clear limits on the extent that these can be utilised.

2. *Budget discipline* – this includes legally-binding agricultural guidelines.

3. The Inter-Institutional Agreement (IIA) – this was an agreement between the Council, the European Parliament and the Parliament. It was a non-legally binding text which set a series of ceilings on EU spending, and was in effect a seven year financial plan for the EU. The IIA was put in place in 1988, ran to the end of 1992, and was replaced in 1993.

4. The UK Abatement – this was carried over from 1984 and incorporated into the Own Resources Decision. It reduced the UK's VAT contribution to two-thirds of the difference between its share of VAT payments and its percentage share of EU expenditure. It does not apply to expenditure outside the EU (about 6 per cent) which is largely for aid.

Budgetary decision-making

The major decisions with regard to the EU budget are inevitably monitored closely by the Member States. The Council of Ministers has the most important role to play in the annual budgetary round, but the longer term strategies have been set by the European Councils. Here the leaders of the Member States resolve their competing claims. In 1984 the Fountainebleau Council found a solution to the difficulty of UK contributions, and in 1988 the European Council set in place the strategy for the period to the end of 1992. While the Edinburgh Summit set in place guidelines designed to last until the end of 1999, these were modified in the light of the accession of new members.

The legal basis

Articles 199 to 209 of the Treaty of Rome give the legal basis for the EU's financial provisions. One of the most notable features of this, which was reinforced by the Treaty on European Union, has been the enhanced role in budgetary decision-making given to the European Parliament. Parliament has the right to do the following.

1. Propose modifications to compulsory expenditure. Increases in total expenditure must win a qualified majority in the Council of Ministers. Where modifications do not involve

any increase in total expenditure, a qualified majority must be found if Council members wish to oppose the changes.

2.   Propose amendments to non-compulsory expenditure, which Parliament can attempt to reinstate even after rejection by the Council.

3.   Reject the budget and call for a new one, if the final draft is not to its liking.

Political controversies

The budget has often dominated the politics of the EU, because of three main areas of overall concern:

1.   the size of the budget

2.   how the burden should be distributed

3.   how well the money is spent.

The first issue is at the heart of the debate on the shape of the EU. If political and economic integration is to be taken further, there is a need to transfer appropriate functions to the centre and away from the Member States. This should of course only take place with the full agreement of all concerned, and it is to be hoped that the principle of subsidiarity will be observed. The principle of subsidiarity assumes that EU competence should be exercised when it can achieve a better outcome than the Member States. This may mean a shift of resources, with more spending decisions being made at the EU level and presumably fewer being made at the national level. Any increase in membership will also increase total spending at the EU level, although not necessarily the level of spending per head of the population.

Secondly, it is not easy to achieve agreement as to the equitable sharing of burdens, because of the way that policies have evolved and the disparities in income levels throughout the EU. All the Member States can easily construct a case for altering the pattern of expenditure and income in such a way that the result would be more equitable from their viewpoint. Any equitable solution must take into account not just budgetary aspects, but the wider benefits and costs of membership.

Finally, there are concerns about the effectiveness of policies, and problems related to maladministration and fraud. However, the stability of the funding mechanism may also facilitate better planning in the use of resources.

The role of the budget

The role of the budget within any organisation is strongly related to the aspirations that members have for the organisation. The pressing need has been to keep the funding of the EU on a firm basis, either for reasons of financial prudence or to enable long-term planning. In the past, the Member States were unwilling to permit the flexibility and independence in funding arrangements that make long-term planning feasible. However, the Delors I package of 1988 and the Delors II package of 1992 put in place forward-looking structures, although the categories of expenditure were highly specified as a result of the negotiation process. Agricultural expenditure has consistently been a major element of the budget, and its major problem area. Its open-ended nature has often meant that commitments in this area have taken so much of the available resources that there has been only limited scope for other activity.

Relative to the total national economies of the EU, the budget is small. It was estimated to take 1.24 per cent of EU GNP and 4.0 per cent of public spending for 1994.[1] In most cases, the role of the budget can therefore be no more than a stimulus and an incentive which supports the coordination of policy. Despite this, it is significant for the following reasons.

- Many important EU policy areas are influenced by the budget.

- Tangible gains and losses of membership can be identified, although the extent of these may be challenged.

- The net contributions from the EU have a significant impact on the economies of small countries. EU aid represents 3 per cent of GDP in Greece, Portugal and Ireland. It assisted investment in these economies, so that it amounted to 11 per cent of total investment in Greece, 8 per cent in Portugal and 7 per cent in Ireland.[2]

The EU is unusual compared to most other international organisations, because it has a budget that provides funds for areas other than basic administration. However, it is still not like the budgets of the nation states, for the following reasons.

1. It has no overall macroeconomic stabilisation role. Its small size would preclude this in any case.

2. Activities cannot be financed by borrowing except in specific circumstances. The budget must therefore balance, and there can be no deficit financing. Article 199 of the Treaty of European Union re-emphasised this point by asserting that 'The revenue and expenditure shown in the budget shall be in balance'. However, there has been a growth in borrowing off budget, to finance the activities of organisations such as the European Investment Bank.

3. Spending areas are subject to separate sets of operating rules and are seen as being independent of one another. They are agreed separately by the different Councils of Ministers. However, it is the role of the Commission to propose policy within the EU, and it was required by Article 201a of the Treaty on European Union not to make proposals or implement measures that could not be financed within the limit of the EU's 'own resources'.

The case for increasing the size of the budget

The size of the EU budget is likely to increase with the growth in size of the EU, and with a rise in national incomes. In addition to this, increases in the number of tasks carried out at the EU level will lead to more funding being required. The movements of currencies will present strains, as in the case of agriculture. Also, most officials live in high-cost countries. Finally, the burden of pensions for officials will increase as the organisation ages and more officials retire.

As long as the total funding is restricted, Member States can control the extent of important aspects of policy. However, there may be an economic case for increasing the size of the EU budget, although this might well imply a reduction in spending at the national level. The reasons for this are as follows.

1. There may be economies of scale to be derived from operating on a larger scale. However, this is unlikely to be the case when considering the EU's finances.

2. There may be spillover benefits to be gained from operating policies at the EU level. EU policies may be more credible, and less subject to distortions created by interference at the national and local level.

As a counter to these arguments, a larger EU budget, could contradict the principle of subsidiarity, which suggests that it is better to devolve decision-making down to the local level, where the decision-makers are more sensitive to the needs of that particular society.

In the course of time the EU may become more like a federal state, in which case the size of the budget would tend to increase significantly. Many of the items at present subject to the control of the states will fall within the ambit of the EU. In 1977 the Commission published the report of a study group set up to examine this problem. The study group, chaired by Sir Donald MacDougall, examined eight existing economic and monetary unions. Five were federal states (USA, Canada, West Germany, Australia and Switzerland) and three were unitary states (UK, France and Italy).[3] The report, entitled *The Role of Public Finance In European Integration*, found that

● public expenditure by the federal governments was between 20 and 25 per cent of GDP, when total expenditure in the EU states was 45 per cent of GDP

● public expenditure by federal states helped to reduce inequalities between regions, and helped them to overcome economic shocks

● if Economic and Monetary Union (EMU) became a reality, it could pose real strains for many regional economies.

The Report suggested that there needed to be a gradual increase in the size of the EU budget, initially to 2–2.5 per cent of GDP, and eventually to 5–7 per cent of GDP. This, it suggested, could be used to offset regional disparities, with innovations such as an EU Unemployment Fund. The MacDougall Report is of course the maximalist case, but it gives an insight into how far the EU would need to progress in order to achieve a federalist budget of even modest proportions.

If the EU did accept greater responsibility for a greater range of tasks, for example social security payments, this would raise significant difficulties. The Member States have found that in periods of recession their tax receipts fall and expenditure on social security payments rises. This results in significant budgetary deficits, which the EU has been able to avoid.

Income

From 1958 to 1970 the EU was financed by contributions from Member States which, although they were politically determined, were broadly based on ability to pay. Since 1970, the EU has operated on a system of 'own resources', i.e. income it regards as its own as of right. This was added to in 1988 by a fourth resource based on national income. The situation in 1993 and 1994 is set out in Table 7.1.

Table 7.1 EU Budget Own Resources (ECU millions)

	1993	%	1994	%
Agriculture and sugar levies	2239	3.4	2039	2.9
Customs duties	13 118	20.0	12 619	18.2
VAT	35 677	54.5	35 850	51.6
Member States' levy	14 030	21.4	18 989	27.3
Miscellaneous	456	0.7		
Total	65 523		69 498	
Percentage of EU GDP	1.20			

Source : Paymaster General (1994), *Statement on the 1994 Community Budget*

Compared to the Member States, the EU operates with a limited number of income sources, as follows.

1. *Agriculture and sugar levies* – Agriculture levies are taxes on food imports used to keep out cheap imports from EU markets and thereby maintain the income of farmers. Sugar levies are charges on producers which are used to help dispose of excess quantities.[4]

2. *Customs duties* – All duties collected by national customs officers automatically go to the EU. This is known as the Common Customs Tariff (CCT). The argument is that the goods could be destined for any country within the EU, and therefore the duty amounts to a genuine shared income. There has been a fall in the CCT revenues due to the lower tariff levels, in part because of the GATT trade rounds. Also, the movement towards the Single European Market has meant that trade is more inward-looking. In addition, the expansion of the EU in the mid-1980s has meant that the trade with the new members carries no tariff, and costs the budget about ECU 1.3 billion a year in revenue. Overall, in the period from 1988 to the end of 1994, the contribution to the budget from this source was expected to be reduced from 26 to 18.4 per cent of the total income.

3. *Value Added Tax (VAT)* – VAT is a tax on goods and services, which applies throughout the EU. A proportion of this is set aside as part of the EU's 'own resources'. Because countries such as the UK zero rate or exempt certain goods from VAT, the actual payments are made on a standardised basis so that payments cannot be reduced by operating a lower VAT rate. From 1970 to the end of 1985, the ceiling on contributions was the product of up to 1 per cent of the VAT base. This ceiling was raised to 1.4 per

cent as a result of the 1984 Fountainebleau Summit, but reduced as a consequence of the Edinburgh Agreement. From 1994, the uniform VAT rate of contribution was to be reduced by equal steps from 1.4 per cent to 1 per cent. The lost income was replaced by the fourth resource ceiling being raised to 1.27 per cent of GNP.

4. *A levy on member states* – Based upon national income, which is used to balance the budget. This was designed to rise from the maximum total overall contribution of 1.2 per cent of GNP fixed as a result of the 1988 Agreement to a maximum of 1.27 per cent over the period from 1995 to 1999.

The EU's 'own resources' have two sources of income that depend on external trade, and are likely to diminish. The diminishing role of VAT was a conscious choice made by the EU in order to promote greater equity. The fourth resource, which is related to GNP, offers the prospects of increased income if there is an expansion of the European economy.

The diminishing role of VAT as a result of the Edinburgh Agreement in the EU's budget was not regarded with universal enthusiasm, especially by those who saw it as a genuine 'own resource'. However, the VAT was seen as a regressive tax, which placed a greater burden on the poorer states. VAT is a tax on consumer spending. The fact that poorer countries tend to devote a greater proportion of their national income to consumption means that they may contribute more than they should to the EU budget. Correspondingly, states with a high level of public expenditure or investment will pay less tax.

Also, the harmonisation of the calculations, which ensures that all member states pay on the same basis, means that the relationship between the contribution and national structures is not there. Anomalies such as zero rates of VAT on children's clothing are taken into account for EU purposes by assuming that VAT is paid. However, there tends to be no sensitivity between VAT rates and changes in the EU call-up rate. This means that changes in the amount raised by the EU from VAT have little impact on national rates. In this case the citizens of the EU cannot feel a sense of accountability, because they do not know that EU spending is changing.

Contributions based on GNP are regarded as being more acceptable than those based on VAT, because they relate to a country's relative affluence. The growth of any resource based on GNP depends on the rate of growth of the GNP of the EU economy. If growth slows down, income may fail to reach the predicted target. The Commission's proposals for budgetary reform in 1992 assumed that there would be a growth rate of 2.5 per cent, but the slowdown of the economy at that time saw estimates revised downwards over the next two years. This was a result of the worsening economic situation throughout Europe, but of course future growth trends could go in any direction.

Expenditure

In 1952, the first year of the European Coal and Steel Community (ECSC), spending was only ECU 4.6 million. However, by the time the EEC had been formed, the size of the budget had grown rapidly. The upward trend continued as a result of the increased scale of EU operations and the growth in membership. The EU expanded in 1973 from six to nine states, and as a result of Greek, Spanish and Portuguese membership had 12 members after 1986. The unification of Germany increased the EU's land mass by 5 per cent and its population by 16 million. This growth of expenditure is given in Table 7.2.

Table 7.2 Growth of the EU Budget

	Spending (ECU million)	Per capita spending (ECU)	% of public spending in Member States	Annual rate of growth of spending	Spending as % of Member States' GDP
1970	3576	19	1.90		0.74
1980	16 455	63	1.70		0.80
1988	42 495	131	2.30	16.90	1.05
1990	45 608	139	2.00	7.90	0.96
1991	55 156	160	2.20	20.90	1.07
1992	60 501	174	2.20	9.70	1.12
1993	69 233	199	2.40	14.40	1.19
1994	72 304	207	2.40	4.40	1.24
Average 1988–1994				10.50	

Source : Commission of EC (1994) *The Budget of the European Union*

The growth in expenditure revealed in Table 7.2 appears startling, but the range of policies that the EU funds has grown, notably with the introduction of the European Regional Development Fund (ERDF), while others have become of greater importance, notably the European Social Fund (ESF).

The expenditure side of the budget is divided into the following two categories which, although they are not mentioned in the Treaty, are of considerable importance.

1. *Compulsory expenditure* – This is regarded as obligatory expenditure in that the programmes are laid down in the Treaties, for example most of CAP spending. This area of spending takes over half the spending of the EU.

2. *Non-compulsory expenditure* – This includes the Regional Development and Social Funds and most new items of expenditure.

The distinction is important because of the degree of control that the European Parliament has over them. In the case of the CAP, expenditure was open-ended until the introduction of quotas and stabilisers in the 1980s, which meant that this expenditure crowded out 'more worthwhile' areas such as social and regional expenditure. This meant that budgetary constraints were holding back programmes that might offer more in terms of promoting integration.

The budget in crisis

Following UK membership in 1973, the EU had many budgetary crises. These were most frequently related to the issues of the level of the UK's contribution to the budget, and the growing cost of the Common Agricultural Policy. The 1984 Fountainebleau Summit agreed to increase the VAT ceiling to 1.4 per cent from 1986 onwards. Additional funds were made available in 1984 and 1985 on the basis of intergovernmental agreement in order to fill the expenditure gap. It was hoped that this ceiling would not be breached for a number of years, and less than 1.4 per cent would need to be collected.

The lack of a clear agreement as to Britain's level of contributions to the EU's budget was to cause many difficulties. These were only partly solved when, as part of the 1984 Fountainebleau Agreement, the UK was given an abatement worth an estimated £12 billion in the period to the end of 1992.[5] The effect of the UK abatement was to reduce the maximum average contribution of all Member States to about 1.25 per cent of the VAT base. The VAT ceiling was reached immediately in 1986.

By 1987, the EU faced a budgetary crisis that would have meant raising the VAT rate to 1.9 per cent, if that had been permissible. In the event, spending levels were above income, with the result that a problem of outstanding debt started to emerge. These problems were resolved by the Delors I package, which was adopted at the Brussels Summit of February 1988. This was a framework covering the period to the end of 1992. It incorporated the funding plans for the policies that derived from the Single European Act. In particular, there was a commitment to increase spending on the structural funds significantly, mostly for the benefit of the Mediterranean states. The package also attempted to limit the costs of the CAP, which continued to absorb up to two-thirds of the budget expenditure.

As a result of the 1988 settlement the EU had available an additional 'own resource' based on Member States' GNP. The settlement was less than the 1.4 per cent of GNP that the Commission wanted, but the 1.2 per cent of GNP represented a 25 per cent increase of resources from an equivalent 0.95 per cent of GNP. Member States were obliged to contribute only to the extent required to balance the EU budget. Actual payments in any one year were restricted to a maximum of 1.17 per cent of GNP in 1989, rising to a maximum of 1.2 per cent in 1992.[6] This sum was to cover the payment of all amounts, including those due from previous years. Commitments to future payments could be as high as 1.3 per cent of GNP to accommodate the fact that some programmes are funded over longer than one year.

The Delors II package

The Delors II package arose from the changes in the circumstances facing the EU in the late 1980s and early 1990s, and was agreed at the Edinburgh Summit in December 1992. This settlement was designed to cover the period from 1993 to 1999. Originally, the Commission had called for an increase of own resources from 1.2 per cent of GNP in 1992 to 1.37 per cent of GNP in 1997. What was finally agreed was an increase to 1.27 per cent spread over the period to 1999. The negotiations that led to the agreement reflected the conflicting interests of the Member States. In order that the hard-won agreements should not be eroded, the final Edinburgh outcomes were expressed in terms of clear headings for commitments, which were subdivided in accordance with those interests. This is illustrated by the agreement concerning the Cohesion Fund (see below).

The final outcome of the negotiations in terms of the proportion of spending under each heading is given in Table 7.3. However, the actual totals incorporate the impact of enlargement:

Table 7.3 The financial perspective 1995 to 1999 for the Enlarged European Union

Financial perspective (million ECU at 1995 prices)	1995	1999
Common Agricultural Policy	38 064	41 668
Structural operations	26 272	32 969
Internal policies	5064	6064
External action	4927	6625
Administrative expenditure	4063	4490
Reserves	1223	1222
Compensation	1427	–
Total	81 040	93 038

Source : Authors' own calculations based upon, Commission (1994), *Adjustment of the Financial Perspective With a View to Enlargement of the European Union*, Com (94) 398 final.

Agricultural spending

In the past, spending on agriculture amounted to over two-thirds of EU spending. It was due to amount to 51 per cent in 1993, and 45.6 per cent by 1999. This reflected the increased size of the budget, not reduced total agriculture spending. Spending on agriculture was increased, due to the changes that were agreed at the Agricultural Council on 21 May 1992. These reforms reduced the guaranteed prices for cereals, beef and milk. While the consumer was meant to benefit from cheaper food, the farmers were compensated by a production subsidy, and rewarded for taking land out of production by a system called 'set-aside'. The impact of the reforms was therefore actually to increase the cost of the CAP.

Budgetary discipline was a major part of the deal as it was in 1984 and 1988. In order to win the support of the sceptics, it was important to show that the increased resources would not be wasted on ever-increasing CAP surpluses. In 1988, it was agreed that the EAGGF Guarantee Section was not to rise by more than 74 per cent of the EU's gross domestic product growth rate. So, if the EU's national income grew by 2 per cent, agricultural budgets could grow by only 1.48 per cent. It was agreed at the Edinburgh Summit in December 1992 that this arrangement would continue. In particular it was required that the Commission should propose action if agriculture spending looked like exceeding agreed limits.

Working against the EU's attempts at budgetary discipline related to the CAP has been the operation of a system of price support based on the strongest currency in the ERM. This system of 'switch-over' (formally know as the Agricultural Central Rate Mechanism) dated back to the Fountainebleau Summit of 1984 and, as a consequence of the devaluation of weaker currencies within the ERM, resulted in a general price rise. Slower economic growth would also restrict the extent to which the EU could put further resources into this area without breaching the budgetary discipline limits. In March 1993 there were serious concerns over the costs of the CAP, and a request from the Commission that ECU 1.8 billion be added to the budget. It had been estimated that 'switch-over' was to cost ECU 1.6 billion of this overrun for 1993, and as a consequence there was speculation that the EU might not be able to meet its salary bill.[7] The collapse of the ERM on 2 August 1993 meant that all currencies became floating currencies. At that time, one estimate suggested that the cost to the budget of compensating fully the farmers in the strong currency countries was in the region of ECU 380 million for every one per cent of revaluation. This would have taken the budgetary costs of agriculture out of control. It was therefore decided to suspend 'switch-over' until a more acceptable mechanism could be found. In 1995 a more market-based system of green currencies was introduced and 'switch-over' was abandoned.

Structural funds

The structural funds of the EU were doubled in the period from 1988 to the end of 1992. This was meant to promote the development aspirations of the poorer regions of the EU, to facilitate a balance of benefits from the single market process, and to compensate for the misallocation effects of the CAP. However, if further convergence was to be achieved as part of the move towards EMU, it followed that there needed to be yet another real increase in the resources devoted to the structural funds.

As a consequence of pressures from poorer states, the largest area of increased spending in the 1992 reform was structural funds for economic and social cohesion, which were to grow from 31 per cent of the total budget to 36 per cent in 1999. The use of the European Social Fund (ESF) and the European Regional Development Fund (ERDF) in order to improve the lot of disadvantaged areas is well established. This was extended to include the new German Länder and East Berlin.

In June 1991, Spain asked the EU to consider the move towards an equalising budgetary fund, or interstate compensation fund. This would have invested in the physical and human capital of states with a per capita income of less than 90 per cent of the EU average. In addition, it was seeking an even more progressive taxation system for the EU Budget. Finally it proposed a more generous system of regional support. In addition to these general aspirations, there is a consistent demand that where EU decisions require funding by Member States, for example environmental measures, EU funds should also be available.[8] (This idea eventually matured into the Cohesion Fund adopted at Maastricht.)

The major innovation that came with the 1992 package, was the adoption of a Cohesion Fund, which was implemented in advance of the ratification of the Maastricht Treaty. It is possible to offer a rationale for the Fund, based on the need for the poorer states to be offered help towards catching up, both in particular policy areas and in income per head terms. However, the reality was that the Cohesion Fund represented the price of winning the agreement of the poorer states to the outcomes of Maastricht. In this sense it was similar to the abatement that the UK gained in 1984, which depended on national bargaining power rather than an even-handed application of EU policy.

With the existing structural funds the member states were required to make a contribution of something approaching half the cost of the projects they assisted. The new Cohesion Fund did away with this condition. This fund was designed to pay the substantial part of the costs for environmental projects and transport infrastructure. Preliminary studies and technical support for projects could be financed to the extent of 100 per cent, while 80 to 85 per cent of the actual cost of projects could be met from the Fund. The Fund was to be an addition to the structural funds, and the amount allocated for the period 1993–1999 was ECU 15 150 million, expressed in 1992 prices.[9] The annual allocations are given in Table 7.4.

Table 7.4 Cohesion Fund (ECU million)

Year		Year	
1993	1500	1997	2500
1994	1750	1998	2550
1995	2000	1999	2600
1996	2250		

Source : Commission of the EU (1992), COM (92) 599, final, 23 December, p. 20

The fund was designed to assist the four poorest states of the EU, with the dividing point being set at a GNP per head of less than 90 per cent of the EU average. While the UK might have qualified on the basis of falling relative national income due to an early entry into the recession in 1990 and 1991, and the devaluation of the pound in 1992, these events were considered to be too recent. A review of eligibility was set to take place in 1996 and in 1999. At this point, any state that caught up to the 90 per cent point would lose its eligibility, while new states might be added. The fund was to be divided on the basis of the size of the state, so that the allocations were: Spain, 52 to 58 per cent of the total; Greece and Portugal, 16 to 20 per cent; and Ireland, 7 to 10 per cent.

Internal policies

Article 130 of the Maastricht Treaty made the need for industrial competitiveness a central issue. Despite the success of the single market campaign, there was a real concern that Europe's relative competitive position had become blunted, and that this was reflected in the decline of the EU's balance of payments in manufactured goods falling from ECU 116 billion in 1985 to ECU 50.5 billion in 1990.

In 1991, the EU was spending only 2.1 per cent of GDP on R&D, compared with Japan at 3.5 per cent of GDP and the USA at 2.8 per cent. At the same time, advanced technological goods accounted for 31 per cent of US exports and 27 per cent of Japanese exports, compared to only 17 per cent for the EU.[10] The strategy for implementing the drive towards greater industrial success was laid down in the EU's fourth Framework Programme.

External policies

The success of the EU as an economic bloc was a marked contrast to some other areas of the world economy. This brought with it greater responsibilities, especially towards the states of Central and Eastern Europe. These states wished to transform their economies and achieve closer relationships with the EU. As a consequence, a series of agreements was reached with them which offered both better trading relationships and financial help.

A great deal of the aid to be given to the former Eastern bloc was to be in the form of technical assistance rather than hard cash. This was in order to

1. encourage progress towards a market economy and liberal democracy with the promise of physical aid later

2. ensure the maximum benefit from the limited funds available – loans to help with the problems of balance of payments deficits were to be considered only as short-term, because they would do little for the structure of economies

3. tie the aid, so that the donors also benefited.

The EU has historical and geographic links with the Mediterranean region. It is in the Community's interest to maintain close links with these states, to promote development as an alternative to migration to the EU. The same is true of relationships with the EU's former colonial territories in Africa, the Caribbean and the Pacific (ACP). Also under this heading has been the need for the EU to respond to humanitarian needs around the world, especially when natural disasters occur.

Winners and losers

A feature of the EU budgetary arrangements is that there are both winners and losers in terms of net payments. This has led to a long-running debate about the extent to which the balances are satisfactory. The fact that the EU has always had policies with differing regional impacts means that redistribution between the Member States is inevitable. The issue that brought Member States' contributions firmly onto the agenda of the EU was the accession of the UK in 1973.

The UK case was different to what had gone before, because the UK was a net contributor despite the fact that it was poorer than other states that were net gainers from the budget. In 1994, GDP per head was 99.8 per cent of the EU average based on purchasing power parities. This estimate is based on an adjustment of the GDP of countries, based on comparable prices.[11] The reasons for the UK being a net contributor were related to its reliance on imports from outside the EU, which meant that it paid more in import duties. Also, a higher propensity to consume meant greater VAT payments. However, the main problem was the inability of the UK to benefit from the CAP. The small size of the UK's farm sector meant that there was less to be gained from farm price support. In addition to this the UK lost out heavily in a non-budget way because of the purchases of high-priced farm goods from EU partners. The 1992 reforms did little to overcome the undesirable redistributional effects of the CAP.

As part of the 1984 reforms, the UK won an abatement based on its VAT contributions, worth £16 billion in the period to 1994. This was justified on the basis of the net contributions that the UK made to the EU budget, which were disproportionately high. It was to generate continuous friction, because it created an exceptional provision for one Member State. Also it was felt that it discouraged the UK from participating in EU expenditure plans. Any increased expenditure that benefited the UK financially simply reduced the size of the abatement.

The estimated position with regard to winners and losers from the budget in 1993 is indicated in Table 7.5.

Table 7.5 The winners and losers in the 1993 Budget

	GDP per capita 1994[1]	1993 ECU million[2]
Net contributors		
Germany	115.5	11 830
UK	99.8	3125
Italy	104.5	1525
Netherlands	100.3	1327
France	109.5	1020
Net recipients		
Greece	48.5	4135
Spain	75.4	3090
Portugal	60.5	2508
Ireland	80.0	2372
Denmark	108.6	377
Luxembourg	133.8	190
Belgium	106.3	60
EU	100.0[3]	

Notes
1   GDP per capita at current prices and current PPS (EU 12 = 100), *Source : Europe*, 16 May
     1994, p. 3
2   Court of Auditors (1994) Annual Report 1993, *Official Journal of the European
     Communities*, C327, Vol. 37, 24 November 1994
3   This table does not take into account all expenditure or all sources of income.

The above estimates may be criticised on the basis that the budgetary balance represents only the formal and not the real situation, for the following reasons. Firstly because of what is known as the Rotterdam effect. This is where customs duties are collected on entry into the EU at the point of entry, but may be destined for another Member State. In the case of Rotterdam, many of the goods that enter may be destined for Germany, for example. Secondly, some kinds of expenditure may be more directly beneficial to an economy than others. So, for example, it has been estimated that spending in the form of administrative services may be only half the value to an economy of transfers payments. This is because the administrative services may well have been employed elsewhere. In effect, therefore, the opportunity cost is not taken into account.[12] Finally, the effect of policies is more far-reaching than the individual Member State, so farmers may benefit from measures taken to support farm prices outside their country. However, as we have seen above, high farm prices are also disadvantageous to Member States that are net food importers and lose out because they can no longer exploit cheaper food on the world markets.

In 1994, the UK government estimated that its contribution to the EU budget would amount to £2.5 billion, rising to £3.55 billion in 1999, despite its abatement.[13] However, the reduced reliance on VAT as an 'own resource' may diminish the impact of the abatement. The UK had always argued that it was not reasonable to expect it to pay more, because of its relatively poor standing in the national income tables. The concept of *juste retoure* has frequently been debated with regard to the above situation. There was little enthusiasm for the UK's retaining its budget abatement in the discussions at Edinburgh in 1992, but the UK was able to maintain its position.

The UK argued that the way EU policies were constructed meant that there were long-term inequalities built into the budget. The gains that the UK had from policies such as the Single Market did not fully compensate for the welfare loss caused by excessive budgetary contributions. The counter view was that it was not only difficult to calculate the geographic incidence of the budget, but some redistribution was to be expected if even poorer states were to make progress. The fact that the four poorest states gained from the Cohesion Fund, which was based upon their relative income levels, indicates a trend away from the position where net benefits can be substantially out of line with relative prosperity.

Getting better value for money

Getting better value for money involves constantly reviewing all areas of EU activity. This encompasses auditing expenditure, evaluating the success of activities, and making suggestions as to where policy might be improved.

Although restricting expenditure on areas such as agriculture is considered to be a desirable objective, there is also a need to make sure that the budget is well spent. In this context the EU is well aware of the damaging publicity that follows evidence of misuse of money.

The Commission has the responsibility of implementing the EU budget, although in practice this role is shared by member states. Detailed investigations into how money has been spent are carried out by the independent Court of Auditors. This institution came into existence as a result of the 1975 'Treaty Amending Certain Financial Provisions of the Treaties', replacing existing arrangements. The Court of Auditors reports on an annual basis, as well as producing reports on individual problems. By the nature of things the Court of Auditors' work is retrospective, although its reports provide important pointers to improved procedures in the future.

One of the non-contentious aspects of the Treaty on European Union was that the Court of Auditors was to be given full institutional status (Article 4). As a consequence it acquired additional powers within the EU's legal structure. Article 188 C charges the Court of Auditors with the task of examining and reporting on the revenue and expenditure accounts of the EU. It is expected to comment not only on the lawfulness of the payments, but also on whether financial management has been sound. In addition, the European Parliament's powers to investigate maladministration were increased, and the Court of Justice could fine states for having not complied with a judgement against them.

The fight against fraud

The complex multinational nature of the EU's activities makes it vulnerable to fraud. This is compounded by the complexity of EU regulations, and the lack of effective controls in some Member States. The extent of fraud can only be guessed at, because measurement tends to reflect the efficiency of the detection systems. Estimates have suggested that the level of fraud might be between 7 and 10 per cent of the EU budget. Between 1991 and 1993 ECU 976 million of fraud was detected by the Commission and the Member States, nearly half of which was spent in Italy. Of this only a fraction was recovered.[14]

The adverse publicity that derives from the reporting of fraud in the European press is a source of concern because

1. it weakens the support for increased EU spending (which may be beneficial), among the general public and by national governments

2. it highlights the weaknesses of the CAP support mechanisms

3. it illustrates a more general problem of cross-border crime, which has yet to be resolved.

The area most subject to the activities of fraudsters has been the CAP.[15] An example of the kind of fraud coming to light concerned maize from the USA. This was allowed into Spain at a reduced levy because of Spain's Accession Agreement. Large quantities were then sold into the rest of the EU, but without paying a higher levy, which applied elsewhere. In total ECU 1.5 million was recovered in this case. The reason for the fraud was, typically, that the regulations were different throughout the EU.

The issue of monitoring of fraud can be resolved only if all players take the issue seriously. A report of a major fraud involving two multinational companies and the water content of cheese was highly sanitised. The companies were not named, despite the fact that irregularities involved ECU 16 million. The companies in question had not been audited by their home authorities for four or five years, despite their being in receipt of 10 per cent of all the refunds in the milk export sector.

While the primary responsibility for the detection of fraud lies with the Member States, the EU has become increasingly involved in the process of detection and prevention. In order to combat fraud, the EU increased its budgetary resources devoted to the task from ECU 76.5 million in 1992 to ECU 133.2 million in 1993. It appears that because EU funding is involved, it is sometimes considered to be less important to check for fraud.[16] While controls are often lax, convictions for fraud are often difficult to achieve because of differing national judicial procedures. As the size of the EU budget has grown, so has the need to establish a specialist fraud unit for the EU. This would be needed not only to investigate fraud, but also to liaise with national judicial authorities to ensure that prosecutions are successful.

Misuse of resources

The Court also points out the way in which EU policies are often contradictory, and as a result waste money. For example, the prices and quotas for the sugar regime were set too high. This led to sugar being produced in unsuitable areas, and increased the problem of overproduction. In addition the EU allowed the production of sugar for export only, presumably on the basis that it had no impact on the domestic European market. This sugar however, helped to depress world market prices, which meant that as the EU produced too much sugar for domestic use, it was effectively spoiling its own export markets.[17]

Another area where it was considered that there might be scope for better use of resources was the Structural Funds. Here money had tended to be handed out on an ad hoc basis, without any real sense of overall strategy. In order to combat this the Integrated Development

Areas were introduced, with the idea of linking the moneys received from the various structural funds.

Aid offered to the Third World and Central and Eastern Europe has also been the subject of criticism. For example, the Court highlighted the fact that 7500 tonnes of skimmed milk sent to Bulgaria, to mitigate domestic shortages, were largely misused. It found that 740 tonnes of this were sold by the Bulgarian State Trading Company via Greece to Egypt, in order to earn foreign exchange.[18]

A report published in 1992[19] noted the difficulty in implementing aid, even in countries where aid was being applied as part of an official programme. The Court felt that many projects were jeopardised by vague objectives and badly evaluated difficulties. This had the result that they 'do not attain their objectives and do not lead to stable economic activity', the reason 'often being not too realistic appreciation of the project from the outset or inability by the beneficiary to supply its contribution or take the necessary action to remedy the distortions'.[20] This report added that many of the EU credits to Central and Eastern Europe were 'characterised by improvisation'. While the Commission responded to these criticisms, clearly if the feeling is that money is not being well spent, the arguments for increased levels of funding become less convincing.

In addition to the work of the Court of Auditors, each policy area is reviewed on a regular basis by the Commission and the Parliament. Many of the reports produced tend to make a particular case, and perhaps lack the objectivity of those produced by the Court. An example was the Review of the Structural Funds published in March 1992.[21] This supported the Delors II package proposals in that it showed that the reform of the Structural Funds in 1989 might well have created 500 000 jobs in the less prosperous regions by 1993. This kind of report is beneficial, in that concentrating on positive outcomes can help to improve the EU's reputation.

The budgetary consequences of enlargement

The most predictable source of change with regard to the EU's budgetary strategy would be an enlargement of the EU. The extent to which new states will contribute towards, or become a burden on, the EU's finances depends on the structure of their economies. In addition, any changes in policy design and methods of revenue raising will affect the final position. Clearly, the Edinburgh Summit agreement in December 1992 could not predict the success of future negotiations, or any transitional arrangements that would form part of the Accession Agreements. The budget arrangements fixed in Edinburgh were therefore always likely to be qualified, and subject to change.

The inclusion of the three EFTA states brought a degree of uncertainty with regard to the resources that were expected to be generated. Austria, Finland and Sweden were all seen as very desirable members, not only because of their democratic traditions but also because they had relatively high incomes per head. In 1994, while GNP per head was ECU 17 247 for the EU 12, it was ECU 21 220 for Austria, ECU 19 498 for Sweden and ECU 15 335 for Finland. In 1995 the three EFTA states may increase the maximum available for own resources by ECU 506.7, rising to ECU 577.3 in 1999. This is rather less than was hoped for (the actual availability of resources depends on economic performance). In 1999 the EFTAns will contribute at their maximum of ECU 1.7 billion, which is about half of what was originally predicted.

The reasons for the shortfall are as follows:

1. The new states experienced a significant drop in relative GDP per head compared to the
    1980s. This was caused by the recession, and in the case of Finland by the collapse of
    trade with the former Soviet Union. In 1994 Finland had a per capita GNP which had
    fallen to 89 per cent of the EU average.

2. The aggressive negotiating stance taken by these countries. The entry negotiations
    resulted in the budget rebates given in Table 7.6 being agreed, which means that the EU
    will see only a limited financial benefit in the early years of the expansion. These rebates
    come on top of more generous provision for disadvantaged regions, and other
    expenditure items designed to assist these states in their transition to EU membership.

Table 7.6 Rebates to New Members (ECU million)

	1995	1996	1997	1998
Austria	583	106	71	35
Finland	476	163	63	33
Sweden	201	128	52	26

Source : *Act of Accession* (1994)

The budgetary costs of absorbing new members will have an impact on determining the
desirability of new Member States in the future. In the case of the Mediterranean States, while
the small states do not represent a significant additional burden, Turkey clearly does.

Table 7.7 Possible budgetary consequences of enlargement (the Mediterranean States)

	Net receipts (million ECU per annum)[1]	Net receipts (% of GDP)[2]
Cyprus	50	1.0
Malta	20	1.0
Turkey	12 000	15.0

[1]   At 1991 prices
[2]   Estimates based on market exchange rates
Source : House of Lords, Select Committee on the European Communities, 1992–93 Session,
First Report, *Enlargement of the Communities*, HL Paper 5, 1992, p. 25

Small states with few problems may be acceptable, given that the total cost of sustaining their
membership is not great. However, states such as Turkey with large agricultural sectors would
be a substantial burden given their relative poverty. The estimates in Table 7.7 have
implications for the existing states' net contributions, because they imply that there will be
changes in burden-sharing. If richer countries join, the individual burden of the structural
funds will be less. However, the impact of a large poor state such as Turkey joining could well
cause significant disruption to the budget.

Conclusions

There is still no consensus about the role of the budget within the EU. However, significant progress has been made with regard to ensuring that sufficient resources are available to the EU to adequately meet its commitments. The Edinburgh Agreement of 1992 mapped out an agreed pattern of expenditure over the seven years that will provide for a degree of redistribution of resources to poorer states.

The importance of agriculture within the EU economies has declined significantly since the EU was formed. However, spending on agriculture remains the largest part, and an unpredictable element of the budget, despite the 1992 reforms to the CAP. Spending on this policy area should decline as a proportion of a larger budget in the period to 1999. However, there will be a real increase in total spending in order to compensate farmers for the measures introduced to restrain production. The inability of the EU to overcome the problems caused by monetary instability in 1992 and 1993 meant that the 'switch over' mechanism operated when currencies within the ERM changed parity. The need for further reform of the CAP is therefore still apparent, if the EU budget is not to be drained.

The operation of the budget also continues to be a problem, with money poorly spent or, in some cases, major fraud. To an extent this could be avoided by a simplification of the rules, whose complexity offers ample opportunities for misuse. Indeed it might even be argued that the central problem is that the Member States feel a lack of ownership of the problem. This could be resolved by simply agreeing monetary transfers to poorer states, and not bothering with a centrally administered budget except to fund minimum levels of the bureaucracy. However, this would risk destroying any momentum towards integration, which the budget must be a central part of.

Two events may cause significant changes in budgetary strategy. The first would be caused by real progress being made towards EMU. The Edinburgh Agreement was not an adequate response to the challenge of monetary union. If there is to be EMU, the size of the Structural Funds will need to be looked at again. Similarly, the issue of expansion of the EU was not properly addressed, largely because this was still a hypothetical issue at Edinburgh. Both these developments will require a new strategy towards the distributional aspects of the budget. However, in 1984 it became apparent that addition of the EFTA states would not bring forth the extra resources, at least in the short-term, that might have been expected.

Notes and references

1. **Commission of the EC** (1994) *The Budget of the EU*, p. 2.
2. *Europe*, 12 March 1992, 8.
3. **MacDougall D** (1992) Economic and Monetary Union and the European Community Budget, in *National Institute Economic Review*, May, 64–68.
4. Member states hand over 90 per cent of the amounts they collect, keeping back 10 per cent to cover the cost of collection.
5. **House of Lords** (1992) *Commission Proposals for Community Finances 1992*, Select Committee on the European Communities, 11th Report, 1992–93, HL paper 38, p. 12.
6. Some of the problems of calculating real GNP will always remain given the existence of the black economy. However, the EU has a statistical guide to the collection of national statistics, which dates back to 1970, helping to rule out some of the irregularities.

7. *The European*, 18 March 1993, 1.
8. **Gardner D** (1991) Southern discomfort, *Financial Times*, 18 June 1991, 6.
9. **Commission of the EC** (1992) Revised draft proposal for a Council Regulation (EEC) establishing a Cohesion Fund, COM (92) 599 final, 23 December 1992.
10. **Commission of the EC** (1992) *From the Single Act to Maastricht and Beyond – the Means to Match our Ambitions*, COM (92) final, 1992, p. 24.
11. *Financial Times*, 16 February 1993, 2.
12. **Smith S** (1992) Financing the European Community: a Review of the Options for the Future, *Fiscal Studies*, Vol. 13, No. 4, 121.
13. **Paymaster General** (1994) *Statement on the 1994 Community Budget*, Cm 2486, p. 10.
14. **Marsh P** (1994) A labyrinth of loopholes, *Financial Times*, 19 May.
15. **Commission of the EC** (1991) *The Fight Against Fraud*, a survey of the activities against fraud prevention in 1991. SEC (92) 943 final, p. 24.
16. *Europe*, 15/16 February 1993, 13.
17. **Court of Auditors** (1991) Annual report concerning the financial year 1990 together with the institutional replies, *Official Journal of the EU*, C 324, Vol. 34, 13 December 1991, 83–90.
18. **Court of Auditors** (1992) Annual report concerning the financial year 1991 together with the institutions' replies, *Official Journal of the EU*, 15 December, 61.
19. *Europe*, 22/23 June 1992, 13.
20. Ibid.
21. *Europe*, 12 March 1992, 8.

Further reading

Commission (1991) *The Community Budget: the Facts in Figures*, 3rd edition, Situation 1990, Luxembourg.
Court of Auditors (1993) Annual Report for 1992, *Official Journal*, C309, Vol. 36, 16 November.
Commission (1993) Stable Money – Sound Finances, *European Economy*, No. 53.
Franklin M (1992) The EU Budget: Realism, Redistribution and Radical Reform, Royal Institute of International Affairs, Discussion Paper No. 42.
House of Lords (1993) *The Fight against Fraud*, Select Committee on the European Communities, Session 1992–93, Report 13, HL paper 44.
Shackleton M (1990) *Financing the European Community*, Francis Pinter.
Strasser D (1992) *The Finances of Europe*, Commission, 3rd edition.

CHAPTER 8

The reformed Common Agricultural Policy

Introduction

In most advanced economies the agricultural industry is subject to considerable government intervention. Within the EU, the Common Agricultural Policy (CAP) aims to support agriculture on an EU-wide basis, thus replacing many national policies and supplementing others, in an attempt to ensure a balance of benefits to both producers and consumers. It is regarded as the most developed of the EU's policies and covers over 90 per cent of agricultural products; yet there have been constant calls for fundamental reform. The major reasons for these demands have been as follows:

1. Agricultural prices are high, which stimulates uneconomic production and disadvantages the consumer.

2. The budgetary cost of the CAP – it has absorbed about 60 per cent of the EU's budget, and as a consequence starves other policy areas of adequate funding.

3. The pricing system results in substantial resource transfers which can be attributed to the CAP but do not show up in the budget. The food importing countries within the EU have to pay higher than world market prices for food, while surplus producers gain privileged access to these markets.

4. Surpluses are dumped on world markets. This disturbs the markets for other agricultural exporters without benefiting the EU's consumers. It is also a source of conflict which spills over into other areas of trade.

5. Farm incomes have failed to keep pace with expectations, resulting in great dissatisfaction with the policy from the very people it was designed to assist.

6. Little emphasis has been placed on the environmental aspects of agricultural policy. Attempts to exploit the soil with ever more intensive production methods have resulted in damage to the land and to the water supply.

7. Intensive farming methods that take little account of animal welfare have been encouraged by the CAP.

At the heart of the debate, is the surplus production of particular products that the CAP generates. The EU, as in the Grimm fairy tale, seems to have forgotten the magic word that will stop the opulent cup from overflowing.

These criticisms are particularly relevant to a country such as the UK, which in 1992 had only 2.2 per cent of its working population employed in the agricultural industry compared to a EU average of 6.2 per cent. Despite substantial gains in productivity, the major food importing states such as the UK have to pay a high price for the CAP. First they pay via the EU budget, and then their citizens pay via high food prices.

There have been many attempts to reform the CAP in the past, most of which have had little positive impact on its problems. This chapter is concerned with the attempts to reform the CAP in the 1990s, although the causes of many of the problems date back to the establishment of the EU. In 1992 the MacSharry Reforms (named after the Irish Commissioner for Agriculture) were finally agreed. The EU began the process of reform in earnest by introducing significant changes, which were to be implemented from 1993 onward. The basis of support was altered to address the needs of both the farmer and the consumer. Prices were lowered and aid was given directly to the farmer, in such a way as to discourage increasingly intensive farming methods, and to promote an environmentally sound policy of extensification (the use of less concentrated farming techniques). The EU settled its disagreements with the USA in December 1992, when it was agreed to contain the extent of support given to agriculture. This was designed to satisfy the USA, that the EU would limit its unfair trading practices. In 1994, when the Uruguay Round of the GATT was completed, a comprehensive set of rules covering agriculture was agreed (see chapter 16).

These reforms were not without their critics, because they aimed simply to constrain surpluses rather than to eliminate them. They also increased the immediate budgetary cost of the CAP, although there was a potential for the consumer to gain through lower food prices. A number of the methods designed to control production were also criticised. Many farmers felt that any attempt to restrict production amounted to a betrayal of the industry.

This chapter discusses the changes that have taken place, and argues that the CAP has to move further if it is not to hold back the development of the EU. Although significant progress has been made in the process of introducing reform, the CAP is unlikely to be able to move the agricultural sector to a point where its operation can be left to the market. Detailed intervention in the sector seems bound to continue, despite the unsatisfactory results gained from the process.

The rationale for agricultural support

Agriculture is an industry that does not function well in a free market environment. Demand tends to be price inelastic, and in the short term supply is also price inelastic. Actual supply may vary by as much as 25 per cent, due to factors such as climate, pests and disease. The fluctuations in supply, plus a lack of market knowledge, mean that agricultural markets may behave erratically. That is, farmers are small producers compared with the size of the market, and as a consequence are price takers. They tend to respond to market signals without realising their true significance, so they produce more or less of a commodity in response to a price change, rather than responding to actual demand changes.

This can be partly explained by economic theory through the use of the cobweb theorem also known by its appropriate picturesque nickname of the 'hog cycle'. In agriculture there is frequently a supply lag of over a year, so that if prices rise, supply does not respond for some time. (In the case of pigs, the lag used to be 2 or 3 years because of the time it took to breed the animals.) This means that shortages are not readily accommodated in the short term. However, a period of high prices may bring about an exaggerated response from producers in the future. The result is a glut of the product and a period of low prices. Figure 8.1 illustrates the process.

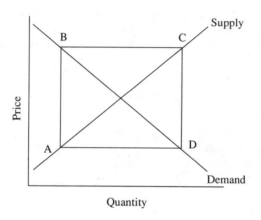

Figure 8.1 The cobweb

If there is a shortage this year, supply will be at A, and that will mean that prices will rise to B. Because supply cannot be increased in the short term, prices will stay high for some time. The period of high prices will, after a delay, produce increased supply, but at a level C that corresponds to the high prices. Production will now be too high, and a glut will result in prices falling to D. The equilibrium between supply and demand is never reached, and agricultural markets will lurch between shortage and glut.

The demand for food also depends on consumer behaviour related to general eating habits. In the 1980s eating habits changed rapidly; for example, between 1985 and 1989, the per capita consumption of butter fell by 40 per cent in Ireland and 20 per cent in the UK and Germany. In 1989 alone, the per capita consumption of butter fell by 19 per cent in the UK and 10 per cent in Germany. This, along with a series of major health concerns related to particular foods such as beef and cheese, has meant that the markets for foods have become more unpredictable. The instability created by these shifts in consumer demand has meant that parts of the industry have suddenly faced a crisis. The result has been political pressure for governments to intervene. In the early 1990s, the most important example of this was bovine spongiform encephalopathy (BSE), which was commonly known as mad cow disease. This caused the German government to question the safety of British beef and led to a general fall in the sale of beef, as there was a fear that the disease could be transmitted to humans.

Added to these problems, there may be periods of over-supply that are general and long-term. In developed nations, where better technology has led to increased productivity in farming, even in times of economic expansion the demand for food does not tend to rise as rapidly as incomes. This is because consumers do not simply eat more because they are better off. Typically, the UK has an income elasticity of demand for food of 0.14, which implies that demand for food will grow only by 0.14 per cent with each 1 per cent increase in income. Income elasticity of demand will, however, be higher for some luxury foods.

The challenge for the EU is to reduce surpluses, but at the same time avoid the all-too-familiar scenario found in the manufacturing sector, where production facilities that are no longer required simply fall into dereliction. If rural incomes become depressed, this will cause migration from the countryside to the cities. Aid given to the agricultural sector may therefore be seen as a tool of development. Supporting the industry may be one method of ensuring that help is given to the less advanced parts of some economies.

In theory, a great deal could be done to stabilise markets by better market information. The majority of states do not take this view, however, and they attempt to stabilise the industry either by physical controls or by supporting the market process. The fact that governments are intervening in the market mechanism means that the area becomes politicised. It gives scope for governments to determine prices and incomes in the industry and encourage production. The method and extent of intervention will depend on the strategic role of the industry. This will be influenced by factors such as the size and structure of the industry, the importance of food supplies, and the contribution to the balance of payments. Other factors will also be important, such as the value placed on the rural way of life.

The development of the CAP

When the CAP was being formulated, the agricultural industries of the EU6 were undergoing considerable change. The degree of mechanisation had increased substantially in the post-war period and large numbers of workers were leaving the countryside attracted by higher industrial wages. The agricultural industry of the Six was not as developed as that of the UK. In 1958 about 20 per cent of the working population were employed in agriculture in the Six compared to 5 per cent in the UK; the average size of holdings was only 10.4 hectares compared to 32 hectares in the UK. The result was predictably a major difference in productivity between the Six and the UK, given that broadly the same kind of crops were being produced. The difference in the size of the holdings still existed in 1990, when the amount of utilised agricultural land per holding in the EU12 was 13.3 hectares compared to 64.4 hectares in the UK.

The reason for the huge differences in size is largely historical. The system of inheritance in the UK had always encouraged the consolidation of farms, while in countries such as France holdings were often split on the death of the landowner. Also, factors such as greater exposure to international competition helped to spur change in the UK, while continental producers were often protected by tariff walls.

The early development of the CAP was influenced by the experiences of food shortages, and an absence of security of food supply caused by two world wars. The main concern was to ensure that food production was encouraged, so that the Member States, and later the EU, would be (as far as possible) self-sufficient.

The general objectives of the CAP when it was established were those set out in Article 39 of the Treaty of Rome. They would have been broadly acceptable to almost any country within Western Europe at the time, and were to:

1. increase agricultural productivity by promoting technical progress and by ensuring the rational development of agricultural production and the optimum utilisation of the factors of production, in particular labour

2. ensure a fair standard of living for the agricultural community, in particular by increasing the individual earnings of persons engaged in agriculture

3. stabilise markets

4. guarantee the availability of supplies

5. ensure reasonable consumer prices.

Article 39 (2) noted the special social structure of agriculture, and the need to bring about adjustment by degrees. This was probably meant to refer to the situation facing the industry in the late 1950s, but could equally be seen as an important guiding principle today. It should be noted that there was no reference to the need to consider environmental factors or to contribute to the stability of global agricultural markets. Both of these issues were essentially later concerns.

It took 10 years of negotiation to translate these objectives into a workable policy, and get rid of much of the national price support mechanism, so that it was not until 1968 that the CAP could be regarded as established.

Prior to the formation of the EU, all the Six had farm policies that contained varying degrees of protection. In order to gain agreement, the overall level of protection from imports was increased. In the early years there were no significant surpluses, so it was the consumer, not the taxpayer, who paid. This redistribution could be justified to some extent, because the economies of the EU6 were growing rapidly.

In contrast, the system of support for agriculture in the UK was traditionally based on the concept of cheap food. The primary method of support was deficiency payments. This involved paying farmers subsidies so that they could compete with cheaper imports, and had the effect of encouraging production at the taxpayer's expense. It was feasible because the UK industry was relatively small and efficient. However, by the 1960s, as agricultural productivity rose and world prices fell, the system became an increasing burden on the taxpayer. Attempts were then made to control the cost of subsidies by raising import prices, so that at the time of UK accession the two systems were, to a limited extent, starting to converge.

The structure of EU agriculture

The addition of Spain, Portugal and Greece to EU membership in the 1980s increased the diversity with which the CAP has to cope. It increased the production of Mediterranean crops, such as citrus fruits and tomatoes, and caused real concern about the wine lake. The situation was made more complex by the addition of East Germany in 1990, in the sense that it took time to adjust to market-oriented farming. Finally, the addition of Austria, Finland and Sweden gives even greater diversity, with some farms operating in very extreme conditions. An example of the diversity of EU agriculture is given in Table 8.1, which compares the profile of cereal production in five Member States.

Table 8.1 Diversity of cereal farming in 1990 (producing soft wheat)

	Total output per hectare	Average area (hectares)	Yield (tonnes per hectare)	Total assets per hectare	Hectares per unit of labour
France	82 535	65.6	6.61	2629	51.4
Greece	14 813	12.9	3.02	4720	9.0
Italy	17 323	14.6	4.92	8870	13.8
Spain	20 499	44.8	2.39	3469	48.2
UK	133 696	126.6	6.84	5604	61.2

Source : Commission of the EC (1992), *Farm Incomes in the European Community 1990/91*, p. 28

These very considerable differences in the industry's structure and development reflect differing social priorities, and the need to take account of the natural soil and climatic advantages that some countries possess. They make it easy to understand the problem of trying to develop a single policy that meets the needs of the sector.

The importance of agriculture

The need for reform of the CAP has rarely been doubted. However, the fact that it is a sector that costs increasing amounts of taxpayers' money, but has undergone a decline in its relative importance, may have contributed to the process of change. Table 8.2 shows the importance of agriculture to GDP within the EU. It illustrates that even in traditionally strongly agrarian societies such as France, agriculture is no longer dominant.

Table 8.2 Agriculture's percentage of GDP in 1991

Austria	3.2
Belgium	2.1
Denmark	3.5
Finland	5.5
France	3.0
Germany	1.3
Greece	16.1
Ireland	8.1
Italy	3.9
Luxembourg	1.9
Netherlands	3.9
Portugal	4.7
Spain	4.1
Sweden	2.7
UK	1.4
EU12	2.8

Source : Commission of the EC (1994), *The Agricultural Situation in the Community: 1993 Report*, p. T/23, and other Commission sources for the 1995 enlargement and OECD

The reason for the decline as a percentage of GDP is that other sectors have grown in relative importance. However, although fewer people are employed in agriculture, structural changes mean that it now operates more efficiently.

During the 1980s the size of the agricultural labour force in the EU12 diminished by 2 million. At the same time, the number of holdings diminished by 1.2 million to 8.2 million. However, the actual land under cultivation decreased by only 1.4 per cent, because of the consolidation of farm holding. This led to the average size of holdings increasing by 1.6 hectares. This trend was to continue: for example, the UK Ministry of Agriculture was to report that employment in the sector had diminished by 24 000 (−4.3 per cent) in 1992. The Sustainable Agriculture, Food and Environment (SAFE) Alliance suggested that the MacSharry reforms might contribute to job losses. It estimated that one farm job would be lost for every 130 hectares devoted to set-aside, as a result of less land being cultivated.[2]

Decision-making in agriculture

Decision-making for the CAP is essentially the same as in any other policy area of the EU. However, the stakes are higher, because of the historic importance of the CAP and the amount that it absorbs of the EU's budget. Although the consumers' interests are represented at both a national and an EU level, the farmers have a very powerful voice. In most EU states, this is a result of the traditional role of agriculture in European society. Even if agricultural sectors are small, many people are only one generation away from the land. Added direct action by farmers can be a very effective way of influencing governments in some countries, such as France.

National organisations in the Member States, such as the UK's National Farmers Union (NFU), are effective in their organised response to developments. At the EU level, farming interests are more coherently represented than those of industry, under the leadership of the Comité des Organisations Professionnelles Agricoles (COPA). In exceptional cases there may be bilateral collaboration between national farming organisations. An example is the Presidents of the Fédération Nationale des Syndicats d'Exploitants Agricoles (FNSEA) and the Deutscher Bauernverband (DBV) jointly declaring their opposition to the Blair House Agreement on agriculture.[3]

The EU's annual price package should be agreed by the Council of Ministers just before the marketing year commences on 1 April. This Council is also meant to be the main focus of debate and decisions about reforms. In reality, issues of reform tend to take anything up to 18 months or more before they are resolved. The MacSharry proposals, for example, were made public informally for the first time in December 1991, but not formally adopted until 30 June 1992. Usually a range of issues are linked, so that all groups of proposals have something in them for each Member State. The Agricultural Council takes about 100 decisions per year, with a major reform such as the MacSharry package requiring 25 regulations.[4]

It is often difficult for the general public to see why agriculture reform should be so intractable. However, the EU decision-making process is difficult to reverse, so that once a system is in place it wins vested interests, which are difficult to overcome. Spending on agricultural support has tended to remain high because

1. support has tended to come as a result of a crisis facing the sector, or because of the need for security of supply – once the crisis has passed, support is difficult to remove

2.   any removal of support reduces the value of the sector, and makes valuable investment redundant, because the returns on investment fall

3.   it is difficult to reallocate agricultural resources to other uses – in particular, environmental concerns tend to hold back this process

4.   the fact that the EU has assumed responsibility for the policy means that it is a burden that has to be shared by all the Member States. This means that the burden of supporting farmers is shared by net importers of other states' surplus production. Likewise, the budgetary cost will be distributed to include states with small agricultural sectors.

Operating the CAP

The operation of the CAP is designed around three main principles:

1.   EU preference against imports

2.   EU free trade

3.   shared financial responsibility.

The responsibility for financing price support and structural change is vested in the European Agricultural Guarantee and Guidance Fund (EAGGF), which typically has taken 60 per cent of the EU's total budget. The Guarantee element predominated, normally taking 95 per cent of funds for price support, while only around 5 per cent has been spent on the Guidance section. Most Guidance payments are made to Member States, in the form of refunds for spending on structural improvements and aid to less favoured areas.

The mechanism for support

For a number of key agricultural products, the EU supports the price by intervening in the market, and where feasible storing the commodity or selling it onto world markets. The following is a description of how the mechanism works with regard to cereals. There are three EU-wide prices in operation, target price, threshold price and intervention price.

Target price

In theory this is the ideal price for the EU, offering farmers the living standard they should be entitled to while taking account of the needs of consumers. In practice, however, because of over-production, it has ceased to be meaningful. The exception is when there is a worldwide shortage of a particular commodity. The target price is based on grain prices delivered into store at Duisburg, the place in the EU where grain is in shortest supply. The price for other areas is calculated by allowing for transport costs.

Threshold price

This is the price at which imports of grain come into the EU. It is set at a similar level to the target price. The aim is to ensure that imported grain does not flood into the EU. A tax called a variable levy is placed on imported grain. It is calculated on a daily basis by taking the difference between the lowest world market price (delivered to the EU) and the threshold price. So the variable levy goes up when international prices fall, and falls when international prices rise. The price moves up over the season to encourage orderly marketing.

In the very unlikely event of world prices being above the EU price, a variable tax is placed on exports from the EU. This is to try and keep prices down within the EU.

Intervention price

This is the theoretical minimum price for grain within the EU. The intervention price is meant to be related to the market conditions in the French Department of Ormes, which is said to be the area of greatest surplus of grain within the EU, and therefore the place where prices should be at their lowest. In practice farmers are likely to be paid less because of

● delivery and handling costs

● delayed payments. In order to encourage sellers to find alternative markets, payment is not made for 3 months after selling into intervention.

As with the threshold price, intervention prices move up over the season to encourage orderly marketing.

Selling into intervention

The EU's intervention authorities are required to purchase all grain that meets the set standards of quality at a minimum price, provided it falls within the intervention period, which normally lasts from November to the end of May.

Grain is withdrawn from the market either by taking it into store or by subsidies being paid to traders to export onto the world market. The EU spends about twice as much on export subsidies as on storage. Traders have to tender for the subsidy (refunds) which they receive only after proof that the grain has been exported. This system is open to a great deal of abuse, as commodities that have been exported find their way back on to the EU's market.

The effects of the intervention system on the grain market are illustrated by Figure 8.2.

Left to itself, the market equilibrium is at E1, which is below intervention price. As grain is purchased, the demand curve shifts from D1 to D2, which gives a new equilibrium point E2. Prices rise from P1 to P2, which is the intervention price. The farmer can rely on a stable price for his grain, but the disadvantage for the EU is that prices are constantly fixed above the level where demand equals supply. The farmer can produce as much as he wishes, regardless of the fact that there is surplus production.

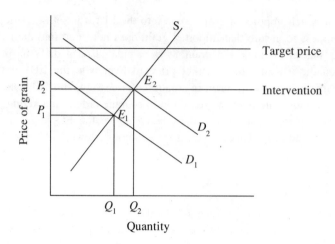

Figure 8.2 The intervention mechanism

The relationship between intervention and threshold prices

In reality, two prices are important: the intervention price, which puts a floor on the market, and the threshold price, which determines the ceiling. The threshold price ensures that EU producers are normally free from competition within their domestic market. The market element for cereals is between the threshold price and the intervention price. These two are bargained about by the various lobby groups including the farmers and the food industry. In addition, financial constraints are significant, given the wish to limit the growth of the EU budget. National governments of states that gain significantly from the CAP or have a vocal agricultural sector, such as the French, are most likely to argue for greater support, while the UK has consistently argued for restraint.

Representative rates (green money)

The advent of the EU's Single Market, with the removal of border controls, offered the opportunity for reform in the way that the levels of agricultural pricing policies had developed within the EU. In the system that had evolved since 1969, the price of agricultural goods could vary considerably because of a system of artificial money, known as green money (or more correctly as representative rates). There were in fact three types of green currency. The first type was a national one, which arose from the changing value of national currencies. The second was a refinement of the first, where differing green currencies applied to particular products within a Member State. The third arose as a result of the switch-over mechanism, and was called the green ECU.

The 1993 Single Market reforms resulted in

1. the removal of border controls designed to maintain different price levels

2. a common support price throughout the EU, with the retention of the green ECU but a reduced role for national green currencies.

The common system of support prices throughout the EU requires a monetary system that will permit it to operate effectively. The ideal situation would be where there was a monetary union, so that there would be no changes in the relative values of currencies. Failing this, a high degree of monetary stability, such as that provided by the European Monetary System (EMS) in the late 1980s, would be an advantage. The currency instability of the early 1990s saw the EU move away from this situation.

Background

The early development of the CAP took place in an era of low inflation and monetary stability. As a consequence, the aim of creating a common price structure for agricultural products looked realistic. In 1962, the EU set into place the rules for expressing EU prices in national currencies. The price of agricultural products was expressed in agricultural units of account (AUA), which were equivalent in value to the US dollar.

However, by the late 1960s, just as the broad framework of the CAP had been agreed, the Bretton Woods system of fixed change rates started to come apart. In 1967 the British pound was devalued; this was followed in 1969 by the devaluation of the French franc and the revaluation of the German mark. The early 1970s saw inflation rates increase dramatically throughout the world and the replacement of fixed exchange rates by floating exchange rates.

The implication for the CAP of the new era of floating exchange rates was that the system of common prices was abandoned. The setting of farm prices is external to an economy. When an exchange rate changes, if there is no intervention, agricultural prices within a country that revalues will fall, in the same way as all imported goods. When a currency is devalued, agricultural prices rise. This era of floating exchange rates threatened the stability of domestic agricultural prices. In order to maintain domestic price stability, measures had to be taken to counteract this.

Currency instability led to the introduction of green rates, initially on a temporary basis, as an artificial method of converting EU prices into national currencies. Despite the benefits to the consumer of falling food prices following revaluation, the German government opted to keep its agricultural prices higher than those in the rest of the EU, in order to protect farmers from the consequent fall in income. In France, the opposite tactic was followed. The French government kept agricultural prices low in order to prevent a windfall gain from going to its farmers when its economy was going through difficult times. The devaluation should have meant rising food prices, which would have added to inflation.

The artificially high or low prices could not be maintained without additional intervention to stop produce moving from the lowest priced markets to the highest priced markets. In order to stop this a system of subsidies and taxes called monetary compensatory amounts (MCAs) was introduced. In the case of a French devaluation and a German revaluation, exports to France from another community country would benefit from a subsidy paid by the EU. In the case of Germany, border taxes on imports would be charged in order to maintain the higher prices.

National prices

Over the years, the green money system developed considerably, so that it became a tool of national policy. By devaluing the green rates it is possible to raise prices for farmers, while revaluation would lower them. Normally the UK operated with a single green rate, but some other countries operated on a number of different rates, which depended on the product. For example, the national green currency might have been at a more favourable rate for pigs than for sheep.

The case for the national green rates system was that it permitted agricultural prices to reflect the needs of the country concerned. This was seen as a way of ensuring that the differing production conditions that exist in farming between the Member States were accommodated. They were regarded as essential given the absence of monetary stability.

The Commission was against national green rates remaining, and their removal was a priority for the completion of the Single Market. The way forward inevitably involved progress towards full involvement of all states in the EMS, and progress being made towards Economic and Monetary Union (EMU). Without this the problem of monetary instability could not be resolved. Green rates meant that the principle of free trade was violated, because they could be enforced only by collecting MCAs at the frontier. They also gave scope for fraud, as animals were smuggled across borders in order to cash in on price differentials. MCAs created a national as against an EU price system for agriculture, which meant that farmers in high-price countries benefited. This distorted both consumption and production patterns. The differing green rates applied within some countries also resulted in distortions, because they targeted assistance towards particular commodities.

Reforming green money

The first step towards the reform of the green money system came with the creation of the EMS in 1979. From that time on, the CAP's price system operated on the basis of the European currency unit (ECU). The ECU was an artificial currency, made up of a basket of the Member States' Currencies calculated on a trade weighted basis. The composition of the ECU was changed with the addition of the Greek drachma in 1984, and the escudo and peseta in 1989.

The EMS was designed to promote monetary stability, although in its early years it was subject to some turbulence. The basis of the system was that group of currencies were tied in a narrow band as part of the Exchange Rate Mechanism (ERM), which did not allow them to fluctuate more than 2.25 per cent either side of the central rate for the ECU. However, some currencies stayed in a wider 6 per cent band within the ERM, including the Italian lira, the British pound, the Spanish peseta and the Portuguese escudo.

The ERM changed to a 15 per cent band as a result of speculative attacks in August 1993 (see chapter 6). This permitted a theoretical divergence of up to 30 per cent between the strongest and weakest currencies. This made a nonsense of claims for stability, especially as the UK pound and the Italian lira had already suspended their membership of the ERM as a result of the crisis of 1992.

The second step was the introduction of the Agricultural Central Rate Mechanism (switch-over) in April 1984. It was a strong currency system, based on the Dutch guilder and the German mark. Whenever currencies were realigned, the ECU was revalued for agricultural purposes, so creating a Green ECU. By September 1993, there was a 21 per cent difference between the green ECU and the market ECU. The aim of the mechanism was to move to a system of common prices based on the strongest currency. This was to ensure that farmers in the countries that revalued their currency did not face a fall in price.

The system survived the introduction of the Single Market in 1993, although it was to be subject to review. However, the crisis of the ERM and the move to 15 per cent ERM margins on 2 August 1993 led to the switch-over mechanism being suspended on 10 September 1993. It was realised that the cost of honouring a system that guaranteed prices to farmers in strong currency countries would inevitably place a considerable burden on the EU budget. In October 1993, the EU Agriculture Commissioner René Steichen described switch-over as being a 'crude and ineffective instrument which raises prices for producers in all Member States in order to avoid price reductions in two Member States'[5] (the two states being Germany and the Netherlands, which stayed within their original narrower currency bands). At that time, the Commission estimated that for every 1 per cent revaluation of the strong currencies, the switch-over mechanism would cost ECU 176 million in 1994, and this would rise to ECU 343 million in 1995 and ECU 360 million per year thereafter.

Farmers in the member states that had a downward realignment benefited from adjustments in support prices to compensate for the devaluation. There seems to have been little objection by national governments to farmers benefiting from higher prices, perhaps because of the impact of the 1992 MacSharry reforms. Farmers in countries such as Germany and the Netherlands, which had strong currencies, enjoyed no benefit from the turbulence and were subject to the full impact of the MacSharry reforms.

In countries with a devalued currency, intervention prices were higher than had been expected, as well as area payments for set-aside. While the intervention prices were adjusted on a continuing basis, the area payments were determined by the green rate of the currency on 1 July each year. These increased payments were not related to costs in the case of cereal farmers, and amounted to an automatic increase in profitability. Farm incomes consequently became unpredictable, and depended on currency fluctuations. Table 8.3 gives one estimate of the impact on an individual farmer's income, made by the UK's Home Grown Cereals Authority. At this point the pound was at a particularly low point, with a devaluation of 16 per cent against the Deutschemark.

Table 8.3 Estimated income on a 200 hectare cereal farm in the UK

Pre-CAP reform	£30 000
Post-CAP reform	£20 000
Post-reform and Green £ changes	£42 000

Source : Farming News, 19 February 1993, 3

In the above example, the farmer would have experienced a 33 per cent drop in income as a result of the MacSharry reforms. However, the combination of a double advantage of increased intervention and area payments resulted in the farmer's income rising by 40 per cent. On 1 July 1993, the area payments were fixed for the coming year. A 1.1 per cent revaluation of green rates cut area payments for cereals by a similar amount. The actual payments were £140.64 per hectare, which was a cut of £6 from the peak position. However, UK farmers were still 18 per cent better off than they would have been prior to the UK pound's devaluation in September 1992.[6]

A rise in intervention prices has an impact on the overall price level within any Member State. However, the precise impact is difficult to estimate because it depends on the extent to which food processors and retailers are able to pass on the price increases. So, for example, the price of bread bought in the shop reflects the baker's labour and capital costs, along with an element of profit. A similar situation applies to the shopkeeper. Also, the impact of the price increase will be restricted to the per centage of our income that is spent on food. In the UK, this is about 15 per cent of income.

For the EU overall, the effects were that the cost of the CAP rose with the operation of the switch-over mechanism. When the switch-over mechanism was formally abandoned on 15 December 1994, it was estimated to have cost ECU 6 billion in the period it had been in operation.[7] In addition, international agreements designed to restrict farm subsidies under the GATT had been in danger of being broken by the additional support given. It was replaced by a system of compensation for farmers which operated if real exchange rates moved 5 per cent above or 3 per cent below the green currency rate.

If all states operate on the basis of free-floating exchange rates, individual gains in competitiveness may be short-lived in the commodity areas where markets are not supported by intervention buying. Where currency movements have given advantages to one Member State's farmers, the losers who find themselves driven out of their own national markets will protest. French farmers burnt truck-loads of lamb from Britain in the early 1990s because they thought that the competition was unfair.

The CAP depends on monetary stability to retain its common pricing system. In periods of stability, the switch-over mechanism is not required, and if there is instability the EU cannot afford to sustain the cost within the current budgetary arrangements. Failing this, there may be no alternative to either making farmers in strong currency countries suffer price falls or permitting national aid to farmers to compensate them. National schemes would, however, be contrary to the common support system of the CAP.

The crisis of over-production

Despite the fact that the EU is a net food importer, there has been a crisis of over-production of certain products which will not go away. The degree of self-sufficiency within the EU is illustrated in Table 8.4, and this indicates the extent of the problem.

Surpluses are not general; indeed, if the EU wishes to be self-contained with regard to agricultural products, then in some years there must be output above self-sufficiency levels to counteract the periods of shortage. As Table 8.4 indicates, the problem is that there is an overall surplus in particular areas. Products such as meat and cereals are consistently in surplus, and it is these that have to be disposed of.

The CAP system of price support had the effect of offering, for most products, the guarantee of an unlimited market at a certain price. This incentive, coupled with improved technology, meant that agricultural production in the EU increased dramatically. In the first 20

Table 8.4 Self-sufficiency in certain agricultural products (percentage of consumption in 1991)

	Cereals (excluding rice)	Fresh milk	Butter	Meat	Fresh fruit	Wine
Belg and Lux	51	134	99	150	40	38
Denmark	151	104	165	319	20	0
France	226	103	98	105	86	93
Germany	114	113	96	90	22	88
Greece	93	97	27	71	171	123
Ireland	104	101	1225	299	15	0
Italy	84	96	75	73	114	127
Netherlands	28	88	248	230	63	0
Portugal	51	90	108	90	84	138
Spain	99	97	170	96	94	106
UK	124	98	60	87	19	0
Eur12	120	102	115	102	85	103

Source: Commission of the EC (1994), *The Agricultural Situation in the Community: 1993 Report*, p. T/170

years of the CAP, agricultural production increased on average at about 2.5 per cent per year, despite 10 million workers leaving the land. Consumption has increased by only 0.5 per cent per year, so almost inevitably, the EU has moved into a crisis of overproduction. The CAP was devised when EU agricultural markets were either in balance or in deficit, so the system provided no mechanism for adequate control of production.

As the EU has acquired new members, the stimulus of high prices has further encouraged production. This was the case with the 1973 expansion and the expansion to the south in the 1980s. Given the catching-up process among many of the backward agricultural producers, the trend towards increased productivity compounds the problem. This can be seen with the example of the former GDR, where agricultural productivity was low because of the system under which the land was managed.

The stimulus that price support gives to production has caused a number of related problems. Large-scale producers of cereals see that hedgerows do not give a sufficient return, and have turned parts of the rural landscape into prairies. The frequent use of chemicals to stimulate food production brings into question the purity of the food we eat.

It is the mountains and lakes of unused foods that tend to focus public anger on the waste of resources created by the CAP. Producing food that no-one wants, that lies in warehouses awaiting buyers that never come, is one of the scandals of the EU's CAP. Even attempts to give away surplus food to the poor and needy have been a source of problems.

The situation shown in Table 8.5 reflects what was to become a pressing problem for the EU in the period from the late 1970s onwards. As surpluses grew, stock levels increased and action had to be taken to reduce them. The cost of warehousing rose substantially, and a storage industry grew up tailored to the needs of looking after the surpluses. The problem was compounded by the deterioration of many of the stocks, so that they were not worth their book value. Attempts to sell intervention stocks of beef that were six years old led to a major scandal in the UK in September 1993. There were fears not only about the extent to which the beef had deteriorated, but also that it was stored at a time when less was known about bovine

Table 8.5 Quantity and value of agricultural stocks in the EU

	1990		1991		1992	
	Quantity (1000 tonnes)	Value (ECU million)	Quantity (1000 tonnes)	Value (ECU million)	Quantity (1000 tonnes)	Value (ECU million)
Cereals	14 378	832	17 237	1044	21 842	1388
Milk products	585	520	683	562	227	232
Beef	529	662	837	996	1166	1116
Olive oil	73	94	18	23	56	57
Tobacco	104	24	106	27.4	10	4

Source: As Table 8.4, p. T/96

spongiform encephalopathy (BSE). In 1993, the EU had over 1 million tonnes of beef in storage, of which 164 000 tonnes were stored in the UK.[8]

The cost of the CAP

Surprisingly, little is known about the burden the CAP places on the citizens of Europe, despite the continuous clamour for the budgetary cost to be brought under control. There is a temptation to see the costs of the CAP only in terms of the EU budget, because it is easily measured. This is a narrow and essentially flawed view of the resource cost of the policy. The actual costs are much more widespread, and include

1. the Budgetary cost of market support, including export subsidies and storage costs

2. payments made by the Guidance section of the EAGGF towards structural improvements in the industry and to help disadvantaged areas

3. national governments' budgetary support for research, infrastructure and advisory services

4. transfers from consumers via higher prices being paid for food within the EU.

In the 1988 budgetary settlement, attempts were made to bring the cost of the CAP under control by setting an upper limit on expenditure. While in the past expenditure had been virtually open-ended, because of the cost of disposal of surpluses on to world markets, a ceiling was placed on the EAGGF Guarantee Section of ECU 27.5 billion for that year. In future years the cost was not to rise by more than 74 per cent of the EU's GDP growth rate. So, if the EU grew by 2 per cent, agricultural budgets could grow by only 1.48 per cent. This arrangement was continued after the Edinburgh Summit in December 1992.

Table 8.6 gives a breakdown of the budgetary costs of the CAP, and indicates that prior to the MacSharry reforms the budgetary cost of the CAP was rising.

Table 8.6 The budgetary cost of the CAP in the EU12

	1990	1992	1993	1994[1]
EAGGF Guarantee ECU million	26 453	32 107	35 352	36 465
EAGGF Guidance ECU million	1846	2938	2946	2864
Other Expenditure ECU million	102	139	128	127
Total Expenditure ECU million	28 402	35 185	38 426	39 456
CAP charges[2] ECU million	2084	2209	2488	2265
Net Cost of the CAP[3]				
ECU million	26 318	32 976	35 937	37 190
percentage of GDP	0.56	0.61	0.66	0.65
ECU per head of population	76.6	95.2	103.3	106.5

[1]   Estimates
[2]   The EU's market policy also generates income, firstly from the variable levies on imports, and secondly from payments for organisation of the market for sugar and isoglucose (a sugar substitute)
[3]   Figures are rounded
Source : As Table 8.4, p. T88

The budgetary costs of the CAP were due to increase further as a result of the MacSharry reforms, although as a result of the Edinburgh Agreement in December 1992 agriculture spending was set to decline as a proportion of a larger budget (see chapter 7). In Edinburgh, the 1993 commitments to the CAP were set at ECU 35 230 million with an expected rise in real terms to a maximum ECU 38 389 in 1999, although this figure will increase to take account of the enlarged EU. The MacSharry reforms were expected to cut the cost of the CAP in an indirect way, by reducing the cost of food to the consumer and moving towards the prices that rule in world markets.

The cost of actually improving agriculture via the guidance section of the budget has always been small, while the main budget cost has been the support of prices. However, while the visible budgetary costs of the CAP appear to be high, they do not tell the full story. The extent of national government support can be calculated if the mechanisms of support are transparent, but the issue of state aid has never been fully resolved, because a variety of state services are offered to farmers either at low cost or free of charge. The range of services offered by the Member States also varies, sometimes for the good reason that production conditions are different.

Some of the most interesting estimates of the cost of the CAP have been calculated by the OECD, and are given in Table 8.7. This shows producer subsidy equivalent (PSE), which is a measure of the value of payments made to the farmer as a result of the agricultural policy. These payments come in the form of market support, direct payments and other support. Total PSE is in the form of support measured in ECU, while the percentage PSE relates to the support per unit.

What Table 8.7 illustrates is that the total help (PSE) being given to the farmer is considerably higher than that shown in the EU budget in Table 8.6.

Table 8.7 Agricultural support in the EU to producers (ECU billions)

	1979–1986	1988	1990[2]	1991[2]	1992[2]	1993[2]
Assistance to producers – total PSE[1]	39.58	59.64	64.8	68.3	66.0	67.9
Percentage PSE		37	46	46	49	47	48

[1]   Producer Subsidy Equivalent
[2]   1990 figures onward include East Germany
Source : Agricultural Policies, Markets and Trade – Monitoring and Outlook 1991 & 1993, OECD
1991 & 1993, pp. 121 and 18

National compensation schemes

The existence of national schemes to assist farmers within the Member States has been a feature of the CAP since its inception. Agriculture ministries existed in all Member States, and were expected to promote the development of the farm sector using funds from the national exchequer. Although this intervention made sense in terms of national priorities, it distorted market forces, creating differing sets of national rules for the industry, which offered some countries' farmers a competitive advantage. When surpluses became a problem, they often had the effect of working contrary to EU policy by maintaining and encouraging production. While attempts were made to eliminate these effects, they existed even in the period after MacSharry and the completion of the Single Market; however, they were subject to the agreement of the Council of Ministers.

Germany, for example, offered an aid scheme to compensate its farmers that went well beyond the completion of the Single Market. Its scheme was originally introduced in March 1992 as a one-off payment limited to DM 2.2 billion, based on the utilised agricultural area of each farm. The purpose was to compensate farmers for the loss of a previous scheme based on their being able to charge and retain a VAT supplement. The new scheme was extended in December 1992 for a further three years, with the amount of assistance declining in steps to DM 750 million in 1995, and no further compensation beyond that time.[9] It remains to be seen whether yet another scheme, supported by another strong national priority, is introduced to replace it.

The cost to the consumer

The CAP imposes a considerable burden on the consumer. The consumer subsidy equivalent (CSE) measures this implicit tax imposed on the consumer by agricultural policy. The main component of this is the higher prices, due to market support, that transfer to producers. This amounts to a tax on consumers, which can be seen as a total or a percentage in Table 8.8.

Table 8.8 indicates that it is the consumer within the EU who has to pay prices well above those that rule in world markets. A simple way of measuring the impact would be to compare consumer prices, which would show that in a number of cases EU prices in the shops are 50 per cent higher than those in the USA or Australia. This is perhaps a flawed argument, because

Table 8.8 The cost of agricultural support to EU consumers (in ECU billions)

	1979–1986	1988	1991^2	1992^2	1993^2
Implicit tax on consumers – total CSE[1]	30.05	47.63	52.7	51.3	48.7
% CSE	30	41	42	40	39

[1] Consumer Subsidy Equivalent
[2] 1990 figures onward include East Germany
Source: OECD, *Agricultural Policies, Markets and Trade – Monitoring and Outlook*, various

of the influence of exchange rate movements and the efficiency of national food distribution systems. Attempts to compare EU prices with those in force on the world market are equally flawed, because the EU, along with other exporters, forces down price levels.

The CAP operates in a highly regressive way, in that the burden of the higher food prices generated by the CAP falls disproportionately on the poorer citizens. This is because they have to spend a higher percentage of their income on food. If the MacSharry reforms work, some of this imbalance will be corrected because food prices should fall, and the increased cost of budgetary help will be met by taxpayers. Table 8.9 illustrates how the poorer members of society are disadvantaged by the system.

Table 8.9 Percentage of income spent on food

	Average household	Low-income household
France	19	32
Germany	20	46
Italy	19	43
Spain	28	52
Ireland	23	45
United Kingdom	32	38

Source: *Are You Paying Too Much?* (1991) Australian Government

Agriculture incomes

In the period between 1989/90 and 1990/91, the average farm income within the European Union fell by 11 per cent in real terms. The actual value of output dropped by 6 per cent, but there were increases in cost. Farm incomes declined by a further 3.5 per cent in real terms between 1991 and 1992, despite a 2.9 per cent increase in volume output and a 16.5 per cent increase in the level of subsidies. The CAP therefore not only was increasingly costly, but could not prevent the fall in income levels.[10] The detailed situation for the Member States is given in Table 8.10.

Table 8.10 Real changes in family farm income 1989 to 1990/91

Belgium	−21%	Ireland	−16%
Denmark	−59%	Italy	−5%
Germany	−22%	Luxembourg	−24%
Greece	−11%	Netherlands	−23%
Spain	−8%	Portugal	−27%
France	−1%	United Kingdom	−15%
EU12	−11%		

Source: Commission of the EC (1992), *Farm Incomes in the European Community 1990/91*, p. 11

It was also significant that farm incomes were very unevenly divided, with the bottom 10 per cent of farms having negative incomes, while the top 10 per cent had incomes of over ECU 60 000 in the period 1989/90 to 1990/91. The system could therefore not even claim to assist the small farmer adequately.[11]

The inequality is not just in overall income levels: the system is biased towards the producers of certain products. The major gainers of the CAP are the producers of crops that thrive best in the north of Europe, while the control regimes are strictest in the South. This is illustrated when we examine how total budget spending is divided between products (Table 8.11).

Table 8.11 Percentage EAGGF Guarantee expenditure by product (main items of expenditure only)

	1990	*1991*	*1992*	*1993*[1]
Cereals	14.6	16.1	17.4	18.3
Milk	18.8	17.6	12.7	14.9
Beef	10.7	13.2	13.7	11.7
Oils and fats	13.1	11.0	12.9	8.6
Sugar	5.3	5.6	6.1	5.9
Olive oil	4.4	5.8	5.5	6.5
Sheep and goats	5.5	5.5	5.4	6.44
Wine	2.8	3.2	3.4	4.7

[1] Estimate only
Source: Table 8.4, p. T90

Reform of the CAP

There has been a long history of unsatisfactory attempts to reform the CAP. Initially, most of the concerns were to modernise the structure of agriculture, so that productivity levels could be raised and farm sizes could be made viable. While some progress was made in improving structures, this concern was replaced at the top of the reform agenda by the need to take action to control the rising tide of surplus production.

Reform based on the free market, with only a limited amount of Member State or EU support, is a distant prospect. It is second nature to intervene and try to manage the industry in most European countries, including the UK. The extent of the intervention required to promote reform is a source of debate, but in general most schemes have been based on a regulated and interventionist solution.

Reform in action – the case of milk quotas

Milk quotas are an example of one of the longest running techniques employed as part of the CAP to physically limit production of a commodity. While market elements have become part of the system of quotas, it is an illustration of how the agricultural industry has had to become increasingly regulated in order to operate at an acceptable level.

In 1983, milk products took 30.4 per cent of EAGGF's Guarantee section, in turn was a significant drain on the EU's budget. With production predicted to grow at 3 per cent per annum, it was clear that urgent action needed to be taken. The Commission estimated that a price reduction of 12 to 13 per cent was required to make any impact on production. As this was unacceptable, the EU agreed in April 1984 to the introduction of milk quotas that would apply immediately. The system was to run for five years, with a review after three years. In fact the system remained in place, with some modification to be incorporated into the MacSharry reforms.

On 14 April 1984 it was decided to base the quota for UK farmers on output for 1983 less 9 per cent. The intention was to cut production by 6 per cent and allow 3 per cent to cover special cases, for example for farmers who had been out of production temporarily for that year. Excess production was to be subjected to a super-levy, but only if the quota had been exceeded. The penalty that operated in the 1990s was 115 per cent of the target price, which was well above the market price. Farmers therefore risked a considerable financial penalty if they exceeded their quota.

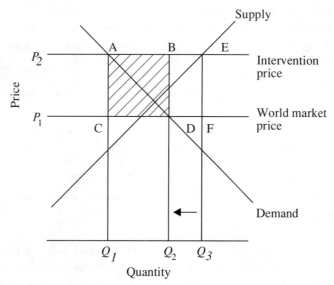

Figure 8.3 The effects of quotas

The operation of quotas is illustrated diagrammatically in Figure 8.3. Q3 is the level of production before quotas are introduced, and Q2 is the level after quotas. In this situation there is still surplus production: the gap between Q1 (consumer demand) and Q2 (the new level of production). The level of export subsidy required to dispose of surplus production would be the gap between P1 and P2. The EU would still have to finance exports to the extent of the shaded area ABCD, but this is an improvement on the situation before quotas, when the cost was ACFE.

The result of imposing quotas was initially encouraging, in that the production of milk did decline, although at the expense of some farmers who found that their business was no longer viable. The consumption of dairy products within the EU remained fairly constant throughout the late 1980s and early 1990s, but there was a trend towards products with reduced butterfat content such as skimmed milk. Despite the introduction of quotas there was still over-production of milk, and the 1984 agreement simply institutionalised surplus production rather than removing it.

This meant that a further cut in quotas was required, and in December 1986 it was agreed that quotas should be cut by a further 9.5 per cent. Between 1985 and 1990, despite an annual reduction in the size of the dairy herd of 2.8 per cent, there was still an increase in yield of 1.6 per cent. In 1991, a further cut of 2 per cent in the total milk quota was introduced in order to move supplies further into balance. This proved to be effective, with a reduction in the herd size in that year of 4.4 per cent and a fall in productivity of 1.6 per cent.

Penalties were not applied rigorously so, for example, if individual farmers over-produced they might well have found that because of under-production elsewhere in their area they did not pay anything. It would have also helped the situation if there had been complete cooperation from the Member States in the implementation of the quotas. However, Italy, Greece and Spain made no progress with their introduction until 1991. In 1993, a total of ECU 2310 million was clawed back from these states. However, this compares with ECU 5380 million that these states received in the form of EU excess spending. In addition, to win agreement, the EU offered for one year only an increased quota of 900 000 tonnes to Italy, 500 000 to Spain and 100 000 tonnes to Greece.

The situation as indicated in Table 8.12 shows that progress was indeed slow, and was made only when the quota was cut. This naturally required a considerable act of will on the part of the Council of Ministers.

Table 8.12 Milk deliveries (production minus farm use and direct sales, million tonnes, EU12 (minus the former GDR))

1986	1987	1988	1989	1990	1991	1992	1993
107	102	99	99	99	97	96	97

Source : As Table 8.4, p. 83

Improvements in technology and the exploitation of new and different breeds of animals can still contribute to significant increases in productivity. Developments like the widespread adoption of the Friesian cow were welcomed in the past, but are now regarded as something to be actively discouraged, because their ability to produce high milk yields adds to the problem of surpluses. In July 1993, the EU prohibited the use of bovine somatotrophine (BST), a hormone that encourages cows to increase their milk production by between 6 and 20 per cent. This was despite evidence that it was safe to use. The reason for the ban was the social and economic disruption its adoption might cause. It was felt that it would reduce further the need for dairy farmers, which in turn might have meant a move towards beef production, which would also be a problem.

The lesson that appears to have been learnt from milk quotas is that it takes time to implement an effective system of reform. Milk quotas have been in place since 1984, and are an important indication of both the strengths and weaknesses of the new regime of resorting to administrative solutions to solve the problem of market imbalance. The MacSharry reforms extended the system of milk quotas until the year 2000, with a reduction of the quota by 1 per cent in 1993–1994 and by a further 1 per cent in 1994–1995. The price of butter was to be reduced by 2.5 per cent in 1993–1994 and in 1994–1995.

The MacSharry reforms

In 1992, the EU agreed a far-reaching package of reforms, covering the organisation of markets in all the principal sectors. These were introduced progressively from 1993 onwards, and covered 75 per cent of the value of EU agriculture. They were an attempt to deal with pressing issues that had been causing concern for some time. If they are successful, these reforms will be seen as a watershed for the CAP.

The purpose of the reforms was seen as being to achieve:

1. a better balance in the markets, by the control of production and by stimulating demand

2. a more competitive European agricultural industry, through a substantial reduction in support prices

3. more extensive production methods, in order to reduce output and preserve the environment, i.e. to discourage very intensive agricultural methods

4. more help and support to the more marginal and vulnerable farmers

5. the maintenance of high levels of employment on the land, while at the same time ensuring that modern efficient structures are created

6. better relations with major international agricultural producers such as the USA and the Cairns Group – these states complained bitterly about the unfair competition, and the USA offered a real threat of damaging the EU's trading interests in other sectors.

The reforms were to be introduced progressively over a period of three years in order to allow farmers time to adjust to the new situation. A range of measures had to be introduced in order to address the multiple objectives of the reforms, including the following:

1. A 30 per cent reduction in the support prices of cereals. This should help the consumer by lowering the price of raw materials to the bakers, and assist livestock farmers by reducing the cost of feed. This in its turn would permit the lowering of beef support

prices by 15 per cent and butter prices by 5 per cent. Pig and poultry producers were expected to benefit to an even greater extent.

2.   A wide-ranging system of taking land out of production would be introduced. This system, called set-aside, had been used in the past but to nowhere near the same extent. All but the smallest farms (those producing not more than 92 tonnes of cereals) were expected to participate by leaving at least 15 per cent of their land fallow.

3.   Payments to farmers to compensate for the lower prices and also for the set-aside land. For those rearing cattle, payment was limited to a maximum headage per hectare of available fodder area. It was not to be made on the basis of the total number of cattle, which would have simply rewarded the farmers who reared their animals intensively.

4.   Aid to farmers who adopted more environmentally sensitive methods, and who were involved in countryside preservation and the conservation of natural resources.

5.   Aid for planting and maintaining forest areas.

6.   An early retirement scheme, particularly aimed at farmers who operated on unviable holdings. The aim was to ensure that consolidation of holdings would make them viable.

Cereals

Trying to reduce the growth of cereal production had been a policy objective for the CAP well before the 1992 MacSharry reforms. In 1988, the EU had tried to use a mechanism called stabilisers, which reduced the price of cereals whenever they exceeded the set target production level. At the same time, there were co-responsibility levies (a kind of tax) which were used to help pay for the disposal of surpluses on the world market, if the target level of production was exceeded. This was not effective, and stabilisers were not part of the 1992 reforms.

Set-aside was first used for the control of cereal production in the EU as part of the 1988 reforms. By 1991, 130 000 hectares of land had been set aside in the EU, which was 2 per cent of the EU's arable land. Ansell and Tranter[12] found in their assessment of set-aside that it allowed many farmers to reduce fixed as well as variable costs of running a farm, and provided a predictable source of income at a time when other sources of income were less predictable.

When the MacSharry Reforms of the CAP were considered, it was believed that set-aside could make a better contribution to the process of controlling production. In particular it was felt that it needed to be more efficiently applied, and at the same time the incentives to participate in the process needed to be increased.

The EU decided to make the basis of set-aside rotational, so that all land was included, not just marginal land. If the set-aside was to be permanent, it would need to cover a larger area. Farmers who chose not to participate could receive compensation for the fall in support prices, to the extent of 92 tonnes. However, the only way of receiving compensation for more than 92 tonnes was to participate in the scheme.

The 1992 version of set-aside was much more inclusive, and was fixed at 15 per cent of the total farm holding on a rotational basis. The advantage of a rotational system was that it reduced the possibility of poor-quality land always being chosen. Farmers could, if they wished, set aside 18 per cent of their land on a fixed basis, as an alternative. The larger area for the non-rotational set-aside reflects the belief that this method of restraining production will be less effective. The land set aside could not be used for producing food products, but it could grow crops with an industrial purpose, such as biofuel.

The 1992 reforms envisaged that assistance to farmers should be given by a mixture of support for prices and direct help. Table 8.13 gives the declining intervention prices within the EU for cereals.

Table 8.13 The fall in cereal prices due to EU reforms (ECUs per tonne)

	Target price	Intervention price	Threshold price
1993–94	130	117	175
1994–95	130	108	165
1995–96	110	100	155

Source : Commission of the EC

Along with the price gained by selling grain in the market, farmers were to receive a direct payment which was to compensate for the falling prices. This was calculated on the basis of ECU per tonne for the whole of the EU. It was set at ECU 25 for 1993–1994, ECU 35 for 1994–1994 and ECU 45 for 1995–1996. Later this was raised to ECU 57 per tonne.[13] This was then translated into payments for farmers based on the historic yields in the region. This gave a higher payment per hectare for farmers in high-yielding regions. It also avoided disputes about the individual productivity of farms. Each of the members was free to decide on the size and number of regions, so the UK opted for five, while France chose to have 90, and Italy 274. In the UK, the system worked out as follows.

1. Farmers were given an area payment per hectare for cereals. In 1993–1994, this was set at ECU 148.25 per hectare for England, where the average yield was 5.93 tonnes per hectare, but only ECU 116.25 for Wales, where the average yield per hectare was 4.65 tonnes per hectare.

2. A ceiling was imposed on the total area payment, based on the average area used to grow the crops in the period between 1989 and 1991. This was to stop areas that had been used for livestock farming, for example, being declared as areas for cereal production. A quota of arable areas could be given to individual farms, if Member States wished it.

3. A condition for the receipt of payments for farms producing more than 92 tonnes in total was that 15 per cent of the arable area of the land be left fallow, and set aside on a rotational basis. The same area of land could not be set aside more than once within a five year period.

4. The set-aside land was also eligible for an area payment. In this case for the crops that were not produced. In 1993–1994 this was 45 ECU per tonne, the actual amount farmers received depending on the average yield in that particular region.

Animal products

The intervention price of beef was to be reduced by 15 per cent over the three years from July 1993. To compensate for the loss of income, those who farmed intensively would gain from the fall in cereal prices. For those rearing the cattle on grassland, a premium (payment) would be paid, once when the cattle were 10 months old and again when they were 22 months old. The amount of the premium would be increased over the period until 1996, but on the assumption of a falling number of cattle per hectare of fodder from 3.5 to 2 over the period from 1993 to 1996. This was therefore aimed at maintaining incomes but encouraging less intensive rearing on grassland. In addition, the amount that the EU would buy into intervention was set to be reduced from 750 000 in 1993 to 350 000 tonnes in 1997. This would have to be high-quality beef only. Beyond this there was a safety net, but only at 60 per cent of the intervention price.

Measures to support the reforms

These come under three main headings: environmental protection, afforestation of agricultural land and early retirement.

Environmental protection

These agri-environmental arrangements were claimed as being a major step towards the integration of environmental policy objectives into the CAP. The measures had a dual purpose of limiting agricultural production and recognising the role of farmers as guardians of natural resources.

This legislation was to be implemented by the Member States, and to compensate farmers who for a period of five years adhered to one or more of the following requirements. They had to:

- substantially reduce the use of fertilisers, use plant protection products, or introduce and continue with organic farming methods

- change to more extensive crop or livestock production

- assist with the maintenance of the countryside

- introduce long-term set-aside for environmental reasons

- make land available for public access or recreation.

Afforestation of agricultural land

Farmers could be paid for planting and maintaining trees, but the programme was to be implemented as part of national or regional plans.

Early retirement

An early retirement was to supplement the national retirement schemes, and was designed to assist farmers and farm workers over 55 to leave the land. The idea was to try and improve the structure of holdings by allowing small farms to expand, which would help to promote their viability. Encouraging early retirement might also help to create more opportunities for young farmers.

The impact of the reforms

It will take many years to assess fully the impact of the reforms agreed in 1992, not least because they were to be implemented gradually over a period to 1996. This meant that there would be short-term responses to an evolving situation. While the intervention price of cereals is due to fall by 29 per cent, the price of beef will fall by only 15 per cent. The budgetary costs were due to rise, and competition within the EU would be restricted by maintaining EU preference. Also, any significant cut in production would have the effect of reducing external competition, because world market prices would rise as dumped supplies fell.

The income that farmers receive will no longer be directly related to the volume of production. That is, farmers will find that it is not always in their best interest to maximise output in order to maximise income. The hope is that most farmers will feel that it may not be worth while to use more and more chemicals or equipment on the land in order to gain only a minor increase in output. It has been suggested that less intensive use of land could reduce output by as much as 5 million tonnes per year. However, it may still be worth while for efficient farmers to maximise output, simply because they can sell the extra production on the open market at the new lower prices and still make a profit.

The effectiveness of the set-aside arrangement is also the subject of debate. The rotation of the set-aside should work in an ideal world, but it may take some time to take the best land out of production. As small farmers are excluded from the process, there may be some scope for circumventing set-aside by the splitting of holdings. In any case, small farmers produce 33 per cent of the EU's cereals, and cultivate 40 per cent of the area. This means that the potential for reducing production via set-aside is reduced to 9 per cent, or 10 per cent if we take account of the higher yield of larger farms. It has been estimated that the combined effects of set-aside and lower yields could reduce output by as much as 12 million tonnes per year, which compares with a surplus in the region of 30 million tonnes per year.[14]

The situation in 1993 was, however, something of a disappointment. The cereal harvest for that year declined by only 1.1 per cent. The reason for only a small fall in production was the exemption from set-aside enjoyed by small farmers who produced less than 92 tonnes per year. At the end of the 1994 harvest, the situation was very different. The Council of Ministers voted to reduce the area subject to set-aside by 3 per cent to 12 per cent. This decision was based upon a concern that cereal production had dropped to 162 million tonnes, compared to 185 million tonnes prior to the introduction of the MacSharry Reforms. It had led to cereal prices rising to a higher point than was felt desirable. The stock of cereals had fallen from 33 million tonnes in July 1993 to 18 million tonnes in July 1994, and was expected to fall to 10–11 million tonnes by July 1995. It was expected that there would be little impact on the EU's budget as a result of the decision, but that output of grain would increase by 3.5 million tonnes. This decision was a recognition that control of agricultural production is a very uncertain activity. It also showed a resolve on the part of the EU to maintain its self-sufficiency in the production of cereals.

The reduction in prices also has the potential to increase the use of cereals for animal food. The effect of a 30 per cent cut in prices depends to an extent on world market conditions, because many of the cheap substitutes have good access to EU markets. Suggestions are that the increased consumption could be between 4 and 12 tonnes per year. This would still leave the EU as a producer of surpluses. However, the cost of disposing of the surpluses would decline, if world market prices rose significantly. The rise in world market prices might, however, encourage non-EU producers to increase their output.

The process of regulation of set-aside is complex, because of the need to monitor the activities of farmers very closely. For that reason it requires increased administrative resources to make it work. Modern technology can assist the implementation of the scheme, for example by using satellite surveillance to ensure that farm land is being used for the purposes claimed. However, farmers find that they are under increasing pressure because of the need to account for their activities.

In addition to the technical issues, the control of production by the use of set-aside has created some more general concerns. Farmers involved in set-aside may feel that they have been deprived of their primary purpose, which is to cultivate their land to its maximum potential. Individually, therefore, farmers were always likely to wish to reduce the impact of the measures, although collectively they might wish to control total production. For society in general, the reforms may be cause for some alarm if the countryside's amenity value is lessened by tracts of land not being cultivated. For that reason, it is important that a maximum area is set for taking land out of cultivation. It is important that significant numbers of farms are not abandoned as part of the process.

The 15 per cent reduction in the support price for beef should encourage consumption. Estimates range from an increase in consumption by 5 to 7 per cent, but this depends on tastes being consistent and there being no changes in the tastes of consumers caused by switches towards healthier diets, or health scares such as 'mad cow disease'. The price of substitute meats is also significant. The organisation of direct payments to farmers means that farmers should be encouraged to maintain herds at more or less the same level.

The income effects of CAP reform

The income effects of the CAP reforms agreed in 1992 are difficult to judge, in part because of the uncertain impact of monetary changes and the differing views of the impact of GATT reforms, and the technical methods of production. The EU Commission tends to take an optimistic view.

The estimates of farm incomes given in Table 8.14 were not released initially by the Commission, but were reported in the *Financial Times*. They show the effect of the MacSharry reforms to be very beneficial to farmers, bearing in mind the decline of incomes in the period prior to the reforms.

The impact of monetary instability is not felt just within the EU. The value of the ECU rises, or falls, relative to the currencies of other agricultural trading nations, because of international monetary turbulence. If the value of the ECU rises against the US dollar, for

Table 8.14 Income effects of CAP reform (% change)

	Total output	Net farm value added	Net[1] value added	Net[2] farm incomes
Small cereal farms	−13	−2	+15	+19
Medium cereal farms	−26	−8	+5	+8
Large cereal farms	−27	−8	−5	−14
Dairy farms	−4	−10	+6	+8
Extensive beef production	−14	−6	+11	+16
Intensive beef production	−13	−9	+11	+16
Mixed dairy/beef	−6	+9	+9	+12

[1]   Revenue before deduction of salaries and rent
[2]   After the deduction of salaries and rent.
Source : The European Commission (1993), reported in the *Financial Times*, 2 April 1993, 4

example, the EU needs to subsidise its agricultural exports to remain competitive in third markets.

In 1993, the first year of reform showed that agricultural income had declined by 1.2 per cent, but in areas affected by the MacSharry Reforms, incomes rose. Incomes in the beef sector rose by 25 per cent, cereals by 11 per cent, and dairy products by 7 per cent.[15] In the UK incomes rose steeply, as the impact of devaluation and the switch-over mechanism took effect. It was suggested that farmers might have seen their incomes rise by as much as 60 per cent.[16]

Impact on related industries

One of the earliest victims of the 1992 reforms was the agrochemicals industry. In 1992, it was estimated that the EU market for agrochemicals declined by between 10 and 12 per cent, although only half of this was related to the reforms: the rest was concerned with the weather. Further declines amounting to 8 per cent were expected over the next two years. Professor Klaus Pohle, Deputy Chairman of Schering, a major chemical company, stated that 'The CAP reforms have really changed the conditions of life. The lower subsidies mean that farmers are unwilling to increase purchases of agrochemicals. At the same time, demands for increasing environmental performance mean higher R&D costs. We have to adapt to a smaller market.'[17]

Other industries will also be affected, for example the sale of tractors and farm machinery will probably be reduced on a permanent basis, although improved farm incomes may mean increased purchases in the short term. The storage industry should also find less use of its services, as surpluses are reduced. However, industries that use food as a raw material will benefit if the price reductions are sustained.

Conclusions

The process of bringing about a successful reform of the CAP is a major economic, political and social task. The industry has been facing a crisis of over-production for some time, which has been created by high levels of support prices. Reducing the level of help that the industry receives is a difficult task, because there are those who argue that it is important to maintain security of food supplies, or who believe that it would be a social disaster if even greater numbers of workers leave the countryside. Indeed, the expansion of the EU to include the Nordic states and Austria increases the number of vulnerable agricultural communities that require support.

The MacSharry reforms will not reduce the total costs of the CAP, although it will take a smaller proportion of an enlarged budget. Prices within the EU will therefore continue to be determined by a political process rather than market forces. This inevitably raises the prospect of conflict if difficult budgetary decisions have to be made. Instability within the European Monetary System could well add further to the cost, given that farmers within countries whose currencies have revalued are likely to continue to press for compensation for falling support prices. The need to ensure that land is set aside and that quotas are adhered to means that the industry will remain highly regulated, which will be a source of frustration to farmers. Indeed, the high incidence of fraud will cause the EU to tighten its monitoring of the industry.

At the end of 1994, the EU had stabilised production levels, and made progress towards eliminating surpluses of cereals. This was achieved by the use of set-aside, which imposed an artificial limit on production. As this situation can only be sustained by maintaining an artificial control on output, the EU needs to move forward by replacing this with more market based mechanisms. The EU should make progress in ensuring that food prices are not artificially high, and that the industry adopts more environmentally friendly production methods. Less land will need to be cultivated in order to maintain current or reduced production levels, especially if technology continues to improve. This means that a rural policy designed to offer alternative employment in the countryside is essential if the fabric of the countryside is to be maintained. The workers who remain as part of the agricultural workforce will have to be used to produce a wider range of products. For example, there is a clear case for planting more trees, where the climate and soil are appropriate.

The widening variety of problems that the agricultural sector faces, may mean that too much reliance is being placed on the EU to sort out the problems. It could well be more effective to leave the support of the industry to the individual Member States. They could then decide how much they were prepared to pay to maintain this important industry. If this does take place, however, there is a danger that national subsidies will destroy the Single Market in agriculture, which is one of the major achievements of the 1990s.

References

1. **OECD** (1992) *Agricultural Policies, Markets and Trade – Monitoring and Outlook 1991*, OECD, Paris, p. 42.
2. *Farming Weekly*, 2 April 1993, 16.
3. *Europe*, 2 September 1993, 7.
4. **Meester G and Van Der Zee F A** (1993) EC decision-making, institutions and the Common Agricultural Policy, in *European Review of Agricultural Economics*, No. 1, 145.

5. *Europe*, 14 November 1993, 6.
6. *Farmers Weekly*, 2 July 1993, 25.
7. *Financial Times*, 16 December 1994, 2.
8. *The Sunday Times*, 5 September 1993, 1.
9. **House of Lords Select Committee on European Communities (1993)**, *The Implementation of the Reform of the CAP*, 24th Report, Session 1992–93, Hl 79 xxiv, p. XXXVI.
10. *This Week in Europe*, 1 April 1993.
11. **Commission** (1992) *Farm Incomes in the European Community 1990/91*, p. 19.
12. **Ansell D J and Tranter R B** (1992) The five year set aside scheme in England and Wales: an initial assessment, in *Farm Management*, Vol. 8, No. 1, Spring, 19.
13. *The Week in Europe*, 9 September 1993.
14. **Roberts I and Anders N** (1992) Market effects of the 1992 EC reforms for cereals and beef, in *Agriculture and Resources Quarterly*, Vol. 4, No. 4, December, 595.
15. *Financial Times*, 2 February 1994, 34.
16. *Financial Times*, 30 January 1994, 16.
17. **Abrahams P** EC reforms hurt agrochemicals, *Financial Times,* 13 May 1993, 27.

Further reading

Commission (1992) *Agriculture in Europe: Development, Constraints and Perspectives.*
Commission (1993) *Possible Developments in the Policy of Arable Land Set Aside: Reflection Paper of the Commission*, COM (93)226, final, 18 May.
Commission (1993) *The Agricultural Situation in the Community 1993 Report.*
Commission (1993) *Our Farming Future.*
European Parliament (1992) *The Agrimonetary System of the European Community and its Prospects after 1992,* Directorate-General for Research, Paper E1, Office for Official Publications, Luxembourg.
Swinbank A (1993) CAP Reform, 1992, in *Journal of Common Market Studies*, Vol. 31, No. 3, September, 359.

CHAPTER 9

The Common Fisheries Policy: a failure of implementation

Introduction

Fishing is an unusual activity in the modern economy because it is one of man's few remaining commercial hunting activities. In the past the sea's fish were mistakenly regarded as being inexhaustible and available to be exploited by all. Due to modern technology, however, man found ways of significantly increasing the rate at which fish are caught. Given the fact that fish stocks are finite, this inevitably led to a resource crisis. The obvious response was to attempt to control catching effort, a task that was not suitable to be left to the free market. The fact that fish move around the ocean, often breeding in one place and maturing in another, means that control is best exercised on an international basis. Fisheries would therefore appear to be one of the most promising areas for the EU policy-makers. The process of developing the policy proved particularly difficult, however. A combination of national sentiment, the pursuit of national interest, and a basic distrust of international fishing organisations meant that it took 13 years for a stable and comprehensive regime to materialise.

After many years of controversy, the Common Fisheries Policy (CFP) was introduced in its present form in 1983, for a 20 year period. Despite its comprehensive nature, it failed to deliver satisfactory results, to the extent that when the ten year review took place many in the industry felt threatened. The CFP has failed to resolve the problems of

1. over-capacity of the fleet

2. chronic depletion of stocks

3. wastage of fish

4. providing a reasonable standard of living for fishermen

5. an excessively complex set of rules and regulations.

The EU had some success in putting legislation into place, but all the fishing nations have been critical of the implementation of the policy in the Atlantic region, while complex national rivalries meant that there was little progress towards a satisfactory agreement covering the Mediterranean. In 1994 the Commission expressed the hope that this might be in place by 1999.

The EU is not alone in having a problem with its fishing industry. The Food and Agricultural Organisation (FAO) noticed an actual fall in the levels of world fish catches in 1990 and 1991. This was a volume measure, and there had been a decline in the catches of the more popular species during the 1980s. Catches were being maintained by placing a greater emphasis on the lesser known species. In 1989, the fishing fleets of the world lost an estimated $22 billion. The Commission estimated that the cost of poor regulation within the EU was $2.5 billion per year, while the FAO estimated the global cost to be $15–30 billion. This was despite the existence of 200 mile exclusive economic zones.[1]

This chapter examines the reasons why attempts to implement a comprehensive fisheries policy have failed. It has not proved possible to reconcile the contradictory policy aims, including the conservation of fish stocks and the need to ensure that fishermen are employed and their social infrastructure is sustained. In addition, the consumer and the fish processors have not had their needs fully considered. The reason is that there has been an inadequate link between attempts to change the structure of the industry and attempts to promote conservation. There is a need to define the Union's priorities for fishing, in order to ensure that expectations are not out of line with what can be achieved. There has, however, been a reluctance to do this, which has led to a view that although collective action by the EU is desirable, it is unachievable in a practical sense. There is a shared responsibility between the Member States and the EU, which allows decisions to be made but not adequately enforced at the national level. National governments can either choose not to enforce EU law fully or circumvent the policy by offering assistance to their national industry. In part this is based on the belief that the industry is still nationally based, despite the existence of the CFP and an increasing international dimension.

The structure of the industry

The fishing industry is not important in terms of its overall size, although it is of significance to some areas in terms of employment. Table 9.1 gives the comparative size and structure of the industry.

Table 9.1 Structure of the EU fishing industry

	Number of vessels	Gross registered tonnes	Landings (ECU million)	% of GDP
Belgium	205	25 445	78	0.057
Denmark	2 291	122 265	454	0.487
Germany	591	47 900	138	0.013
Greece	21 894	129 729	504	1.023
Spain	20 759	619 329	1764	0.518
France	10 361	205 303	943	0.109
Ireland	1796	55 822	111	0.363
Italy	Not known	282 567	1252	0.160
Netherlands	668	Not known	Not known	Not known
Portugal	16 195	195 879	275	0.670
UK	8283	206 934	622	0.083

Note : The above figures relate to 1989, and exclude the five new German Länder
Source : Commission of the EC (1992), *Community Structural Policy: Assessment and Outlook*, COM (92), 18 March 1992, p. 13

The differences in the average size of vessels and the relative importance of the industry within the Member States is demonstrated in Table 9.1. Only in Greece is the industry worth more than 1 per cent of national income. Although there are more vessels in Greece than in any other Member State, the value of catches is only one-fifth of the Spanish fleet's. The 1995 enlargement added two Nordic states with fishing fleets, however the Finnish and Swedish industries are of minor importance. Only Norway, which rejected membership, had an industry of real importance.

The rationale for a Common Fisheries Policy

There are examples of concern about particular fish stocks being over-fished dating back to the 19th century. The first major investigation into the depletion of stocks of fish available was in 1863, when a British Royal Commission was appointed to 'ascertain firstly, whether the supply of fish is increasing, stationary, or diminishing; secondly, whether any modes of fishing which are practised are wasteful, or otherwise injurious to the supply of fish; and thirdly whether the said fisheries are injuriously affected by any other legislative restrictions'. The report that appeared in 1886 concluded that fish stocks had actually increased, and suggested that fishery statistics be collected to try to avoid unfounded panics.[2]

In the post-World War II period, not only was the scale of fishing operations increased, but it was combined with improved technology. Better design of fishing vessels, improved fish finding equipment, and technological advances in net design and winding gear have meant that catching capacity increases at a rate of around 2 per cent a year, without any increase in gross registered tonnage. Even small boats of under 10 metres, which did not originally require a fishing licence under the CFP, are capable of making a significant contribution to the level of catches. The use of factory ships, which shorten the time spent in transit to ports and process the fish at sea, further enhances efficiency.

Table 9.2 Fishery decline of more than 100 000 tons: peak year to 1992

Species	Peak year	Peak catch (million tons)	1992 catch (million tons)	Change (%)
Pacific herring	1964	0.7	0.2	−71
Atlantic herring	1966	4.1	1.5	−63
Atlantic cod	1968	3.9	1.2	−69
Southern African pilchard	1968	1.7	0.1	−94
Haddock	1969	1.0	0.2	−80
Peruvian anchovy[1]	1970	13.1	5.5	−58
Polar cod	1971	0.35	0.02	−94
Cape hake	1972	1.1	0.2	−82
Silver hake	1973	0.43	0.05	−88

[1]   The catch of Peruvian anchovy hit a low of 94 000 tons in 1994, less than 1% of the 1970 level, before climbing back to the 1992 level
Source: The Times, 27 July 1994, 7, quoting FAO sources

Nations saw fish as a useful supplement to human diets, and also recognised that it had industrial uses for animal food and fertilisers. The industry was encouraged to such an extent that some fish stocks started to collapse. By the 1960s the problem was widespread. As a consequence, some types of fish started to become scarce (Table 9.2).

Fish stocks can decline for purely biological reasons, but there are strong indications in Table 9.2 that over-fishing caused the problem. If fishing is kept at a low level, a large number of fish survive to grow to maturity and breed. Consequently the average size of each vessel's catch will rise as the fish become more plentiful. If fishing increases to the point where the breeding stock is affected, then the size of fish tends to be smaller and the age is younger. The primary problem with the CFP is that there is over-fishing of a finite resource.

The decline in supply need not make an industry unprofitable in the short term, if demand is inelastic or increasing. Indeed, falling catches may even stimulate investment because the product is more valuable. The problem of relating capacity to the available stock is illustrated in Table 9.3 below.

Table 9.3 Value of landings in the UK compared with active fleet size

Year	Real value of landings in 1992 prices (£ million)	Annual average active gross tonnage (000s)	Ratio of opportunity to capacity (1983 = 100)
1983	476.7	185.8	100
1985	505.7	163.1	120.9
1987	619.8	157.1	153.8
1989	517.6	176.0	114.6
1991	445.8	173.0	100.5
1992	404.2	181.4	86.9

Source : House of Commons (1993) Agriculture Committee, Sixth Report 1992–93, *The Effects of Conservation Measures on the UK Sea Fishing Industry*, p. 69

What Table 9.3 shows is that there were two periods for the UK fleet. Up to 1987 the size of the fleet was falling, but the value of the catch was rising. After that the value of the catch fell, while the fleet increased in size, presumably attracted by the rising earnings in the previous period. The trend in the second period reflects the difficulty in adjusting capacity in the short term, because owners are locked into their investment.

Increasing the catching effort may not seem sensible in a time of falling stocks, but from the point of view of the individual fisherman or nation state it could appear perfectly logical if there is a free-for-all. With no agreed rules of management, anyone increasing catches does so largely at everyone else's expense. If any individual decides to control catch levels, the existence of 'free riders' means that the sacrifice merely benefits others. The answer, therefore, must be some kind of collective management of the resource which offers tangible benefits to those who participate in conservation.

Any collective action must take account of biological constraints. The basis of most modern discussion of fisheries economics concerns the following model, Figure 9.1, which sets out some of the broad objectives of fisheries policy.

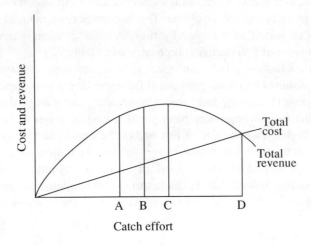

Figure 9.1 Objectives of fisheries policy

This simple model suggests possible targets. It does not, of course, take account of social and regional considerations, which can be very important for isolated communities totally dependent on fishing.

Point A is the profit maximisation position, with the greatest gap between total cost and total revenue. Point B is the suggested optimum sustainable yield (OSY) This allows margin for error. Point C is the maximum sustainable yield (MSY). Beyond this point any increased fishing simply reduces stocks, and less is available for the future. Point D is the point that the industry would operate at if there were no regulation.

Apart from man's activities, other factors such as disease affect fish stocks, so that biological estimates can never be exact. This has led to a consensus that the most desirable objective is OSY, because it allows a margin of error. The problem is that there is no exact agreement as to where it is, except that it lies to the left of MSY. All those interested in the sea-fishing industry agree that the industry should be organised on a sustainable economic and biological basis, but it is not clear what this means in practice.

The lack of scientific certainty has, in the past, been exploited by non-conservation minded states to justify fishing in excess of the MSY. The objective of OSY can therefore never be realistically achieved unless there is an agreement about resource management and its enforcement. This implies that the concept of free access to the fish stock must be abandoned. However, the problem of adjusting fleet sizes and social considerations means that, unless stocks are near collapse, there must be time to adjust.

Conservation policy has historically been on a biological rather than an economic basis. This has therefore amounted to stocks being managed by either controlling the rate at which fish are caught or regulating the size of fish that can be caught. The difficulty is that there is still an economic incentive to cheat on the systems of control that are put into place.

Failed attempts at international cooperation

In order to achieve any kind of fisheries policy with objectives not compatible with open exploitation, there must be an effective method of imposing controls on catching effort. Attempts were made to do this by international cooperation. Most notable within European waters was an organisation called the North East Atlantic Fishing Commission (NEAFC). This had a wide membership, including Eastern European states. Typically NEAFC ignored scientific advice in setting total allowable catches (TACs), because it wished to accommodate all claims to stocks in order to gain agreement. Added to this, the will to enforce agreements did not exist. An example of NEAFC's inability to act was its failure to stop herring fishing, despite the depletion of the Atlanto-Scandian stock. Only in the 1970s did it introduce closed seasons, but these simply resulted in increased fishing for the rest of the year. NEAFC failed as other similar organisations did because:

1. it had no real control over stocks – the fish existed in the high seas or within national territorial waters

2. there was no source of pressure to encourage a realistic agreement

3. sanctions could not be easily imposed.

The NEAFC was disbanded in the late 1970s, only to be resurrected in the early 1980s as a forum for consultation.

Extending fisheries limits

Until the 1950s the seas were largely free for all, with only three mile limits in force. This allowed the development of distant water fleets which could exploit fishing grounds far away from home. The pressure on fish stocks helped to bring about rapid changes in the international law of the sea, and we are now in a position where 200 mile exclusive economic zones (EEZs) predominate. The sovereign states have the right to exploit the resources within the EEZs. What is left outside these areas, about two-thirds of the world's oceans, is of relatively minor importance, given that fish stocks tend to be concentrated on the continental shelves, which are generally within 200 mile limits. The 200 mile limit meant that the effective jurisdiction of states with long coastlines has increased dramatically. In the case of Iceland, the extension to 200 miles was the final stage of a 30-fold increase in the area under its control.

Not surprisingly, these developments caused conflict as they tended to be in advance of international law. It was not until 1982 that the United Nations Law of the Sea Conference number three (UNCLOS III) agreed to 200 mile EEZs, and yet they were firmly part of the scene by 1977, the year that the EU members extended their limits. The agreement had not been formerly ratified even in the early 1990s.

The enclosure of much of the world's fishing grounds had three important consequences:

1. some countries became net beneficiaries in terms of the areas they could fish without competition, while others lost out by being excluded

2. it led to the displacement of many of the distant water fleets from what had become their traditional fishing grounds

3.   it gave the opportunity for firmer control over fisheries

4.   in most cases control based on 'ownership' was the only realistic alternative to the failed attempts at cooperation.

All the above points had implications for the CFP: in particular, the displacement of distant water fleets meant that some compensation was sought in domestic waters. The UK distant water fleet had caught 239 634 tonnes in 1974, or about a quarter of the national catch. By 1981, catches by this part of the fleet were down to 10 726 tonnes. The distant water vessels largely waited to be scrapped or did other work, as they were not suitable for domestic operations. Their decline was not attributable to the EU, yet it soured relations with the UK demands for compensation. The nationalisation of fishing grounds meant that the states of the EU could move towards the rational exploitation of fishing resources. This, however, depended on being able to find an adequate mechanism for their allocation amongst member states. It also meant that when the Spanish and Portuguese became members in 1986, access to additional fish stocks had to be purchased by the EU, largely from developing countries. These were predominantly states that felt unable to exploit the full potential of their fishing assets.

Objectives of the CFP

The CFP relies on the objectives set for the Common Agricultural Policy (CAP) in Article 39 of the Treaty of Rome. This states that there should be a rational development of production and the optimum utilisation of the factors of production, in particular labour. There should also be a fair standard of living for those who work in the industry, markets should be stabilised, supplies should be available and they should reach the consumer at reasonable prices.

The above objectives were refined in Article 1 of Regulation 170/83, which set in place the new regime as being:

'...the protection of the fishing grounds, the conservation of the biological resources of the sea and their balanced exploitation on a lasting basis and in appropriate economic and social conditions'.

The development of the CFP

The lack of a specific reference in the Treaty of Rome reflects the fact that the industry was small relative to the economies of the Six, and there were more urgent priorities. Also, the industry was subject on the catching side to the influence of other international agencies. However, as trade liberalisation started to affect the less efficient French and Italian fleets, it was clear that help would be required. It took from the mid-1960s to 1970 to agree on a policy. The spur to agreement was the possible accession of new members.

When the original six launched the CFP in 1970, it was not the ideal organisation to run a fisheries policy, especially on the catching side. One member had no coastline at all, three had only short coastlines, and one was a Mediterranean state and was not involved in regulation of fish in the area covered by the CFP.

Not only did EU officials lack experience of the area but, more importantly, the major European fishing nations were not members. To compensate for this, however, the EU had certain advantages. Firstly, the EU could win agreement over a broader range of issues than just fishing, so that losses and gains could be traded. Secondly, the EU had some mechanisms to ensure that policies were actually carried through. So, despite its imperfections, the EU was superior to organisations like NEAFC. It could of course be argued that the best possible solution would be to leave it to nation states once 200 mile limits had been declared, but such a declaration seemed only a distant possibility in 1970.

The regulations adopted in 1970 introduced, first of all, a marketing policy, which involved withdrawing surplus fish in order to support prices, in a method similar to the CAP. Secondly, the principle of non-discriminatory access to Union fishing grounds was introduced. This implied that Union fishing grounds were a shared resource and fishing fleets could operate up to the beaches of Member States. Agreement as to the basis of policy came on the very day of the formal application for EU membership of Britain, Denmark, Ireland and Norway. As the four applicants had by far the largest stocks of fish within their 12 mile limits, the move was to generate considerable resentment. Non-discriminatory access took away an important source of protection from foreign boats afforded to inshore fishermen, many of whom lived in communities highly dependent on the industry. Britain, Denmark and Ireland were able to delay full application to the CFP for 10 years as part of the Accession Agreement, but Norway, partly as a result of the proposed CFP, opted to stay out of the EU. This decision was repeated in 1994, when Norway again decided to remain outside the EU, partly because of a fear that EU conservation measures would not be adequate to protect fish stocks.

The movement from 12 to 200 mile limits in 1977 increased substantially the EU's role in fisheries management. It caused the creation of Directorate General XIV within the Commission in order to manage the process. It had been hoped initially that fishing rights could be renegotiated for the distant water fleets. There was very little progress in this direction, and so they went into sharp decline. The EU had then to allocate fish largely from its own resources within the communal 200 mile limits. Non-EU fleets were, however, largely excluded from these waters.

The EU's main policy instrument after 1977 was the total allowable catch (TAC). This is simply a target level of catches devised on the basis of what fish of each particular type are thought to be available for exploitation within Union waters. The TAC is then broken down and distributed to national fishermen on some agreed basis. It is a highly administered solution of allocation, and modified considerably the principle of open access agreed in 1970. The long-term objective of this kind of policy should be a move towards the goal of OSY so that fish stocks would not be depleted, but it was recognised that it would take time to adjust fleet sizes.

Allocation by quotas involves difficult political choices, especially when demand for fish exceeds the supply thought to be available. The EU started with no established basis for policy, consequently the process of decision-making was often very acrimonious, largely because of what appeared to be incompatible claims to the limited resources. For the UK and Ireland, the ideal solution would have been allocation based on the quantity of fish available within national 200 mile limits. The UK, with its very long coastline and rich fishing grounds, probably had 60 per cent of the EC's North Atlantic stock. Traditionally, however, the UK's exploitation of these stocks was not as great as it might have been because of the reliance on its distant waters fleet.

The initial proposal, put forward by the Commission in 1977, was based on traditional fishing patterns. It offered the UK only 24.4 per cent of the volume of catches. This gave no real compensation for losses of catches off Iceland, and did not reflect the UK's contribution of about 60 per cent of the fish. It became clear at that time that the CFP was even more disadvantageous to the UK than had been first thought. As a consequence it took six years of bitter dispute to establish the basis of a permanent policy. Three factors helped to bring about the eventual settlement on the 25th January 1983:

1. the recognition that the UK case had some merit

2   the end of the 10 year postponement of fully open access imposed by the Accession Agreement

3. the threat posed by the very large Spanish fishing fleet having access to EU waters as a result of membership.

The settlement was actually an agreement of quotas for 1982, the year past, but it established the basis for future annual allocations. Table 9.4 gives one version of the settlement: the EU did not publish its own, thus allowing different nations to put their own complexion on things.

Table 9.4 Allocation of quotas for 1982: the basis for future settlements

	Tonnes	%
Belgium	28 900	2.0
Denmark	344 000	24.2
France	183 000	12.9
West Germany	182 000	12.8
Ireland	60 700	4.3
Netherlands	100 800	7.8
UK	509 500	35.8
EU10	1 424 000	99.9

Note : The above apply to what are known as cod equivalents. This is a formula that allows the worth of fish to be standardised as follows: cod (1.0), haddock (1.0), redfish (0.87), whiting (0.86), saithe (0.77), mackerel (0.3). If all fish were taken to be of equal value, the UK's would be something like 30 per cent
Source : Eurofish Report, 27 January 1983

The allocation in Table 9.4 gave a relative stability to the industry:

1. it avoided an annual debate on how the TAC was to be allocated

2. it did not guarantee actual tonnages, because these depended on the state of fish stocks.

The agreement was to last 20 years. In addition to the quotas, for a period of 10 years, extra protection was given to some communities particularly dependent on fishing by an exclusive national 6 mile limit, and a larger area where restrictive 12 mile limits applied. Also, in an area off the Shetlands boat sizes were restricted, and in other areas industrial fishing was prohibited.

Assimilating the fleets of the new members

The accession of Spain and Portugal in January 1986 created the most important challenge facing the CFP, for as a consequence the Union had to cope with:

1. a doubling of the number of fishermen

2. a 75% increase in catching capacity

3. more complex external relations, as Spain and Portugal (especially Spain) take a significant portion of their fish outside EU waters.

The Accession Agreements allowed for a seven year period for the industries to adjust to the EU regime, although they were originally not due to become full members until 2003. This was reconsidered as part of the Scandinavian enlargement negotiations, when it was agreed that they would become full members in 1996.

The fishing industries of Spain and Portugal were not similar. The Portuguese fleet was old: about 75 per cent was over 15 years old, and only 6000 of the 16 000 vessels were motorised, the rest being powered by oar and sail. Not unnaturally, the fleet mostly confined its activities to the 12 mile coastal limit from where about 80 per cent of the country's catch came. A good deal of the rest of the catch was made up of distant water catches, but most of the fish was sold fresh, because of a lack of freezing and storage capacity. The problem of Portugal's industry was a lack of modernisation and investment.

In contrast, the average size of the 17 500 vessels that made up the Spanish fleet was very much larger. It contained 2500 trawlers and 500 freezer ships. The fleet operated in many parts of the world, and had an annual catch of 1.1 million tonnes. This complicated the EU's external fisheries relations, as the Commission had to negotiate with many more non-EU countries to maintain Spanish access.

Within the Union, the problem was the lack of discipline shown by the Spanish fleet. The fleet has the reputation of frequently ignoring regulations, for example not declaring catches and fishing without licences. Many Spanish fishermen saw membership of the EU as a way of unlocking the riches of EU fishing grounds. Countries such as Britain, France and Ireland wished to keep them at bay as long as possible.

The unification of Germany caused some renegotiation of the CFP external relations, as did the collapse of the Soviet Union. However, the greatest potential for change came with the enlargement negotiations in 1994. Both Sweden and Finland had fishing fleets, but Norway created the prospect for greatest change to the CFP. Sweden was a net importer of fish, and the catching side of the industry contributed only 0.06 per cent to GDP. The problems of over-exploitation of the Swedish fishing grounds were similar to those faced by the EU. In contrast, fishing was important to Norway, where the industry contributed 6 per cent of the country's exports and landings were in the region of 2 million tonnes per year. The addition of the Norwegian fleet would add 17 per cent to the EU fleet tonnage, and increase the number of fishermen by 10 per cent. Norway's conservation policy was not only more stringent than that of the EU, but also more effective. Membership of the EU threatened to weaken its system of fisheries management, but had the advantage of offering tariff-free access to Norway's most important market.

Operating the CFP

Budgetary costs

The cost of the CFP has risen considerably since the early 1980s. In 1983, the total cost was ECU 29 million, but by 1986 it had risen to ECU 97 million. By 1992 the CFP was costing ECU 502.8 million. While in 1983 ECU 25.8 million was spent on market support, this was only a small percentage of the cost in 1992, as is shown in Table 9.5.

Table 9.5 Distribution of CFP expenditure in 1993

	ECU million
Market support	33.0
Structural measures	221.4
International agreements	216.3
Marine inspection	32.1
Total	502.8

Source : Court of Auditors (1993), Annual Report: 1992, *Official Journal of EC*, 16 November, p. 93

The cost of structural measures rose, in order to meet the problems of excess capacity and to make a contribution towards the modernisation of the fleet. Also of considerable significance was the cost of buying into the rights to exploit non-EU fish stocks. Not unnaturally, there was some debate as to the desirability of the EU's meeting these costs, when it was commercial fishing vessels that were benefiting from access to the stocks.

Market support

The market support system of the CFP has been in operation since 1970. It has generated less controversy than the catching side of the policy. The policy is carried out by producer organisations (POs) whose members are the union fishermen. Membership of the POs is voluntary, and fishermen pay a levy to belong. The Council of Ministers fixes a guide price for different species of fish annually. From this is derived a withdrawal price, and the POs will not sell their members' fish below it. The surplus fish must be disposed of in a way that does not interfere with normal marketing practices, and must not be used for human consumption. Compensation is paid, but on a sliding scale to discourage catching that will result only in the fish being dumped. POs are expected to pay a limited amount towards any compensation, the rest being made up by EU funds.

The cost of the market support is low, partly because of the digressive system of compensation. Also, the EU is a net importer of fish, so that tariffs can be used to discourage cheap imports and maintain prices. For example, in order to maintain fish prices, the EU reintroduced minimum import prices in March 1994.

Management of fish stocks

Council Regulation (EEC) 170/83 set down the basic policy for the management of stocks, and carried forward some of the existing regulations, which had been in place since 1977. It provided for:

1. setting an annual total allowable catch (TAC) for each stock of fish where there is a need to restrict the level of catch – this is based on scientific advice

2. sharing the TAC among the Member States, according to an agreed formula

3. setting specific rules for particular areas, such as the type or nationality of boat

4. laying down standards with regard to fishing gear

5. establishing minimum landing sizes for fish

6. restricting the amount of fish caught.

The EU sets TACs for 103 stocks of fish based on the scientific advice it receives from the Advisory Committee on Fisheries Management of the International Council for the Exploration of the Sea (ICES). The Member States are responsible for monitoring the fishing activities and enforcing Union law within the 200 mile limit off their coasts. Fishermen are required to record the level of catches and the areas that they have fished in a European Union logbook. Member States are then required to report to the Union the level of catches on a monthly basis. The efforts of fishermen are monitored by the national fishing inspectorate, which in its turn is monitored by a very small number of EU inspectors.

The management of catching capacity to the existing stock is carried out by a Multi-Annual Guidance Programme (MAGP) which is formulated after discussions with the Member States. This sets targets for the reduction of the fleets. Incentives can be made available for the retirement of fishermen, and the disposal of their vessels either by scrapping or by disposing of them outside the EU. States that do not meet the targets do not receive funding towards the building and modernisation of their fleets. However, in the past this has proved an empty threat to countries such as the UK, which did not seek funds for this purpose. Indeed, in the period 1987–1991 the UK failed to meet its objectives by 11 per cent. The EU planned a reduction of 8 per cent in the gross registered tonnage in the period 1992 to 1996.

Conservation of fish stocks

No conservation measure is painless to the fishermen. Given the finite nature of the resources, conservation will always be the major issue concerning the operation of the CFP. The EU has used quotas and controls over fishing methods to try to balance catches with the supplies available. The Fisheries Council of Ministers has shown a willingness to respect scientific advice, and some tough decisions have been taken, which should be of long-term benefit to the industry. However, the EU started to control catching at a time when it had over-committed its stocks. This was because of an overestimation of what was available, plus the rather cynical way in which the 1983 agreement had been reached. This was another occasion when 'paper fish' had been conjured up to ease the negotiation process. From 1985, catch quotas were agreed prior to the start of the year, and some stocks, once under pressure, started to shown signs of recovery, thus making more fish available for distribution. Regrettably, this has not been the case universally.

The setting of the TACs was criticised on the grounds that:

1. there is inadequate information about the precise nature of the fish stocks

2. they are often fulfilled early in the year, which is disruptive for both the consumer and the fishermen – it leads to situations of glut and shortage

3. they are set without taking full account of the wider social context of the fishing industry.

Wastage of fish

Information about the level of catches is difficult to obtain, because often as much as 40 per cent of the fish that are caught have to be discarded at sea. This is because they are not part of the right quota, or are undersized. They have to be thrown back because the alternative would be to permit fishermen to land these catches, which would reward those who had broken the regulations. To make matters worse, the fish normally die when they are rejected.

Part of the reason for the discards is that fish are sometimes mixed, so that efforts to catch one kind of fish means that others are caught. If the quota has run out, then these fish cannot be landed. This seems to suggest that there may be a case for some flexibility between quotas. With regard to the fish rejected because they are undersized, there is a clear case for improved net design.

Enforcement

The fact that the Union relies on regulation to control the level of catches means that the supervision of the industry is a major issue. This is an industry where there is between 25 and 40 per cent over-capacity, and there is a strong temptation to break rules with regard to the level of catches. This can only be resolved in the long term by reducing capacity, but in the short term the EU relies on the Member States to monitor the industry by the use of national inspectors, who are in turn supervised by 22 Union officials. The Commission has taken active steps to try and improve the quality of inspection, but in 1989 the European Parliament pointed out that many still did not wholeheartedly cooperate. It observed that:

'...the lack of uniformity in the application of Community rules by Member States gives rise to unacceptable differences in the treatment of fishermen, all the more so in that some Member States are stricter with fishermen from other Member States than with their own nationals'.[3]

The UK devotes most resources to the enforcement of regulations (Table 9.6). This is in part a function of the large sea area that the UK has within its fishing limits. There are many examples of deliberate under-recording of catches, with boats having secret holds and fraudulent logbooks. By its nature the extent of illegal fishing is almost impossible to measure. However, a number of boats record only half their actual catches.

Table 9.6 Comparison of Member States' enforcement

	Shore-based inspectors	Inspection days at sea	Inspection planes	Aerial surveillance hours
Belgium	3	30	1	15
Denmark	200	200	0	0
Germany	20	200	0	0
Spain	12	0	–	50
France	20	850	–	500
Ireland	7	1000	2	700
Netherlands	180	100	0	0
Portugal	12	–	3	100
UK	152	2500	5	4800

Source : House of Commons Agriculture Committee, Sixth Report 1992–93, *The Effects of Conservation Measures on the UK Sea Fishing Industry*, p. 71, based on Commission of EU figures

Minimum net size regulations are similarly ignored. With poor enforcement comes the prospect of the fines being inadequate to deter boats that are caught contravening the rules. Finally, in a number of Member States, there is little possibility of action being taken if illegal catches are landed. There is for example an active market for undersized fish in Spain, where they are considered to be something of a delicacy.

The uneven enforcement encourages others to break the rules, and the Commission has criticised the lack of adequate resources in nearly all the Member States. The worst case is that of Spain, which has the largest fishing fleet but where the inspectors are based in Madrid.

The solution to these difficulties lies in increasing the number of Union inspectors, and at the same time considering the viability of establishing a Union fisheries service. This must be accompanied by a willingness of the Member States to cooperate fully in the system, and a change in attitude by the fishermen themselves. In the short term, it would be helpful if national inspectorates were able to operate within the territorial waters of another Member State. This may not be acceptable because it would threaten national sovereignty, but it should be recognised that over-catching means that all fishermen suffer in the long term. Suggestions that satellite-based systems might be used to resolve some of the problems have not been met with great enthusiasm, because they would do little to deter many of the present illegal practices, such as the use of wrongly sized nets.

Reducing capacity

Ideally a fishing fleet should be kept occupied most of the time in order to ensure profitability. If the main problem is that there are too many boats chasing too few fish, the solution is to reduce the capacity of the fleet. This can be done by allowing the market mechanism to operate, which suggests that the fleet would decline as the operators of the boats either left the industry to move into other areas of work or went bankrupt. This strategy would almost inevitably bring about social hardship, which might be concentrated in remote areas that are very dependent on fishing. It could also be very damaging to fish stocks, as it increases the risk of cheating on quotas, as a means of survival.

Planned decommissioning to bring the fleet's capacity into line with available stocks requires funding. In the past, this has had only a limited impact, because only the oldest and least efficient ships are taken out of commission. The cut in the fleet's catching capacity must also take account of the improved technical efficiency of the fleet. Also, there would be a need to take out of service the very smallest boats, which are an important part of some fleets, and to ensure that all vessels are licensed. In the late 1980s, of the ECU 253 million given for multi-annual guidance programmes, only ECU 98 million was given for capacity reduction. However, the measures, by increasing efficiency, actually increased the catching potential in the areas of heaviest fishing. This took capacity out of the EU fleet, but many of the vessels were simply used outside the EU.

The funding of decommissioning should ideally be shared, in order to encourage full participation. All states would benefit from the reduction in the size of fleet. However, if one state refused to participate fully, it might gain at the expense of the states that took active steps to reduce the size of their fleet. This is because the remaining fleet should benefit from higher catches. The decommissioning of boats has also been accompanied by help to restructure local economies and to retrain the labour force. Simply compensating the boat owners does not ensure that the fishermen are going to be fully compensated for their loss of livelihood. This is especially true for those who do not own a significant stake in the vessel they work on.

Some of the over-capacity in the EU fleet did disappear, for example the distant water fleets of Britain and West Germany. This was under a scheme that ran from 1983 to 1986, where EU funds were used to supplement national scrapping schemes. More EU money was made available, but Member States were slow to take it up because they believed the EU contribution was inadequate. Also, at times it did not appear to be required. By the time the severe crisis of over-fishing became apparent, the funds made available at a national level were still not adequate to reduce capacity quickly enough.

Restrictions on the number of days at sea

This has the benefit of ensuring that the activities of the fishing boats can at least be monitored. It is an inferior solution to decommissioning, because it means that vessels are kept unproductive for any purpose. It means that there is a temptation to concentrate all the effort into catching days. Also, the restrictions on days will have a limited impact if they are simply the days when boats would have been confined to port because of poor weather. Measures of this kind need to be related to realistic quota restrictions on catching. They also tend to be regarded as highly unjust by fishermen, who regard them as yet another attempt to constrain their livelihood. Attempts to introduce restrictions on the number of fishing days in the UK resulted in a legal challenge in 1994. The case was referred to the European Court of Justice to give its view on the legality of the measure.

Technical restrictions

It would be an ideal solution to a number of problems associated with over-fishing if nets were designed to catch fully mature fish. At the same time, the nets need to be less of a hazard to wildlife. In 1992, the minimum mesh size was increased from 90 to 100 mm for catching white fish (e.g. cod and haddock) in the areas off the west coast of Scotland and in the North Sea. While some immature fish could escape capture, the nets tended to close up when being pulled.

Reforms as a result of the mid-term review

As part of the 1983 agreement, the EU was committed to a mid-term review of the CFP. This was to bring some incremental reforms, which came into effect on 1 January 1993, with the replacement of Regulation 170/83 with Regulation 3760/92 . The main features were:

1. the retention of the 12 mile limits for Member States, and the principle of relative stability which allocated the fish as per the 1983 agreement

2. more emphasis on the control of fishing by the use of multi-annual guidance programmes

3. a new system of Community licensing was to be introduced not later than 1 January 1995, to be operated by the Member States

4. limitations on the days boats can spend at sea.

Completion of the Single Market

The single market impinges on fisheries policy in a number of ways. The first is in the area of state aids. As with most EU policy areas, national governments are involved in promoting the interests of the industry. In the past, a multiplicity of national schemes helped the industry. Some of these, such as fuel subsidies, not only were harmful in that they slowed down the shake-out of excess catching capacity, but also resulted in excess supplies of fish and depressed prices. The amount and scope of national aid is now restricted in order to avoid this. Money can, however, be spent by national governments improving marketing and developing new fishing grounds, but this is subject to Commission approval.

The free movement of goods will offer a competitive threat to the areas that rely on fishing and yet are not fully competitive with either imports or other producers within the EU. A typical example of this problem is the sardine fishery in Portugal. Here there are many small-scale fishermen who eke out a living with tiny boats, many of which are still built in a traditional style. If the industry's catching effort becomes more efficient, many of these boats will not survive, and gone with them will be many jobs that will not easily be replaced. However, if the industry does not become more efficient, the tide of imports will see off the marginal producers also.

Perhaps the most emotive issue concerning the Single Market is that of quota-hopping. The 1983 system set in place a system of TACs, which were then allocated to Member States in the form of quotas. These quotas were designed to be fished only by vessels of that nationality. Quota-hopping refers to the practice of foreign vessels registering under another flag in order to attain access to that country's quotas. It is a problem in the sense that it reduces the amount of fish available for the genuine nationals. Also, because there is often no real economic link between the vessel and the state it is operating in, there are no benefits for onshore industry of the country. Finally, the extent to which quotas are being complied with is difficult to judge. The main victims of quota-hopping have been the British and the Irish, especially off the south-west coasts. Quota-hopping started in the late 1970s as a result of the extension of fishing limits to 200 miles, and became a serious problem in the 1980s. The Spanish boat operators saw that there were significant opportunities in catching fish such as hake. Prices can sometimes be five times higher in Spain for this fish, which is relatively undervalued in Britain.

The first attempt to prevent quota-hopping came with the passing of the British Fishing Boats Act in 1983, but this was not a success. By the time Spain had become a member of the EU in 1986, the British had toughened their provisions with the requirement that British vessels must also have licences. This was subject to a legal challenge, so that in 1988 the British adopted a radical policy via the Merchant Shipping Act. This removed Spanish boats from the register, as it required that the owners and operators be British nationals or, if a boat was operated by a company incorporated in the UK, 75 per cent of the directors and shareholders had to be resident in the UK. This was overturned by the Factortame Judgement of the European Court of Justice, which found that it contravened Community law by preventing business from establishing itself anywhere within the Community. The restrictions were found to be damaging to the idea of the free movement of business within the Single Market.

Of the 150 vessels deregistered as a result of the 1988 Act, 90 were reregistered by 1992. The problem this posed for the CFP was that it meant the end of the strict national quotas which were a feature of the 1983 agreement. In a number of cases, the new arrangements have meant that Spanish vessels have two skippers: the unofficial Spanish skipper who is responsible for directing the crew and the commercial operation of the vessel, and a British national who acts as the official skipper, completes the log book and confers nationality on the vessels. British skippers with this role on Spanish vessels have a rather dull, but well-paid existence.

Conclusions

Although a number of Member States might reflect that they could have done better from the negotiated policy, there seems to be a general acceptance that a reasonable compromise has been achieved in terms of the distribution of the fish stocks. The CFP's success can be measured in two ways. Firstly, its cost is clearly under control, providing reasonably secure marketing arrangements. This does not mean that prices are always satisfactory to the fishermen or the consumer. As long as catches are poor, there will be pressure to raise prices to compensate for this by raising the price of imports. Secondly, there has been a willingness to agree to cuts in fish quotas, although they have not been fully adequate. Where the CFP has failed has been in the actual implementation of the policy. There has been a willingness to agree to one course of action at the EU level and to ignore this at the national level. Conservation polices can work, but only if they are thoroughly implemented, as in the case of Norway.

There clearly must be a reduction in the catching effort by the Member States. This implies that there will be a reduction in the number of fishermen, and that there can no longer be an assumption that this occupation can be passed on from father to son. The only way that the industry can be reduced to the right size is if there is further intervention. Although maintaining grants to scrap vessels can help, the fishermen should see some benefit from an industry that has been reduced in size.

One suggestion is to award quotas to individuals that can be accumulated and transferred across national boundaries. That is, to make the right to fish a valuable commodity that those leaving the industry can cash in. This may give fishermen an incentive to adhere to conservation laws. At the same time, it would mean that capacity could be cut by state or EU action to purchase quota.

Finally, over-fishing damages the wider marine environment. Certain species that live in the sea have been badly affected, such as dolphins, which get caught in tuna nets. The tendency towards the increasing use of drift nets, which can be up to two miles long, means that sea birds often get caught. Nets that drag along the sea bottom can disturb and destroy the wildlife there. The fact that fish are caught to be used for industrial reasons makes matters worse. Some species are caught simply to be processed for oil or fish meal which is used to feed animals. While the industrial fish may have little use as human food, they support important species of bird life. More concern should be shown for environmental issues, although these will perhaps remain less important to the policy-makers as long as the fishermen are dissatisfied.

References

1. *The Economist*, 19 March 1994, 27.
2. Report of the Commissioners appointed to inquire into the fisheries of the United Kingdom, Vol. 1, 1866 (3596), quoted in the House of Commons Agriculture Committee Sixth Report, *The Effects of the Conservation Measures on the UK Sea Fishing Industry*, HC 620, p. IX.
3. **European Parliament** (1989) *Report Drawn Up on Behalf of the Committee on Agriculture Fisheries and Food on Monitoring the Enforcement of the Common Fisheries Policy*, Document A 2-0389/88, 8 February, p. 12.

Further reading

Commission (1991) *Report 1991 from the Commission to the Council and the European Parliament on the Common Fisheries Policy*, SEC (91), 2288, final.

Court of Auditors (1993) *Special Report 3/93 Concerning the Implementation of the Measures for the Restructuring, Modernisation and Adaptation of the Capacities of Fishing Fleets in the Community.*

House of Commons (1993) *The Effects of the Conservation Measures on the UK Sea Fishing Industry*, Agriculture Committee, Sixth Report, HC 620.

House of Lords (1992) *Review of the Common Fisheries Policy*, Select Committee on the European Communities, Session 1992–93, 2nd Report, HL paper 9.

CHAPTER 10

Competition Policy in the EU

Introduction

The EU was founded on the basis of a belief in the free market, although the commitment to this has always been qualified in such areas as agriculture. The free market bias of the EU is most obviously reflected in its Competition Policy. The development of the EU has brought new dimensions in the way in which the economy operates. Competition Policy has become increasingly important as businesses operate on a Europe-wide basis rather than being restricted to an individual Member State. Although merger activity and collaboration will in the short term rise and fall with the ups and downs in the business cycle, the long-term trend will be for the coming together of firms in a way that makes it best for them to exploit the benefits of the Single Market. This could give economies of scale if mergers take place, or firms may benefit from a joint approach to distribution. While these arrangements may bring benefits, they may not always be seen as being in the best interest of the EU.

Competition Policy was an important part of the Treaty of Rome. Article 3(f) calls for a system that ensures that competition in the market is not distorted. The actual rules of competition are set out in Articles 85 to 94 of the Treaty. These rules are directed against the activities of both companies and states. This chapter deals predominantly with Articles 85 and 86, and seeks to demonstrate that the EU Competition Policy has been a positive development. The issue of state aids is dealt with in chapter 11.

The completion of the single market of the EU offered the prospect of a more competitive environment within the EU. Many of the dynamic gains from completion will, however, be lost if restrictions on company activities or abuse of dominant positions are allowed to interfere with the market mechanism. The responsibility for Competition Policy within the EU is shared with the Member States, although the division is not clearly defined between the two. In the UK the Office of Fair Trading and the Department of Trade and Industry deal with the bulk of cases, along with the Monopolies and Mergers Commission.

Competition Policy within the EU involves the monitoring of and intervention into markets to ensure that there is an adequate level of competition. The purpose behind this in economic terms is to ensure that there is an efficient allocation of resources. Underlying this is the belief that the market economy is a more effective way of allocating resources than alternatives such as the state-run economies that were typical of Eastern Europe until the late 1980s. The basis of much traditional economic theory is that the market mechanism works best when there are many buyers and sellers of goods, and consumers are well informed. Under these circumstances all consumers pay the same price, because both the buyer and the seller are aware of what the correct price should be. Any attempt to charge more than the market price will result in a loss of business. It means that suppliers of goods are encouraged to be efficient, and this in turn promotes growth in the economy.

At one extreme some industries might operate under conditions of perfect competition, but examples of this form of market structure are difficult to find. The reality of the modern economy is that there is a tendency for firms that are efficient to grow larger, and that the number of potential rivals is limited. Market economists believe that, unless firms are free to contest (enter) a market, there is a danger of abuse of monopoly power and a lack of sufficient reason for firms to increase their efficiency.

The modern economy contains many firms that are huge and may dominate a national economy. This might not be a problem, as firms may achieve a position of dominance because they are more efficient than their rivals. Provided other firms can contest the market, there is still a threat to even the largest of firms. Even if the source of competition is not immediately apparent, the dominance of all firms comes to an end eventually. This is because the passage of time brings new technology and replaces old products. Competition might not be domestic in origin, indeed in sectors such as the manufacture of airliners there may be room for only two or three producers in the world. In this case, the cost of entry into the market was so high that the only way to make it contestable, was to encourage collaboration. The Airbus was created by bringing together major European companies, supported by a significant level of state aid, to meet the challenge of the US company Boeing.

In its approach to the issue of Competition Policy, the EU has shown itself to be a skilled political actor. While this area is governed by rules that appear to be detailed, the task of the EU, and particularly the Commission, is to interpret these rules in such a way as to ensure that business operates on a European-wide basis. That is, Competition Policy should not constrain the actions of business unless an activity is perceived as being harmful.

The most recent innovation in terms of policy was Council Regulation (EEC) 4064/89, which set out the EU's Merger Regulation. This was an important step, in that it put in place an EU merger policy which:

● established a jurisdiction for the EU intervention

● conceived criteria for EU intervention

● provided a timetable in which decisions are to be taken.

Some evaluation of the above policy is provided in order to demonstrate the way in which policy has moved and developed to take account of the evolution of the Single Market.

Restrictive practices and Article 85

This article prohibits activities that are incompatible with the operation of the market, affect trade between the Member States, and have the effect of restricting, preventing or distorting competition. The article does not come into force unless the activities have an impact, or potential impact, on the normal pattern of trade between the Member States. So, for example, the resale price maintenance on books that operates within the UK, is not forbidden, because it is limited to the activities of book publishers within the state. However, even where an agreement appears to impact on just one Member State, it may infringe Article 85. This is a risk that all businesses have to be aware of. The case of the UK Net Book Agreement[1] was dealt with by the Court of First Instance in 1992 on this basis.

In particular, paragraph (1) forbids agreements that

1.   fix prices or trading conditions

2.   control or limit production, markets, technical development or investment

3.   share markets or sources of supply

4.   make the conclusion of contracts subject to the acceptance by the other parties of supplementary obligations which by their or according to their commercial usage, have no connection with the subject of such contracts.

It is worth noting items 1, 2 and 3 above are dependent on one another, as any practical attempt to fix prices and trading conditions depends on the suppliers having a considerable share of a market. If they do not, attempts to restrict the market will be ineffective. Item 4 refers to attempts to force customers to accept conditions of sale that they might not wish to if they had a free choice. Article (2) declares that agreements or decisions that are prohibited shall be automatically void.

An example of a case under Article 85 paragraph (1), is that of the Belgian brewery, Interbrew. The European Commission announced in April 1994 that the brewery had renounced its exclusive rights to distribute the Danish beers Carlsberg and Tuborg in the Belgium market. The hope was that this would give an impetus to competition in the luxury beer market. The Commission's belief was that the agreement was one of market sharing, which prevented the structure of the market from changing. It allowed Interbrew to maintain its dominance of the national market, at the expense of small and independent producers. As a result of the Commission's intervention the Danish beers then moved on, creating a new distribution company as a joint venture with N V Haelterman SA, another Belgium company.[2] This created another source of competition in the Belgian market.

There may be cases where some restrictions are considered to be a benefit. Paragraph (3) states that the provisions of paragraph (1) may not be applied if there is evidence to suggest that the agreement improves the distribution or production of goods, or facilitates technical or economic progress. However, the consumer must gain a fair share of any of the benefits. Although there is no compulsion to do so, companies are requested to notify the Commission of any agreements that might infringe Article 85. Large numbers of firms have done so in order to be considered for exemption from its effects. There is no guarantee that an agreement can be exempt, even if the Commission initially indicates that it does not intend to challenge it. If the Commission is not informed of an agreement, exemptions are not granted.

An example of an agreement being allowed under Article 85 (3) is that between the 16 Dutch brick manufacturers, which were collaborating to reduce capacity in the industry. The industry was facing a production over-capacity of 217 million bricks, and the agreement was designed to preclude new capacity and to close down seven brickworks. The benefits were said to be that this would make the industry more efficient, and restructure the industry under socially acceptable conditions. The buyers would benefit by choice being maintained, but from a more competitive industry. The agreement was acceptable, because it was time-limited.[3]

Dominant firms and Article 86

This article concerns the activities of firms that abuse their dominant position in the market. The existence of large firms that dominate markets is not in itself a bad thing. Dominance can come about because of a firm's superior efficiency. Having market power by virtue of being better at producing a particular product can be of benefit to consumers, and can be essential in order to be competitive on a worldwide basis.

Article 86 prohibits the abuse of a dominant position, in so far as it may affect the trade between the Member States. It does not make it clear what it considers a dominant position to be, which is sensible given the difficulty of defining these things. What the article does is to set out the kind of practices that a dominant firm should not resort to. Dominant firms should not impose unfair prices or trading conditions on their trading partners. If they use their market power to exploit or maintain their dominance, they can be enforced by the Commission. Unlike the case of Article 85, firms are not expected to report their dominance to the Commission. Prosecutions depend on either the Commission's investigations, or complaints about firms' activities.

The Commission has had less success with the problem of dominant firms, than it has had with restrictive practices, perhaps because of a lack of resources to investigate these activities thoroughly. A case that attracted a great deal of attention in the late 1970s was that against the Swiss multinational Hoffman-La Roche. The company was the dominant producer of vitamins. In the case of vitamins B2 and H, it had something like 80 per cent of the market. The company used fidelity payments as a means of keeping customer loyalty. If customers bought exclusively from Roche, they could expect better prices than if they bought only a few of their requirements from it. These fidelity payments were not related to the quantity purchased, but to loyalty. This restriction had the effect of excluding competitors that might have been able to offer certain products more cheaply. It therefore helped to maintain the company's dominance.

Although Article 86 does not mention merger activity as a method of gaining dominance, it appears that this does fall within the ambit of the Article, in that it may be used to establish dominance. This issue was taken up by the EU's Merger Regulation.

Implementing policy

The implementation of Articles 85 and 86 is the responsibility of the European Commission, and is dealt with by DG IV. The Commission learns about cases from information given by firms, from complaints from third parties, or by acting on its own initiative. It prefers not to act directly on its own initiative, because this is administratively more difficult. Inevitably there are conflicts between the legislation of Member States and that of the EU, given that most Member States have some kind of legislation in this area of policy. While members can deal with cases concerning Articles 85 and 86, they are expected to bow to the superiority of the EU if the Commission decides to take up a case.

The Commission faces difficulties because it is dealing with the activities of companies across 12 national boundaries. The amount of research it can do is limited, and so it tends to find itself restricted in the ground it can cover. The Member States have their own competition rules that seek to regulate activities within the national borders. These are supplemented by EU rules, not replaced by them. Generally it is better for competition cases to be dealt with by national courts because

1. only they can award damages, the threat of which is likely to be a powerful deterrent against abuse

2. cases can generally be dealt with more speedily

3. it is possible to pursue a claim under national and EU law at the same time

4. some national courts have the right to award costs.

The above are strong arguments for the majority of competition cases being dealt with at the national level. However, there is a need to improve on the general consistency of national remedies, so that injunctions and interim measures are applied in the same way, and fines are imposed on a consistent basis.

The Commission prefers to tackle the competition cases that have relevance and importance for the EU. Not only does this reduce the possibility of conflict with the Member States, but it also saves on resources. Publicity is via the *Official Journal*, the monthly *Bulletin*, the annual *Report on Competition Policy*, and press releases. All this helps to ensure that there is regular reporting in the media. The fact that the results are accompanied by significant publicity gives a demonstration effect.

The role of the Commission

The Commission has a very powerful role in the implementation of Competition Policy. Regulation 17 of 1962[4] sets out many of the procedures as they apply to the competition elements in the Treaty. It gives the Commission the power to request information from companies, and to carry out investigations. This may involve examining books and papers, asking for oral explanations on the spot. The method for applying these is described as the 'dawn raid', when Commission officials, along with those from the Member State, enter the premises of companies subject to investigation. After collecting information and ascertaining that an infringement has taken place, the Commission can

● impose fines of up to 10 per cent of the company's turnover of the previous year

● take interim measures to halt damaging behaviour.

An example of a firm refusing to comply with the Commission's request is the long-running dispute concerning Schoeller, the German ice-cream producer. In May 1994, the company was threatened with a fine of ECU 1000 per day if it continued with its exclusive purchase agreements with German shops. This denied other suppliers access to selling ice-cream in those shops, and as such was a restriction on non-German as well as German producers. The formal ban on this practice came into effect in 1982, and in 1992 Schoeller was formerly asked to stop the restriction. Despite this, Schoeller continued, signing 14 000 agreements in 1993 (the Commission threatened to deal with this at a later date). The company argued that it was justified in ignoring the Commission on the grounds that the agreements were for a fixed term of not more than five years.[5]

In the early years of the EU, the Commission had a huge backlog of cases, which was an indication that the Commission was inadequately resourced to enforce the legislation. Resources were increased, and the backlog of cases was reduced from 1700 cases in 1992 to 1231 in 1993. In 1993, of 723 cases being examined by the Commission, 60 per cent were notified by the parties involved, 25 per cent were complaints, and 15 per cent were cases where the Commission initiated proceedings.[6]

The introduction of block exemptions under Article 85 also helped to reduce the workload faced by the Commission, and at the same time offered greater certainty to businesses. These agreements are justified on the basis of an overall benefit. An example concerns motor vehicles, which should ensure that the consumer gains from a distribution system that is fully supported by the car manufacturers. This Regulation has been criticised on the grounds that it has permitted higher car prices in some countries than might have been the case if there had been a free market. Another block exemption concerns research and development agreements, which are the backbone of the EU's policy concerning high technology.

Judicial control of the Commission

The European Commission has frequently been criticised for being both investigator, judge and jury in competition cases. However, the European Court of Justice (ECJ) has the power to review the decisions taken by the Commission, and to confirm or reduce fines and penalties and change all formal decisions. Appeals can also be made against the decision not to investigate a formal complaint. The process of review was improved by the establishment of the Court of First Instance (CFI) in 1988. Its position was formalised under Article 168a of the Treaty on European Union, which attached the CFI to the Court of Justice. One of its tasks was to deal with competition cases. Generally it has been widely praised because it subjected the Commission's decisions to greater scrutiny, and helped to maintain confidence in the process of regulating competition.

Despite the improvements in the way that justice is implemented, there are some areas where the process could be better. A House of Lords report suggested that there was a need for a greater explanation of the Commission's actions, and that the appeals process should be simplified.[7]

Mergers and acquisitions

The completion of the Single Market changed the nature of competition within the EU. Firms faced many more challenges within their home markets, as the borders became more open and non-tariff barriers were removed. A natural part of the adjustment to a larger market was the growth in the size of firms, in order to gain economies of scale in terms of production and research and development. This was in some cases done to protect home markets from the threat of competition from the rest of the EU. In other cases it was an aggressive strategy to try and take the opportunities offered by the enlarged market. While some firms were happy to grow within their own resources, others felt that there were significant benefits to be gained from the acquisition of other businesses.

Some firms consolidated their home base, but aimed to move later into cross-border acquisitions. In other cases, the pace at which firms could expand from their home base was limited. To generate resources for acquisitions, some firms divested themselves of certain assets and concentrated on their core activities. This allowed firms to expand geographically, and one of the quickest methods of doing this was to merge with firms in other states. The sale of assets also generated opportunities for other firms to acquire further assets.

The value of cross-border merger activity increased dramatically after the launch of the Single Market campaign. In 1989 it reached a peak of ECU 44 billion, which was three and a half times the level of 1986. After that time the value of bids went into decline, in part because of the impact of the recession. The merger wave was expansionary, and a way of achieving a presence in the markets of other Member States quickly. In 1986 half the mergers were essentially defensive, being justified on the basis of synergy and rationalisation. In 1991, only 16 per cent of mergers were for this reason, and the strengthening market position and expansion emerged as the major reason.[8]

The conditions in the macro-environment within the EU assisted the growth in mergers. Important factors were

1. an improvement in business profitability

2. stability in exchange rates

3. the opportunities offered by the Single Market.

It should also be noted that a similar trend was observable in the USA, which suggests that some of the activity related to a general fashion in favour of cross-border activity. The national balance of mergers and acquisitions, related to the size of GDP, is given in Table 10.1.

The national involvement in mergers and acquisitions activity has not been uniform. The UK has actively participated in the trend towards acquisitions, to a greater extent than might have been expected from the relative size of its economy. This reflects the experience of companies in this activity, and the openness of the UK market in quoted company securities. In contrast, German involvement in mergers and acquisitions was relatively low: there was an increase in the acquisition of German companies in the early 1990s, but this was more a product of the East German privatisation. National traditions towards investment in other states mean that some states are less involved. Also, the conditions for hostile takeovers vary considerably between the Member States. Structural and technical barriers to contested takeovers, including the extent of state ownership, the role of supervisory boards and the problem of identifying the ownership of shares, are such that hostile bids are virtually certain to fail in certain states, such as Germany.[9]

Table 10.1 Share of cross-border mergers and acquisitions by Member States

	1986–1992		1993		
	Target	Purchaser	Target	Purchaser	GDP %
Belgium	6.1	2.6	4.9	3.6	3.2
Denmark	3.4	3.6	4.4	4.8	2.1
Germany	25.6	11.7	28.6	18.0	29.4
Greece	0.4	0.0	0.3	0.1	1.1
Spain	9.2	1.4	9.0	2.0	7.4
France	15.1	19.6	15.2	18.4	19.7
Ireland	1.2	3.5	1.0	2.7	0.7
Italy	7.5	4.8	8.5	5.2	15.5
Luxembourg	0.5	0.9	0.5	1.1	0.2
Netherlands	9.6	7.3	8.5	10.5	4.8
Portugal	1.4	0.1	1.1	0.0	1.2
UK	19.9	44.5	18.0	32.6	14.6
EU12	100	100	100	100	100

Source : *European Economy*, Supplement A, Recent Economic Trends, February 1994, pp. 6 and 10

Merger legislation

The introduction of merger legislation in 1989, at the EU level, was a recognition that merger control had become an increasingly important issue. This was particularly important following the movement towards the completion of the Single Market and the liberalisation of capital and equity markets. It was accepted that the process of corporate reorganisation should continue, but it was felt that this should not impede the competitive process. There was a fear that while national legislation was not suitable to deal with the potential emergence of pan-European monopolies, Articles 85 and 86 of the Treaty were not adequate for the purpose.

It took 17 years to negotiate an EU Merger Regulation and to decide what powers the Commission should have. There were major problems in deciding which mergers should be brought under EU control and the division of responsibility between the national and EU authorities. Any regulation should preclude, except in exceptional circumstances, cases being dealt with on a national *and* an EU basis. This was resolved on the basis of the size of the deal involved, with the scope of EU legislation being limited to the largest deals. This was seen as a victory for the UK and Germany, the two states with the most developed merger legislation. The EU's Merger Regulation came into effect in September 1990.[10] The Regulation dealt with the effects on competition that arose when two or more previously independent undertakings merged. This was given legal authority under Articles 87 and 235 of the Treaty.

Its main features were that mergers should be notified to the European Commission if:

- the worldwide turnover of the combined undertakings was in excess of ECU 5 billion

- the EU-wide turnover of at least two of the undertakings was over ECU 250 million.

(Unless each of the undertakings concerned achieved more than two-thirds of its aggregate EU-wide turnover within one the same Member State).

The above thresholds were set at a high level, which limited the number of cases that the EU dealt with to around 50 to 60 per year in the period 1990 to 1993.[11] Of the 58 cases handled in 1993, 50 were not seen as being problematic, four were outside the definition of the Merger Regulation, and four were permitted to go ahead, but three of these were subject to modifications. The reasoning behind the high thresholds was that it would not be desirable for the EU to be involved in monitoring a large number of small-scale merger operations. In any case, if there were problems associated with competition, these might be taken up by the Commission under Articles 85 and 86.

The appraisal of concentration was to take account of:

● the need to maintain and develop effective competition, taking account of the structure of the markets involved, and the existence of actual or potential competition

● the market conditions of those concerned, and their economic and financial power, the alternatives available to suppliers, and the access to markets.

The requirement was that the EU be informed not more than one week after the announcement of the conclusion of an agreement, the announcement of a bid, or the acquisition of a controlling interest. Once the decision has been made to merge, the deal is suspended and the procedure is then as shown in Figure 10.1.

The procedure shown in Figure 10.1 does not, of course, mean that the merger activity is considered satisfactory to individual Member States that may be involved. However, the number of cases covered by this requirement will be limited. The first case was the Tarmac/Steetley merger in the UK. In this case, it was decided that the merger impacted only on the UK, because the cost of transporting building and construction materials meant that this was a distinct market.

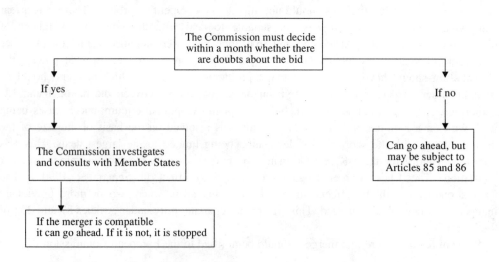

Figure 10.1 EU merger procedure

Only about 10 per cent of cases go to the point where the EU investigates the case in detail. Any decision taken on the basis of the above criteria must always be subjective, and the application will tend to depend on the way things are viewed by the Commission at a particular time. That is, the enthusiasm for large-scale mergers seems to vary over time. Following the investigation, most cases have gone ahead, although after some modification. However, there was one notable case of a bid being blocked. This was the case of the bid by France's Aerospatiale and Italy's Alenia for the Canadian aircraft manufacturer De Havilland. This decision caused enormous controversy even within the Commission, because there was a belief that free market doctrine had won a victory over commercial realities. This small number of cases makes the process manageable. The Merger Task Force, operating as part of DG IV, met all deadlines in the first three years of operation, but the reports were not as thorough as those of the UK's Monopolies and Mergers Commission. While there was controversy surrounding the decision to permit certain mergers to go ahead, the Regulation provided both a quick response and a high degree of certainty, which were not features of some national regulation.[12]

The EU's merger legislation has become well regarded by European business. The Centre for Economic Policy Research examined the impact of the Regulation, via a survey of firms involved in mergers and of law firms handling merger cases. It found that:

1. firms were pleased with the speed and flexibility of the implementation of the Regulation

2. there was no evidence of potential mergers not going ahead because of the procedures involved

3   there was some evidence of 'forum shopping', i.e. firms changing the nature of deals in order to fall into the ambit of EU legislation

4. the European Commission appeared keen to do deals wherever possible.[13]

There have been regular calls for a lowering of thresholds so that more cases can be dealt with at the EU level, and these thresholds were to be subject to review after a period of four years. It was estimated that lowering the threshold from ECU 250 million to 100 million would have doubled the case load.[14] However, a lowered threshold presented the danger that it would capture many mergers that had a purely national impact. In July 1993, the Commission announced that it would not be proposing a reduction in the threshold, but this would be subject to review in 1996. Generally, EU business was thought to be strongly in favour of the status quo and it was felt that its support was needed to make it work.

Conclusions

The current EU Competition Policy works well, despite the fact that it is a shared responsibility with the Member States. In a single market, there would normally be just one competition authority covering general business activity. The present policy can accommodate the different commercial traditions within the Member States, and is not excessively intrusive. If all Competition Policy issues were transferred to Brussels, the whole process would become excessively bureaucratic.

However, it is possible to envisage a situation where the confidence in the EU competition process continues to increase, and its scope widens. That the Commission is so central to the process is a source of concern. That the Commission has a role in investigating, prosecuting, and imposing penalties may not be acceptable if a wider role is assumed. In the future, it may be desirable to create a separate competition authority, which is not so tied to the central bureaucracy.

References

1. **Bright C** (1992) The Court of First Instance and the Net Book Agreements, *European Competition Law Review*, 266.
2. *Europe*, 29 April 1994, No. 6221, 9.
3. *Europe*, 4 May 1994, No. 6223, 9.
4. *Official Journal of the EC*, (1962), No. 204.
5. *Europe*, 4 May 1994, No. 6223, 9–10.
6. *Europe*, 20 May 1993, No. 6234, 7.
7. **House of Lords** (1993) *Enforcement of the Community Competition Rules*, Select Committee on the European Communities, 1st Report, 1993–94, HL Paper 7.
8. *European Economy* (1994) supplement A, Recent Economic Trends, February, 6.
9. **Davison L** (1994) The myth of the level playing field: the case of contested take-overs within the EC, in Barnes I and Davision L, *European Business; Text and Cases*, Heinemann Butterworth, Oxford.
10. **Commission of the EC** (1990) Council Regulation 4064/89 on the control of concentrations between undertakings, in Community Merger Control Law, *Bulletin of the EC*, supplement 2/90.
11. As Ref. 8, p. 2.
12. **Rice R** Marriages made in Brussels, *Financial Times*, 19 January 1993, 14.
13. **Neven D** *et al.* (1993) *Merger in Daylight: the Economics and Politics of European Merger Control*, Centre for European Policy Research, pp. 6–7.
14. As Ref. 7, p. 33.

Further reading

Commission of the EC (1990) *Community Merger Control Law*, Bulletin of the EC, supplement 2/90.
Commission of the EU (1993) *Report on the Implementation of the Merger Regulation*, COM (93) 385, final.
Commission of the EU (1994) *Report on Competition Policy*.
European Economy (1994) Competition and Integration – Community Merger Control Policy, No. 57, Spring.
Ehlermann C D (1992) The contribution of EC Competition Law to the Single Market, in *Common Law Review*, Vol. 29, No. 2, 257–282
Oxford Review of Economic Policy (1993) *Competition Policy*, Vol. 9, No. 2, Summer.
Singleton E S (1992) *Introduction to Competition Law*, Pitman, London.
Steiner J (1992) *Textbook on EEC Law*, Blackstone Press.

CHAPTER 11

Industrial Policy in the EU

Introduction

There are very few actions of the state with regard to the economy that do not have some implications for industry. However, despite the need for advanced economies to maintain a competitive industrial structure, policy is rarely constructed in a coherent way. Industrial policy is designed to solve the problems of structural change, and is intended to affect the supply side of the economy. Some policies are designed to improve the environment in which industry operates, and have a less specific effect. Examples of this are deregulation measures, which improve competition. At an EU-wide level, measures to promote the Single Market (see chapter 4) affect the environment in which business operates, and it is hoped will produce a change in the structure of industry in the longer term. This chapter discusses the EU's policies that are designed to have an impact on a particular sector of the European economy. Many of these policy initiatives emerge as the result of crisis throughout the EU. (Initiatives concerning new technology are dealt with in chapter 12.) The attempts by states to act independently to deal with structural problems frequently lead to undesirable results, especially where state aids are given.

Industrial policy can be used to

- defend and preserve the current structure of the economy

- adapt and facilitate change to match current market conditions

- initiate change to gain an overall advantage in the market place.

The EU needs to ensure, given that it does not have the resources itself to conduct an independent policy, that Member States' activities are not contradictory. That is, there should be common goals, given the degree to which industry depends on the Single Market.

The purpose of this chapter is to analyse the way that the EU has dealt with industry in order to meet the challenges of the Single Market and global competition. There is a debate as to the extent to which the EU should involve itself in industrial questions. One simplistic solution would be to leave the adaptation process to market forces. Free market enthusiasts might favour this view, but the reality is that, even after offering assistance to overcome pressing social problems, there is a need to take account of the political agendas of the

Member States. Many European states combine a free market with political intervention to assist the process of change. There are many examples of useful intervention, such as the investment in modern transport systems. However, some intervention can retard development. An example of this was the telecommunications sector, where public procurement (buying) policies were often designed to support national champions. As a consequence there was less incentive to innovate and become efficient.

A new emphasis on policy emerged in the mid-1990s. The need to address the issue of international competitiveness became even more apparent. This now overlays the reaction of the EU to the completion of the Single Market. It means that the EU needs to think of ways of going beyond overcoming the negative effects of restructuring its industries, and now must look for ways in which it can compete globally. As yet, this aspect of policy needs to be further developed. Despite many brave pronouncements about the need to be competitive, in some sectors attempts to create a truly Europe-wide policy have failed. In this respect, the steel industry is an interesting case study. It is a sector where the EU has very wide-ranging powers, yet appears to have failed to find a lasting solution to a pressing industrial problem.

National policy

All Member States of the European Union would claim to have an industrial policy, although there are differences in the emphasis that particular measures are given. Some countries, such as France and Italy, have traditionally taken a more interventionist stance with regard to their industry. Others, such as Germany, have tended to rely more on a market-based strategy. The use of the term 'policy' is misleading: it implies that there is a deliberate and carefully thought out strategy, but in most Member States industry is dealt with in an *ad hoc* way. Some national industrial policy refers to a particular industry, while the term may refer to a complete strategy, although this is not often the case. Some policies have simply been designed to counteract the actions of other states. On occasions this has led to an almost indecent auction to attract the limited amount of footloose international investment available. On other occasions, the level of state aid to assist an ailing industry in one state has led to similar measures being adopted wastefully elsewhere in the EU.

What is surprising is the level of involvement of the Member States of the EU in their industries. This includes:

1. influencing the distribution of resources between industry, for example by the manipulation of energy prices

2. using regulation to control monopoly and restrictive practices

3. influencing the location of industry, by planning regimes and regional assistance

4. offering state assistance to old or declining industry

5. using public ownership to maintain industry that might not be viable in the market economy

6. environmental controls

7. setting conditions of employment

8.   fiscal and monetary policy.

The scope of EU policy

There is frequently a conflict between the role of the Member States and the need to keep within the rules of the EU. National actions should be consistent with the rules of the EU, although there must be scope for national initiatives that suit local conditions. Many firms are involved in activities that are largely concerned with national markets, yet governments may wish to assist with their development on the basis of social goals such as maintaining employment.[1]

It is difficult to see the EU in the short term being able to replace the role of the Member States, because it lacks the resources and a mandate to intervene at the micro level. Detailed involvement may also not be desirable for technical reasons, including the facts that at the EU level

● the detailed information required to conduct policy may not be available

● there may be too many parties involved

● policy cannot be constructed to suit the local need.

Under these circumstances, the EU's role is restricted to trying to set an overall framework for industry to operate within. This may involve either dealing with industries facing a Europe-wide crisis or encouraging industries with the potential to expand.

The rationale for an EU Industrial Policy

The origins of the EU's involvement with industrial policy can be traced back to the European Coal and Steel Community (ECSC), which put the coal, iron and steel industries of its six members under one High Authority. Although based on one group of industries, the ECSC was primarily political in its purpose. It was seen as a way of encouraging the integration process, by coordinating one of the principal (groups of) industries of the six Member States. Under the Treaty of Rome, which set up the European Economic Community (EEC), the main emphasis was on Competition Policy. There was no specific mention of Industrial Policy. However, there were important sectoral policies for agriculture and transport, and great hopes for Euratom, which was designed to promote research and development in the peaceful use of nuclear power.

An emphasis on Competition Policy was understandable in the early stages of the EU's development. Generally speaking, industry was growing rapidly, and the main concern was for the operation of a competitive market as a vehicle to promote economic and political integration. It was only in the 1970s that the industries of the Member States started to face a general crisis. In response to this crisis, a number of measures were adopted by members, and it was clear that some kind of EU response was called for. Industrial policies adopted by Member States tended to renationalise problems of the European economy, and so reduce the benefits from integration.

An EU-wide policy would:

1.   eliminate many of the conflicting rival national policies

2.   reduce the unfairness of national policies, where the stronger states gain at the expense of weaker states

3.   create a Europe-wide strategy for industry based on improving international competitiveness.

This does not mean that the EU has to intervene in all cases where an industry faces a crisis. The history of many Member States has shown that attempts at industrial intervention can result in expensive failures. This means that the EU has to take care not to back too many losers. Before intervention takes place, the following questions should be answered.

1.   Is EU industrial intervention really needed?

2.   What is the purpose of the intervention?

3.   How will the goals of policy be achieved?

Given that there are many examples of failed government interventions, the state should always consider if any intervention is superior to the market. However, there may be few realistic alternative policies, given that the EU is part of a democratic society, which may wish to have certain industries. Indeed, the social aspects of intervention may be more important than those designed to show clear overall economic benefits.

Promoting competitiveness

In the period after the completion of the Single Market campaign, the priority for EU Industrial Policy became to increase the international competitiveness. The idea that European industry should be competitive in world markets is something that everyone can agree on. The debate about Industrial Policy in the EU therefore developed into how to realise this concept. However, as Martin Bangemann, the EU's Industry Commissioner, was to observe: 'I understand "industrial policy" to mean creating international competitiveness. There is no simple method to do this.'[2]

The EU's most comprehensive approach to a policy for industry emerged out of the White Paper *Growth, Competitiveness, Employment – the Challenges and the Ways Forward into the 21st Century,*[3] which was published in December 1993. This identified a number of issues concerning EU competitiveness. It pointed out that, in the 20 years before the White Paper was published:

● the European economy's potential growth rate had shrunk from 4 per cent to 2.5 per cent per year

● unemployment had risen from cycle to cycle

● the investment ratio had fallen by five percentage points

- the competitive position in relation to Japan and the USA had worsened with regard to

  o employment
  o shares of export markets
  o R&D and innovation and their incorporation into goods brought into the market
  o the development of new products.

Rather than being concerned with comparative advantage, which relates to the endowment of natural resources, the White Paper stated that the EU's strategy was to promote competitive advantage. It was claimed that

'In such a context, factor mobility and the capacity to combine factors effectively and to organise the social consensus on the share out of the value added are becoming much more important than the initial factor endowment.'[4]

A key aspect of the EU's Policy toward greater competitiveness was to help firms to adapt to the new globalisation and interdependent competitive situation. The priorities for action identified in the White Paper were to

- capitalise on the community's industrial strengths

- develop an active policy of industrial cooperation

- establish a concerted approach to strategic alliances

- target measures to ensure the competitive functioning of markets.[5]

This would mean that the pursuit of national champions at the expense of competitive Europe-wide businesses was to be avoided. The Single Market should be promoted in order to prepare firms for the global trading environment. Support would have to be given to the development of small and medium-sized enterprises, and that social dialogue would have to be maintained with the different sides of industry. It would also mean that the development of infrastructure networks would have to continue. Finally, the foundations would have to be laid for the information society.[6]

A great deal of the content of the White Paper was designed to gain an overall consensus. This meant that it was capable of interpretation from a number of levels. Martin Bangemann, for example,[7] believed in a much more pragmatic approach to policy, suggesting that there was a need to move the orientation of products from just European markets, and to think in terms of global needs in areas such as motor vehicle manufacture. He also believed that large firms do not always have a monopoly, because of the existence of global competitors. Under these circumstances, companies should generally determine what they believe to be their optimum size. However, a rational industrial policy should not circumvent competition.

The European Round Table of Industrialists[8] suggested that industry had the prime responsibility for competitiveness, innovation and wealth creation, while it saw the role of the state as being to enable industry to do its job. This was to be by measures that assisted the lowering of costs, reduced regulation and raised quality. In addition, an adequate infrastructure was important. Overall, it was the uncertainty that made investment difficult, in which case the state must show a commitment to consistent economic policies which generated confidence.

However, in order for industry to be effective it needed

- a stable political and economic framework to encourage investment and innovation

- a strategic approach to industry that rebuilt confidence

- specific policies that enabled industry to become competitive, raised quality and liberated the efforts of management.

A similar message came from the Union of Industrial and Employers Confederations of Europe (UNICE).[9]

State aids

State intervention in the management of economies has been a feature of industrial development, particularly since the end of World War II. The trend towards greater state involvement in the activities of business met with some resistance at the national level, with the growth of the monetarist school of economic thought. The UK was early in its commitment to privatisation as a solution to the rising costs of maintaining the state sector. It tried to reduce the extent of subsidy given to private industry. At a simple level, the abolishing of national aids to industry would appear to be a desirable response to the creation of the Single Market. However, the issue is complex, although a consensus exists for a more consistent level of involvement across the EU.

In this section, the following issues are addressed.

1. Why do the nation states assist industry with subsidies of various types?

2. Why does this bring them into conflict with the EU?

3. The EU's own role in supporting industry as part of the development of a more coherent industrial policy at European level.

State aids are subsidies given by the government sector to enterprises, which are designed to affect the expected outcomes of the market. They are transfers, which are normally specifically targeted, but this can be done in a number of ways. It is difficult to define precisely what state aids are, but they may include one of the following measures:

- direct cash grants

- tax concessions

- soft loans

- direct investment by the government

- use of land or facilities at preferential rates

- buying of shares in companies

● not expecting a return on public investments in what would normally be a market-oriented exercise.[10]

Economic theory has normally been hostile to state subsidies of all kinds in closed economies operating under perfect competition. However, there may be cases where state aids are justified, where the market fails to give the optimum result. This happens where there are externalities (over-spill effects), for example where help is needed to save jobs and to overcome the short-term effects of a slump. Other examples include the help required to expand a sector of the economy that investors are sceptical about.

The reasons given for national support for industry include the following.

● The failure of the market, which may result in an inappropriate level of activity.

● Domestic distortions caused by the taxation system.

● The protection of 'infant industries'.

● To gain positive externalities that can result in a particular industrial activity, because its development has a wider spin-off.

● Public goods and strategic industry, for example defence industries.

● The creation or maintenance of employment.

● To alleviate balance of payments problems by encouraging exports or reducing imports.

State aids are tied to the state sector. Governments are prepared to assist industry, because they see that there may be political benefits to be gained from this. The immediate benefit of state aid is often easy to identify, while the costs are spread among the taxpayers. However, the fact that the help given by one state gives an industry a competitive advantage in international markets is of concern. It may result in less efficient firms surviving. Firms that are not subsidised, but are viable under normal conditions, may find that they lack the resources to survive in a battle of subsidies. Finally, state aids may create or maintain firms that cannot survive except on the basis of state assistance. This creates a long-term dependence culture, which may retard economic development.

The EU is taking an increasingly tough view of countries that subsidise certain industries, because this may influence effective competition within the EU and may distort the way in which the common market operates. Yet at the same time the EU is developing a role in the supporting of certain industries because they may be in declining areas or may be needed to enhance the competitiveness of the EU internationally.

The EU and state aids

The granting of state aids can give a substantial competitive advantage to domestic producers, and as a consequence many are regarded as being incompatible with the Common Market. Under Article 92(1) of the EEC Treaty, state aids are not permitted if they affect the EU in any way. However, Article 92(2) exempts certain state aids such as those designed for a social purpose. If the state gives school children free school milk, this is allowable, providing any supplier within the EU can tender for the contract. Also, aid was given to relieve the effects of a natural disaster. Finally, aid was allowed to assist with the problems caused by the geographical division of Germany. Article 92(3) considers that certain aid given by the Member States may be compatible if it

1.   promotes economic development in areas of abnormally low living standards or serious underemployment (there is no specific heading for regional policy)

2.   promotes projects of common European interest, or to remedy a serious disturbance in the economy of a Member State

3.   helps industry facing a crisis, although the aid should not be regarded as permanent.

In addition to the above, the Council could permit other categories of aid, acting by qualified majority. Finally, the Treaty on European Union allowed aid to promote cultural and heritage conservation as long as it did not affect trading conditions.

Member States should inform the Commission of any aids being given to industry, and these aids must conform to the requirements of the Treaty. If they do not conform, the Commission can issue a Decision requiring the member either to amend or abolish the scheme. In theory, the aids should be transparent, i.e. their effects on industry should be easily understood. In practice, many of the effects of policy are difficult to understand, and states seek to muddy the ground in order to win an advantage.

The European Commission deals with around 1000 cases of state aid per year. Under half of these are concerned with industry and the service sector; the rest relate to transport, agriculture, fisheries and coal mining. In 1993, the Commission raised no objections to 399 of the 435 state aids cases it dealt with that related to industry. Of the 36 remaining cases, 19 were allowed to proceed after investigation, and 7 were turned down. The remainder were still being investigated when the 1993 Report on Competition Policy was published. A fuller picture of the trend is given in Table 11.1.

Table 11.1 Notified state aid (excluding aid to agriculture, fisheries and transport)

Year	Number of Proposals notified	Number of objections raised
1986	124	98
1987	326	205
1988	375	311
1989	296	254
1990	429	352
1991	472	383
1992	459	393
1993	435	399

Source : Commission, Reports on Competition Policy, various

In the period 1988 to 1990, an average of ECU 89 billion per year was given, with about 40 per cent of this going to manufacturing (Table 11.2). Many countries still break or bend the rules either by not informing the Commission or by giving the aid first and asking for permission afterwards. At any time, a number of cases will be subject to detailed investigation by the Commission's investigators into state aids. The number of staff in this area is however, nowhere near adequate to the task.

Table 11.2 State aid to manufacturing industry 1988–1990

	As a percentage of value added	ECU per person employed	Million ECU
Belgium	4.1	1655	1211
Denmark	2.1	634	333
France	3.5	1380	6106
Germany	2.5	984	7865
Greece	14.6	1502	1072
Ireland	4.9	1734	368
Italy	6.0	2175	11027
Luxembourg	2.6	1270	48
Netherlands	3.1	1327	1225
Portugal	5.3	758	616
Spain	3.6	936	2499
UK	2.0	582	3133
EU12	3.5	1203	35 503

Source : Commission (1993), Third Survey on State Aid, quoted in Commission of EC (1993), *XXIInd Report on Competition Policy 1992, p. 214*

State aids are a sensitive area of activity for the EU. All the Member States find it easier to see the purpose behind the giving of aid within their own country, and there is generally considerable political support for many of the national decisions. The EU has therefore to move carefully. There is no specific amount of aid that states are allowed to give; indeed the Member States have very different philosophies with regard to the state's involvement in the economy. The Member States are free to decide on the level of aid they give, within EU rules. The Commission monitors the aid being given. Karel Van Miert, the Commissioner in charge of Competition, suggested that the approval process involves trying to determine an overall common interest. He stated that:

'...if the Commission wants to approve the granting of aid, it must ultimately be able to argue plausibly to the eleven other Member States that the aid awarded in the twelfth Member State is in the true interest of all, even if competition in the common market is affected. Ultimately, therefore, and this is much too rarely recognised, the Commission plays the role of the referee, a role which is quite important for the completion of the single market.'[11]

The Commission tries to avoid financial interventions that give particular firms a competitive advantage. The Commission therefore intervenes only where there is likely to be a distortion of trade flows between the Member States. For this reason, the Commission decided that small amounts of aid do not require monitoring. In 1993, the limit was set at ECU 50 000 per item of aid, with an overall limit of ECU 100 000 over a three year period.

Aid is judged to be acceptable if it is:

- necessary, and the changes could not happen without the assistance

- finite and in proportion to the task it is meant to assist with

- meant for restructuring, and not for the day-to-day operation of the business

- of benefit to the EU as a whole

- a coherent fit with the policies of the EU, i.e. aid to businesses in an industry where there is already over-capacity should be given only under strict conditions.[12]

There are still special problems concerning the unification of Germany. These are dealt with by Article 92 (2C) of the Treaty, and were designed for the time when Germany was a divided country. However, this Article has been used to deal with problems post-unification. In 1994, the Commission approved of aid given by the German state of Bavaria to support the maintenance of a wagon-carrying trailer connection between Tettau and the railway station in Steinbach am Wald. (The rail connection had been disrupted in 1952, when the infrastructure network of Germany was divided.) The payments of DM 363 000 per year until the end of 1995 were to be transitional, until the time when alternative, self-financing arrangements could be made.[13]

State aids and the national political process

The issue of state aid tends to be highly political, given that the decision to offer aid means that the Member State has decided to make a political commitment to a project. The existence of the EU's role in monitoring the process can be resented, but it has the advantages that:

- it may limit the extent to which inward investors can play one Member State off against another for the best financial offer

- it can protect the Member States from lobbyists, who seek to gain ever-higher levels of subsidy.

The Commission is aware of the political realities within the Member States, and for that reason does permit projects to go ahead that do not meet with a strict application of the rules. An example of this was the decision to build a £157 million synthetic fibres plant in Northern Ireland, built by the Hualon Corporation. This was to supply materials to low-cost clothing producers in Europe. State aids of £61 million were approved by the Commission in 1994, despite some opposition within its own ranks. The synthetic fibres industry in Europe already suffered from considerable over-production, and the addition of 23 500 tonnes of extra capacity did not appear to make sense. There was felt to be little reason to offer aid to a mature industry, especially as the production was unlikely to be a substitute for production from outside the EU.

The case for the project was that it would employ some 1800 people, with an extra 500 associated jobs. This was in an area of extremely high levels of unemployment, where wages were 20 per cent below the UK average. (Wages were not as low as many of the Asian producers; for example, in Taiwan, Malaysia and Vietnam, they were 57 per cent, 12 per cent and 4 per cent of UK rates.) The decision to permit the aid was granted on the basis that the manufacturing process in Northern Ireland was labour-intensive, and therefore did not compete with the output of what was a high-technology industry in the rest of Europe.[14]

Nationalised industries

A particular problem of concern was that of the relationship between the governments of the Member States and state-owned industry. Article 90 makes it clear that the nationalised industry sector is subject to competition rules, but this is one of the most difficult areas of state aids to police. In many of the Member States they have received very significant levels of support, often by means of indirect assistance. This can cause severe problems for the part of the industry that is not in state hands, either within the national market or elsewhere within the EU. This has been a particular problem of the steel industry, which is dealt with later in the text. Even the privatisation process, which is supposed to reduce state involvement, has caused problems. An example of this was the sale of the Rover Group to British Aerospace.

The British government's holding in the Rover Group was sold in August 1988. The company had originally fallen into the state's hands in 1975, after a period when it looked doomed to go out of business. This would have resulted in the loss of many thousands of jobs, both within the company and among its suppliers. By the time the company was sold, it had a much smaller share of the UK market than in the past, but had started to look like a worthwhile asset. In 1994 the company was sold to BMW.

The sale to British Aerospace had required the approval of the European Commission, as it involved giving state aid to the company. The UK government had proposed an £800 million cash injection. This was reduced because of the objections of the Commission, so that the apparent cost to the UK taxpayer was £422 million. However, other deals were on offer that were not made known either to the UK Parliament or to the Commission. This meant that the total cost of the privatisation was £460 million. Not unnaturally, the Commission demanded that some of this be paid back, once the deal became known.[15] There is no reason to believe that the behaviour of the British government was unique, but evidence of this kind of abuse is not generally well recorded.

State aids and the international economy

While the EU wishes to reduce Member State involvement in industry which distorts the Single Market, it is rather less scrupulous about the subsidy of European champions and global competition. This is largely because global competition is less well regulated than that within the EU, although the World Trade Organisation may eventually change this. If any one state appears to be gaining an advantage because of subsidy to its domestic industry, the likelihood is that the source of pressure for reform will be bilateral rather than multilateral. Trade disputes and the threat of retaliation are frequently the outcome, with anti-dumping duties or other sanctions being taken against the products suspected of benefiting from unreasonable state assistance.

One of the longest running disputes concerns the Airbus, with the USA and the EU arguing about the legitimacy of aid being given to establish a viable manufacturer of commercial airlines within the EU. An agreement was reached between the USA and the EU in May 1992 to limit the extent of help that was meant to be given.[16]

These rules were subject to review as part of the Uruguay GATT Round, but no agreement was reached on a permanent solution. Issues of further conflict included the need to restrict the extent of indirect support, control on subsidies given to aero-engines and parts, and the exempting of aid to current projects.[17]

The restructuring of EU industry – the case of steel

The restructuring of the steel industry is an important example of the problems of operating an EU-wide Industrial Policy because the sector is

- a traditional area of intensive national involvement and state ownership

- an area where the EU has considerable formal powers to intervene

- subject to increasingly serious crisis.

While the EU's Competition Policy has gone some way towards discouraging cartels and indiscriminate use of state aids, the policy towards the steel industry represents a substantial contrast. Here the EU has involved itself in a detailed way in the restructuring of an industry, by coordinating and providing financial aid and, in the past, by restricting competition.

Since 1960, the EU's share of world steel production has declined, as Japan and the newly industrialised countries introduced capacity. Europe's steel industry remains largely national in character, with few companies producing in more than one country. In the UK, France, Italy and Belgium, a significant proportion of the industry is nationalised. Although some modernisation took place in the years of rapid economic growth to 1974, generally costs of production were higher than those in Japan at the time, because of the failure to build really large plants in order to gain economies of scale. The stimulus to change was not as great as it might have been, because of the protective environment in which the industry operated.

The recession caused by the 1974 oil crisis reduced the world demand for steel by 14 per cent. This caused fierce competition, as producers tried to maintain market share, which in turn reduced the price of steel by between 35 and 45 per cent. In response the European Commission introduced voluntary restrictions on production. In 1980 mandatory production quotas were introduced in response to a second bout of recession. Along with this there were attempts to achieve 'recommended' prices, although the success of these was limited. Once demand fell in 1982, so did prices.

The rationale for EU restructuring of the steel industry

EU measures to restructure the steel industry have been designed to bring about an orderly reduction in capacity, in order to promote efficiency and a return to profitability. There can be no doubt that if adjustments are left to unregulated international market forces, the process can be very painful. The demand for steel depends on the demand for the products that use it: it is not a final production good. If steel prices fall, demand tends to be inelastic, i.e. the quantity demanded from the whole industry hardly increases at all. On the production side, the industry is highly capital intensive, and requires between 70 and 90 per cent usage of capacity to ensure profitability. If demand falls, the tendency is for steel producers to cut prices in order to maintain the tonnage going through their plants. If all producers do this, the intense competition results in even the most efficient losing money. Producers frequently just cover their day-to-day costs, without getting any return on their investment. Added to this, because steel plants are frequently located in traditional heavy industrial areas where jobs are scarce, governments feel the need to step in. Survival depends more on the availability of financial resources than on the efficiency of production.

In the above situation some control of state aids as part of a restructuring programme is essential. The EU needs to encourage the closure of outdated capacity in order to stay internationally competitive. It also has to adjust the industry to the reality of a generally lower level of output due to some loss of international market share. Added to this there has been a trend towards the replacement of steel by newer materials such as plastics and ceramics, or simply to use less steel to make products such as motor cars.

The EU's measures

The legal basis for Community action is based on the Treaty of Paris of 1951, which set up the European Coal and Steel Community (ECSC). The High Authority of the ECSC (forerunner of the Commission) was given extensive powers to forbid cartels and promote research and development, as well as finance retraining. It also had the power to prohibit excessive investment. With the agreement of the Council it was able to declare a state of 'imminent crisis' and set minimum prices. If conditions in the industry warranted it, it was also possible to declare a state of manifest crisis, in which case production quotas could be imposed. It was not until the mid-1970s that these powers were first used. In 1980, a state of manifest crisis was declared under Article 58 of the Treaty of Paris. This was called the Davignon Plan (named after the Commissioner responsible) and introduced a system of production and delivery quotas which, if they were exceeded, could lead to a fine being imposed.

The impact of attempts to reduce capacity by the steel companies, Member States and the EU over a longer period is given in Table 11.3 which shows that there were differences in the way the industry evolved through the difficult years of the 1970s and 1980s. In particular, there was an expansion of capacity in Spain, in the period up to 1988, reflecting the pace of its industrial development. This meant that capacity nearly matched that of the UK in 1988. Greece, Ireland and Portugal also expanded their industries, but from a very low base, which reflected their lack of an established industrial base. The main producers all followed a trend towards reducing capacity, with the exception of Italy, which subverted the trend.

By the end of 1985, the crisis was thought to be largely over, and the EU prohibited the use of state aids, except for environmental purposes and the closure of inefficient plants. The industry was, however, still operating at less than full capacity, although it did gain some benefit from the upturn in the European economy. The system of quotas was disbanded between 1986 and 1988. During the period of 'manifest crisis', capacity was reduced by 19

Table 11.3 Changes in the EU crude steel capacity 1975–1992

	Changes 1976–1992 (percentage)	Changes 1976–1992 (million tonnes)	Changes 1986–1992 (percentage)	Changes 1986–1992 (million tonnes)
Belgium	−23	−4.2	5	0.7
Denmark	−29	−0.4	−	−
France	−28	−9.2	−15	−4.1
Germany[1]	−26	−17.4	3	1.2
Greece	42	1.1	−16	−0.7
Ireland	245	0.2	−	−
Italy	16	5.4	10	3.7
Luxembourg	−37	−3.0	−5	−0.3
Netherlands	−16	−1.2	−18	−1.5
Portugal	29	0.2	10	0.1
Spain	35	5.2	−9	−1.9
UK	−27	−7.8	−5	−1.2
EU12	−14	−31	−2	−3.9

[1]   The figures for Germany are for West Germany. Capacity in the East was 10 million tonnes 1988–1991, falling to 7.6 million tonnes in 1992
Source: House of Lords (1993), *Restructuring The EC Steel Industry*, Select Committee on the European Communities, 24th Report, Session 1992–93, HL paper 111, p. 43

per cent (51 million tonnes). Employment in the industry fell by 40 per cent between 1980 and 1990. The social cost of restructuring was therefore very high, but at least the industry appeared to be ready to move towards normal trading. It was also more efficient as a result of greater investment and better use of manpower. Table 11.4 gives a comparison of the costs of the industry relative to its international competitors.

Table 11.4 Comparative costs of producing steel (March 1993)

	US $ per tonne CRC shipped
United Kingdom	413
France	493
Germany	558
Japan	572
USA	513
South Korea	511
Taiwan	511

Note: The above assumes 90% capacity
Source: Peter Marcus and Donald Barnett. *World Steel Dynamics*, Paine Webber, New York 1993, exhibit 14. Quoted in House of Lords (1993), *Restructuring The EC Steel Industry*, Select Committee on the European Communities, 24th Report, Session 1992–93, HL paper 111, p. 2

The use of production quotas was generally regarded as a success at the time, and the EU's policy for the industry appeared to work well in the short term. However, demand was unlikely to grow significantly. This meant that there would be future adjustments to get rid of out-of-date capacity, which would lead to job losses and future states of crisis. Quotas were also a poor long-term policy instrument in that they can perpetuate over-capacity. The Davignon Plan was thought by some to be an 'output fixing cartel'[18] which fixed the structure of the industry rather than assisting with its change.

Crisis returns to the industry

As the European economy turned down again, the steel industry drifted back into a crisis situation. Between 1991 and 1993, steel prices fell by 30 per cent. In October 1992 the 16 major steel producers wrote to the Commission, and in 1993 the EU confirmed that a crisis existed in the industry. The EU had a capacity to produce 185 million tonnes of crude steel, but the actual production was 132 million tonnes, giving a capacity utilisation of just over 70 per cent. The EU initially suggested that there was a need to cut crude steel capacity by 30 million tonnes, which would increase capacity utilisation to 83 per cent. After protracted negotiation, a deal appeared to be have been struck in December 1993.[19] The agreement appeared to cut the capacity of the industry by between 19 and 25 million tonnes. The hope was that if the state-owned sector cut capacity by 4.6 million tonnes, this would bring forth cuts in the private sector. The state-owned sector was to be permitted to be awarded ECU 7 million of state aid on the basis of 'one last time'. Also, the British government was able to gain agreement concerning investigation of the awarding of illegal aids.

The problems with the deal soon became apparent.

1. The actual agreed cutback in the state-owned sector was no more than 2.5 million tonnes.

2. The private sector appeared unwilling to cooperate without a more complete commitment from the public sector.

The state sector was really a prisoner of domestic interests. The location of steel plants, frequently in areas of high unemployment, meant that the concessions offered were always likely to be limited. The EU's contribution towards the social cost of closure was never adequate. An ECSC grant of ECU 9000 per job lost to assist with the impact of redundancy was made available, and there were schemes for retraining and encouraging investment into areas of high unemployment caused by steel closures. The EU made available an indicative ECU 240 million in the period 1993–1995.[20] However, in this area it has had little success. Throwing money at areas of high unemployment through retraining schemes does not replace the jobs lost. Inevitably these areas are likely to remain in a depressed state for a long time to come, especially in an era of generally high unemployment.

For the private sector, the cutbacks were important because of their very high levels of losses.[21] The private sector disliked intensely the subsidies offered by the state sector, because they were seen as a waste of public funds and they amounted to an unfair trading advantage. However, while the private producers had been keen to see EU involvement in 1992, this unity started to evaporate in 1994. With the prospect of an improving market situation, and what amounted to a very poor response from the state sector, they were reluctant to cooperate.

Despite the EU's best intention, no lasting solution appeared to be on offer. The best that could be hoped for was that the market would continue to revive, with the adjustment taking place by market means, i.e. economic pressures forcing either the public or the private sector to accept the inevitable. The problem with this solution is that many of the steel plants are located in areas of high long-term unemployment. When demand recovers with an upturn, the willingness to take action diminishes; when the next major slump occurs, the crisis talks are resumed.

Given the difficulty of creating a satisfactory solution based on voluntary action, despite the assistance the EU was able to offer, a number of possible alternative models present themselves:

1. to offer even more assistance with closures, via voluntary action

2. to move towards a permanent cartel, along the lines that were tried in the 1980s

3. to permit the free market to operate, and force closures as needed.

The first two have not delivered a lasting solution, while the third can work only if state aids are really abolished. Some states will benefit at the expense of others. Table 11.5 gives a comparison of steel-making costs. In this situation the UK will clearly do well. Hence there will always be support for the free market in the UK, given that it is an industry that has undergone considerable reorganisation associated with its privatisation.

Table 11.5 The breakdown of steel-making costs in Europe (US $ per tonne CRC shipped, March 1993)

	UK	France	Germany
Materials			
coking coal	41	41	44
iron ore	62	61	69
scrap	39	39	38
other materials	153	160	179
total materials	295	301	330
Labour			
costs per hour	18.0	27.5	33.0
hours per tonne	5.4	5.2	5.3
total labour	97	143	175
Financial costs			
depreciation	20	36	42
interest	1	13	11
total financial	21	49	53
Total pre-tax cost	413	493	558

Note : The above assumes 90% capacity
Source : As Table 11.4, p. 3

What Table 11.5 demonstrates is that although it takes slightly more man-hours to make a tonne of steel in the UK, overall costs there are lower. British Steel gains from lower material costs, lower wage rates, and the fact that it has lower debts than its rivals. If efficient producers such as British Steel are permitted to operate in a free market, they will no doubt gain market share and so gain economies of scale.

It can be argued that the special case made for state intervention with regard to steel has simply run its course. There is little evidence that any of the alternatives to the market really work. This is because there is a lack of willingness to face up to the reality of adjustment to a mature market structure. The EU has a role in providing funds to assist with the closure of surplus capacity. Member States should also be permitted to help their industries, but the aid they give should be tightly controlled. The model the EU suggested in June 1994 was that:

- aid must be given for the closure of surplus capacity and the retraining of workers only

- the closures of steel plants as part of the restructuring must be permanent

- the closed plants must not be relocated

- new capacity must not be opened elsewhere using state funds

- the process must be monitored.[22]

This aid must be used, but once rationalisation has taken place it should be possible for the industry to adjust to the competitive environment. This will certainly save taxpayers' money. However, there is an implied social cost attached to closures. Clearly there will be very high pockets of unemployment, and perhaps severe political unrest, unless the process is dealt with in a sensitive way.

Other policy areas

Apart from the steel industry, the EU has been involved in a number of industrial sectors. The adjustments required for the coalmining and shipbuilding industries are typical of the problems facing industries in decline. In both cases there has been a need to keep control of the extent of state aids, which have a tendency to cancel each other out. Generally the EU has shown tolerance, recognising that these industries require time to adjust from a social point of view. The only long-term schemes that the EU has envisaged are for these areas. However, the level of aid was reduced from 25 per cent of contract value to 9 per cent in the early 1990s.

In the case of shipbuilding, the competition in subsidies could not stop closures and Europe losing ground to non-EU competitors. Very fierce international competition saw the EU share of the world market drop from 25 per cent in 1988 to 20 per cent in 1990. By 1992 this share had fallen to 18 per cent of the world market. The problem for the EU was that its yards were 20 per cent more expensive than those in the Far East.[23] The high levels of fixed capital required for a modern shipyard mean that if they close, they cannot easily be reopened. However, if the subsidies continue, there is no incentive to modernise and structural change will be held back. With this in mind, the EU agreed to an Organisation for Economic Co-operation and Development (OECD) initiative which comes into effect in 1996. This will end direct subsidies to the industry, but permits aid of up to 100 per cent towards a shipyard's research cost. As shipyards only spend 1 to 2 per cent of their turnover on research, this is not a significant concession.

If Europe wishes to make the industry more competitive perhaps the policy might be widened, and a maritime policy be created, which links the building of vessels with a policy of European carriers having to use domestically built vessels. It would only work if there was also a sharing of cargoes destined for EU ports, and this suggestion from Martin Bangemann would carry a risk of retaliation.[24]

A more market-oriented approach is possible in the case of motor vehicles. As we have seen in chapter 10, the European industry is protected from Japanese competition by a voluntary export restraint. The industry employs 1.8 million in the supply of parts and manufacturing, with a further 1.8 million employed in distribution and repair. It is an industry that has suffered with the downturn of the economy, so that in 1993 the Commission estimated that the market for cars and light vehicles might have shrunk by 15.9 per cent to 11.74 million vehicles. However, it was expected to grow to 15 million units by 1999.[25] The opportunity to maintain domestic producers' share of the market depended, it was felt, on improving quality, meeting environmental standards, adopting innovation and reducing costs. This meant a restructuring of the components industry, and improving productivity so that a 30 per cent shortfall in productivity compared to the Japanese was made up.

A series of proposals was put forward that was much more market-oriented than that being adopted for the steel industry. This included:

- improving the operation of the Single Market

- training and retraining the work force

- research and technological development

- orderly liberalisation of access to the EU market

- ensuring access to third markets.

These policy initiatives all have problems, but they represent what many believe to be achievable. They are a repackaging of what is available across a range of sectors, and do not involve the EU in many of the detailed commercial decisions that apply for industries such as steel which are either in decline or have reached maturity. So, for example, the EU could decide to liberalise the market by not renewing Regulation 123/85 in 1995, which prevents the large-scale movement of cars from one EU state to another except by the manufacturer. The Regulation is meant to ensure a balance of benefits, including an adequate support for the customer by the distributors, but it leads to a significant variation in price levels. Taxes on cars could be brought into line, as the VAT has been, and environmental standards could be improved.

Conclusions

The application of Community Industrial Policy changes with the times. There is little confidence that it is possible to operate the kind of active and directive policy that was fashionable in the Member States in the 1970s. The case of steel demonstrates that, even with a major crisis developing in an industry, there is not a willingness to act in a cohesive way to ensure that restructuring is a success. It is much more likely that the policy instruments that have worked for the EU, such as the Single Market and the Common Commercial Policy, will be acceptable.

This suggests that the EU is really mainly involved in the setting and supervision of the rules that control the conduct of the Member States. There is scope for flexibility: for example, it is appropriate, in periods of slow economic growth, that the Commission is more likely to be tolerant of agreements that involve the restructuring of industry. The task for the EU is to ensure that the Member States recognise a collective interest in ensuring that policy in one Member State does not offset the actions taken by another.

References

1. **Geroski P A** (1990) European Industrial Policy and Industrial Policy in Europe, in Cowling K and Tomann H, *Industrial Policy After 1992*, Anglo German Foundation, p. 265.
2. **Bangemann M** (1992) *Meeting the Global Challenge*, Kogan Page, London, p. 13.
3. **Commission** (1993) *Growth, Competitiveness, Employment – the Challenges and the Ways Forward into the 21st Century*, COM(93) 700 final.
4. Ibid., p. 60.
5. Ibid., p. 72.
6. Ibid., p. 18.
7. As Ref. 2.
8a. **European Round Table of Industrialists** (1994) *Beating the Crisis: a Charter for Europe's Industrial Future.*
8b. A report from the House of Lords (1994) *Growth, Competitiveness and Employment in the European Community*, Select Committee on the European Communities, 7th Report, Session 1993–94, HL paper 43, p. 53
9. As Ref. 8b, p. 39.
10. *European Economy* (1991) Economic rationale for subsidy control, No. 48, September p. 17.
11. **Karel Van Miert** (1993) in a speech to economists in Bonn, quoted from *Europe*, Document, 9 July 1993.
12. Ibid.
13. *Europe*, 16/17 May 1994, No. 6231, 13.
14. *Financial Times*, 31 May 1994, 8.
15. **House of Commons** (1991) *Sale of the Rover Group to British Aerospace*, First Report, Session 1990–91, No. 34, HMSO.
16. For further information see **Barnes I** *et al.* (1994) European collaboration in aircraft manufacture, in Barnes I and Davison L (Eds), *European Business; Text and Cases*, Heinemann/Butterworth, London.
17. *Financial Times*, 19 May 1994, 5.
18. **House of Lords** (1993) *Restructuring the EC Steel Industry*, Select Committee on the European Communities, 24th Report, Session 1992–93, HL paper 111, p. 9.
19. *Europe*, 20 December 1993, 10.
20. **European Commission** (1994) Intermediate report on the restructuring of the steel industry, *Europe*, 28 April, 4.
21. Choice of cuts or catastrophe, *Financial Times*, 15 February, 1994, 17.
22. *Financial Times*, 16 June 1994, 22.
23. *The European*, 17 June 1993, 40.

24. As Ref. 2, p. 98.
25. **Commission of the EU** (1994) Memorandum on competitiveness and the prospects for the European automobile industry, *Europe*, Document, 25 February 1994, 2.

Further reading

Emerson M (1988) *What Model for Europe?* MIT Press, Cambridge, MA.

House of Lords (1994) *Restructuring the EC Steel Industry* (supplement to the 24th Report 1992–93), Select Committee on the European Communities, 5th Report, Session 1993–94, HL paper 30.

Jacquemin A and Wright D (Eds) (1993) *The European Challenges Post-1992: Shaping Factors, Shaping Actors*, Edward Elgar, Cheltenham.

Pearce J and Sutton J (1985) *Protection and Industrial Policy in Europe*, Routledge and Kegan Paul, London.

CHAPTER 12

Promoting new technology in the European Union

Introduction

The developed world is going through another industrial revolution, in which new technologies are generating fierce international competition based primarily on knowledge, information and networks. This poses a challenge to the European Union to the extent that there is an enormous potential to increase productivity and to improve living standards. At the same time, the penalties of falling behind are considerable.

The promotion of new technology forms part of the EU's industrial policy, and as such is designed to affect the supply side of the economy. Having an economy based on advanced technology is regarded as an important way of contributing to raising living standards. This chapter is concerned with industrial research and technological development (R&TD) and the promotion of innovation which, it is hoped, will make European business competitive with its major global rivals, the USA and Japan. This excludes activity that takes place for military reasons, but this situation may change in the future if the extent of political integration permits the inclusion of defence activities.

The EU's response to the global challenge has been to adopt an active role in the promotion of new technology on a Union-wide basis. This is because of the belief that the challenge of rapid technological change is best met at the level of the Single Market, and because of the threat posed by individual Member States. The blind support for national champions and the pursuit of narrow nationalistic goals will not only slow down the full completion of the Single Market, it will also diminish Europe's ability to compete on a global basis. Although initiatives date back to the early 1980s, the Union's response was first formally articulated in the Single European Act. Article 130 was amended in the Treaty of European Union, and set out a more complete view of the EU's broad strategy with regard to the promotion of new technology. It recognised a weakness of past policy by calling for

'Fostering better exploitation of the industrial potential of policies of innovation, research and technological development.'

Article 130f goes on to state that

'The Community shall have the objective of strengthening the scientific and technological bases of Community industry and encouraging it to become more competitive at international level, while promoting all the research activities deemed necessary by virtue of other chapters of (the) Treaty.'

This was to be achieved by strategies that

1.   encouraged cooperation between industry, research centres and universities across Europe

2.   enable firms to exploit fully the internal market.

In many cases the Union has tried to solve a pressing problem with only limited resources. Indeed, most of the shortcomings of European industry are a result of problems within the Member States. Despite this

1.   the EU has consistently demonstrated an ability to propose potential solutions to common problems facing industry

2.   industry has been mobilised in a way that might only have been possible in a forum designed to restrict competition

3.   the EU has put forward an agenda which, despite areas of controversy, has won a high degree of agreement

4.   compromises have been found to difficult problems, especially concerning appropriate levels of funding and the selection of new standards.

However, the continued poor showing of the EU in the global battle for supremacy in high-technology goods has led to a number of criticisms of the strategy. These include the following:

1.   Inadequate funding.

2.   Excessive bureaucracy in procedures.

3.   A lack of access to many of the programmes for small and medium enterprises.

4.   Slowness to win agreement among the Member States.

5.   The strategy has become less useful as a result of a movement towards globalisation of history.

6.   The outcome from projects has often been of limited value.

This chapter demonstrates that while many of the criticisms of the policy can be substantiated, the EU has at least made an attempt to resolve the issues of nationalism that have held back the competitiveness of European high-technology industry. However, despite these valiant efforts of the EU, the longer term viability of many of its solutions will be questioned.

Not all areas of new technology and scientific research are considered directly, for example those that support agriculture and the services sector are left aside. The main concern is with the EU's Framework Programmes and their constituent parts. The specific example is the European Programme for Strategic R&D in Information Technology (ESPRIT). In addition, the case of Union support for high-definition television (HDTV) is examined.

Europe and global competition

The promotion of new technology has been a constant theme in industrial society since the industrial revolution. Industrial society is in a continuous state of change, although there are periods in which the pace of change is more rapid than in others. In the period from 1946 to 1973 high rates of economic growth were achieved relatively easily, helped along by an increased working population and productivity growth. This growth in productivity was achieved by better working methods, a movement of labour into the more productive areas of the economy, increased investment, and the adoption of new technology. From 1973 onwards it became more difficult to achieve satisfactory growth rates. As part of their strategy to overcome this situation, many governments increased support for industry to promote new technology, either by directly funding R&TD or by indirectly funding it by devices such as public procurement programmes. Also, attempts were made to improve the general environment for developing and adopting new technology.

A related issue was that of competitive advantage. In the 1960s the technological gap between Europe and the USA was a source of continuing debate, but this issue was largely forgotten in the 1970s. It re-emerged in the 1980s, when there was an increased concern about the challenge coming from Japan in addition to that from the USA. The three global trade blocks are in essence competing with similar goods, and the ability to manufacture and design products that win greater market share is central to the overall process.

In particular there was a feeling that Europe was falling behind in the area of high-technology trade, and that this was affecting the growth of the economy. The extent of the challenge facing the EU is illustrated in Table 12.1.

Table 12.1 High-technology products as a share of EU trade in manufacturers (%)

	1978	1988	1990
Imports			
Extra EU	27.1	30.8	31.4
USA	44.9	51.6	52.2
Japan	34.7	44.2	42.9
EFTA	17.1	18.5	18.6
Exports			
Extra EU	20.5	20.3	20.7
USA	19.1	23.2	25.6
Japan	19.4	15.2	12.2
EFTA	16.5	17.0	16.6

Source : European Economy (1993), No. 52, 213

Table 12.1 illustrates the extent to which the EU has failed to make real headway in world markets in high-technology trade, especially with its major trading competitors. The worst possible case is that of Japan: the European market is flooded with Japanese products, but the percentage of high-technology exports to the Japanese market continues to fall. This is in part a market access issue, and is therefore related to the Common Commercial Policy.

Europe's poor performance in exports could be strongly related to the level and quality of investment in R&TD. The EU did badly in terms of investment in R&TD, as Table 12.2 demonstrates.

Table 12.2 Comparison of spending on research and technological development (R&TD) in 1991

	Total R&TD spending (ECU billion)	R&TD spending per head of population (ECU)	Total R&TD as % of GDP
USA	124	493	2.8
Japan	77	627	3.0
EU12	104	302	2.0

Source: Commission (1993) *Growth, Competitiveness and Employment in the European Community: the Challenges and Ways Forward into the 21st Century*, COM (93) 700, p. 97

Table 12.2 shows that the EU is not matching the level of commitment shown by its major trading rivals. Although total spending in the EU appears to be at a reasonable level, the EU does badly when spending per head of population is taken into account, and spending is compared as a percentage of GDP. However, investment in R&TD varies considerably between the EU Member States, with Germany spending 2.6 per cent of GDP and Greece and Portugal investing only 0.7 per cent of GDP. The more affluent a country is, the lighter is the real burden of higher expenditures.[1]

There are also likely to be significant variations in the effectiveness of spending programmes. In particular, the R&TD spending by the private sector of the economy is likely to give better commercial results than that funded by the state. In Europe, business funds only 52 per cent of research, compared to 78 per cent in Japan.

For a number of countries, the extent of state involvement in R&D is complicated by defence spending. Military research amounted to 44 per cent of all research in the UK, 37 per cent in France and 17 per cent in Spain. Often this kind of work is designed for a specific purpose, and has limited use in civilian projects. Also, defence-related research may not be available to a wider circle of industrial users. In addition, some of the usefulness of defence-related R&D may be reduced if the movement towards peace continues.

Europe appears to be less well placed in terms of the key workers required for its high-technology industries, as Table 12.3 below demonstrates.

The growth in the stock of such key members of the workforce has tended to be lower in the EU. However, care has to be taken with such tables, because the comparisons of skills and qualifications are not always valid. Given the higher number of US researchers, it is not surprising that they won 143 Nobel Prizes for medicine, physics and chemistry between 1940 and 1990. The Europeans did reasonably well with 86, but the Japanese gained only 5.

Table 12.3 Comparison of the number of researchers and engineers 1991

	Total number of researchers and engineers	Number of researchers and engineers per 1000 of the working population
USA	950 000	8
Japan	450 000	9
EU12	630 000	4

Source: As Table 12.2

There can be no doubt about the ability of the Europeans to invent. Despite the success of the USA in areas such as semiconductors, the growth of its economy was related more to the ability to generate jobs. It is the Japanese who have gained most from the application of new technology and who have shown the greatest ability to bring it speedily on to the world's markets. It is in the development and production stage that the trade battle is won and lost, and this is one area where Europe is poor. A rough rule of thumb is said to be that for every £1 spent on research, £10 must be spent on development and £100 on production.

The rationale of intervention in promoting new technology

The promotion of new technology is often regarded as a private sector concern, and indeed if the market gave the desired results in terms of economic progress there would be no need for the state to intervene. However, the main argument in favour of intervention is that left to itself the market under-produces in terms of this key element of economic development. The collective benefits gained from a wide range of organisations being involved in R&TD tend to be cumulative, and go beyond short-term gains of immediate profits. Specific skills are developed, and the new innovations that result may be of benefit to other sectors of the economy.

For the individual firm, the risks involved in spending on the R&TD sector may be high. Unless new ideas can be adequately protected, and there is sufficient finance to bring them to fruition, firms may stay shy of heavy involvement in these activities. Often firms will not wish to undertake basic research because experience has shown that in some sectors it is the firms that enter second into the field, and take advantage of others' efforts, that succeed. In particular, small and medium firms may not feel that investing significantly in R&D is worth the risk. In recent years, it has also been argued that the stock market tends to undervalue firms with heavy R&D programmes. In countries such as the UK with very liberal rules with regard to share dealings, there is a danger that unless profits are kept at high levels companies will be taken over.

Firms may, of course, be able to license new patents. Here the Japanese have had great success, but there is a limit to the extent to which this free riding can continue. There may not be access to new developments. Also, some firms would argue that in a number of areas it is important to participate in the development stages in order to get full value from research and development. Smaller firms may not have the access to the patents or may be incapable of exploiting them without the help of governments. Domestically based firms may find that they are overwhelmed by large multinational corporations that use new technology as a competitive weapon. These multinationals can use their financial power to switch to high-growth sectors and maintain their dominance on a worldwide basis.

The purpose of state intervention should be to increase the extent of R&TD activity and to promote innovation, so that industry is able to achieve benefits in addition to those provided by the market economy. Help given to support pure research or basic research, where the results become widely available, is clearly desirable. This is especially the case if it means that duplication by numerous private firms is avoided. It may also lead to useful research being carried out where it might not have been due to an inability of individual enterprises to exploit the results fully. The nearer we get to the market in terms of research activity, the more it appears that the private sector should take a greater responsibility. This is because there is an increased danger of interfering with the competitive process. However, there is little point in carrying out research if it does not have commercial potential. Help for near-to-the-market research may be justifiable where firms in a sector are clearly in need of remedial help in order to catch up with international competition. The issue of how close a project should be to market application can never be fully resolved, simply because it is subjective. However, the Union has some protection against the misuse of state aids, with the enforcement of Articles 92 and 93 of the EEC Treaty.

Collaboration as a strategy

A strategy based on collaboration between businesses and research institutions across Europe has the advantage that it brings the participants into regular contact. It places the Union at the centre of the process, and offers an opportunity for greater understanding and the exchange of ideas. In that sense it helps to deepen both political and economic integration, and moves away from the excessive dominance of Japan and the USA. For the individual Member State, collaboration offers an opportunity to gain from a much wider experience. New technology is difficult to develop fully nationally and in isolation. Even the most inventive of societies produces only a fraction of the total of new patents and processes required.

European firms, with a lack of a unified market, have been at a disadvantage to the Americans and Japanese in the past. It remains to be seen whether the completion of the Single Market has helped such problems as the need to produce for a multitude of differing technical standards. National governments tend to make things worse by their insistence on trying to promote a number of national champions, which holds back market forces. The challenge for Europe is to use its resources to the best advantage. If there is excessive competition in R&TD, firms may be duplicating research. Within the EU, it is suggested that the Member States would all benefit from a sharing of information, and a greater degree of specialisation on aspects of technology they feel most comfortable with. Each successive stage in developing new technology becomes more expensive, and individual Member States may not have the resources to compete adequately. The arguments for greater collaboration include the following:

1.   Cost reductions, for example economies of scale and experience-based savings.

2. The ability to share technology across national boundaries, so that there is no need to duplicate high R&TD costs.

3. Sharing risks, especially with large-scale projects, where there may be a risk of failure. This is especially true of projects such as the Joint European Torus (JET), a nuclear fusion programme.

4. Reduced problems with technical standards, in that where new standards emerge they do so in more than one Union state.

5. Increased market power, so that whatever emerges as a result of collaboration is less likely to be lost due to the lack of size or a presence in other markets.

For the EU, the hope is that the dependence on US technology will be reduced, and that the overall technological gap will be reduced.

It would be wrong to assume that collaboration was a universal panacea. The increasing use of collaboration as a method of operating within the European market has revealed the following significant problems.

1. A lack of control over vital parts of the project. There is often a lack of understanding of foreign business cultures and working methods, which leads to very different outcomes to those expected.

2. No sense of ownership, because the costs and risks are being shared, means that in some cases projects do not receive the same priority as those generated domestically within the organisation.

3. Costs can increase very substantially at the early stages of programmes, often because of the need to travel and develop adequate communications. Also, compromises frequently have to be made about alternative methods of working.

4. Setting up and running collaborative projects can take a great deal of time, especially for senior managers.

5. State or EU funding is required to make projects viable, and even then the levels of funding do not always compensate for the extra costs involved, especially where funding is available only on a competitive basis.

The decision to collaborate therefore depends on the extent to which the positive aspects of collaboration can be said to outweigh the negative aspects. Also, it might be said that even if there is a balance of advantage in terms of collaboration as against the 'go it alone' option, this might be a second-best solution to the creation of just one or two European firms in key sectors. In some sectors even greater specialisation is required, and not all Member States can maintain firms in all sectors.

What a EU policy in this area cannot do, in the short term at least, is to eliminate national interventions. The recognition that industrial performance is not satisfactory makes state help to industry inevitable. Indeed, where the issue of defence technology is concerned, the EU's role can only be regarded as peripheral. Added to this, the Union simply does not have the funds to launch initiatives in all sectors. From an EU-wide perspective, policy towards new technology should:

1. eliminate many of the conflicting rival national policies

2. reduce the unfairness of national policies, where the stronger states gain at the expense of weaker states

3. create a Europe-wide strategy for new technology.

Collaboration in action

European industry has learned to cooperate on a limited basis by the development of collaborative projects. The British and French national electricity grids are linked by a cross-Channel cable in order to pool resources to relieve peak loads, for example. Also, the Channel Tunnel is a significant example of collaboration in providing improved transport links, on a bilateral basis.

In aircraft production, there has been a long, if not always successful, history of collaboration. The most famous example here is the Anglo-French Concorde. A more successful example from a commercial point of view is the Airbus project, which involves the collaboration of Britain (with British Aerospace holding a 20 per cent stake), France (with Aerospatial holding a 38 per cent stake), Germany (with Deutsche Airbus holding 38 per cent), and Spain (with CASA holding 4 per cent). The establishment of the Airbus was an attempt to provide a viable alternative to the dominance of the American airframe industry, which in 1978 had something like 90 per cent of the world market. The success of the project in terms of sales can be judged by the increase in market share. In 1993, the European collaborative project had seven models under production or under development. It had increased its share of the world market from 5 per cent in the mid-1970s to over 30 per cent.

In part, the success in terms of sales has been due to very favourable market conditions. The aircraft produced by the consortium are regarded as being technically advanced, particularly with regard to their 'fly by wire' technology. This system has allowed the mechanical systems of flying the aircraft to be replaced by lighter and more precise electrical equipment. The overall fuel efficiency and quiet running of the aircraft are also important selling points.

Despite its commercial virtues, the US government has always protested that the competition from the Airbus was unfair because of the levels of subsidy that it received. The full validity of this claim is difficult to judge, because of the unwillingness of the member governments to release adequate accounts.

The US government has constantly sought to reduce the extent of direct aid for the development of a new aircraft in Europe, in order to protect US market dominance. It has, however, been pointed out that European companies do not have the access to indirect help towards development costs that is available in the USA. This is said to be worth $1 billion per year. The Europeans have claimed that McDonnell Douglas and Boeing received up to $41.5 billion in state aid over the past 15 years, while the help given by European governments towards Airbus is estimated to be in excess of $13.5 billion. In addition, the fact that both the French and German national airlines are required to buy the planes discriminated against the US competitors.

In May 1992, an agreement was reached between the USA and the EU to limit the extent of help that was meant to be given. This stated that there were to be:

1.   no direct subsidies in the manufacture of aircraft

2.   a limit to subsidies towards development of 3 per cent of annual turnover

3.   a timetable for paying back the development costs

4.   a limit on indirect subsidies, fixed at 5 per cent of a manufacturer's civil aviation turnover

5.   transparency about the help given

6.   rules in force concerning inducements.

This agreement came under pressure in the GATT negotiations in 1993, when the USA requested further cutbacks in aid. This was not granted as part of the main settlement in December of that year, but there was agreement to talk further about the issue.

The European partners in the project regarded the assistance they received as being launch aids, and claimed that these would be paid back once the aircraft were delivered. However, even if the return on the investment was low, the arrival of a European rival aircraft at least provided an alternative to the monopoly power of the US producers. Airbus has been able to be innovative in its development of new aircraft. The Airbus A340, for example, with its capacity of 295 passengers, showed itself to be a major competitor for the Boeing 747. Although the 747 had a capacity of 380 seats, it cost $150 million to buy, as against $117 million for the A340, which had a similar long-haul capacity. In addition, the A340 was more suitable for routes with lower passenger density.[2]

The internal organisation of the project was criticised. Many of the decisions were subject to political intervention, which led to greater inefficiency. The division of work between the four partners also caused considerable problems, because the parts of the aircraft had to be carried to Toulouse or Hamburg (depending on the model) to be assembled. This not only added to costs, but also made the project vulnerable. For example, Airbus ran into considerable difficulties due to a strike in the UK in 1990. This lasted several weeks and closed down production elsewhere, because of the lack of the British-made wings.

The additional costs involved in the way Airbus is organised became more difficult to carry in the 1990s. Competition became more intensive with a downturn in demand, and a general over-capacity in the industry emerged. The challenge facing Airbus was that Boeing, its main rival, adopted a strategy of reducing its manufacturing costs. This had to be matched by Airbus, but it was difficult to reform the organisation's working patterns because of the structure that had been adopted. Working in a consortium made it difficult to win agreement about the measures needed to increase efficiency. There were attempts to move Airbus from a consortium to a limited company that owned its own assets, in order to get over the deficiencies in decision-making. This, it was hoped, would allow decisions to be made on a commercial basis rather than a political one.

Despite reservations concerning the collaborative model within Airbus, the individual members of the consortium sought other alliances in the area of smaller regional jets. At the same time Boeing sought an alliance with Airbus in the development of a very large passenger airliner.

The European Union's response

Attempts to promote a response to the challenges of new technology have a long history in the EU. The Jean Monnet Action Committee for a United States of Europe, which was established in 1955, had as an explicit part of its programme the idea of a European Technology Community. The European Atomic Energy Community (Euratom) was created in 1958, and was designed to promote research and development in the peaceful use of nuclear power. However, the encouragement of new technology was not part of the treaty that established the EEC, and there were no specific powers to promote R&TD. This meant that initiatives in this area were subject to the need to gain a unanimous vote in the Council of Ministers.

It was not until 1967 that the Council of Science Ministers first met. It commissioned studies into the potential for action to promote technological development in six broad areas: transport, oceanography, metallurgy, the environment, information technology and telecommunications. Its activities were held up by negotiations to expand the Union, but in 1971 the COST (European Co-operation in the Field of Scientific and Technical Research) grouping was established. This covered the six areas investigated on behalf of the science ministers plus medical research, food technology, meteorology and agriculture. Despite providing a useful framework for applied research on a pan-European basis, its weakness was that it included all 19 Western European members of OECD. This wider membership shifted the emphasis away from the EU and towards separately negotiated agreements for cooperation relating to each project. In the 1980s COST was overshadowed by the EUREKA programme, which once again had a wider membership and tended to be national government-oriented. The EUREKA programme was designed to be the broader European response to the US 'Star Wars' programme, but has since become a much wider vehicle for collaboration.

In 1973, the energy crisis gave an impetus to step up this area of activity. In 1974, it was agreed that the Union should have an involvement in all fields of science and technology apart from those affecting military and industrial secrets, and the Commission was given the task of coordinating national science policies. While these were important developments, real progress was limited until 1979, when Commissioner Davignon got together a working group of the 12 largest electronics companies. These companies became the European Information Technology Industry Round Table, and along with the Commission were able to develop the ESPRIT programme. The establishment of ESPRIT led to the development of a model for the majority of EU high-technology programmes. This promoted collaboration between organisations across the EU with the following features.

1.   Partners from more than one Member State.

2.   Up to half the funding coming from the EU budget.

3.   Projects with specific objectives and limited time spans.

4.   Spending as a supplement in addition to national efforts.

While at first it may appear that measures to promote competition and free trade contradict strategies designed to encourage collaboration, these two strategies may be complementary. The motive behind the EU's wish to advance cooperation or collaboration across frontiers is that firms should be able to compete effectively against companies from outside the Union. However, it is important that European business does not see this process as an opportunity to become complacent and try to shelter behind a protectionist shield.

The Framework Programmes

The EU's broad strategy with regard to the funding of new technology programmes has been produced under the Framework Programmes. This concept was first formalised under the Single Act, and reinforced by the Treaty on European Union. The First Framework Programme predated the Single Act and was for four years. Further Framework Programmes covered five year periods, which overlapped to accommodate ongoing projects. The Framework Programmes set out a broad set of objectives and identify expenditure priorities. Examples of programmes are ESPRIT and RACE (R&D in Advanced Communications Technologies for Europe), which fall under the heading of information and communications.

Table 12.4 The first three Framework Programmes

	I 1984–1987 (%)	II 1987–1991 (%)	III 1990–1994 (%)
Information and communications	25	42	39
New industrial technologies	11	16	16
Energy	50	23	14
Biotechnology	5	9	13
Environment	7	6	9
Human capital and mobility	2	4	9
Total amount (ECU billion)	3.8	5.4	6.6

The broad categories of expenditure for the first three programmes are given in Table 12.4. The total EU spending amounted to only 4 per cent of the spending of the Member States. Even adding other spending on joint schemes, such as EUREKA and CERN, the total European spending was no more than 10 per cent of national budgets.[3]

Following from the above, the general guidelines that informed the development of the Fourth Framework Programme were:

1.   the orientation of programmes to areas that were important to the EU's industrial system

2.   an increase in resources, with greater coordination with national programmes.

The Fourth Framework Programme was agreed at a time when most EU economies were going through a period of economic stagnation. While there was a recognition that the overall amount spent on R&TD was not sufficient, the budgetary constraints were considerable. The general agreement with regard to the level of funding of the IV Framework Programme was not arrived at until March 1994, with the final agreement not being ratified by the European Parliament until the end of June 1994. This was after a period of protracted debate, and helped to ensure that there was a late start to the projects. The Programme does not compare directly with the previous ones. Funding was allocated on the following basis in December 1993.

- First Action – Research, development and demonstration programmes = 87.8 per cent.
- Second Action – Cooperation with third countries and international bodies = 3.5 per cent.
- Third Action – Disseminating the results = 2.5 per cent.
- Fourth Action – Stimulation of training and researcher mobility = 6.25 per cent.

The total amount devoted to the Programme was agreed at ECU 12.3 billion, with the possibility of a further 0.7 billion to be added in 1996. This was to depend on the progress of the Programme, and the general economic situation at the time the decision was taken. The amount devoted to the IV Framework Programme was higher than the earlier ones. Over the period, even allowing for inflation, spending had risen from 2.6 per cent of the Union budget in 1988 to 3.8 per cent in 1992. The hope was that, under the Delors II package, expenditure on this kind of area would rise to nearly 6 per cent of the Budget.

The balance of expenditure changed over time, with an increased emphasis on information and communication technology, and a reduced emphasis on energy, which predominated in the First Framework Programme. This trend continued with the First Action (part) of the IV Framework Programme (Table 12.5).

Table 12.5 Distribution of resources within the First Action of the Fourth Framework Programme (%)

Information technology	28.2
Industrial technology	16
Environment	9
Life sciences and technology	13.1
Energy	18.65
Transport	2
Socio-economic research	0.65
Total	87.8

The process of moving the allocations in Table 12.5 into actual spending programmes was expected to take up to 18 months, which meant that the Framework Programmes took some time to be effective. The method for allocating the money from the EU tended to follow common patterns, as follows.

1. Expert opinion is used to devise a work plan for a particular programme.

2. Expressions of interest are requested through an announcement in the EU *Official Journal.*

3. A formal call for proposals appears in the EU *Official Journal.* Many of the interested parties will have knowledge of the project prior to this stage as a result of the consultation process.

4. After proposals have been submitted they are evaluated by expert panels, taking account of the ability of the consortiums to achieve their aims.

5. An assessment of the overall balance of the expenditure takes place, which ensures that the member helps in this part of the exercise. This tends to mean that consortiums with partners from the Southern states may benefit, given their disadvantage in high technology.

6. The Commission then negotiates with the consortium before agreeing a contract.

The overall process can be quite time-consuming, and those who wish to succeed need to ensure that they have plenty of time to construct the bid. Many organisations will have representatives in Brussels to see them through this process.

Information technology and collaboration

The first attempts at collaboration among European computer companies date back to the 1960s, when they were an attempt to meet the challenge of US multinational International Business Machines (IBM). They met with little success, however. In 1972, the Unidata scheme was launched. This was also an initiative to counter the dominance of IBM, by CII of France, Siemens of Germany and Philips of the Netherlands. Once again it came to nothing, due to a lack of commitment. As a consequence of these and other companies not working together, industry in the EU failed to establish an adequate platform to attack the world market and became vulnerable to imports in many areas where it should have performed well.

In 1973, the energy crisis gave an impetus to step up this area of activity. In 1974, it was agreed that the Union should have an involvement in all fields of science and technology, apart from those affecting military and industrial secrets, and the Commission was given the task of co-ordinating national science policies. While these were important developments, real progress was limited until 1979, when Commissioner Davignon got together a working group of the 12 largest electronics companies. These became the European Information Technology Industry Round Table, and along with the Commission were able to develop the ESPRIT programme. The importance of this industry was becoming apparent in that 5 per cent of Europe's working population was working in the information industry, and it was influencing something between a half and a third of all those who were economically active. With the newly industrialised countries overtaking Europe in the traditional industries, it was important to look to growth areas like this. The need for the EU to concentrate on this sector became even more apparent when the Japanese announced their Fifth Generation Computer Programme in 1981. Their aim was to obtain 40 per cent of the world computer-related market by 1990.

The ESPRIT programme

ESPRIT was the first of the major EU collaborative projects, and was all the more important because it was generated by industry rather than by the bureaucrats. It was designed to overcome the fragmentation of the R&D effort in the EU, but was more selective than many national programmes. Its aim was to bring together firms or institutions from more than one EU country. At least 50 per cent of finance was to come from the participating partners, for what was described as 'pre-competitive research'. This avoided some of the problems that might have arisen due to the EU's Competition Policy. It meant that any of the results of the work would not be immediately applicable, at least in theory. In practice, however, it seems unlikely that firms would involve themselves in this kind of activity without some thought as to its pay-off, although universities and other non-commercial organisations might. Indeed, the pretence that the projects were entirely pre-competitive was later abandoned.

The programme was launched in December 1982 with a pilot scheme, and the contracts for the first of the 38 projects were signed in May 1983. These were incorporated into the main programme when it got under way in 1984. ESPRIT was designed to be in two five year phases. The first was given a ECU 750 million budget by the Union, and this was to be matched by a similar amount from industry, making the potential total amount of funds available ECU 1500 million. It covered advanced microelectronics capability, software technology, advanced information processing, office systems and computer-integrated manufacture. The programme was a huge success in terms of the number of applications it generated. By January 1987, ECU 1.36 billion had been spent, and almost the whole allocation had been set aside for the ten years that ESPRIT was designed to run.

The popularity of the first ESPRIT programme encouraged the launching of ESPRIT II in 1989, with a potential ECU 3.2 million being available, split between the EU's contribution and that provided by the participants. The programme contained three research areas: micro-electronics, information technology processing systems, and the applications of new technology. The greater emphasis on applied aspects reflected a greater commitment to the more competitive aspects of research, and is perhaps a better use of resources. In any case, ESPRIT II was certainly popular among the manufacturers and researchers, in that it was ten times oversubscribed with its first tranche of projects. ESPRIT was carried forward into the Third Framework Programme, and similar work went on into the Fourth Framework Programme.

The best feature of ESPRIT was that it has promoted cooperation between firms, which has not happened often enough in the past. In spirit, it was meant to move the Member States away from support for national champions and create a European industry capable of competing in global markets. There were concerns that non-European firms might benefit from the research that had been designed to make European industry more competitive, even though firms had to have substantial European research facilities in order to participate in the scheme. Indeed, non-EU firms have not been welcome unless there were reciprocal rights to participate in their national research programmes.

The resources allocated to ESPRIT have been relatively small compared to those devoted to similar areas of research by Europe's global competitors. This may have resulted in Union support being spread too thinly to be of real use to many businesses. This is a criticism of the Council of Ministers, which consistently curbed the Commission's spending ambitions. The largest US companies were often spending $2 billion or more per year on research in this area, while the EU devoted a fraction of the money being given to even the smallest parts of the CAP.

However, national programmes of support for this area of work have continued, so it could be argued that it is the total funding levels that are important. Member States such as the UK have suggested that the principle of 'subsidiarity' should apply. They have argued that it is only reasonable to transfer spending to the Union where it is most effective. Many projects in the area of new technology, they believed, could be carried out more effectively at the national level. For this reason the UK government has seen EU spending in this area as an extension of national policy. Also, it has taken the view that if more is spent on Union projects, less should be spent on that area nationally.

The failure of national governments to allow Union expenditure on R&TD to be fully additional might seem reasonable if the area were adequately funded. However, in an area where public expenditure appears to be low, the situation could be judged as unsatisfactory. If national governments cut support because EU funding exists, there may be a disincentive to apply for Union funding. The overall value of the EU's policy will also be reduced, and there will be a watering down of the commitment to a truly European approach.

When ESPRIT was first launched, it was felt that it was difficult for small and medium firms to participate, although they were not excluded. However, in an industry dominated by large firms, it was to be expected that small firms would find it difficult to participate. This was especially the case given that only 5 per cent of the Union's SMEs tend to be involved in R&TD. By the 1990s, sufficient progress had been made with the task of integrating small firms into the programme for this complaint to lack some of its earlier substance. In 1992, it was claimed that half the industrial contractors in ESPRIT were SMEs.[4] A similar picture of involvement emerged with the Basic Research in Industrial Technologies (BRITE) programme, but this should not be regarded as a source of complacency, as SMEs' participant rate has been significantly lower in the biotechnology programmes. Also, large firms have often been involved in a multiplicity of projects, which makes them still the dominant force in all programmes.

Despite the claim that SMEs are given access to research, that they might not normally come into contact with, and that they benefit from the mobility of researchers, there are complaints. Small firms in particular feel that it takes far too long to fill in the forms for some of the collaborative projects, and they complain that the officials in charge change too frequently to establish long-term relationships with them. In addition, the funding frequently just seems to run out. The shift towards more market-based research has, however, been welcomed by many small firms as they feel that they cannot afford to participate in activities that do not show an immediate return.

Evaluating the success of ESPRIT

The ESPRIT programme has been judged a success by the European Union. The basis of this evaluation has tended to be subjective, because objectives such as the need to involve SMEs and the promotion of contact between organisations across the Union are essentially political. It is difficult to determine what extra value has been added by any particular project, in part because there are not normally exactly similar national projects to compare them with. The fact that there has been such a high degree of willingness by companies and research institutions to participate indicates that they see advantages, and as long as this enthusiasm continues new initiatives are likely to be forthcoming.

In the early years, it was argued that the improved flows of technical information that resulted from the ESPRIT programme produced little commercially useful technology. However, in an area where there are major problems related to diverse standards, it can be argued that companies by working together have produced compatible standards. The move towards more open systems in the area of information technology is regarded as an essential prerequisite for more developed collaboration. An example of this is the Portable Common Tool Environment (PCTE) project, which made it possible to develop a standard programming environment for software technology. Where standards are incompatible, systems remain closed, and sharing of technology is difficult. By 1992, the Union was able to claim that ESPRIT had led to the development of 700 IT prototypes, tools or standards. Products that emerged out of the programme included a system for storing and retrieving information that was used in the Philips compact disc interactive (CDI) multimedia products. In October 1993, ICL was able to launch an advance computer system based partly on technology developed under ESPRIT.

Globalisation as an alternative

Without further help from the Member States or the EU, the threat was that production capacity would have to be reduced, or companies would have to move closer to non-EU partners. The purchase from STC of ICL (the largest and most profitable British computer company) by Fujitsu the largest Japanese computer group in 1990, is an example of how vulnerable European industry can be. ICL and Fujitsu had been working together since the early 1980s. The merger put ICL with a far stronger parent company, and one that had a compatible range of interests. For Fujitsu the benefits of the purchase were expected to be a greater global coverage, and in particular access to the European market and technology. Following the acquisition, ICL became a much more credible entity, and the computing interests of the Nokia Group were taken over. ICL then became part of a worldwide group, including Amdahl, the US mainframe manufacturer, Poqet, a US maker of handheld computers, and Hal a specialist in advanced computer technologies.

Significantly, the takeover of ICL caused great concern to the EU, as ICL was participating in 36 ESPRIT schemes at the time. In response the major European computer companies attempted to isolate ICL by forcing the company out of the 12 member European Information Technology Industry Round Table, set up in the late 1970s to advise the European Commission. The group said it wished to remain truly European.

Siemens became the EU's largest computer company as a result of a merger caused by a financial crisis in Nixdorf. However, it was still a national champion rather than a truly European one. In 1991, Siemens created further cracks in European solidarity when it contemplated a joint venture to develop a 64 megabyte chip with IBM, the largest global computer company. In 1992 further deals were announced, so that IBM, Toshiba and Siemens announced collaboration to develop 256 dynamic random memory chips. In the 1990s it became normal practice for companies in the sector to collaborate. These collaborations were often between large multinationals and smaller companies with specific skills.

These trends towards global collaboration cast doubt on the value of strategies that are geographically limited and designed to promote just European interests. Globalisation made initiatives such as ESPRIT look not unlike the nationally based schemes that they were designed to counteract. It gave the impression that EU schemes were designed to be in some way protectionist, and that they created a culture that depended on subsidies and defending inefficiencies in Europe.

The European computer industry in the 1990s

In 1993 the European Union's highest placed company came tenth in the global league, the other nine places being occupied by Japanese and US manufacturers. Despite the EU spending on ESPRIT, the computer and electronics firms within Europe went through a period of crisis. Philips, the European leader in electronics, was facing major financial and managerial problems. Bull SA, the French computer company, made massive losses and the other major French company, Thomson, was also in difficulty despite state subsidies. The German company Siemens-Nixdorf, the largest computer company in Europe, was not making money from its microchip manufacture. Its semiconductor division lost DM 500 million (£180 million) on sales of DM 2 billion in 1991. The Italian company Olivetti had similar problems. This raised questions as to the overall value of the programmes, for if Philips and the other major companies were in trouble despite being major beneficiaries of grants and heavy involvement in collaboration, the strategy could not be working well.

The problems faced by the industry were not, however, derived from just technological disadvantages. IBM, the dominant US producer, faced massive losses and had to be subjected to considerable rationalisation. Globally, all producers suffered from falling prices for their products, which was a gain for the consumer but imposed a harsh environment on producers. European labour costs were a great deal higher than the competition from the Pacific Rim, and overall costs in 1992 were thought to be between 10 and 20 per cent higher than those in the USA and Japan. The three largest EU producers – Philips, SGS-Thomson and Siemens – recognising the extent of the competition they faced, attempted to concentrate on their recognised energy, and reduce their diverse product lines. Philips concentrated on multimedia products, Siemens on automotive applications and SGS-Thomson had strengths in the area of communications. This was seen as alternative to the creation of true European champions, although the company specialisation may lead to this in the longer term. The main players or their national governments were not prepared to adopt a Europe-wide solution, and recognise that the main source of competition was global.

Alternative responses

The alternative to leaving the European computer industry to the influences of global market forces would be to adopt a more directly interventionist strategy. Without an acceptable European solution, individual nation states often feel driven to take action on their own behalf. Bull, the French computer company, had state involvement in its activities from 1966, and became state-owned in 1982. Despite Ff 37 billion in state aid in the period to the start of 1994, it was still in need of further help to prevent its collapse. This was because of accumulated losses of Ff 18 billion in the four year period to the end of 1993. As a consequence of these losses, the French requested that the EU grant permission for further state aid, amounting to Ff 8.6 billion. Competitors argued that this payment might unfairly distort competition, although the French government hoped that it would move the business onto a firmer foundation.

The French government had frequently shown itself willing to come to the aid of national companies. Commenting on an earlier decision to assist Bull and Thomson in 1991, in direct response to the fear of major job losses and factory closures, *Le Monde* had argued

'Is it not time...to do what one can to save Bull, Thomson and the others, knowing that there is nothing to hope for from a semi-impotent Europe?'[5]

From the point of view of other Member States, the problem is that there may be a need to protect their industries against the subsidies of rivals. At the same time, a desirable wider restructuring of the industry might be prevented.

High technology and protectionism – the case of HDTV

Attempts to anticipate the development of technical standards within the EU have proved to be difficult, because of the range of national interests involved and the speed at which technology can change and develop. HDTV was considered of strategic importance to the EU's consumer electronics industry, as well as for television and film production. The older television standards within Europe had been diverse, and were felt to have made for an inefficient production of consumer products as well as holding back the cultural aspects of integration. The purpose of the HDTV initiative was to create a Europe-wide strategy, which would result in a new standard for the next generation of television. The notion of permitting the system to develop incrementally was rejected on the grounds that it would produce national solutions that would fail to bring about a satisfactory European solution, or that it would result in the kind of wasteful investment that had occurred with the introduction of video standards. Consumers who had purchased the European 2000 system or the BETA format found themselves with technology that had to be replaced in its entirety.

In 1986, Europe was poised to accept a Japanese standard for the high-quality HDTV system of the future. However, the notion of being dependent on the Japanese for the licensing of patents caused the Europeans to seek to develop their own standard. A consortium of 30 companies, led by Philips, Thomson and Bosch, was given four years to develop an alternative. This was to develop further the common satellite standard developed within the framework of EUREKA. The hope was that it would result in advantages for the European audiovisual and electronics industry. It took 20 months to develop a workable prototype, and this was demonstrated in Brighton in September 1988. Broadcasts took place of the Olympics at Albertville and Barcelona, but the audiences were very limited because of the lack of available sets.

By 1993, this strategy was all but abandoned. A number of satellite operators were able to circumvent the MAC standard which led to a loss of confidence in the project, although they did indicate a willingness to consider its adoption if there was a sufficient financial reward. This was proposed by the EU, but Britain in particular regarded it as a waste of money. As time went on, however, it became clear that digital technology, which was in its early stages in the mid-1980s, had advanced sufficiently to permit this to be used both for satellite and ground station broadcasts. The technology moved on, to the point where it was the USA that was able to gain an advantage, and the Europeans had to be satisfied with a process of upgrading existing standards and moving towards the development of wide-screen television.

Few people complained about the actual quality of the European HDTV, but the implementation was criticised, largely on the grounds that the policy became dated. However, there was also a view that the European public might not have been prepared to pay for the technology anyway. It was not a case of a radical change like the move from black-and-white television to colour, it was more a question of a move from good quality television pictures to better ones. These might have been of interest to commercial users, such as the computer industry, or for medical reasons, but this did not amount to a new mass market. Added to this was the failure to impose the MAC standard on satellite broadcasters.

There is still a need for a European standard to replace the Pal, Secam, Pal plus and D2 Mac standards that have grown up. There will also be a need for Europe to move towards digital technology, which makes it likely that the analog version of HDTV will never reach its full potential. The lesson to be learned from this is that it is unwise to go too early in the process of imposing standards, and that it would be advisable to consider the merits of adopting a more global standard. However, without a clear guide as to what the new standard is likely to be, there will never be the level of consumer demand required to make investment in the next generation of technology viable.

Conclusions

The need to resolve the problem of how to collaborate to generate solutions to technological problems was never more sharply illustrated than with the attempts to put into place the Schengen Agreement. In January 1994, it was decided that Schengen could not go ahead for some time to come because of the failure to put into place the computer system needed to keep track of drug traffic, criminal elements, terrorists and illegal migrants. The central computer was installed in Strasbourg by Siemens Nixdorf, with Bull providing the telecommunications, and Sema, the Anglo-French computer services group, providing the software. Each of the nine members was then to link its computer systems to the system, but the deadline was put back repeatedly because of a failure to do so. Although there were attempts to distribute the blame across a number of the participants, the episode demonstrated the difficulty of trying to create an information superhighway across Europe.

The EU has moved some way in its attitude towards industry. It no longer sees its role as being limited to preventing restrictive practices and helping declining heavy industries to adapt, although these are still important functions. It now rightly sees that it has an important role to play in promoting change, either by developing the internal market or by promoting R&TD. It would be a mistake to expect too much from collaborative schemes, however, unless the Union can devise methods of translating the success of research into viable commercial products. Also, there is a real danger that collaboration will result in retaining weak national champions that rely on subsidies or protection to survive. It is clear that the global trend towards collaboration can be fully exploited only by large Europe-wide businesses that are flexible enough to take advantage of the emerging global situation. Without the restructuring that is required, the danger is that European companies will be picked off one by one and will not become European champions. This points to the EU fully accepting the logic of the Single Market, with very large organisations operating within it. This means that attempts to preserve companies on just a national basis by the use of state aids can only hold back changes. The structure of companies in the industry considered here was not sufficiently large to gain economies of scale in both production and R&TD.

There is a need for the EU in the long term, and that is for the maintenance of competition policy, to overcome the excessive use of state aids. It is also important to ensure that the infrastructure to support high-technology industry is maintained, so that small and medium firms are also able to gain access to the technology. Training and education are also important, to ensure that the capacity to respond to the new developments is retained. Finally, if European companies are to keep their manufacturing base, the costs of production within Europe must be competitive.

References

1. **Commission of EC** (1993) *Growth, Competitiveness and Employment in the European Community: the Challenges and Ways Forward into the 21st Century*, COM (93) 700, p. 97.
2. *Sunday Times*, 9 January 1994, Section 3, 4.
3. As Ref. 1, p. 98.
4. **Commission of EC** (1992) Evaluation of the Second Framework Programme for Research and Technological Development, SEC (92) 675 final, p. 12.
5. Quoted in the *Financial Times*, 5 April 1991, 2, from *Le Monde*, 4 April 1991.

Further reading

Commission (1992) Research after Maastricht: an assessment, a strategy, *Bulletin of the EC*, Supplement 2/92.

European Economy (1994) European competitiveness in the Triad, No. 54, 131–133.

Sandholtz W (1992) ESPRIT and the politics of international collective action, in *Journal of Common Market Studies*, March.

Sharp M and Pavitt K (1993) Technology policy in the 1990s: old trends and new realities, in *Journal of Common Market Studies*, June.

CHAPTER 13

European Union Regional Policy: narrowing the gap?

Introduction

An effective regional policy is crucial to the development of an integrated EU. If the EU does not have a commitment to reduce the disparities in income differences and living standards, the future of the integrative process will be undermined. It is unacceptable for citizens in differing parts of the Union to be subject to significantly different standards.

It is, however, unrealistic to attempt to equalise all conditions throughout the EU, which are the result of different resource endowments and historical factors. The measures adopted by the EU in the form of Regional Policy are not intended to do that. The objective is to achieve economic and social cohesion. This is defined in unique terms within the Treaty on European Union as '...reducing disparities between the various regions...' (TEU Art 130a) in order '...to promote economic and social progress' (TEU Art B).

In order to achieve these objectives, financial assistance is made available, through the Structural Funds, for regions and groups in most need. There is no fixed numerical value attached to the level of unemployment or per capita GDP that is the desired objective. It is much more important to ensure that the economic benefits of membership of the EU are apparent to all than to fix absolute numerical targets.

However, the nature and distribution of the support has become a politically sensitive issue within the European Union. For some states, in which the poorest regions are located, payments have come to be considered as the means to ensure their national government's support for potentially damaging EU actions. For other states, which are the net contributors to the European Union Budget, payments from the Structural Funds are seen as a way of 'clawing back' some of those contributions.

Despite the significant increase in the levels of funding available since 1993, the steps being taken by the EU to achieve economic cohesion are still very hesitant. Overall levels of funding for regional development remain low in comparison with the levels of spending in the individual states. The disparities in income and unemployment within the EU between the most prosperous and least prosperous regions remain greater than those within the USA. The forces that accompany greater economic integration within the Union have the potential to exert unequal pressures on the regions.

The increasing levels of unemployment within the EU in the mid-1990s were a cause of grave concern. Unemployment in some states rose to over 20 per cent. The enlargement of the

EU in the mid-1990s increased the disparities. Action at the supranational level was therefore concentrated on ensuring that the mechanisms were in place to transfer sufficient funds to assist the development of the regions that were most likely to be adversely affected by the changes taking place within the EU.

This raised a series of crucially important questions about the nature of the European Union Regional Policy.

1. Did the political will exist within the national governments to see the formulation of an effective EU Regional Policy?

2. Were adequate mechanisms in place within the EU to reallocate the massive sums of regional assistance required?

3. Apart from the tools of the Structural Funds, what else could be done to achieve the EU's objectives?

4. What could be done to ensure that the citizens of the Member States were aware of the benefits of EU membership?

5. How could be the most effective use made of the funding that was available?

It was intended that the 1993 revisions of the regulations for the Structural Funds would address some of these issues. However, as this chapter demonstrates, the revisions have not been far-reaching enough to reduce the disparities between the regions of the European Union.

The regional problem

There are wide disparities in living standards and levels of economic development across the European Union. Regions with high per capita incomes contrast with economically backward regions. These backward regions tend to have a more peripheral location and are often characterised by low standards of public services and communications.

By the mid-1990s the ten least developed regions of the EU had average incomes less than one-third of the average of the ten most advanced regions in the European Union's northern core. Comparisons made with the USA show the limitations of the tools the EU has at its disposal. Regional disparities remain at least twice as wide within the EU as those within the single currency area of the USA. The federal government of the USA has been able to play a much more active role in reducing income differentials by about 35 per cent. The success of EU Regional Policy depends on having in place the mechanisms of a single nation state or a federation to transfer resources directly to specific regions within the Member States. EU Regional Policy can therefore be seen as potentially the most federal of all the policy areas.

The continued existence of regional disparities has raised the whole question of EU Regional Policy to a more central role in the debate about the future of integration. For the EU the goal has been set of achieving social and economic cohesion at the same time as economic, monetary and political union.

Article B of the Common Provisions of the Treaty on European Union (TEU) states that

'the Union shall set itself the following objectives to promote economic and social progress...'

and Article 130a (amendment to the articles of the European Economic Community Treaty) states that

'...the Community shall aim at reducing disparities between the levels of development of the various regions and the backwardness of the least favoured regions including the rural areas...'.

The Treaty on European Union therefore contains the continuing commitment of the EU to reducing the disparities. However, there are many concerns that this goal cannot be achieved without releasing forces that would widen the disparities further.

The challenges for the EU of the 1990s related to the progress towards greater economic integration. There was a risk that the southern economies would not benefit from the liberalisation of the Single Market. A region's development is the result of many influences which change over time. Some of these influences may be contradictory and counteract the levelling out of disparities. For some of the more peripheral regions of the EU, increased integration pulling development into the core area of the EU posed a threat. There was a perceived need for a more active European Union Regional Policy, which would have the tools to be able to resist the effect of market forces in the poorer and more peripheral regions of the EU.

The Member States were not prepared to support the development of a mechanism for a direct and automatic transfer of funds from the richest and poorest regions of the EU. Additional funding was made available instead for regional assistance. This raised the profile of ensuring that questions about the most effective ways of utilising the existing funds for regional support were resolved.

The arguments for radical changes are not new. The MacDougall Report of 1977 recognised the need for a considerable increase of funding and changes to the transfer mechanisms. It concluded that in the Community of nine states there was a need for an input equal to 7 per cent of total EU GDP to reduce 40 per cent of the disparities in existence then. The proposals for the period from 1994 were designed to address some of these problems, but were not far-reaching enough.

The primary aims of European Union Regional Policy are therefore to:

1. invest in the backward regions

2. encourage future growth in these areas.

The main tools the European Union has at its disposal to achieve its objectives are the Structural Funds.

The Structural Funds include:

1. the European Regional Development Fund (ERDF), established in 1975

2. the European Social Fund (ESF), created in 1957

3. the Guidance section of the European Agricultural Guarantee and Guidance Fund (EAGGF), established in 1957

4.   the Financial Instrument for Fisheries Guidance (FIFG), established in 1993 by
       Regulation (EEC) No. 2080/93.

In addition to these Funds, the Cohesion Fund was established in 1992 as a specially directed
Fund for the four poorest states of the EU. There are a number of other financial instruments
at the disposal of the EU. The European Investment Bank (EIB) is the most important. The
tasks of the EIB are set out in Articles 129 and 130 of the Treaty. Its primary objective is to
assist the less prosperous regions of the Union.

Monitoring of national regional policy and the coordination of the efforts of the ERDF,
ESF and EAGGF by the Commission also form an important element of EU Regional Policy.

Regional policy within the Member States

The Member States have carried out active interventionist regional policies since the 1920s for
a number of reasons.

Political

The level of inequality may lead to a lack of confidence in the government in power.

Social

There are unacceptable social consequences of high levels of unemployment. Patterns emerge
in the less developed regions of high unemployment, increasing levels of illness, child abuse,
infant mortality and inadequate housing.

Economic

Many regional imbalances are the result of long-standing and deep-seated difficulties.
Differential economic growth rates have an adverse effect on more prosperous as well as less
prosperous regions. The pressures in areas of high unemployment are more apparent.
However, as workers move to regions of low unemployment and low housing stock, this may
result in inflationary pressures growing in the more prosperous regions. A rise in wage
inflation may result from the increased demand for skilled labour and other prices will also
rise. Inward migration becomes curtailed as the stock of housing is taken up by new arrivals.
The problem of regional imbalance therefore continues.

In reviewing the effectiveness of the policies adopted by the national governments, it is
clear that many of the regions where the first policies were adopted are still the problem
regions. The national governments have more tools at their disposal to eradicate these
disparities. In setting the goal of reducing the disparities between the regions, the EU has
therefore embarked on a strategy that requires a great deal of concerted action over a very
long time.

The rationale for a European Union Regional Policy

If the Member States are already taking action, why is there a need for the EU to introduce measures to reduce the disparities between the regions? There have been clear calls from the larger states of the EU to 'renationalise' the policy on the regions. A frequently repeated theme in this chapter is the lack of funding for regional investment, which comes from the lack of commitment to the policy by the Member States.

The EU is not replacing the role of the nation states in regional policy. Instead, the EU's efforts are concentrated on assisting national regional policies to stimulate economic growth by granting *additional* financial aid. It is apparent that granting money for various schemes in the Member States will have little impact on the scale and nature of the regional disparities. The Member States spend much greater funds nationally than the EU has at its disposal. The role of the EU Regional Policy is to provide a framework for coordinated action.

Within the constraints set for it by the Member States, EU Regional Policy has become progressively more interventionist since 1972. The reasons for this development mirror the reasons why national governments intervene in the less prosperous regions.

Reasons for EU intervention to assist the regions

The most important argument in favour of an EU policy is the necessity to have an active device by which the welfare benefits of economic integration are spread throughout the European Union. There is no guarantee that this will occur if market forces are allowed to operate freely. Evidence would suggest that the opposite effect might result, and that development would become even more concentrated in the centre of the EU, with severe social consequences.

Social

The EU aim was an avowedly economic objective: to create greater growth and development through the integration of economic policies within Europe. However, there is little to be gained from greater economic integration if the citizens of the states do not feel that they are benefiting. The progress of greater political as well as economic integration in the EU requires everyone to feel that they are sharing the results of the growth.

Political

The development of EU Regional Policy has been encouraged throughout its history by its forming the 'bribe' to a state or group of states to accept what was for them a potentially damaging change within the EU.

- The ESF was the means by which the redundant mineworkers received support in the European Coal and Steel Community (ECSC).

- The EIB was established by the Treaty of Rome to channel funds to the south of Italy.

- The ERDF was the result of pressure from the UK during the accession negotiations in 1972, when the UK, Ireland and Denmark were preparing for membership of the EU.

- When the states of the Iberian Peninsula were being considered for membership of the EU, the bribe to Greece, France and Italy was the Integrated Mediterranean Programmes.

- The Cohesion Fund was the result of the need to convince the four poorest states, led by Spain at Maastricht, that despite the potential implications of EMU for them, they should ratify the Treaty of European Union.

- A new Objective 6 was added to the Structural Funds to meet the concerns of Sweden and Finland about the most northern regions close to the Arctic Circle when they joined the EU in 1995.

Economic

It is possible that coordination of the regional policy at the supranational level may remove the contradictory influences of policies in neighbouring states. This is a particular concern where the neighbouring states have regions of different types close to one another. It is in such a situation that the Community 'own initiatives', such as the INTERREG programme, have played a role.

Economic growth may be impaired within the EU as a whole by the presence of the less prosperous regions which need support. As the arguments presented in this chapter will show, it is in times of economic growth that the lagging regions have shown most convergence.

Regional impact of other European Union policies

It is of vital importance in any evaluation of the effectiveness of regional policy to consider the impact of other areas of policy. The impact of the EU policies may have an adverse effect on the less prosperous regions. Neither at EU level nor at national level do economic or financial policies have aims that are exclusively to promote investment in the less prosperous regions. Difficulties therefore emerge when the objectives or the results of other policy areas run counter to the objectives of Regional Policy. The potential impact of agriculture, monetary and economic and competition policies on regional competitiveness forms the basis of the arguments in favour of an EU Regional Policy.

The completion of the Single Market

The full impact of the completion of the Single Market on the regions will not be felt for some time. The national governments' ability to protect a region by the use of regulations such as export subsidies, import restrictions, local preference in public procurement and infrastructure should disappear over time. This removal of the non-tariff barriers will increase the competitive pressures on the least prosperous regions.

To take advantage of the benefits of the completed Single Market, the less prosperous regions of the EU will have to make any adjustments to the new environment of the completed market more rapidly than the more prosperous regions. But as Tables 13.1 and 13.2 show, this would be very difficult to achieve.

Table 13.1 Economic growth

Change in GDP per head (Index, EU12 = 100)		Time period (years)		
		10	15	20
From (A)	To (B)	Required deviation of regional growth from EU average		
50	70	3.5	2.25	1.75
50	90	6–6.5	4–4.5	3
70	90	2.5	1.75	1.25

Note: For a region with an index GDP per head of half the EU average (50) to move to 70 within 10 years, the region's growth of output per head must be 3.5 points higher than the average growth rate of the EU. Assuming the European Union growth rate per head to be 2% per annum during this time-span, the region's rate would have to be 2% + 3.5% = 5.5 % per annum

Source: *Community Structural Policies – Assessment and outlook*, COM (92) 84 Final, Statistical Analysis, Table 11 p. 10

Table 13.2 Employment growth

Change in unemployments rates (%)		Time period (years)		
		10	15	20
From (A)	To (B)	Required employment growth (% per year)		
20	15	2.25	1.5	1.5
20	10	3.5	2.25	1.25

Source: As Table 13.1 (Table 11)

What these tables show is that it would take a region with a per capita income 50 per cent of the EU average, an average of 20 years to reach 70 per cent of the Union average. To do so would require the lagging region to achieve a growth rate 1.75 per cent that of the EU average. For a region with a rate of unemployment of 20 per cent, it would need an employment growth rate of 2.25 per cent per year for ten years to reduce the rate to 15 per cent.

This raises a series of questions for the less prosperous regions.

1. How sensitive is the region to the changes in the economic environment?

2. Can the region make use of the employment opportunities that result from the completion of the internal market?

3.   Can the region diversify its product base?

4.   Can the region increase income at an above-average rate?

5.   Can the region achieve a target of full employment?

In the short run the less prosperous regions may have a wage cost advantage, but if it is concentrated in low-technology sectors, or in sectors that do not have good long-term prospects, the result will be a widening and not a reduction of the disparities. The less prosperous regions are those where there is already a concentration of low-technology development and infrastructural deficiencies. Assistance is needed in a number of areas to develop the skills base of the workforce.

Impact of other policies on the lagging regions

Gains

Gains may come to the lagging regions of the EU in the future from the operation of the integrated Single Market and the Economic and Monetary Union. This will be as a result of greater economic growth and development in the EU as a whole. These gains will not, however, occur if the redistributive mechanism remains relatively ineffective.

The Single European Act and the 1988 Reforms laid the foundation for a Common Regional Policy. The agreement at the Edinburgh Council in 1992, and the revisions of the Structural Funds regulations in 1993, provided for a regional policy that will take 36 per cent of the EU Budget by 1999. The regulations in 1993 contained a requirement for a five-yearly review of effectiveness. This will be of vital importance to assessment of the policy and ensuring that the direction of future policy is appropriate. But in comparison to actions that have been taken in the individual Member States, the EU's attempts at Regional Policy are still in their early stages.

Losses

● Competitiveness will suffer as a result of greater economic integration. The lagging regions are not competitive and do not on their own have the ability to improve their competitiveness. The sectors of economic activity present in the lagging regions are characterised by low potential to achieve the economies of scale that would enable them to take advantage of the completed Single Market.

● The lagging regions have a large number of sensitive sectors of economic activity concentrated within them.

● Improving the opportunities to migrate leads to a loss of the human capital that performs a crucial role in the development of a region.

● Technology support tends to concentrate in the richer Northern states of the Union. The firms with the resource base to co-finance research and development are located there.

● Agricultural support still focuses 75 per cent of funding on 25 per cent of the EU's most competitive farmers.

The development of European Union Regional Policy

It is possible to identify a number of phases in the development of the European Union's Regional Policy.

First phase, 1957–1972

EU Regional Policy between 1957 and 1972 had the following characteristics:

1. measures were meagre and rudimentary

2. there was little coordination of the policy at EU level

3. vague objectives were set.

The potential regional impact of economic integration was recognised in a number of articles of the Treaty of Rome. These articles did not provide for a Common Regional Policy.
    Instead the regional dimension was included in:

1. improving living standards (Art 2)

2. Agricultural Policy (Art 39)

3. Transport Policy (Art 75)

4. decisions about the level of state aid to industry (Art 92).

    Certain financial instruments were also established that had a regional impact:

1. the European Social Fund (Art 123)

2. the European Investment Bank (Articles 129 and 130)

3. the Guidance section of the European Agricultural Guarantee and Guidance Fund. This took about 5 per cent of the total agricultural budget.

Despite this implicit recognition of a need for developing measures to help with regional disparities in the EU6, no specific chapter was added to the Treaty of Rome. In 1957 the underlying rationale was that the process of integration, plus the general economic expansion that would accompany the completion of the market, would automatically close the gap between the richest and the poorest regions. It was recognised that there might be some worsening of regional problems as a result of economic integration. However, the main task of the EU was to ensure that national policy did not interfere with the needs of economic development throughout the whole of the EU.
    Each of the states had a long history of assisting its lagging regions, but in different ways. The task of the Commission was seen to coordinate these policies into a coherent pattern of national assistance which would not interfere with the operation of the EU. There was a commitment to preventing the adverse side-effects of the EU policy. However, much of the

activity undertaken by the EU until 1972 was aimed at preventing the governments from abusing the provisions on state aids to industry rather than active interventionist-type regional measures.

The situation in the EU in 1957 sharply contrasted with 1972 which was a major 'break' point in the development of the European Union and the need for regional policy.

Second phase, 1972–1979

In 1973 the enlargement of the EU to include the UK, Denmark and Ireland increased the magnitude as well as the nature of the disparities. In Denmark and the United Kingdom, the range of disparity had been increasing during the late 1960s and early 1970s. Table 13.3 gives a comparison, based on national per capita GDP, between Denmark, the UK and Ireland and the EU6 in 1973. Denmark's per capita GDP was 11 per cent above EU average, but the Irish position was very much worse. At the time of accession to the EU, the Irish per capita GDP was about 60 per cent of the EU average. While the situation has improved, as the figures for 1986 and 1995 indicate, Irish per capita GDP remains some 20 per cent below the EU average. In the UK, from a position of 5 per cent above EU average in 1973, per capita GDP had fallen in 1995 to below the EU average.

Table 13.3 GDP per capita (EC =100) at current prices and current PPS

	1960	1973	1986	1994	1995
Belgium	98.0	104.1	103.3	106.3	106.2
Denmark	116.5	111.5	115.2	108.6	109.6
Germany	123.2	115.8	118.4	115.5	114.3
Germany[1]				103.4	103.2
Greece	34.9	51.4	50.7	48.5	47.7
Spain	59.0	76.7	70.6	75.4	75.5
France	106.2	111.6	111.3	109.5	109.8
Ireland	59.9	58.1	62.8	80.0	81.6
Italy	86.9	93.7	102.6	104.5	105.2
Luxembourg	153.3	139.4	124.9	133.8	134.6
Netherlands	115.5	110.2	103.9	100.3	100.0
Portugal	37.9	54.6	52.1	60.5	61.0
UK	123.8	104.7	102.3	99.8	99.9
EU	100.0	100.0	100.0	100.0	100.0
EU[1]				97.90	98.0
USA	18.7	154.2	146.3	148.2	148.2
Japan	54.5	93.6	105.8	120.4	120.7

[1]   EU+ includes figures for unified Germany
Source : Europe, 16 May 1994, 3

The first enlargement of the EU was made against a background of global economic recession. This was the result of slowing of growth, decline in world trade, the collapse of the world monetary system, and the oil price crisis. An added economic pressure came from the newly industrialising states. As a consequence there was a rise in the level of structural unemployment within the EU. The necessity to strengthen regional policy was apparent. In 1972 the EU acted to counterbalance the vagueness of the Treaty of Rome. In the Paris Summit meeting of the Heads of State in 1972, agreement was reached to establish the European Regional Development Fund (ERDF).

The objectives of the ERDF were to:

1. provide subsidies to stimulate investment

2. develop infrastructure in the less prosperous regions.

The first task for the EU was to define what was a problem region in need of assistance. A Report presented in 1975 by the then Commissioner for Regional Policy, Lord Thomson, proposed the following broad definition.

Problem regions included:

1. agricultural regions with 20–40 per cent of the population employed in agriculture, a high degree of out migration and a low level of productivity

2. industrial regions where coal, steel, shipbuilding and textiles had been concentrated

3. peripheral regions

4. congested regions where severe environmental problems or diseconomies of scale would come from further concentration.

The national governments were left to identify which regions would need additional assistance. The regions which they identified had the following characteristics:

1. high levels of unemployment

2. poorly developed infrastructure

3. high levels of out-migration.

However, a great deal of dissatisfaction was expressed about the way in which the ERDF was operated. From 1975 to 1979 all the ERDF money was allocated in fixed national quotas based on the national definitions. As a result some 60 per cent of Germany was classified as eligible for assistance. The UK government led the criticism about the use of the different national criteria. It was pointed out that as a result, all the ERDF aid granted to Germany was going to richer regions than some of those in the UK. As Table 13.3 shows, Germany, in 1973, was the second richest state of the EU after Luxembourg. The bureaucracy involved also led to much criticism. Overall, the early Fund was not very effectively used. Of the initial allocation made in 1975, only 60 per cent of the £126 million funds were actually used.

Third phase 1979–1988

The Council of Ministers issued a series of guidelines on regional policy in 1979:

'Regional Policy is an integral part of the economic policies of the Community and the Member States. It forms part of the various elements which contribute to the attainment of a high degree of convergence of the economic policies of the Member States.'[1]

This clear recognition of the problem of convergence and the impact of greater economic integration was crucial at the end of the 1970s, as the EU of nine states (EU9) was about to absorb the newly democratised state of Greece. Within the EU9 the disparities appeared to be worsening rather than improving. Development in the EU9 was concentrated in the 'golden' industrial triangle formed between Rotterdam, Milan and London. Greek membership of the EU opened the gap between the regions even further. In 1986 Greek per capita GDP was 50 per cent of the EU average (see Table 13.3). In Luxembourg, in contrast, the per capita GDP was 24 per cent above the EU average.

The ERDF was reformed in 1979 in preparation for Greek membership. The Fund was divided into quota/non-quota sections. There were certain advantages to the division. It was one way of ensuring that the greater proportion of the ERDF funding went to the poorer regions of the EU. The non-quota section was a small separate section of the Fund which was approved by the Council of Ministers in February 1979. Five per cent of the ERDF Budget, worth about £45 million pounds, was allocated to this section.

Unemployment increased in intensity during the mid-1980s. This rising level of unemployment had a different effect on different regions. Certain sectors of the older traditional heavy industries such as steel, shipbuilding, agriculture, textiles and clothing had seen major job losses. Service sector employment had grown, but this had not offset the overall losses. The levels of disparity therefore increased within the Community. This was not as a result of the increased development in the strong regions pulling away from the poorer. Some of the former strong regions had in fact grown weaker.

There was clearly a need for radical reforms to be introduced. Despite this, a major round of reforms was not undertaken. Instead, the 1984 reforms of the EU Regional Policy concentrated on increasing the level of funding in the non-quota section to 20 per cent of the Regional Fund budget.

The impact of the third enlargement of the European Union

The pressures for reform were increased because of the prospect of the third enlargement of the EU to include Spain and Portugal. Their economies were characterised by:

1. below EU average economic performance

2. above-average rates of unemployment

3. large inter-regional differences in development

4. relatively high levels of agricultural employment.

In order to prevent further widening of the disparities in the EU, these new states had to have an above-average level of growth in output and employment. The EU therefore needed to introduce a major reform of its Regional Policy to support these states. The background conditions to such a major reshaping and redirection of regional policy were not good. However, a major reform was begun in 1988.

Fourth phase – increased intervention

Reforms of the late 1980s

The series of reforms of the Structural Funds and their operation begun in 1988 marked the beginning of a more interventionist approach to Regional Policy by the European Union. The new strategy was based on a doubling of the funding available in the three Structural Funds. The effectiveness of action was increased by greater coordination between the Funds. This was combined with multiannual and integrated regional development plans which were the result of a partnership that included the local authorities, national governments and the Commission.

The reforms came into force on 1 January 1989. A number of forces had propelled them.

1. The Single Act of 1986 had included the objectives of economic and social cohesion in Arts 130a and 130d. As a result the Council of Ministers had called for the Commission to make a proposal for an amendment to the rules of the Structural Funds.

2. The accession of Spain and Portugal had brought a considerable widening of the disparities between the regions of the EU. The number of people in the least favoured regions (i.e. those with a per capita income of less than 50 per cent of the EU average) had doubled.

3. Levels of unemployment were still higher than they had been in the late 1970s.

4. It was recognised that the adaptation process that had to be undergone as the Single Market Programme was completed would impose severe strains on the objectives of achieving social and economic cohesion.

In a move towards a more coherent EU Regional Policy, European Union-defined criteria for the allocation of funding were agreed.

European Union-defined priorities for action

The criteria chosen were based on per capita GDP (75 per cent of EU average being taken as the benchmark) and unemployment rates. These criteria are not without their difficulties. There may be differences in the calculation of unemployment rates between the Member States. The use of GDP as a measure somewhat overstates the differences, unless some account is taken of the differences in purchasing power between the regions. The calculation of purchasing power parity is a very imprecise method for comparison.

Five objective priority regions were identified.

Objective 1

To promote the development and adjustment in the regions where development was lagging behind (i.e. per capita GDP less than 75 per cent of the EU average).

Objective 2

Converting the regions or parts of regions seriously affected by industrial decline (based on an above EU average unemployment rate, industrial employment above EU average, decline in industrial employment).

The programmes for Objective 2 regions covered three years rather than the five year coverage given to the objective 1 regions. This was because industrial conversion problems were considered to be more susceptible to rapid change than the equivalent problems of the lagging regions and the rural areas.

Objective 3

Combating long-term unemployment (above the age of 25, unemployed for more than 1 year).

Objective 4

Assistance for schemes concentrating on the young unemployed (below the age of 25).

Objective 5

This was split into two:

5a. speeding up of adjustment of agricultural structures

5b. promoting the development of rural areas.

An important consequence of the identification of these regions was the possibility of concentrating and coordinating all the Funds that were available. Table 13.4 gives the allocations to each priority area and the Funds from which they were to come.

Table 13.4 Structural Fund Instruments and allocations 1989–1993

%	Objective	Instrument	ECU billions
63	1	All Funds	38.3
12	2	ERDF, ESF	7.2
12	3	ESF	7.5
	4	ESF	
6	5a	EAGGF	3.4
5	5b	All Funds	2.8
2	Other		1.1
			Total 60.3

Source : New Strategy for Social and Economic Cohesion after 1992, p. 34

It was expected that the Member States themselves would contribute to the objective of economic and social cohesion in two ways:

1. by bringing their economic policies together

2. by working in partnership with the Commission to ensure that cohesion objectives were taken into account in the formulation of all EU policies.

The reform was based on five principles. These were designed to ensure that greater care was taken about the methods being adopted to reduce the disparities between the regions, and also to ensure better coordination with the national policies.

1. Assistance was concentrated on EU-defined priority objectives.

2. Partnership between all tiers of government – Union, national, regional, local and interested groups in the regions in the development of multiannual programmes. Development plans were submitted by the national governments for each of the objectives and then negotiated with the Commission for allocation of funds. Community support frameworks (CSFs) were then produced outlining the strategy that was being adopted.

3. Measures taken were to be consistent with the economic policies of the Member States.

4. Measures were to be introduced to ensure that EU actions were consistent with the economic policies of the Member States.

5. The operational procedures were to be simplified, monitoring was to be a priority and the overall objective was to maintain a flexible approach that would take account of the needs of the individual regions. Further flexibility came from the allocation of some of the funds to the EU's 'own initiatives'. These were specially targeted programmes, which in the period from 1988 to 1993 took 3.9 billion ECUs.

Effectiveness of Regional Policy 1988–1993

The long-term nature of the problems being tackled and the nature of the strategy adopted by the 1988 reforms, made the socioeconomic impact of the funds difficult to assess. For some states the impact has been greater than for others, as Table 13.5 shows. The impact of the EU funding was very important for Greece and will continue to be so under the revised funds following 1993.

Issues that emerged following the 1988 reforms

1. The need to ensure that further simplification of the procedures and mechanisms of transfer of funding took place.

2. The need to increase the level of funding available to the Structural Funds. The Funds had undergone a significant change between 1988 and 1993, so that they became equal to 25 per cent of the total European Union Budget. However, the pressures on the regions were increasing and therefore more funding would be needed.

3.   The need to introduce more flexibility to assist the four poorest states.

4.   The application of the principle of additionality.

Table 13.5 Commitment of the ERDF and the other Structural Funds as a percentage of investment and GDP in Objective 1 regions (1989–1999)

Objective[1]	ERDF (% investment GFCF[1])	ERDF (% investment GFCF[1])	ERDF (% investment GFCF[1])	ERDF (% GDP)	ERDF (% GDP)	ERDF (% GDP)	All funds (% GDP)	All funds (% GDP)	All funds (% GDP)
	1989	1993	1999	1989	1993	1999	1989	1993	1999
Gr	7.3	11.0	12.6	1.4	1.9	2.2	2.5	3.3	4.0
Sp[2]	2.6	4.0	6.6	0.7	0.9	1.5	1.0	1.5	2.3
Ire	5.2	9.3	7.8	0.9	1.5	1.2	2.1	3.1	2.7
Por	5.3	7.0	8.0	1.4	1.8	2.1	2.7	3.3	3.8
EU 4	3.9	6.0	7.8	0.9	1.3	1.7	1.6	2.3	2.9
(of which Cohesion Fund)								(0.4)	(0.6)
New Länder[3]	n.a.	(0.9)	1.8	n.a.	(0.4)	0.8	n.a.	(0.8)	1.7
It [4]	1.7	3.6	4.0	0.4	0.7	0.8	0.6	1.1	1.2
Other [5]	2.0	3.3	2.5	0.4	0.6	0.5	1.0	1.4	1.1
All Obj 1	3.0	5.0	4.7	0.7	1.1	1.2	1.2	1.8	2.1
EU 12	0.4	0.6	0.9	0.1	0.1	0.2	0.1	0.2	0.3

[1]   GFCF Gross fixed capital formation
[2]   1999 figures include Cantabria
[3]   Figures in brackets refer to amounts provided under EEC Reg 3570/90
[4]   1999 figures exclude Abruzzi
[5]   For 1989 and 1993 Northern Ireland and Corsica, for 1999 also including Hainault, the Arrondissements of Douai, Valenciennes, Avesnes, Flevoland, Merseyside, Highlands and Islands
Source : Commission (1994) *Fifth periodic Report on the Social and Economic Situation and Development of the Regions*, p. 131

The principle of additionality

Regional Policy is not to replace national policy. The additionality requirement had always been there as part of the allocation of Funds, but it was explicitly stated for the first time in 1988 in Article 9 of Regulation No. 2052/88. The Commission and the Member States must ensure

'...that the increase in the appropriations for the Funds...has a genuine additional economic impact in the regions concerned and results in an equivalent increase in the volume of aid in the Member State concerned...'

Simply stated, this principle of additionality was based on the idea that EU action to assist the regions should be a complement to and not a substitute for national government actions. It has proved more difficult in practice, and the source of much controversy. The controversy has focused on two aspects of the principle.

1. The requirement for the nation state concerned to match the EU funds. The macroeconomic climate of the Member State in question may leave the government unable to fulfil this requirement.

2. The flow of the funds to the region for which they are intended.

Matching of the Funds

The whole of Greece was designated under the 1988 reform as eligible for Objective 1 priority status (see Table 13.5). This meant that transfers made to the national government for assistance to the affected regions immediately reach the affected region!

On the other hand, the matching of the funding provided more difficulty for Greece. The devaluation of the Greek national currency relative to the EU Budget made matching the Funds more difficult in the 1990s. Meeting the additionality requirement of the Structural Funds implies a greater financial effort by the Greek government. The tight fiscal control that the requirements of EMU have imposed has further constrained the Greek government.

The transparency of the mechanisms by which funds are transferred to the regions

'We do not have problems with other governments in the way we have had problems with the United Kingdom Government...' (Bruce Millan, Commissioner for Regional Affairs, 1991)[2]

Acting on the advice of Bruce Millan during 1992, £100 million of regional grants were withheld from the UK government, because of dissatisfaction about the way in which the transfers of funds were made to the regions for which they were intended. The Commission recognised that in the UK local government financing is very complicated, but the concern was that as a result of the procedures, the grants for the regions were being allocated throughout the whole country and not to the regions for which they were intended. Many of the UK local authorities were not in a position to apply for grants as they did not have the necessary borrowing consents made available to them by the national government to utilise the grants.

The argument of the UK national government was that the additionality principle did not apply to the UK for the following reasons.

1. Prior to 1988 it was not stated in the legislation.

2. The UK national government had ensured that spending equivalent to the grants from the Structural Funds was made in the regions. It therefore did not matter if the funds went to the area for which they had been intended. The regions were receiving the intended level of assistance anyway.

3. As a net contributor to the European Union Budget, it would be less wasteful of money and time if the UK were to reduce its contribution to the European Budget and use the difference to finance its own national regional development programmes.

Clearly these arguments were not acceptable to the Commission. The Commission had been working to ensure the continuation of the Structural Funds, to find ways to improve the administrative arrangements of the Funds, and to encourage the Member States to establish effective systems of financial control.

Agreement about the release of the withheld funds for 1992–1993 for industrially depressed regions was reached with the UK government shortly before the 1992 UK General Election. The rising levels of unemployment in the regions of Strathclyde and Merseyside put additional pressure on the UK national government, and the appropriate levels of funding were made available to the local authorities to enable them to take advantage of the EU allocations.

Regional support 1994–1999

A major problem for the Community of the mid-1990s was the weak performance of the European economies and the resulting problems. Growth slowed from 1.1 per cent in 1992 to –0.3 per cent in 1993 (Table 13.6). Although some improvement is shown in the forecast, it was not a return to the levels of growth of the late 1980s.

Table 13.6 Economic forecast (real GDP growth)

	1988/90	1991	1992	1993	1994	1995
EUR12	3.6	1.5	1.1	−0.3	1.6	2.5
Ger. 1	4.3	4.5	2.1	−1.2	1.3	2.4
France	3.8	0.7	1.4	−0.7	1.6	2.8
Italy	3.0	1.3	0.9	−0.7	1.5	2.8
UK	2.5	−2.3	−0.5	1.9	2.5	2.3

EUR12, Ger. 1 from 1991 including the five new German Länder.
Source: Europe, 16 May 1994, 3

In the Fourth Periodic Report on the Social and Economic Situation in the Regions, the Commission had highlighted a trend that had emerged within the regions. Between 1980 and 1990, the Member States saw their per capita GDP move towards the EU average, with two exceptions: Luxembourg, whose lead widened, and Greece, where the situation worsened. Also, as Table 13.3 shows, the relative positions of each state within the EU had remained little changed since the 1960s. Luxembourg was the richest and Greece the poorest of the states.

When the Fifth Periodic Report on the Regions was presented in July 1994, it confirmed the findings of the Fourth Report that there had been some convergence, with 40 per cent of the regions having a per capita income closer to the EU average.

The other main findings of the Fifth Report were that:

1. Some of the lagging regions had begun to catch up, especially regions in Ireland, Spain and Portugal. Since 1986 Ireland's growth rate had been the most improved as a result of the ability of the Irish government to impose budgetary discipline. At the same time the country had attracted a considerable amount of foreign direct investment. The results for

Greece, southern Italy and Northern Ireland were in contrast disappointing, especially those for Greece.

2. The countries with the least driveable roads were Greece, Spain and Portugal, but major road building programmes were under way.

3. Investment from the other EU states was being attracted to Spain, Ireland and Portugal because of the advantages these states had of expanding markets and low labour costs. Greece was less attractive because of lack of infrastructure, e.g. telecommunications.

4. Little attention was paid to research and development in the four poorest states of the EU. The Commission view was that the richest Northern states should be encouraged to help with these developments (see chapter 12 for discussion of the problems of doing so).

5. The Northern states had been able to alter their regional policies and had abandoned automatic large-scale aid in favour of more selective small-scale aid.

6. The new states, except for Austria, had seen a major fall in their per capita GDP since the early 1980s. Finland's economic position had worsened when its Soviet markets were lost, and its per capita GDP in 1993 was 86 per cent of the EU's average.

In his conclusions to the Fifth Report the Commissioner for Regional Affairs, Bruce Millan, concluded that

'The economic recession has accentuated inter-regional disparities in unemployment rates, starting in 1991...The economic analysis contained in the Fifth Report provides confirmation of the importance of the regional dimension in matters of competitiveness and job creation.'[3]

The unemployment situation in the mid-1990s had continued to worsen. The period of the latter half of the 1980s had been one of growth, with more than 9 million jobs being created. Those gains had been lost in the mid-1990s. Within the EU as a whole the unemployment rates by the end of 1994 were in excess of 18 million. The trends suggested that there would be 30 million unemployed by the end of the century. The unemployment rates for the under 25s averaged over 25 per cent in most states of the EU. Those who had been unemployed for a year or more were in an even worse situation. The long-term unemployed rate was over 40 per cent of the total.

While the picture was severe across the whole EU, some regions suffered more than others. The Commission Report on the Employment Situation in the EU in 1993 showed that unemployment rates in the Objective 1 regions rose more rapidly than in the other regions during the early 1990s. Investment in the regions therefore continued to be an EU priority. In 1993 the regulations governing regional assistance were revised to take into account the growing economic difficulties.

The main objectives of the revision were:

1. to ensure simplification of the procedures and mechanisms covering the policy area

2.   to increase the level of funding available to the Structural Funds – it had undergone a significant change between 1988 and 1993, so that it was equal in the period to 25 per cent of the total Union budget, but the pressures on the regions were increasing and therefore more funding was needed

3.   to introduce more flexibility to assist the four poorest states.

These revisions incorporated the more flexible approach to the objective criteria that had been agreed in December 1992 at the Edinburgh Summit.

The revised criteria included:

1.   the GDP of the Member State and the region concerned

2.   the population of the region concerned

3.   the level of employment

4.   the rate of economic activity

5.   the rate of agricultural activity.

This did not alter the designation of the priority areas a great deal. The biggest differences from the 1988 regulations were in the designation of Objectives 3 and 4.

Objective 3

This combined and extended the 1988 Objectives 3 and 4. Action was to be focused on combating long-term unemployment and facilitating the integration into working life of young people and those socially excluded from the labour market. The primary source of funding was to be the Social Fund.

Objective 4

To facilitate the adaptation of workers to industrial changes and to changes in production systems. This Objective was concerned with preparing workers for expected industrial changes, anticipating market trends and occupational requirements. For the period 1994–1999 14 billion ECUs was allocated to this Objective (at 1994 prices).

Measures for the adjustment of fisheries structures were included in Objective 5a. A new financial instrument was created for support to the regions where the fishing industry was encountering difficulties, the FIFG (Financial Instrument for Fisheries Guidance).

Objective 6

Following enlargement of the EU in 1995, a new Objective 6 was added. The criterion used for deciding which areas were to receive this support was based on a low population density of below 8 inhabitants per square kilometre. The eligible regions were identified in the two Scandinavian states. This was to focus assistance on the areas of the EU north of the line of latitude 62 degrees north.

Until 1999, when the Structural Funds will be reviewed, the aid given to the Objective 6 regions will be regulated through a Protocol in the Treaty of Accession. Table 13.8 shows the total to be allocated to the new Member States from the Structural Funds.

Specific allocations of the funds to the Objective 6 regions will be made as follows.

Total allocation 1,109 million ECUs (1995 prices)

1.   In Sweden the designated regions are the three northern counties, with a population of 450 000. The aid given between 1995 and 1999 will be equivalent to 101 ECUs a year for each inhabitant.

2.   In Finland 837 000 people living in the areas bordering Russia and Lapland are included. Amounts of regional aid equalling 122 ECUs per person per year from 1995–1999 were agreed.

Table 13.7 The Structural Funds and the new Member States 1995–1999

	Austria	Sweden	Finland	EU 8 (excl. Gr, E, Ire, P)
Population (000)	7699	8559	4998	283 365
Objs 1,6 Pop (000)	269	450	837	45 036
Objs 1,6 (as % of national pop)	3.5	5.25	16.7	15.9
Structural Funds 1995–1999				
1995 prices MECU	1623	1420	1704	67 247
Objs 1,6	184	230	511	32 247
Other Objs	1439	1190	1193	35 000
Structural Funds per head (ECU)	211	166	341	237

Source : Adapted from Commission (1994), *Fifth Periodic Report on the Regions*, p. 133

Effectiveness of the 1993 revisions of the Structural Funds regulations

Changes to the designated priorities

No radical overhaul was carried out of the Objective 1 designation in 1993. The criterion remained that a region had per capita GDP less than 75 per cent of the EU average, measured as buying power on the basis of data from the previous three years. Certain regions, as a result of changed economic performance, were included for the first time as shown in Figure 13.1.

The Italian region of Abruzzi was no longer regarded as an Objective 1 priority, but in order to alleviate any adverse effect from the withdrawal of funds a transitional phasing out of the funding to the region was agreed to last for five years. Other adjustments had to be made to take account of the worsening economic difficulties of the new German Länder. They were included in the Objective 1 list, but excluded from the calculation of per capita GDP, to ensure that the overall number of regions eligible for assistance within the Union remained the same. In the UK, Merseyside and the Highlands and Islands of Scotland, which had been Objective 2 regions, were redesignated as Objective 1.

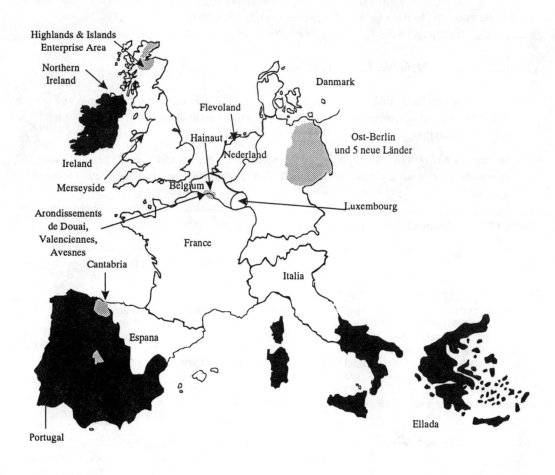

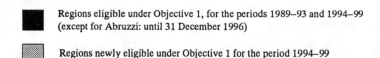

Regions eligible under Objective 1, for the periods 1989–93 and 1994–99
(except for Abruzzi: until 31 December 1996)

Regions newly eligible under Objective 1 for the period 1994–99

Figure 13.1 Regions eligible under Objective 1 (regions whose development is lagging behind)
Source : Commission (1993), *Community Structural Funds 1994–1999, p. 13*

In determining the geographical eligibility criteria, a great deal of emphasis was placed on concentrating on the Objective 1, 2 and 5b regions in order to achieve the aim of cohesion. This signalled a recognition of the need to support the areas of densest population to a proportionately greater extent. 43 per cent of the population of the EU was covered by these three objectives (Table 13.8).

Table 13.8 Percentage of population in Objective 1, 2 and 5b regions

Region	% Population
Objective 1	21.6
Objective 2	16.4
Objective 5b	5
Total	43

Decisions about the designation of regions for priority action led to division among the Member States before the final decision was reached. Spain, Portugal, Ireland, Greece and Italy favoured a strict application of the criteria of eligibility (75 per cent of per capita GDP at national level in relation to the EC average), others shared the Commission view that there should be a certain amount of flexibility. The differing national views were a clear reflection of concern among the four poorest states that funding for them might be threatened. These fears were allayed somewhat by the creation of the Cohesion Fund.

The Cohesion Fund

The agreement for the initiation of a special fund for the four states with the most problems – the Cohesion Fund – had been reached during the Intergovernmental Conferences at Maastricht in 1991. The impact of the progress towards EMU on the least favoured states of the Union was the reason for the creation of the new Fund. The particular frame of reference for the Cohesion Fund was to facilitate real convergence and nominal convergence so that the Member States covered by the Funds would be able to fulfil the conditions of accession to EMU.

Table 13.9 Allocation of the Community's Resources to the Cohesion Fund

1993		1996		1999	
ECU bn	% total EU budget	ECU bn	% total EU budget	ECU bn	% total EU budget
1.5	2.2	2.3	3.1	2.6	3.1

Source: Commission (1994), *Fifth Periodic Report on the Regions*, p. 126

The Cohesion Fund has similar objectives to the other Structural Funds. It contributes to government expenditure. The main emphasis is on strengthening structures to achieve balanced growth in the Member States with the greatest structural weaknesses and limited funding capacity. Projects being financed for the Cohesion Fund have to be concerned with improving transport or environmental infrastructure.

Two requirements are made of the programmes advanced for consideration.

1. They must be in keeping with the objectives of the Union's environmental programmes and the objectives of the TEU to ensure that there is a coherent development of the Union's communications networks. The TEU highlighted the need for the development of Trans-European networks (TENS) in the areas of transport, telecommunications and energy infrastructures.

2. There must be coordination with the other Structural Funds to ensure that the maximum impact is achieved from all the funds.

Allocation of funds

There has been a significant increase in the funding for the Regions as a result of agreement reached in the Edinburgh Summit of 1992 and the creation of the Cohesion Fund. The Structural Funds allocated in 1989–1993 contributed 63 billion ECUs, at 1989 prices, to programmes of investment, restructuring, training and employment in the Member States. The allocation was increased to 141 billion ECUs at 1992 prices for the period 1994 to 1999. This was split so that the Objective 1 regions received 96.5 billion ECUs and the rest 44.5 billion ECUs.

Table 13.10 shows the Financial Allocation by Objective to the Member States as a percentage of the total allocated through the Structural Funds to the EU12 states.

Table 13.10 The Structural Funds 1994–1996/1999: Financial allocations by objective (% of total by member state)

Resources available for the CSFs	Obj 1 1994/99	Obj 2 1994/96	Obj 3/4 1994/99	Obj 5a 1994/99	Obj 5b 1994/99	Total	Total member state % of the EU 12
B	45	10	29	12	5	100	1.3
DK		9	45	39	8	100	0.5
D	73	4	10	6	7	100	14.8
GR	100					100	11.1
E	87	4	6	1	2	100	24.1
F	19	16	28	17	20	100	9
Irl	100					100	4.5
I	78	4	9	4	5	100	15
L		9	31	52	8	100	0.1
NI	8	16	59	9	8	100	1.5
P	100					100	11
UK	26	23	37	5	9	100	7.2
EU 12	74	6	11	4	5	100	100

Source: Commission (1994) Fifth Periodic Report on the Regions, p. 126

Objective 2 allocations were made in two stages: 7623 million ECUs for the period from 1994 to 1996 and 7623 million ECUs from 1996 until 1999. The breakdown of allocations between the Objectives followed the same lines as the allocations for 1992, and did not involve a major increase for Objective 5a in real terms. Some states benefited more than others, as shown in Table 13.11.

Table 13.11 National allocation of Structural Funds 1993–1999 (billions of ECUs at 1992 prices)

	ECU billion
'Cohesion Four'	
Greece	19–20
Ireland	8.1–9.3
Spain	36.5–38.5
Portugal	19–20
Other Obj. 1 Structural Funds only	
Belgium	0.8
Germany	14.0
France	2.4–2.6
Italy	17.1–18.9
Netherlands	0.2
UK	2.2–2.7

Cohesion Four states receive Structural Funds and Cohesion Funds
Source: Europe, 22 October 1993, 5

Predominance of national interests

The overall share of the European Union Budget devoted to reducing the disparities between the regions remains low in comparison to the accelerating problems of the lagging regions. The problem lies in the political will of the Member States' governments to make the commitment to increasing the funds. To bring the four poorest states to 75 per cent of the EU average, the Commission has estimated that it would need an increase in the budgetary capacity of more than 100 billion ECUs per annum, equivalent to a figure in excess of 1 per cent of total EU GDP.[4] The total agreed until 1999 is 141 billion ECUs, or about 0.43 per cent of total EU GDP.

National government opposition built up during 1994 to the agreement that had been reached at the Edinburgh Summit in December 1992. Then it had been agreed that the contribution of the Member States through the Own Resources element of the Budget to the Structural Funds, including the Cohesion Fund, would be increased. It stood in 1992 at a ceiling of 1.2 per cent of the national GDP. It was agreed that this would be raised to 1.27 per cent by 1999.

Both the German national government and the UK government objected to this increase. Germany as a net contributor of EU funds had contributed more than DM 22.4 billion to the European Union budget in 1992. This was a doubling of its commitment of the previous five years. The German Bundesbank, in reviewing the funds being transferred to the EU, was concerned that this would rise to DM 30 billion by 1997. By the end of 1993 the German current account deficit stood at DM 39.5 billion. More than half of this deficit was the result of the support being given to the EU. At the same time the German government was under a great deal of pressure following the 1990 unification of the state.

Within the UK the Edinburgh Agreement precipitated a national political crisis in November 1994, when the Bill ratifying this agreement was debated in the House of Commons. The Conservative administration was forced to make the vote on the Bill a vote of confidence in the national government in order to have it accepted.

Regional Policy in the future

The Structural Funds are the chief means at the disposal of the EU to overcome the socioeconomic problems of the EU. This chapter has concentrated on the measures taken since 1972 to reduce the economic disparities between the regions. Low per capita GDP and high unemployment rates are the twin measures that form the basis of the identification of the problem regions.

How effective have the EU attempts at reducing the disparities between the regions been?

'In summary, statistical data indicate that overall progress over time has been far from satisfactory...regional disparities in the Community remain wider than those within most unitary states or federal systems. Differences...are greater...given the lack of specific distributive mechanisms.'[5]

In order to be effective, mechanisms have to be in place and there must be a commitment to allow transfers of substantial amounts of funding from one area to another in order to stimulate growth. This is not yet the case within the EU. While plans are agreed for a substantial increase in the level of spending on the less prosperous regions, there has been a failure to agree on plans to increase the total EU budget significantly. The total available to the European Union therefore continues to be considerably below the sums being spent within the individual states themselves.

The European Union is not a single unitary state, nor a federal system. The wide disparities within the EU policy require tools that are not at the disposal of the EU. Since the 1988 reforms of the Structural Funds, the EU has been moving towards a more interventionist regional policy. However, as the 1992 Mid Term Review of Regional Policy concluded, it is still a long way from being a satisfactory policy with anything more than a limited impact.

This is not to deny the achievements brought about under the 1988 reforms which are the foundations of the 1993 revisions and the basis of the policy to the end of the century. The Mid Term Review concluded that Regional Policy had made a small but significant contribution to the goal of economic cohesion in some areas. During the period from 1989 to 1992 GDP per capita had grown by 3 percentage points in Spain based on a Union average, 1.7 per cent in Portugal and 1.9 per cent in Ireland, but it had fallen by 2 per cent in Greece. These estimates were attributed by the Commission to the impact of the Structural Funds counterbalancing, in these states, the general slowing of the European economy.

What can be done with the tools at the EU's disposal?

The effectiveness of the EU policy to achieve economic and social cohesion depends on the relevance and the nature of the policy being used. It is not sufficient to double the funding available to the various programmes without some form of control of how the funding is spent. Nor is it adequate to expect that the Structural Funds will be able to counterbalance the actions being taken in other areas of policy on their own. As has been demonstrated in this chapter, there is a significant impact on the regions of other areas of EU policy.

The regional implications of actions taken in other areas have to be taken into account in a more concerted manner. The role of the Commission in coordinating the activities taken at EU level in the different policy areas is crucial to an effective EU Regional Policy.

Four areas are specifically referred to in the revised 1993 regulations that are intended to support the objective of ensuring compatibility with the other areas of EU policies:

1. the observance of the commitment to equality of opportunity between men and women

2. the strict observance of rules on competition, with specific information being made available about decisions on the provision of assistance for productive investment projects exceeding 50 million ECUs

3. the observance of EU rules on public contracts

4. the observance of EU environmental policy

To do this, binding provisions have been introduced into the regulations. In the future all development plans for objectives 1, 2 and 5b '...must include an appraisal of the environmental situation of the region concerned and an evaluation of the environmental impact of the strategy...'.[6]

The impact of the proposed development for the regions has to be assessed to ensure the effectiveness of the measures being taken. This prior appraisal of the plans was an important part of the reform of 1988 and has been strengthened considerably in the 1993 revision. There, a distinction has been made between the processes of appraisal, monitoring and evaluation. From 1993 the prior appraisal has been continued on the basis of the identification of the minimum necessary to carry out the planned programme. The appraisal process is vital to the allocation of the funding, since the assistance will be allowed only 'where appraisal shows medium term economic and social benefits commensurate with the resources deployed'.[7]

The principle of additionality continues to be a controversial area of Regional Policy. As set out in the regulations of 1988, Article 9 presented a definition of what additionality entailed. Member States had to ensure that any funding allocated from the EU for regional assistance resulted in an equivalent increase in the total volume of national aid in the Member State. This has led to a number of disputes with the UK government in 1991 and 1992. In the past the Italian government has also found itself in difficulty because of not having transferred funds to the region for which they were intended.

When the regulations were revised in 1993 an attempt was made to ensure that disputes between the national governments and the EU could not occur again over the principle of additionality. Provisions were built into the regulations which specified that there had to be verification of the principle of additionality at each level of each objective and in the Community Support Frameworks. Accounting has to be done by the Member States more transparently for the Structural Funds they receive, at the time of submission of the plans and also during the implementation of the CSFs.

Each Community Support Framework and Operational Programme (OP) has a Monitoring Committee of regional and national representatives and Commission representatives to ensure that the goals set out in the plans are adhered to. These Committees had their powers strengthened in the 1993 reform.

Conclusions

The basis of Regional Policy to 1999 will be the revision of the Structural Fund regulations agreed to in 1993. A new Objective 6 designation has been agreed following the accession of the former EFTA states.

The Budget for the Funds has been increased so that the 141 billion ECUs allocated are equal to one-third of the European Union budget. The place of Regional Policy as an area of priority action within the EU was affirmed in Article 130b of the Treaty on European Union. The effectiveness has been reinforced by the revision to the regulations in 1993.

The way forward has been charted on the basis of five principles.

1. Concentration of effort on a number of priority objectives for action.

2. Partnership between the Union, the national governments and the local and regional authorities.

3. The quality of the programming and planning.

4. The application of the principle of subsidiarity.

5. The commitment of the Member States to respect the principle of additionality.

However the regional disparities that have been identified will not be eradicated by the actions of the Structural Funds alone. The most effective way that has been demonstrated of overcoming the disparities between the regions is to ensure that there is growth throughout the whole of the EU. Stimulation of the whole macroeconomic environment is needed. Investment in the development of the less prosperous regions is crucial to the overall development of the EU economically as well as politically. The levels of competitiveness of the lagging regions have to be improved. To do that it is necessary to institute a Regional Policy that will counterbalance the adverse effects of other actions of the EU and stimulate investment.

The competitiveness of a region can be improved by better use of the human resources of the regions. Recognition of this has led to an increase of support through the Structural Funds for programmes that include a balance of infrastructural improvement, investment in telecommunications, aid to small and medium enterprises, skills training and investment in new technologies. This has been a major achievement of Regional Policy since 1988, to move away from a one-off project-based approach to the co-financing of multiannual programmes.

The intention is that the Structural Funds should benefit the citizens of Europe, so concerns like infrastructure, health and education are increasingly seen as part of the legitimate EU concern and activity. More funding is crucial to be able to develop programmes that concentrate on the human capital of the regions.

It is not, however, merely a question of throwing money at the problems of the less prosperous regions. There has to be greater coordination of the economic, financial and regional policies. The European Parliament in its opinion on the Mid Term Review of the Structural Funds in 1992 pointed to the danger for the lagging regions that would arise as national regional investment fell. States that are unable to meet the criteria for EMU will be unable to increase funds for public investment programmes, and may in fact have to make reductions. This would in turn reduce the amounts being spent from the EU Structural Funds because of the requirement for matching of funds.

Commission research indicates that, to reduce regional imbalances sufficiently in time for EMU, transfers are needed of 1 per cent of total EU GDP to the less prosperous regions. The Edinburgh Summit in 1992 agreed funding that will equal only 0.43 per cent for the period until 1999. Better value has therefore to be gained from this investment. The 1993 revised regulations and their concentration on better monitoring, evaluation and appraisal of the use of the Funds will assist in this process.

It is apparent that there has continued to be a concentration of development in the centre of the EU: the area bounded by London, Paris and Milan which has been variously described as the 'Golden Triangle' or the 'Hot Banana'. Reforms of the Structural Funds have not been sufficient to counterbalance this tendency. It is also apparent that much structural aid spent in the less prosperous regions has seeped back to the more prosperous in orders for finished goods and machinery. Investment in skill and training within the less prosperous regions may alter this pattern over time.

The Regional Policy of the European Union has developed considerably since the rudimentary attempts of the 1960s. The pressures within the EU have increased considerably as the European Union has grown. The EU has laid the foundations of a more interventionist approach to Regional Policy since 1988. Because of the deep-seated nature of many regional problems, it is unrealistic to imagine that there will be rapid growth and development across the whole EU. On the other hand it is politically, socially and economically unacceptable not to attempt to reduce the disparities that do exist. The Structural Funds can only achieve a limited amount because they continue to represent only a small share of resources. It is important that all the economic policies proposed and adopted by the EU are coordinated to achieve cohesion.

References

1. *Official Journal,* C36, 9 February 1979.
2. **House of Lords** (1992) **EEC Regional Development Policy**, p. 26.
3. *Europe,* 23 July 1994, 15.
4. **Commission of the EC** (1991) *The Regions in the 1990s,* Fourth Periodic Report on Economic and Social Progress in the Regions, COM (90) 609, final, p. 31.
5. **Commission of the EC** (1992) *Community Structural Policies: Assessment and Outlook,* COM (92) 84, final p. 6.
6. **Commission of the EC** (1993) *The Community's Structural Fund Operations 1994–1999. Proposals for Revised Regulations,* COM (93) 67, final, p. 29.
7. Ibid., p. 30.

Further reading

Armstrong H (1993) Community Regional Policy, in Lodge J (ed.), The European Comunity and the Challenge of the Future, 2nd edition; Leicester.

Armstrong H and Taylor J (1993) *Regional Economics and Policy*, Harvester Wheatsheaf, Hemel Hempstead.

Begg I et al. (1991) *A New Strategy for Social and Economic Cohesion after 1992*, European Parliament, Regional Policy and Transport Series, Paper 19.

Commission of the EC (1977) *Report of the Study Group on the Role of Public Finance in European Integration* (the MacDougall Report).

Commission of the EC (1989) *A Guide to the Reform of the Community's Structural Funds.*

Commission of the EC (1989) *Community Support Framework 1989–1993 for development and structural adjustment of regions whose development is lagging behind: Spain.*

Commission of the EC (1990) *Europe 2,000: The Outlook for the Development of the Community's Territory*, COM (90) 544, final.

Commission of the EC (1993) *Proposal for Council Amendments to Regulation EEC No. 4254/88 Laying Down Provisions for Implementing Regulation EEC 2052/88*, COM (93) 124.

Commission of the EC (1993) *The Future of Community Initiatives under the Structural Funds*, COM (93) 282, final.

Commission of the EC (1993) *Employment in Europe 1993*, COM (93) 314.

Commission of the EC (1993) *Community Structural Funds – Revised Regulations and Comments.*

Department of Trade and Industry (1993) *Explanatory Memorandum on the proposal to amend regulation EEC No. 2052/88 laying down provisions on the implementing of the regulations covering the ERDF.*

European Parliament (1990) *Report of the Committee on Regional Policy on a Community Initiative in Favour of Border Areas – INTERREG.*

European Parliament (1992) *Report of Committee on Regional Policy on the Regions in the 1990s.*

European Parliament (1992) *Report of the Regional Committee on the Communication from the Commission on Community Structural Policies – Assessment and Outlook.*

European Parliament (1993) *Report of the Committee on Regional Policy on the Future of Community Initiatives under the Structural Funds.*

Franzmeyer F et al. (1991) *The Regional Impact of Community Policies*, European Parliament, Regional Policy and Transport Series, Paper 17.

Nam C W et al. *The Impact of 1992 and Associated Legislation on the Less Favoured Regions of the European Community*, European Parliament, Regional Policy and Transport Series, Paper 18.

CHAPTER 14

European Union Policy on the Environment: are we all environmentalist now?

Introduction

Article 2 of the Treaty on European Union set a new agenda for the European Union's Policy on the Environment.

'The Community shall have as its task...to promote...sustainable and non-inflationary growth respecting the environment.'

The adoption of the Fifth Environmental Action Programme (EAP) entitled *Towards Sustainability* by the European Union in March 1992 provided the framework of actions to be introduced to fulfil the TEU commitment. The Fifth EAP outlined the EU's actions in its contribution to the global objectives of sustainable development. It set the basic framework for the actions necessary to curb the slow 'but relentless deterioration of the general state of the environment'[1] which was identified in the report on the State of the European Environment that accompanied the Fifth EAP. The Programme also outlined measures to be taken to overcome some of the problems of ineffective implementation of environmental protection measures within the Member States.

The objectives introduced by the TEU and the Fifth EAP to Environmental Policy required a very long-term strategy to be adopted, with no guarantee that there will be a successful outcome to the action. The challenge set in the Fifth Environmental Action Programme was to operationalise the proposed strategy in such a way as to combine economic progress with environmental protection and conservation of resources so that development remains possible into the future.

The aim of this chapter is to ask whether there is the necessary commitment to environmental issues among all groups within the European Union and if the European Union's Environmental Policy is able to meet this challenge. The first part of the chapter concentrates on the development of the Policy; the second part evaluates its effectiveness.

Recent events within the EU have posed additional barriers to the progress of Environmental Policy at the supranational level. The application of the principle of subsidiarity to Environmental Policy has introduced a new uncertainty, as it is seen by some Member States' governments as a curb on EU action. In other states it is seen as the means by which higher environmental standards may be maintained. While there is growing public pressure on governments to put environmental issues higher on the policy agenda, there is also a need to stimulate job creation in the EU. Economic growth and environmental protection are frequently seen as contradictory rather than complementary and therefore have only limited support.

'The full effects of this major overhaul of Community environment policy will only be felt in a few years time *and only if the political will of the Member States* allows the Commission's proposals to be put into practice.'[2]

Achievements of EU Environmental Policy

Environmental Policy was not one of the common policy areas of the Treaty of Rome. Since it was launched in 1972, almost 200 Directives, 40 Regulations, 150 decisions and 94 recommendations and opinions have been adopted by the Member States. These pieces of legislation cover a very wide range of concerns at EU level. Varying standards have been set in the legislation to deal with different problems. For example, environmental quality standards have been used in directives covering drinking water and bathing water. Emission standards have been set for lists of dangerous substances discharged into water courses and the atmosphere.

Legislation has been introduced to cover the quality of water, waste management, air quality, the control of pollution from transport, emission of chemicals, protection of wildlife and the countryside, as well as measures to make the legislation work. As a result, the European Union's policy on the environment has an impact on all aspects of life. Measures are aimed not just at pollution control, but also at the protection of human health and preservation of the environment.

These achievements are the result of an EU approach on environmental protection that has relied on the introduction of legislation from the centre. It has been easy to reach agreement on the need to improve the environment. It has been relatively simple to pass legislation with this aim. But it is much more difficult to ensure that the 15 individual Member States of the European Union put the legislation into action. The need for more effective implementation and enforcement of legislation on the environment is apparent if the EU is to make a contribution to the global objective of reaching sustainable levels of development.

In its participation in this debate, the EU can provide only a broad framework in which action can take place. The centralised regulatory approach of the EU has to be reinforced by other means, if the problems associated with enforcement and implementation are to be addressed. New ways of combining legislation with more market-oriented measures are being introduced by the EU. The aim of environmental actions in the future will be to replace the confrontational stance between the major polluters and the policy-makers, and to encourage cooperation between the different groups, industry, the consumers and the policy-makers.

The search for sustainable development

By 1987 and the adoption of the Single European Act (SEA), there was a recognition within the EU that Environmental Policy would need to be strengthened. The concern was that the increase of economic activity associated with the further removal of barriers within the EU would have an adverse impact on the environment unless there was concerted action throughout the EU to limit environmental damage. The Task Force on the Environment and the Internal Market, set up by the Commission, had reported in 1990 that the increased traffic and economic activity associated with the Internal Market would result in a rise in sulphur dioxide, nitrous oxide and other pollutants. Within the EU, there was therefore a need to redefine environmental policy in a way that would enable economic growth and environmental protection to be combined.

1987 was also an important year in international environmental developments. The same questions of how to combine economic growth and environmental protection were being asked by governments throughout the world. The ideal of achieving sustainability of development was put forward in the 1987 Brundtland Report, *Our Common Future*. There sustainable development was defined as

'...development that meets the needs of the present without compromising the ability of future generations to meet their own needs'.[3]

In the Brundtland Report, empirical evidence was presented that economic growth and development were possible alongside the preservation of environmental systems. This was a radical departure from the view that had existed during the previous 20 years, that strong economic performance could not exist alongside environmental concern. For the environmentalists this report was important because of its view that a way had to be found to combine economic development and environmental protection. The sustainable development paradigm outlined by the Brundtland Report is a more optimistic view. It is more politically acceptable and appears to be more purposeful to electorates.

Since the publication of the Brundtland Report in 1987, policies to achieve sustainable development have emerged. The ideas formed the background to the Rio Earth Summit of 1992, where the Member States of the EU played an active role. Commitments have been made globally to reduce the levels of carbon dioxide emissions in order to restore the thinning ozone layer. Many new measures are being considered globally to ensure that environmental considerations are taken into account by the policy-makers. The measures being introduced by the EU in order to fulfil the commitments to sustainable development are reviewed in detail later in this chapter. Many problems still have to be overcome.

Legal basis of the Policy

In the 1960s and early 1970s there had been a few pieces of European Union legislation concerned with control of atmospheric pollution and noise, but the policy launched in 1972 was more ambitious. It was viewed by the Commission as an attempt to achieve a coherent management plan for the care and protection of the environment of the whole EU. Initially the policy was developed under Article 2 of the Treaty of Rome in combination with Articles 100 and 235. These three Articles of the Treaty contained the right of the EU to initiate new legislation and also to harmonise the laws of the individual Member States if they directly affected the functioning of the Single Market. This provided for the extension of the essentially economic aims of the Treaty to include the protection of the environment.

But as it was based on an *interpretation* of three Treaty articles, the legality of environmental actions was under some question until the 1987 amendment to the Treaty of Rome, the Single European Act (SEA). The SEA included a chapter on the environment. It gave EU Environmental Policy a much firmer legal basis by removing the possibility of the Member States questioning EU environmental directives and measures on the grounds of legality.

The Single Act clearly stated a number of objectives for environmental policy:

- to preserve, protect and improve the quality of human life

- to contribute towards human health

- to ensure a rational use of natural resources.

Action was to be taken by the application of three principles:

1.   that prevention is better than cure

2.   that damage should be rectified at its source

3.   that the polluter should pay to clean up any damage (Article 130 R SEA).

In the United Kingdom these principles were included in the 1990 Environmental Protection Act. The application of the 'polluter pays' principle implied that the polluter should pay the full cost of the damage caused by his activities. In practice this is very difficult to enforce. It is apparent, however, that since 1990 the fines imposed in the UK when the causes of pollution have been identified have increased to a more realistic level which reflects the clean-up costs.

The SEA included the requirement that environmental protection considerations were to be part of other EU policies. This had wide-ranging implications in all areas of EU action: the Common Agricultural Policy, the Common Transport Policy, the development of a Common Policy on Energy, Regional Policy, the developments in Tourism Policy, research and development initiatives. Consultation between groups of policy-makers at EU level and at the national level was necessary to ensure that this requirement was met. It led to a number of initiatives on consultation across the Directorate-Generals within the Commission, which were supported by the information provided by the European Environment Agency.

The SEA contained the first explicit reference in the EU Treaties to the principle of subsidiarity (see chapter 2). The wording of the SEA article introduced an expectation that environmental policy at EU level would be strengthened.

'The Community shall take action relating to the environment to the extent to which the objectives referred to in Paragraph 1 can be attained better at Community level than the level of the individual Member States' (Art. 130r).

The objectives set in paragraph 1 are preceded by the statement that the '...Community...shall have the following *objectives to preserve, protect and improve* the quality of the environment'.

The language used here in the SEA sets the scene for a high level of environmental protection across the EU. The wording of the articles presupposes a centralisation of action, with the European Union responsible for the framework of policy, setting criteria and content. No cases were brought to the European Court of Justice following the SEA on the basis of infringement of Article 130r. The Court's interpretation of the application of the principle of subsidiarity was untested before the Treaty on European Union was adopted.

The TEU strengthened the EU's Environmental Policy in some ways. However, it appeared to be more in the rhetoric of the Treaty than in the reality of action. The TEU did include the term 'policy' in its description of the EC's action on the environment for the first time in Article 3. This replaced the term 'actions' on the environment which had been used in the SEA.

The principle of subsidiarity was extended by its inclusion in Article 3b of the TEU to all areas of EU policy. Article 130r of the TEU was altered to

'...Community policy on the environment shall *contribute to the pursuit* of the objectives of preserving...'.

The language of the TEU suggested a departure from the high expectations for environmental policy that were raised in the SEA.

Environmental Policy was the policy area where there was the greatest extension of the right to apply the majority voting in the adoption of legislation, apart from the following.

1. Provisions that may be of a primarily fiscal nature. The energy/carbon tax would have been subject to a unanimity vote as a result of this proviso.

2. Measures that relate to town and country planning and land use, with the exception of waste management, measures of a general nature and management of water resources.

3. Measures that might significantly affect a Member State's choice of energy resources or the general structure of its energy supply (Art. 130s, Treaty on European Union).

For environmentalists, the exceptions to the extension of the principle of majority voting were disappointing. It is in the areas of energy and urban developments that some of the severest pollution problems are found, yet action here remains subject to the unanimity vote.

The development of an effective EU Environmental Policy was undermined in the declaration issued by the Heads of Government in Edinburgh in December 1992, which stated that:

'The Treaty on European Union does not prevent any Member State from maintaining or introducing more stringent measures compatible with the EC Treaty in order to pursue the objectives of protection of the environment'.[4]

The application of higher environmental standards is possible so long as it does not create an open or disguised barrier to intra-EU trade. If any Member State wishes to apply higher environmental standards, there is a fear for companies within that state that their competitiveness will be undermined. There is therefore pressure within individual states to ensure that standards are applied equally across the EU. This is not the most effective environmental policy to pursue, as it may lead to a lowering and not a raising of standards.

The implications of the adoption of an EU Policy on the Environment are potentially wide-ranging. The rationale for the introduction of such a far-reaching policy is underpinned by potential political and social as well as economic benefits to the EU.

Economic rationale

All economic growth carries consequences for the environment. A number of surveys have been done to try and quantify the costs of environmental pollution. In the early 1980s the damage to buildings from acid rain deposition in the EU was estimated in the range of 540 million to 2.7 billion ECUs per annum. In the late 1980s damage to the forests from acid deposition was around 300 million ECUs a year, while lost agricultural production from the same cause was valued at 1 billion ECUs. More recently the Organisation for Economic Co-operation and Development has estimated that pollution of the environment cost the former Federal Republic of Germany DM 200 billion per annum.[5] Further calculations by the OECD show that overall economic growth rates in the industrialised countries would be between three and five per cent lower if the damage to the environment associated with achieving the existing gross national product were included in the calculations.

By emphasising the economic consequences of environmental policy and linking it to the completion of the internal market, a number of issues have been highlighted.

1. The benefits leading to economic growth stemming from the removal of trade barriers carry the possibility of adverse environmental effects. It is only at the point of zero economic growth that there is no additional impact on the environment. All growth has some consequences. The aim of the Single Market programme is to accelerate economic expansion in the European Community. This will make existing problems more acute as well as introducing new ones. The search is therefore on for a method of ensuring that any additional pollution is controlled. Since this is the result of greater integration within the European Union, the appropriate level for action is the supranational level.

2. The ability of the EU to act to harmonise definitions and standards in an area where differences might cause distortion or barriers to trade. Low standards within a Member State are a way of maintaining an unfair advantage over states where standards are higher. If the low standards are achieved by ignoring the damage to the environment and discharging into a watercourse or the atmosphere then product prices could be lower, thus giving companies an unfair advantage in the Single Market. If a Member State has lower standards then the cost of environmental damage does not have to be taken into account. High standards in a Member State also can act as a non-tariff barrier to the movement of goods. In the area of the control of chemicals the EU answer has been to ensure safety by establishing a classification and labelling procedure for dangerous ones. The companies producing the chemicals are required to supply information on the quantities, safety measures and testing procedures being used. Once that is done in one Member State, the chemical may be marketed throughout the European Union.

3. The need for measures at EU level to ensure the effective implementation of legislation. If this is not done, then despite the existence of the legislation there will be the possibility of trade distortion.

4. The job creation potential of the eco-industry (i.e. the production of the pollution control equipment) as well as the development of the new 'clean and lean' technologies that will bring a competitive edge for the EU's industry in its global trading relationships.

Socio-political basis for EU action

Modern industrial life is increasingly interdependent. Environmental issues are no longer the concern of an individual country. Within the EU it is politically unacceptable that the citizens of one Member State should be subject to:

1. differing environmental standards from the citizens of another Member State

2. pollution produced by the citizens of another state.

The Fifth Environmental Action Programme and its accompanying *Report on the State of the Environment* provided a comprehensive statistical analysis of the problems affecting the whole of the EU. A number of trends were identified that had significant negative consequences and cross-border effects.

- Energy use – a 25 per cent increase by 2010 at the present rate of demand, with a 20 per cent increase in carbon emissions (reference year 1987).

- Transport – a 25 per cent increase in car ownership. A 17 per cent increase in mileage by 2000 (reference year 1990).

- Agriculture – a 63 per cent increase in fertiliser use between 1970 and 1988.

- Waste – a 13 per cent increase in municipal waste between 1987 and 1992.

- Water – a 35 per cent increase in the EU's average water withdrawal rate between 1970 and 1985.

- Tourism – a 60 per cent increase in Mediterranean tourism projected by 2000 (reference year 1990).

Action at the EU level, cutting across national boundaries, has obvious benefits in a search for policy to deal with these issues. The EU has states with a North Sea coastline and states with a Mediterranean coastline; the River Rhine flows through and forms the border of five others. Since 1995 the EU also includes areas that lie to the north of the Arctic Circle. The nature of EU cooperation provides it with a unique opportunity to act in the broader regional context and establish a policy that will effectively protect the environment.

The Member States of the European Union are joined by a Treaty obligation. EU legislation takes precedence over national legislation and the Member States acknowledge the rulings of the European Court of Justice on the implementation of legislation (see chapter 2).

This is in contrast to the various international conventions on the protection of the environment. The EU is a signatory of these conventions, but they lack the legislative tools of the European Union.

The ability to take collective action is very important. This is true not only for the Member States of the EU, but also because it provides a more effective means of support for non-EU European states that are attempting to introduce environmental protection policies.

The most urgent environmental concern in Europe is with the massive problem of environmental degradation in areas of the Central and Eastern European Countries (CEECs). Prior to 1989 in the centrally planned economies of Central and Eastern Europe, no officially recognised environmental problem existed. However since 1989 the extent of the problem in the CEECs has become evident. Some problems are not as acute as in the Western part of Europe. For example, the quality of air in Prague is worse than in Brussels or Frankfurt, but better than in Athens. Overall, however, problems are more acute than in the EU states.

There are a number of causes of environmental degradation in Central and Eastern Europe.

1.   Industrial practices. There was a concentration on the heavily polluting smokestack industries. Investment in heavy industry was regarded as a visible symbol of the success of economic activity in the states under Soviet domination.

2.   In a number of regions brown coal was used as the basis of energy supply.

3.   A lack of infrastructural investment for the environment.

4.   The emphasis in the centrally planned economies on meeting production quotas. This left little opportunity for any other objectives to be achieved.

5.   Low prices were set for energy, basic raw materials and agricultural inputs. There was no mechanism by which environmental costs could be included in the subsidised prices charged to the consumer.

Not all the CEECs are affected by these problems to the same extent. A summary of the most important causes of environmental degradation in each CEEC is given in Table 14.1.

As a result, the concentration of toxic emissions around some of the major cities is considerably above EU levels. The northern region of the Czech Republic has higher concentrations of sulphur dioxide than the Xian region of China, reputedly the world's worst![6] Large-scale industrial activity has also polluted many of the underground drinking water supplies of some states.

Environmental legislation did exist in the states of Central and Eastern Europe. It should have been enforced through a system of charges. However, the major problem was the implementation of the control measures, which was largely ignored. Those dealing with monitoring environmental standards had little or no control over the large state-run enterprises.

Given the relatively small geographical area occupied by the states of Eastern and Western Europe and the trans-boundary nature of pollution, little overall benefit will be gained if action is not taken across all the states of Europe. The EU can help in this clean-up by allocating funds to assist with the various schemes in the Central and Eastern European states. Funding is available through the ERBD and also the PHARE Programme to assist with environmental projects.

Table 14.1 Summary of the main causes of environmental degradation in the states of Central and Eastern Europe

	Former GDR	Czech Rep and Slovakia	Poland	Hungary	Bulgaria	Romania
Transport	**		**	*	*	
Energy usage	**	***	***			*
Lack of environmental technology	**	**	**	*	*	***
Lack of infrastructure	*			*	**	***
Lack of environmental education	*			*	*	***
Poor enforcement of legislation	**	*	*		**	***
Obstacles to environmental improvements	*	*	*	*	*	***

* Significant problem, ** serious problem, *** major problem
Source: Adapted from *Environmental Issues in Eastern Europe: Setting an Agenda*, RIIA (1992), pp. 2/3

The development of European Union Environmental Policy

The European Union's Environmental Policy was launched in October 1972 during the Summit Conference of Heads of State in Paris. The first Environmental Action Programme was adopted at the same time to cover the five year period to 1977.

The five objectives identified in 1972 for the new Policy were:

1. to prevent, reduce and, as far as possible, eliminate pollution and nuisance

2. to maintain a satisfactory ecological balance and protect the biosphere

3. to avoid damage to the ecological balance

4. to ensure that more account is taken of environmental aspects in town planing and land use

5. to work for those ends with non-members of the European Union.

The European Union's Environmental Action Programmes (EAPs)

Five Action Programmes have been issued by the Commission to set out the broad framework of the EU's Environmental Policy. They do not contain an exhaustive or definitive list of legislation, but they do give a clear indication of what the main thrust of the legislation will be. For example, the theme of water pollution control has been a major issue throughout all the Action Programmes.

By briefly reviewing these Action Programmes it is possible to trace a definite development in the European Union's Environmental Policy.

The First Action Programme 1973–1977

The Directives adopted as a result of this EAP introduced remedial measures to deal with specific pollution problems, e.g. the Directive 'on pollution caused by the discharge of certain dangerous substances into the aquatic environment' (Dir 76/464). The First EAP also established one of the basic principles on which the EU Environmental Policy was built – that the person responsible for the pollution should pay.

The Second Action Programme 1977–1982

This Programme marked the beginning of a more proactive rather than merely reactive environmental policy. The main emphasis of the programme's measures shifted away from remedial action in response to specific sources of pollution and specific industrial processes, towards preventive action. Prevention rather than cure was adopted explicitly as a fundamental element of the policy. The high costs of cleaning up after major pollution incidents highlighted the fact that this was the most appropriate approach to adopt. It was recognised that it is more economically sound to prevent pollution or nuisance from pollution at the source than to try to counteract its effects.

The Third Action Programme 1982–1987

Proposals for this period continued to emphasise the 'prevention rather than cure' principle. The economic recession of the middle and late 1970s had led to a need to justify decisions being made on cost grounds – hence the remedial bias of the First Action Programme. But by the early 1980s it was recognised that, despite the worsening economic conditions, environmental protection was not an extra option, but part of sound future management decisions. The Fourth EAP was important as it moved EU environmental policy away from measures to merely control pollution towards establishing a much broader framework for Environmental Policy.

The Fourth Action Programme 1987–1992.

The Fourth EAP was adopted at the same time as the Single Market Programme was launched. There was a clear linkage of the economic and environmental policies taking place within the EU. The inclusion of an environmental chapter to the SEA marked the growing commitment to ensuring that economic integration should not undermine environmental protection.

In this EAP the Commission pointed to the gap developing between the number of pieces of legislation passed and the patchy implementation record of the Member States. Effective implementation of environmental legislation was crucial if the economic growth associated with the completion of the internal market was not to prove environmentally harmful. The Commission view was also that there was clearly little point in preparing new legislation if existing legislation had not been applied. The Commission made certain recommendations to ensure that the Member States became more assiduous in their implementation of directives.

The Fifth Action Programme 1992–2000: the strategy for the future?

The Council of Ministers adopted a declaration setting out the objectives and principles to be the guidelines for this programme in June 1990. The Programme was published in March 1992. It differed in a number of respects from the earlier ones.

Its proposals were to cover a longer period, from 1992 to the year 2000. Agreement was reached that there should be a more enlightened and systematic approach to environmental management. A special emphasis was given to the question of research and monitoring of environmental problems. Greater cooperation with non-EU states was identified as a priority so that action could be taken to deal with threats such as that to the rainforests.

The regulatory centralised approach used by the EU until the Fifth EAP was to be supported by an approach based on a combination of regulation and measures intended to allow market forces to operate. This involved a greater emphasis on encouraging the Member States to use economic instruments such as taxes, charges and tradable permits to protect the environment.

The Fifth Environmental Action Programme established a European Union Financial Instrument for the Environment (LIFE) to complement the legislative and the market-based approaches to environmental protection. This was a radical step, since the European Union did not have a specific fund for the environment.

Financial support from the European Union for environmental protection measures

There are inevitably limits to policy that has no financial backing. Thus, the policy could be made more effective by the provision of more funding from the EU for environmental projects. The high costs for Member States to introduce programmes aimed at improving their environmental protection measures has been recognised within the EU. Funding came from a number of different sources within the EU before the introduction of the LIFE Programme. These sources will still be available; the intention is that their effectiveness will be enhanced as a result of better targeting and additional funds.

Structural Funds

It was possible to obtain European Union funds for environmental projects from programmes aimed at research and development and from the ERDF, the ESF, and the EAGGF (the Structural Funds). But in practice the qualifying criteria of these Funds offered few opportunities for assistance for environmental purposes. The priorities associated with the Structural Funds were not necessarily environmental and this limited their effectiveness. Financial pressures on the Funds meant that the other priorities took precedence.

The 1988 reforms of the Structural Funds (see chapter 13) improved the situation. Environmental questions were included in the criteria under which the Structural Funds could be applied. During the period from 1988 until 1993 one billion ECUs was specifically earmarked for environmental problems relating to economic development. Half of this was used for special purposes including water treatment for communities of up to 100 000, the treatment of hazardous waste disposal, and the protection of nature reserves.

The Cohesion Fund

The TEU established the Cohesion Fund.

> 'The Council...shall before 31 December set up a Cohesion Fund to provide a financial
> contribution to projects in the fields of environment and trans-European networks in the area
> of transport infrastructure' (TEU 130d).

This Fund was introduced to assist the four poorest states of the EU. However, many of the
projects in the initial phase in 1994 had a transport rather than an environmental orientation.

The Financial Instrument for the Environment (LIFE)

This programme was established by the EU in early 1992. The objective of LIFE was not to
establish a separate European Union Environmental Fund, but to be a way of ensuring that
financial support from the different sources was coordinated in a rational way to achieve the
maximum impact.

Five major priorities were identified for support from the LIFE programme:

- promotion of sustainable development, including new clean technologies, management of
  waste, and improving the urban environment

- protecting natural habitats and nature

- administrative structures and services for the environment

- education and training awareness

- technical assistance outside the territory of the EU.

In September 1992 the first group of 42 projects funded in this way was announced. They
ranged from recycling of used plastics in Spain to traffic management in Naples and the return
of migratory birds to the Rhine Valley. The EU contribution was 27.6 billion ECUs to all the
projects. The financing was on a co-funded basis, the EU contribution being between 20 and
50 per cent. 1.2 million ECUs also went to projects outside the EU, e.g. 100 per cent funding
was provided for a technical assistance programme to identify environmental policy and action
programmes in Estonia.

In December 1992 further funding was announced totalling 37.6 million ECUs to go to 49
projects, including 23 nature conservation programmes and 26 designed to promote
sustainable development, including the promotion of clean technology in non-EU states. In
1994 more targeted proposals were agreed in order to achieve a more coherent financial
support for projects. 76.5 million ECUs was allocated for projects in 1994. Despite this
increased financial commitment, the amounts being allocated from EU Funds remain small in
comparison with expenditure by the individual Member States of the European Union.

Table 14.2 gives the amounts being spent by the Member States on pollution abatement and
control. While the levels of expenditure are showing some increase among the Member States
of the EU, the overall picture is that these states are investing less in pollution control than the

Japanese. This is true at the supranational level through the support of the EU Structural Funds and the LIFE Programme, and also for the individual States.

Table 14.2 Examples of pollution abatement and control expenditure (% GDP)

Country	1985	1987	1988	1989	1990
Austria	1.0	1.0	1.0		
Denmark	0.7	0.8	0.9	0.9	1.0
France	0.6	0.7	0.7	0.7	0.5
Germany	0.7	0.8	0.8	0.8	0.8
Italy			0.2	0.2	
Netherlands	1.0	0.9		0.9	
Portugal			0.5	0.4	
Spain		0.5	0.5	0.6	0.6
Sweden		0.7			
UK	0.7				0.4
Canada	0.7	0.7	0.7	0.8	0.9
USA	0.6	0.6	0.5	0.6	0.6
Japan	0.9	1.0	1.0	1.0	1.0

Source : Financial Times, 13 March 1994, 11

The effectiveness of the Policy

The first major problem of effectiveness that had to be overcome in the environmental area was the ability of the Member States to 'ignore' the legislation on the basis that it was not part of the Treaty of Rome. The SEA and the TEU have given environmental policy a firmer legal basis, but the problem of how to ensure effective application of the legislation remains. For any policy to achieve its objectives, implementation and enforcement of the legislation and the supporting measures must be effective. There has been concern within the Commission and the European Parliament since the mid-1980s that EU Environmental Policy was not substantially improving the European environment. A number of initiatives have accompanied the Fourth and Fifth EAPs and the TEU to try to ensure that these concerns are dealt with.

Lack of commitment among the Member States

The European Union produces legislation couched in very specific terms to meet and deal with particular problems. It is then left to the Member States to carry out the policy. Most of the environmental legislation that has been adopted has used the form of the Directive. Directives are binding as to the ends which are to be achieved, but leave to the national authorities the choice of form and method (see chapter 2). As a result, a gap has grown between the drafters of policy and the Member States that have the responsibility to put the legislation into practice. If the Member State lacks commitment to a particular issue, then effective implementation will be uncertain. It is relatively easy to draft legislation, but more difficult to see that it is applied.

Table 14.3 Progress in implementing directives applicable to the environment

Country	Directives applicable on 31 December 1993	Directives for which measures notified	Percentage implemented
Belgium	117	107	91
Denmark	117	115	98
Germany	119	108	91
Greece	119	100	84
Spain	117	106	90
France	117	111	95
Ireland	117	103	88
Italy	117	95	81
Luxembourg	117	108	92
Netherlands	117	108	92
Portugal	117	106	90
UK	117	106	90

Note : not all Directives are included in the table
Source : *11th Annual Report on the Application of EU Law,* p. 83

Table 14.3 gives the Member States' progress on the implementation of environmental directives. The record of implementation appears to be impressive. However the Commission, in the 11th Report on EU Law, concluded that Greece, Ireland and Italy 'could do better'.[7] Some failures to implement directives date from the 1970s. For example, in 1994 the European Court of Justice delivered a judgement against the UK for failure to preserve the quality of bathing water at the resorts of Blackpool and Southport. The standard for bathing water was set in a Directive adopted in 1976.

Table 14.4 shows the actions taken by the European Court against the Member States for failure to introduce national measures to implement legislation. Lack of administrative coordination was the cause of most of the delays. The main problems of practical implementation in Belgium were associated with the water directives. In Germany the main problems were with the practical application of the waste directives and the quality of water in the new Länder.

Table 14.4 Failure to notify national implementing measures

Action	1992	1993
169 letters	95	90
Opinions	26	18
Refer to ECJ	4	7
Terminated	63	53

Source : As Table 14.3, p. 70

Legal compliance with legislation

The transfer or transposition of the European Union's legislation into national laws creates a number of difficulties. Each piece of legislation adopted by the EU contains a timetable for its transposition into the national legislation. The deadlines set by the EU may be missed if Member States do not have the necessary national legislation in place. The ECJ has stated that, in certain circumstances, an individual may sue a national government for damages for failure to implement legislation within the prescribed time (Frankovich and Bonifaci versus Italy, 1991). This ruling has implications for all policy areas. In the case of Environmental Policy, the Commission has encouraged individuals to report infringements of EU directives. The Frankovich ruling provides additional support for individuals and pressure groups who would like to make such a report.

The Commission has taken action against Italy and Belgium because of persistent failure by the national governments to introduce legislation to put the EU's laws into place. The main problems have arisen because there is a high degree of regional devolution of powers in these states. The problem of regional devolution also exists in Germany. The central government has only limited competence within the German federal structure for both formal and practical compliance with EU environmental legislation. In order to implement an environmental directive it is necessary to introduce 16 pieces of legislation in Germany, one in each of the 16 Länder.

Since the unification of Germany, it is becoming apparent that because of the difficulties of clean-up in the new Länder, two environmental standards are emerging. For example, the German government has adopted the lower standard for transport infrastructure which is included in the Directive on Environmental Impact Assessment.

The establishment of the Committee of the Regions (see chapter 2) provided a clear opportunity for progress to be made to ensure that the regional authorities in the Member States do have a direct input to the EU's decision-making process. The CoR may speed the process of transposition and also the commitment of the regional authorities to the EU legislation.

The Netherlands, with its reputation for environmental concern, also has problems in transferring EU law into national legislation. This is not a result of regional devolution, but of the national policy-making procedures. The consultative process between the policy-makers in the Netherlands and the interested groups is a lengthy one. National legislation may take between six and eight years to go through the procedures leading to its adoption by the Dutch Parliament. The timetable set in EU environmental directives is often shorter than this.

The TEU has introduced a new penalty for Member States that fail to take the necessary measures to comply with time limits set in EU legislation.

'If the Member State concerned fails to take the necessary measures...within the time limit laid down by the Commission, the latter may bring the case before the Court of Justice. In so doing it shall specify the amount of the lump sum or penalty payment...If the Court of Justice finds that the Member State concerned has not complied with its judgement it may impose a lump sum or penalty payment on it' (TEU Art 171).

Enforcement of legislation

The Fourth Environmental Action Programme highlighted the problems of lack of enforcement of the environmental legislation for the first time. The proposals of the Fourth EAP laid the foundations for a number of initiatives intended to ensure that environmental protection measures were applied throughout the EU. Accurate information is crucial to effective enforcement of EU legislation. Before any action can be taken against a Member State, the Commission has to be informed of the failure of the state to implement the legislation. The Commission has emphasised the role of individuals in the monitoring of implementation of environmental law.

> 'Incorrect application of environmental law in various parts of the Community is most commonly detected through complaints from Community citizens and through questions put by Members of the European Parliament.'[8]

The number of infringements of legislation notified by individuals increased during the mid-1990s. The Directive on freedom of access to information on the environment held by public authorities adopted in 1990 (Dir EEC 90/313), was intended to support future developments to include the general public in the enforcement of legislation. However, for individuals and the environmental pressure groups a number of frustrations remain when they attempt to use the procedures.

Following a complaint to the Commission, the Member States concerned are warned that a complaint has been lodged. They are then given time to respond. If the response is not satisfactory then the Commission requests the initiation of proceedings by the ECJ using TEU Article 169. (See Table 14.4 for the number of letters issued in 1993 and 1994. As Table 14.4 also shows, few cases become subject to a Court judgement.) One of the criticisms made of these procedures is the length of time taken up. In some instances the Member States had begun the schemes or programmes that were the subject of the complaint before the case reached the Court.

Other criticisms have been made of the limited resources available in the Commission's legal department to deal with complaints.

> 'The process is subject to a political rather than a legislative process and any complaint is likely to disappear into a big black hole. Brussels has lost its ability to enforce its own laws.'[9]

Many of the Directives have contained an obligation for the Member States to report on the progress of implementation of the legislation. This relies on the Member States having the necessary infrastructure in place to make the reports. Some Member States do not have a separate government department dealing with environmental problems, but include the work in other departments which results in delays.

Where scientific data are required to ensure that legislation is being enforced, difficulties can occur if the data are not comparable from one country to another. The Community Information System on the Environment and Natural Resources in the EC (CORINNE) was established to take responsibility for the collation of this type of information. It was originally intended that CORINNE would last until 1991 and that its work would become part of the work of the European Environment Agency.

The European Environment Agency

The need to create a specific Environment Agency to support the enforcement of environmental legislation was based on a proposal made by Jacques Delors in 1989. Its founding regulation stated that the role of the EEA is

> '...to provide the Community and the Member States with objective, reliable and comparable information at European level, enabling them to take the requisite measures to protect the environment, to assess the results of such measures and to ensure that the public is properly informed about the state of the environment...'.[10]

The establishment of the EEA was supported by the French, German and UK governments. However, the European Parliament was very critical of the original proposed Agency. The role of the EEA falls far short of that of the US Environmental Protection Agency. It is not an initiator of legislation or an inspectorate with powers to investigate the response of the Member States to legislation. The main concern of the European Environment Agency is to provide support to the initiators of the legislation and to improve the implementation and enforcement of legislation through the spread of information.

The work of the Agency was delayed when a decision about where it should be located became part of a political 'horse trade' of new institutions and agencies. During 1992 the location of a large number of EU agencies had to be settled. The decision about their sites was delayed when the French government insisted that the European Parliament should continue to use Strasbourg as one of its locations. As the decision about the location of the new agencies was subject to unanimity vote, the French government was able to hold up the decision about all the new agencies. Eventually it was agreed that the EP should move onto a new purpose-built site in Strasbourg.

The final decision about a location for the EEA was made at the end of 1993. It was decided that it should be located in Copenhagen and it was able to become fully operational at the beginning of 1994. The success of its role and work will be reviewed in 1996.

The importance of the role of the EEA has grown considerably since the idea for the agency was proposed, for a number of reasons.

1. The decision to adopt a four year programme for 1994–1997 to develop official and regular statistics on the environment has to be supported by an organisation whose concern is primarily with environmental data. The scale and the nature of such a programme needs specialists.

2. The material that can be produced in this way has a direct and practical application. Clarity in the framing of legislative proposals and a simple presentation of the standards that have to be met would assist industrialists who have to comply with legislation. The need for this clarity was put very succinctly by a representative of the UK Federation of Small Businesses in evidence to the House of Lords in 1993.

'If the Lord's Prayer has 56 words, the Ten Commandments have 297 and the American Declaration of Independence 300, the latest directive on the export of duck eggs will have 26 911!'[11]

3.   The role of the EEA in monitoring the enforcement of legislation will be of greater importance as more legislation is produced subject to the principle of subsidiarity.

The case for an EU environmental inspectorate

The importance of an independent inspectorate within the EU that would work with the EEA to ensure requirements were being met has to be considered. There is no intention to introduce an EU inspectorate to ensure that legislation is implemented. It is an issue that has to be dealt with by the Member States' governments. However, an implementation network was proposed in the Fifth EAP to enable the national authorities with responsibility for practical implementation to meet to exchange views. This network of Member States' officials responsible for pollution control and environmental protection began to meet during the British Presidency of 1992.

The role of industry in the EU's strategy to achieve sustainable development

The Fifth Environmental Action Programme targeted five areas of economic activity where environmental protection had to be given a higher profile in any policy decisions: industry, energy, transport, agriculture and tourism. Each sector had specific problems, and a number of different measures were identified for each sector.

For the energy sector the main thrust outlined in the Fifth EAP for future policy was to concentrate on the improvement of energy efficiency and the funding of technology and research into renewable energy. In the transport sector the main objective was to meet the demands for land for transport infrastructure through greater emphasis on planning and economic development. A number of reforms of the Common Agricultural Policy had an environmental objective. The tourist sector was recognised as the fastest growing sector of economic activity within the EU. The Green Paper presented by the Commission in 1994 to implement the Fifth EAP proposals concentrated on providing guidelines for better implementation of EU rules and controlled management of tourist development.

The following section concentrates on the measures identified for industry. Industrial producers of pollution were the main target of action in the Fifth EAP.

'In its exploitation of natural resources, consumption of energy, production processes, and generation of both pollution and wastes, the industrial sector is among the principal causes of environmental deterioration.'[12]

This sector of economic activity is important for two reasons:

1.   it generates 25 per cent of total EU GDP per annum

2.   it provides a large number of jobs within the EU.

The Fifth Environmental Action Programme put forward the view that as the levels of industrial activity within the EU exceed the tolerance levels of the environment, economic activity will become stalled. As the numbers of unemployed within the EU increased during the mid-1990s it became more important to formulate a strategy that would promote job creation and protect the environment.

This question was returned to in the chapter on the environment in the Delors White Paper on Growth and Competitiveness in 1993. In the White Paper the environmental impacts on growth and competitiveness were analysed within the framework of proposals for tax reforms. Social costs, including environmental costs, were regarded as a burden on employers. If the environmental costs could be calculated as part of the true cost of resource use and recouped through taxation, then the burden on employers would be reduced and jobs created. The result has been to give European Union environmental policy a new emphasis, as initiatives to bring the three pillared approach to environmental protection in the Fifth EAP begin to be adopted. It is not, however, a trouble free shift of emphasis.

Partnership to promote EU environmental objectives

The most radical difference with the EU's Environmental Policy in the future will be the idea of partnership with industry, with consumers and with policy makers. Part of the problem of lack of effective environmental protection was seen by the Commission as the result of a confrontation with industrialists because of the large body of legislation being produced at the supranational level. In the new approach much more emphasis was given to the idea of a partnership to share the responsibilities and duties of protection of the environment. Also, the legislation was to be accompanied by the use of market related measures to encourage the heaviest polluters to change their behaviour.

To develop a partnership between industry and the EU to help to promote the objectives of the EU's environmental policy required the policy to be outlined more carefully. Major criticisms have been made in the past about the way that the legislation has been drafted. If it is badly drafted then clearly it will not be possible to take effective action. Legislation where scientific standards are questionable will also have little effect. Legislation which creates practical difficulties or imposes disproportionate financial penalties will be circumvented. The importance of the role of the European Environment Agency has already been outlined as a means of ensuring that these problems will be overcome in the future.

A Consultative Forum was proposed in the Fifth EAP to provide a vehicle for the exchange of information and consultation between industry, local and regional authorities, environmental pressure groups and consumer research organisations. It began its work in 1994, including in its 32 members the Vice President of UNICE, major industrialists and the leading environmental campaigner, Jonathan Porritt.

Despite the support given to this initiative by such groups as the UK Confederation of British Industry (CBI), there are a number of problems with consultation in a single umbrella forum of such diverse interests. Each of the groups represented has its own priorities for action. If it does not feel that these are being met, the consultation procedure will become devalued as commitment to the procedure is lost.

Market-based instruments to protect the environment

The Fifth Environmental Action Programme advocated the use of market-based measures to reinforce the action of legislation. The range of economic-based instruments proposed by the EU as the way to reinforce the implementation and enforcement of the objectives of its legislation are seen as a means of channelling behaviour of both consumers and producers into a direction that is less harmful to the environment. There are trade-offs to be made between the costs and the benefits of actions. In the case of the proposals on taxation, the trade-off for the target group was that by changing their behaviour the tax could be avoided. If subsidies were introduced by national governments, they would reward those who had changed their behaviour. Voluntary action to introduce environmental protection would follow when the consumer rewarded the company by purchasing from it and not a rival firm.

This approach relies on an ability to fix accurately a cost of environmental damage. To cost the damage done to the environment by economic growth and development is one of the most difficult tasks to accomplish. However, despite the difficulties of assessing the long-term damage, approximations have been made of the costs of environmental damage in some areas. If damage is done to a building it is possible to derive a cost from the costs of cleaning up the stonework. At the level of individual industrial plants, to help with this pricing structure the Commission is advocating the disclosure of information in companies' final reports that will identify the expenses of environmental activities. The requirement will also be to include provision in the accounts for environmental risks and future environmental expenses.

Estimates of environmental costs are also done by governments and international organisations such as the OECD. In the former German Democratic Republic it has been estimated that the cost of treatment of contaminated ground water and soils will reach 16 billion ECUs by the year 2005. The damage to the German economy because of the problem of environmental degradation in the former GDR is estimated to be about 305 billion ECUs of a total German GNP of about 1380 billion ECUs.[13] Taking this into account, the net value of goods and services produced in Germany is reduced to the level of the early 1980s.

By advocating the use of economic and fiscal instruments, the EU's objective is to ensure that a true price is paid for a product and that control is maintained in such a way as to ensure that companies cannot continue with wasteful practices. If they do so, the companies that adopt environmentally friendly technology will be at a disadvantage because of costs. To do this it is necessary to establish a pricing structure that will internalise all the external environmental costs from the beginning of the product cycle to use to final disposal.

One of the first pieces of legislation to result from the Fifth EAP, which incorporated this new approach to environmental protection was the European Union's Eco-Management and Audit Scheme Regulation (EMAR). The EMAR is based on the introduction of a cycle of environmental auditing by a company with the objective of identifying and introducing measures to improve environmental performance over time. Environmental auditing is an internal management tool which should indicate performance with regard to resource management. It can also be used as a market-based instrument since it will provide shareholders, investors, financial and insurance companies with a performance indicator. Companies that register for the scheme have to produce an environmental statement for publication following verification by an independent auditor. The environmental audit will provide information on performance and act as a measure of compliance with legislation.

The experience of environmental auditing in the USA showed that there would be a great deal of opposition to the introduction of a mandatory registration for the scheme. US industrialists' opposition is based on the grounds that the purpose of the audit is to assist a company to identify its environmental problem and to improve its environmental performance. Given these objectives, companies within industrial sectors would not be prepared to support the information gathered in an environmental audit being made public, as it might give information to their competitors. The EU's eco-audit scheme, on the other hand, may receive support as it is a voluntary scheme and companies can choose whether they wish to put together a public statement and apply to use the appropriate logo.

The eco-labelling initiative was adopted as a similar voluntary instrument that would provide information for consumer products and an effective marketing tool for companies. Consumer awareness of the potential damage done to the environment by a number of products has been heightened in recent years by various campaigns. The eco-label is to provide information to enable the consumer to judge a range of different products. However, the eco-label will not be an absolute measure of a product that does no damage to the environment. It is a relative measure of products that are among the least damaging twenty per cent.

Along with its voluntary approach which relies on consumer pressure to change the behaviour of the heaviest polluters, a range of instruments was proposed in the Fifth EAP to control the quantity of pollution. The use of levies and charges is one method that has been used for a long time, particularly in the area of water pollution control. The primary aim of these charges is that a fund can be established for clean-up operations and water treatment facilities.

It is important to ensure that responsibilities for preventing damage to the environment are shared, and that funds are available for the clean-up operations. An integrated approach to environmental liability has been adopted by the policy-makers in the EU. This has been greeted with disquiet by some companies, which are unclear about the implications of proposed legislation on civil liability for environmental incidents, as outlined in a Green Paper in 1993. The Proposed EC Directive includes strict liability for damages, retrospective action, joint and several liability and compulsory insurance cover.

Issues raised by the Green Paper included the following.

1. Concern about the question of who was to be considered responsible for environmental pollution of a site later acquired by another company.

2. The danger that some of the problems found as a result of similar legislation in the USA would also occur in the EU. In the USA more than 80 per cent of funds earmarked through compulsory insurance of this type go to the legal profession dealing with the claims, and not to cleaning up the environment.

The US legislation was introduced in 1980 – the Comprehensive Environmental Response Compensation and Liability Act (CERCLA)-Superfund Act. 33 000 sites were identified for clean-up and 1200 were put onto a National Priority List. The Superfund clean-up was projected to cost between $150 billion and $300 billion, but the long-term ramifications are uncertain. Since 1980 the greatest area of activity has been in legislative action to identify who will pay for the clean-up. This has taken more than 12 years and cost 80 per cent of the funds available. Fewer than 100 sites have actually been cleaned.

A proposed initiative that has had more success in the USA is the market-based incentives of using tradable permits. The Commission is committed to encouraging the Member States to make greater use of this type of permit. Basically, the polluter is given a permit allowing it to produce a specified amount of waste. This is the same as the control and regulatory systems currently in operation, where, for example, firms are given the right to pollute an estuary to a given amount, or a water company the right to pump a specified amount of sewage into a river. The difference is that with a tradable permit the industry can either buy other permits not being used or sell any excess capacity it might have, as long as the total amount of pollution is not being exceeded. It is estimated that in the USA up to $10 billion in compliance costs have been saved in ten years of the tradable permit system.

The use of taxation

The Fourth Action Programme included a chapter on the use of taxes of pollution control, but did not make any specific recommendations. Recently there have been a number of changes in this area of consideration. In the Fifth Environmental Action Programme the advocacy of the use of fiscal incentives was based on the view that it is more efficient to tax activities that damage the environment and to reduce the burden of taxation that has a negative effect on employment and investment. This was also the conclusion of the White Paper on Growth which followed it in 1993.

Taxation is not, however, appropriate in all cases. The nature and the form of the taxation have to be carefully considered, as it may raise the problem of EU involvement in the taxation policies of the individual Member States. However, Member States' approval was given to the national governments' introduction of a tax incentive scheme to accelerate the introduction of more advanced catalytic converters in cars from 1994. This reduced average car pollutant emissions by about 75 per cent.

The Commission has been mandated to examine the introduction of interim taxes on chlorofluorocarbons (CFCs) production to inhibit their use more quickly. These are the group of gases that have been nicknamed the 'greenhouse' gases and are of concern to the scientists who have identified the thinning of the ozone layer of the atmosphere. The taxation of CFC production is to help the EU to progress more rapidly to cut the levels of production. Agreement was reached on an 85 per cent cut by 1 July 1995, with complete phasing out by mid-1997.

Energy/carbon tax

The introduction of this form of taxation has been the subject of much controversy since the idea was first introduced in 1989. A proposal was made for adoption in 1992. As it continued to be difficult to reach agreement on the proposals in the Council of Ministers, a high-level Working Group was set up in March 1994 to consider its implications.

Much of the criticism of this initiative to conserve energy and to protect the environment centred around the fact that it was seen as a blunt instrument that would hit all consumers indiscriminately. The households with the lowest incomes across the European Union would, it was claimed, be hit more severely than other consumers. The Commission, however, was concerned to ensure that the overall pattern of taxation should not be increased. As a tool of environmental protection the proposals were also criticised as ineffective. Many of the major industrial producers of pollution were be exempted from the proposed taxation.

The Working Group reported on five areas to the Council of Environment Ministers held in June 1994:

1. the form of the tax and its scope (excluding renewable energies)

2. the initial level of the tax ($3 per barrel equivalent to be phased in over ten years)

3. the exoneration from its application of the high-consumer industries

4   the review of the system planned for 1997

5. the principle of burden sharing, so that the poorest states of the EU were not disproportionately hit by the tax.

Agreement on the tax continued to be difficult to reach. Failure to introduce some measure to curb carbon emissions within the EU would be contrary to the commitment made in the Earth Summit Conference in Rio in 1992. During the German Presidency of 1994, the Member States turned to proposals to use the existing excise duties as the means of meeting this obligation.

The EU had already introduced a minimum excise tax rate for petrol, heating oil and diesel. The proposal was therefore changed to an extension of this excise rate. It would not fulfil the objectives of curbing industrial pollution.

The fact that the EU's future strategy for the environment couples market-based measures and legislation reflects the fact that many of the environmental problems at present affecting the industrialised world are the result of past failures of an unregulated market. Relying solely on the market-based instruments leaves the way open for pollution to continue. The economic measures outlined are an indirect way of changing behaviour; they allow additional uncertainties to creep into actions to protect the environment. Consumers and producers alike would have to rely on having full information of the costs and benefits of actions before they took them. For a company the freedom to pollute would remain. This would be especially true if continued economic expansion occurred and there were greater benefits to be gained by continuing with already established practices.

Applying the principle of subsidiarity

The economic consequences of Environmental Policy were increasingly recognised during the 1970s and 1980s. When Environmental Policy was linked to the completion of the Internal Market Programme, the Commission gave the policy a new imperative and urgency. The EU is able to act to harmonise definitions and standards in areas where differences might cause distortion or barriers to trade. Effective implementation of legislation is therefore essential to the completion of the Internal Market. If standards are applied differently in the different Member States, it could give rise to unequal conditions of competition or unequal living conditions for the citizens of the Member States.

The Edinburgh Summit of the Heads of Government declaration reaffirmed that the TEU did not prevent any Member State from maintaining or introducing more stringent environmental measures, provided that they are compatible with the Treaty. This raised a number of concerns that:

1. applying the principle of subsidiarity would result in the creation of a barrier to trade because of the continuance of different environmental standards

2. the opportunity to maintain different environmental standards would leave some Member States able to lower standards of environmental protection.

The Commission had stated that

'The environment is a key element in the achievement of the internal market; the adoption of high environmental standards at Community level and their uniform application will strengthen the process of convergence and cohesion and remove the fears for many countries against products of other Member States, allegedly produced under lax environmental conditions.'[14]

The Sutherland Report had identified the possibility that the objectives of the Internal Market will be undermined by the risk of fragmentation of the market from divergent interpretation and enforcement of law or the introduction of national rules that 'needlessly' segment the market. The Report had added that subsidiarity

'...does not and cannot be interpreted as permitting the fragmentation of the market, because of divergent interpretations or enforcement of Community law or from the introduction of national rules which needlessly segment the market'.[15]

Already there have been a number of examples where this has not been the case in practice and it is from these instances that the concerns about market fragmentation gain credence, along with the fears of undermined environmental protection.

In the UK both the Confederation of British Industry (CBI) and the Chemical Industries Association (CIA) have pointed to a vast difference in the way in which the Liquid Beverages Containers Directive 85/339/EEC.OJ.L. 176, 6 July 1985 was implemented.[16] By 1992 four states had introduced legislation, four had voluntary agreements with companies and four had not taken any action to transpose it into national legislation at all. This is a clear example of the way in which a significant market disorientation was allowed to develop.

Some countries, notably the Netherlands and the Federal Republic of Germany, are more careful than others about the implementation of legislation. On the one hand the Dutch and German governments have been called 'protectionist' by other states of the EU, whose standards are different. On the other hand German and Dutch industries, especially power generation and chemicals, have accused their governments of hobbling their competitive position by devoting so much effort to complying with the EU standards. Pressure is being felt by the governments in Bonn and the Hague to demand more stringent monitoring of implementation to ensure that they are not disadvantaged and that standards are applied equally throughout the Community.

In 1994 the controversy about the differences between the German Ordnance on Packaging and the EU Directive on the packaging of waste provided another example. The targets set in the German Ordnance on Packaging compel German producers of packaging waste to take it back for reuse or material recycling. The targets set in the German Ordnance were higher than in the proposed EU Directive on the packaging of waste. The Directive allowed Member States to set higher targets if the Commission confirmed that they avoided internal market distortions and so did not hinder compliance by other Member States. The proviso was added to the Directive that the application of the higher rates must depend on having the facilities to treat the waste without exporting it to other Member States.

This was the subject of much controversy. The German standpoint, if it had been accepted by the ECJ, was that the national legislation was compatible with Article 100a para 4, which permitted national environmental protection measures after a harmonisation measure was passed. The arguments were that there was no restriction of trade in secondary products (i.e. waste packaging) within the EU and no restrictions should be imposed on such trade. Opposition to this view had come from the waste disposal industries of a number of states, which viewed the large surpluses of waste material that the German recycling industry could not cope with, which was then being exported, as a means of dumping into their market of national government-subsidised material. As such it was contrary to the objectives of the Directive which, when adopting the common position of the Council of Ministers, were described as: 'to ensure a high level of protection of the environment and ...the functioning of the Internal Market'.[17]

Following the Edinburgh Summit of 1992, the Commission began a systematic review of the existing European Union legislation to 'simplify, consolidate and update existing texts, particularly those on air and water, to take new knowledge and technical progress into account'.[18]

The intention is to set rules and regulations that would include essential quality and health parameters but leave Member States to add secondary parameters. As a consequence of this review of legislation, water protection within the EU will be based on two sets of directives.

1. A set of framework directives to replace the existing directives on the quality of drinking water, bathing water, freshwater and groundwater protection.

2. A set of framework directives designed to control pollution at source.

Integrated pollution prevention and control

An important development in the mid-1990s was the introduction of a Directive concentrating on a more integrated approach to environmental protection. It was in recognition of the fact that remedying an environmental problem in one environmental medium might transfer it to another. This would reduce the overall benefit of the action being taken and possibly add to the damage in another area.

Each Member State of the European Union, apart from France, Denmark and Luxembourg, where an integrated approach had been adopted from the 1970s, had legislation that concentrated on control of damage in one environmental medium. The primary objective of the Directive on Integrated Pollution Prevention and Control (COM (93) 423 (IPC) was to supplement existing directives by requiring the Member States to adapt their minimum discharge standards to 'best available techniques' (BATs). This means to the latest stage in the development of technology, but in accordance with the principle of subsidiarity the adaptation procedures necessary will be left to the Member States. Each Member State will be required to impose emission limit values for all the substances listed in the Annexes to the Directive. The aim of the Integrated Approach is to prevent damage to the whole environment, rather than allowing it to be transferred from one part to another by protecting one area of the environment and not another.

In the control of emissions into the atmosphere, for example, the IBC approach will provide common air quality monitoring standards and pollution limits for more than 14 air pollutants. These will include sulphur dioxide and nitrogen dioxide, ground level ozone and carbon monoxide, lead and hydrocarbons. Prior to the adoption of the IPC these were covered by five different directives.

Common reporting standards were established, setting pollution limits with a timetable for them to be met within 10–15 years. There were a number of provisional ceilings. An essential requirement of the Directive was that the public was to be informed when the ceilings were exceeded and emergency measures adopted. The whole procedure was to be backed by the publication of regular air quality reports by the Commission. Pollution limits for substances already covered by EU law were set for the end of 1996, with a deadline of the end of 1999 for other groups of targeted chemicals that were being included for the first time.

Conclusions

There has been a considerable increase of interest in environmental issues since the 1970s, and the European Union is uniquely placed to take action. The rationale for action at Community level is quite clear. By doing so it is possible to coordinate efforts to prevent pollution in the broader regional context of Western Europe. Legislation enacted by the EU takes precedence over the legislation of the Member States and provides the possibility of an integrated approach.

The main argument of this chapter has been that there is a urgent need to make the European Union's Policy on the Environment more effective. Each of the means by which that can be achieved has been reviewed. Clearly the European Environmental Agency is an important part of that requirement, but it needs more extensive powers than have so far been suggested. Commitment is necessary from all parties in the EU, at all levels from individuals to industry and business, to local and national government, if a coherent Environmental Policy for the EU is to materialise. The developments associated with the Completion of the Single Market have given a new urgency and a new opportunity for better care and protection of the environment.

In the Fifth Environmental Action Programme, the EC has outlined a strategy for future Environmental Policy. The main objective of that policy was to ensure that development and growth are compatible with and not contradictory to environmental concerns. It will inevitably take some time for current patterns of consumption and behaviour to turn towards sustainability. The Community's strategy will depend very much on the quality of the legislation adopted and the measures for the enforcement of the legislation. Better coordination and cooperation with industry will be essential. More coordination in other policy areas is necessary. Better and more systematic follow-up and stricter compliance are required.

The outline for the future EU action proposed in the Fifth EAP recognises that it is a long-term strategy, to take the European Union into the next century. The legitimacy of action was guaranteed in the Single European Act, and reaffirmed in the TEU with increased opportunities for the use of the qualified majority vote. The Treaty on European Union has committed the Member States to meeting the challenge of sustainable development. Much has been accomplished in the environmental area since 1972, but much remains to be done.

References

1. **Commission of the EC** (1992) *Towards Sustainability,* COM (92) 23, final, p. 3.
2. **Commission of the EC** (1993) *European Union Environmental Policy Background Report*, ISEC B9/94, p. 4.
3. **World Commission on Environment and Development** (1987) *Our Common Future* (the Brundtland Report), Oxford, p. 43.
4. **Council of the European Union, Edinburgh** (1992) *Declaration of the Council on Social Policy, Consumers, Environment, Distribution of Income*, Annex 2.
5. **Commission of the EC** (1992) *Communication on Industrial Competitiveness and Protection of the Environment*, COM (92) 1986, final, p. 2.
6. *OECD Observer* (1993) Volume April/May, p. 34.
7. **Commission of the EC** (1994) *Eleventh Annual Report on the Application of Community Law*, p. 83.
8. Ibid., p. 72.
9. **Sands P**, quoted in *The European*, 29 July 1994, 5.
10. Council Regulation No. 1210/90, *On the Establishment of the European Environment Agency and the European Environment Information and Observation Network*.
11. **House of Lords Select Committee on the EC** (1992/93) 18th Report, *Industry and the Environment*, p. 68.
12. As Ref. 1, p. 28.
13. **European Parliament** (1994) *Report on the Need to Assess the True Costs to the Community of Non-Environment* (Pimenta Report), p. 6.
14. **Commission of the EC** (1993) *Report on Reinforcing the Effectiveness of the Internal Market*, COM (93) 256, final, p. 9.
15. **Commission of the EC** (1992) *The Internal Market after 1992: Meeting the Challenge*, Report by the high level Working Group on the Operation of the Internal Market (Sutherland Report), p. 6.
16. **House of Lords** (1992), 9th Report, *Implementation and Enforcement of Legislation*, p. 27.
17. *Europe*, 12 January 1994, 11.
18. **Commission of the EC** (1993) *Report on the Adaptation of Community Legislation to the Subsidiarity Principle*, COM (93) 545, final, p. 15.

Further reading

Barnes P M (1994) The European Union's Environmental Management and Audit Regulation, in Barnes I G and Davison L (eds) *European Business: Cases and Text*, Heinnemann-Butterworth, London.
Commission of the EC (1992) *Proposal for a Council Directive Introducing a Tax on Carbon Dioxide Emissions and Energy*, COM (92) 226.
Commission of the EC (1993) *Communication on Making the Most of the Internal Market* – Strategic Programme, COM (93) 632, final.
Commission of the EC (1993) *White Paper on Growth, Competitiveness and Employment*, COM (93) 700, final.

Council of the European Communities (1992) *Conclusions of the British Presidency in Edinburgh.*

European Communities (1992) *Treaty on European Union.*

Haigh N (1990) *EEC Environmental Policy and Britain*, Longman, London.

House of Commons Select Committee on the Environment (1988/89), 7th Report, *The Proposed European Environment Agency.*

House of Lords Select Committee on the EC (1992/93) 8th Report, *Fifth Environmental Action Programme: Integration of Community Policies.*

House of Lords Select Committee on the EC (1992/93) 14th Report, *Environmental Aspects of the Reform of the CAP.*

House of Lords Select Committee on the EC (1992/93) 26th Report, *Packaging and Packaging Waste.*

House of Lords Select Committee on the EC (1993/94) 3rd Report, *Remedying Environmental Damage.*

Judge D (ed.) (1993) *A Green Dimension for the European Community*, Frank Cass, London.

OECD (1991) *The State of the Environment.*

OECD (1993) *Taxation and the Environment.*

Official Journal of the European Communities, L.176, 6 July 1985, Council Directive EEC No. 339/85 on Containers for Liquid Beverages.

Official Journal of the EC, L.169, 29 June 1987, *Single European Act.*

Official Journal of the European Communities, L.168, 10 July 1993, Council Regulation EEC No. 1863/93, 29 June 1993, Allowing Voluntary Participation by Companies in the Industrial Sector in a Community Eco-management and Audit Scheme.

Pearce D (1993) *Blueprint 3 – Measuring Sustainable Development*, Earthscan, London.

CHAPTER 15

European Union Social Policy: adding the social dimension to the European Union?

Introduction

For the early days of the European Union, economic integration was the primary objective. However, a commitment was made to the objective of social as well as economic cohesion.

'The Community shall develop and pursue its actions leading to the strengthening of its economic and social cohesion' (Treaty of Rome, Art 130a).

The term 'social cohesion', as used in the Treaty of Rome, is very specific. It includes:

1. the harmonisation of some social measures to enable the movement of workers within the European Union

2. a broader objective to protect workers from the potential adverse effects of the integrated Single European Market

3. a growing concern about specific problems for groups who are at a disadvantage in the integrated market because they find it difficult to obtain employment. This includes the disabled or women workers, or the elderly and retired who are no longer economically active.

Overall, social cohesion means that the economic benefits of the integrated market should be felt equally by all the citizens of all the Member States. The distribution of the social welfare benefits of increased integration was to be left to the governments of the Member States. The expectation was that intervention by the European Union would be necessary only in a limited number of areas. The social protection policies of the individual Member States would gradually come into line as a result of economic integration. It was not the intention that the EU would provide the resources for social welfare benefits such as unemployment benefits, invalidity benefits, pensions and sickness benefits. Nor was it the intention that the EU should take over the allocation of resources for these benefits. This would have been an unwarranted intrusion by the EU on what was perceived to be a major role of the national governments.

Instead the Treaty of Rome gave the European Union competence for a limited number of areas. The greatest emphasis was placed on:

- the protection of workers' rights, for example the Directive on the rights of employees of insolvent employers (EEC 283/80)

- the protection of the rights to social welfare benefits for workers who moved from one Member State to another for employment

- equal opportunities.

The European Social Fund was established to help with the retraining of redundant workers. Provisions were also made for the Economic and Social Committee to be established as a forum in which consultation could take place between the representatives of the employers and the employees.

The scope and range of European Union Social Policy was therefore limited and fragmented. The question of whether the EU needed a Social Policy and, if so, what type of Social Policy had not been answered. European Union Social Policy was not concerned with housing provision, the provision of education, community health services or any of the concerns that are normally classified as 'Social Policy' in a national context. Instead it was based on a model of a European Welfare State where social policy was considered to be an integral part of economic policy. It was an interventionist view that advocated establishing a framework in which governments, organised employers and trade unions are able to act in concert.

The fundamental questions of the need for, and the nature of, EU Social Policy remained unanswered in the mid–1990s. The scope of EU Social Policy had not altered significantly. The use of the term continued to be misleading, as its main emphasis focused on economic integration. The European Union had not found a balance between what could be classed as the 'human face' of the EU and a Social Policy as a means to achieve other strategic objectives. The Commission of the European Union had made proposals to increase the range and scope of the EU policy, but these had met with limited national support.

The increasing levels of unemployment and the inability of the states of the European Union to create employment were a major concern when the Third Social Action Programme commenced in 1995. The dispute that developed within the EU was over the ability and desirability of the Member States' maintaining their traditional social protection systems. The pressure to introduce a more flexible labour market did not include the same safety net of welfare provisions. This was counter to the view of the supporters of the European model of the welfare state, which saw social policy as an integral part of economic policy. As a result European Union Social Policy became riven by political controversy.

The achievements of European Union Social Policy

Some limited success can be credited to the role of the EU in the following areas:

1. ensuring equal pay and opportunities

2. providing a body of legislation to ensure the protection of migrant workers

3. making funding available for schemes to retrain workers.

However, there has been little transfer of competence for Social Policy from the nation states to the EU level. While the twin objectives of achieving economic and social cohesion appeared in the Treaty of Rome and have been repeated since in the Single European Act and the Treaty on European Union, social cohesion remains a secondary consideration to the objective of economic cohesion.

The first sections of this chapter concentrate on the history and development of the EU Social Policy, including an evaluation of the main policy instrument, the European Social Fund. The second part of the chapter reviews the effectiveness of the areas where the EU has been given competence for action by the Treaties:

1. the role of the EU in the promotion of employment

2. the EU's contribution to establishing a framework for industrial relations within Europe

3. the 'success' of equal pay and opportunities legislation and initiatives

4. removing the causes of poverty within the EU and ensuring the objective of social cohesion.

The rationale for European Union Social Policy

Freedom of movement for workers

The creation of the single integrated market was based on the freedom of movement of people, goods, services and capital. The rationale for support for workers who wished to move was therefore economic. Free movement of workers was needed in the integrated market to ensure that no distortion of the market could occur. If workers were free to move from one area to another, any imbalance in employment would be naturally evened out. The right of free movement was therefore not a general one. It was limited to those who were economically active, so that effective use could be made of the labour force as one of the factors of production. Although the right of free movement has been extended since the Treaty on European Union, this is still the underlying rationale.

It was recognised that certain measures would have to be introduced to ensure that the free movement of workers was possible. As a result much of the legislation adopted by the European Union in the period from 1957 until the mid-1970s was concerned with ensuring the protection and social security rights of migrant workers. More recently, measures have been introduced to ensure that other barriers to movement are removed (these issues are dealt with in chapter 5).

Protection of workers' rights

Other action in the social area followed the recognition that increased competition, due to the creation of the Customs Union, carried the potential for restructuring of industry with the possibility of job losses. Protection of workers' rights would therefore be needed. Explicit reference to equal pay for male and female workers had been included in the Treaty of Rome for this reason. There was the potential for considerable job losses in sectors with predominantly female workforces. Safety and health related issues in the workplace were included to protect workers from the worst effects of increased competition, which might lead to an erosion of the safety standards.

The necessity of measures to protect workers and the possibility that their introduction may lead to a loss of flexibility for companies lies at the basis of the current fierce political dispute within the EU. Unemployment rates within the EU states are unacceptably high in comparison with the USA and Japan, and the debate centres on the nature of the measures that must be introduced to overcome this problem. Some states, led by the UK, support a complete removal of the regulations introduced to protect workers. Other states, such as Germany, support the continuance of these and the introduction of additional measures. There is institutional support within the EU from the Commission and the European Parliament for further regulations to protect workers.

Harmonisation of national social policies to avoid market distortion

The national social policies of the individual Member States of the European Union differ markedly. Over time, cultural, political, ideological, economic and institutional differences have meant that different priorities have been identified in each state. Different national decisions are made about:

1. who should be supported

2. the amount of support individuals should receive

3. the balance between public and private sector expenditure on social protection.

If different standards of social protection are allowed to persist from one state to another, then there may be distortion of the market. Differing social protection systems may make it difficult for people to move for employment. One view is that harmonisation of the national social protection systems is unnecessary, since market competition will overcome and even out any distortions. The other view is that, if left to themselves, market forces may cause a downward pressure on social provisions. This would not be politically acceptable in states where there is already a high level of social provision. States where there is a lower level of provision may be able to achieve an unfair advantage within the EU as a result. The EU should therefore take action to ensure that this does not happen.

However, it is not the intention of the EU to harmonise the national social security systems of the Member States. Following the introduction of the Single European Act, any attempt to do so was abandoned. Instead, the national governments adopted a new approach which involved the convergence of social protection objectives and policies (Council Recommendation 92/442/EEC). This Recommendation left the Member States free to operate and decide on the means by which social protection should be financed. It concentrated on providing common objectives for the national policies. It was also agreed that a reporting system would be introduced so that the Member States would have a joint opportunity of developing new ways of providing social protection.

In the first report on the development of social protection policies published in 1994[1] a narrowing of the differentials in expenditure on social protection between the Member States was identified. It was mainly as a result of the spending of the Southern states of the EU increasing and that of the Northern states stabilising (see Table 15.1).

Table 15.1 Current social protection expenditure as % of GDP, 1970–1991 (total social expenditure)

	B	DK	D	GR	E	F	IR	I	L	NL	P	UK	EU12
1970	18.7	19.6	21.5	NA	NA	19.2	13.2	17.4	15.9	20.8	NA	15.9	NA
1975	24.2	25.8	29.7	NA	NA	22.9	19.7	22.6	22.4	26.7	NA	20.1	NA
1980	28.0	28.7	28.7	12.2	18.1	25.4	21.6	19.4	26.5	30.8	14.7	21.5	24.4
1983	30.8	30.1	28.2	17.2	19.5	28.3	24.1	22.9	27.2	33.2	16.1	23.9	25.3
1986	29.4	26.7	28.1	19.4	19.5	28.5	24.1	22.4	24.8	30.9	16.3	24.3	26.0
1989	26.7	29.8	27.5	20.7	20.1	27.6	20.2	23.1	25.2	31.0	16.6	21.9	25.2
1991	26.7	29.8	26.6	NA	21.4	28.7	21.3	24.4	27.5	32.4	19.4	24.7	26.0

Source : Adapted from Commission, *Report on Social Protection in Europe*, COM (93) 531, Final p. 42

All categories of social protection expenditure are included in Table 15.1, e.g. unemployment benefits, pensions, child allowances and maternity benefits, invalidity, housing benefits. There are substantial differences between the spending of the Member States on the different categories. The rising levels of overall expenditure are the result of an increasing number of social problems in the European Union. The rising level of unemployment and the ageing of the population are the two that are causing the greatest concern in the 1990s.

The Report found that there had been no clear evidence of convergence of the social protection systems since the 1980s. Some changes had worked in the same direction, e.g. charges for health care and drugs had been increased in all states. Other changes had worked in opposite directions. There had been some reductions of benefit rates in some states, others had increased levels of benefit. Some states had restricted entitlements to benefits, others had increased them. There were national-based attempts to solve the similar social problems emerging in all the states of the European Union.

The creation of the 'social dimension'

While the articles of the Treaty of Rome were few in number, they contained the potential for far-reaching action at such time as the Member States were prepared to make the increased political commitment. During the 1980s this political commitment appeared to have been made in association with the launch of the Internal Market Programme.

'The European Council stresses the importance of the social aspects of progress towards the 1992 objectives...the Internal market must be conceived in such a manner as to benefit all our people.'[2]

The creation of this 'social dimension' to the Market was to be based on the Charter on Fundamental Social Rights (Social Charter) adopted in 1989. The idea of a social dimension implies a much wider range of social policy actions than the protection of migrant workers' rights alone or employment policy. In the political declaration of the Social Charter commitment was made to introduce programmes that would help the elderly and a number of disadvantaged groups in European society.

The Treaty on European Union stressed the importance of the introduction of measures that would enable all the citizens of the EU to feel that they were benefiting from increased integration, i.e. the process of social cohesion.

'The Union shall set itself the following objectives to promote economic and social progress which is balanced and sustainable...through the strengthening of economic and social cohesion... (Art B, TEU).

'The Community shall have as its task...a high level of employment and of social protection, the raising of the standard of living and quality of life, and economic and social cohesion and solidarity among the Member States.' (Art 2, TEU)

The use of such terminology and the reaffirmed commitment to social cohesion and solidarity among the citizens of the Union in the TEU had raised the expectations of the 1980s.

The main argument of this chapter is that instead of meeting these raised expectations, the development of European Union Social Policy in the mid-1990s is being undermined by economic, political and legal developments. The scope of EU Social Policy has broadened since the earliest actions of 1957, but the competence for social policy remains largely in the hands of the Member States. The commitment of the national governments to EU-level action remains limited, because of fears firstly of the political implications and secondly of the possible consequences of EU policy. For some states the concerns revolve round the possibility of attempts to reduce the standards of social protection. For other states the concerns are about the costs of increased social protection.

As a consequence of these concerns, the role of the European Union in Social Policy has become concentrated into the following areas of action:

1.   to agree to *convergence* of policy in areas that currently remain the exclusive competence of the Member States, such as social protection provision

2.   to use European Union programmes to encourage the development of good practices to assist the retraining of workers

3.   to provide *financial support* through the European Social Fund (ESF) and the work of the European Investment Bank (EIB)

4.   to provide a framework in which to reach *agreement between the social partners* (i.e. the employers, the trade unions and other professional groups) at EU level about improving conditions in the workplace

5.   to develop a body of *legislation* relating to employment protection in the workplace.

These do not represent a comprehensive Social Policy. They are minimal measures designed to support the rhetoric of '*social cohesion*'.

Factors that undermine the development of European Union Social Policy

A number of developments taking place within the EU are contributing to maintaining the fragmented and limited nature of European Union Social Policy. They include:

1. the high levels of unemployment within the EU

2. the fragmented legal framework for action.

Unacceptably high levels of unemployment

The most important socio-economic problem within the Union in the mid to late 1990s was the high level of unemployment and its consequences. By mid-1994 the average level of unemployment within the EU was over 11 per cent. As this was coupled with an expected low growth rate, the likelihood of the problem being solved in the short term was low. A number of EU initiatives were proposed to stimulate growth and create employment possibilities in the White Paper on a Medium Term Strategy for Growth, Competitiveness and Employment published by the Commission in late 1993.[3] (This will be referred to throughout this chapter as the White Paper on Growth.)

In some of the Member States there was opposition to these proposals because of the potential costs. It appeared that national economic concerns were pushing even further down the European Union political agenda the ambitions to create the social dimension and solidarity among the citizens of Europe.

During 1993 and 1994 the Commission published first a Consultative Green Paper on the available options for Social Policy,[4] and then a White Paper[5] containing the framework for action based on these responses. The Third Social Policy Action Programme, based on this consultation process, was adopted by the Council of Ministers in Essen in late December 1994.

The Third Social Action Programme did not include any radical measures. A number of measures were identified, including:

1. the promotion of new higher standards at work, particularly protection for those in part time and non-standard employment

2. the (broader and more difficult to achieve) promotion of integration and an active society, by support for programmes of support for the disabled and the elderly

3. progress on equal treatment of men and women

4. better sources of information about employment opportunities to help people moving to find work

5. better use of the resources of the European Social Fund

6. democratisation of the decision-making procedures through improved consultation and information procedures, so that both workers and employers would be more involved

7. more support for small and medium companies with the potential to create jobs.

The fragmented legal framework for action

This continued concentration of Social Policy at the national level is also seen in the legal framework for European Union action on Social Policy, which had divided the areas of concern. The TEU, which all the states have ratified, sets out the EU concern:

- to create a high level of employment and social protection within the Union (Art 2)

- to raise the standards of living and quality of life and ensure the creation of economic and social cohesion and solidarity among the Member States

- to set objectives on working and living conditions for workers (Art 117)

- to ensure health and safety for those at work (Art 118a)

- to develop the social dialogue between the social partners at European level (Art 118b)

- to put in place the necessary provisions to ensure equal treatment of men and women at work (Art 119)

- to set the provisions governing the operation of the Social Fund (Art 123)

In addition, Art 3 lists the attainment of a high level of health protection, a contribution to education, and the strengthening of consumer protection. This has widened some of the areas of EU activity.

The legal basis of other areas of action is less certain. The Agreement on Social Policy following the TEU, which was ratified by all but the UK, broadens the scope of EU activity into the areas of human resources, employment, social protection and measures for those who are not economically active. These aspects of policy will be subject to new procedures on decision-making. Overall this has weakened the Union's ability to act in the social area, as only 14 of the 15 states accepted the new procedures.

The UK 'opt-out' from the Social Chapter of the Treaty on European Union and the inclusion instead of the Social Protocol, signed by the other 11 states, has introduced the possibility of differences in the working conditions for British workers from the rest of the Union. It has provided the opportunity for the Single Market to be undermined, by allowing companies to operate with different conditions within the UK from the rest of Europe. The result of allowing different conditions to prevail in the labour market has created a potential barrier to the free movement of people within the Union. This dual legal situation will continue until at least 1996, when the review of the TEU in the Intergovernmental Conferences occurs. It is a unique situation in the Union and there will be areas of confusion and overlap where decisions will be difficult about which of the procedures now in existence should be adopted.

Despite the increase of European Union action in the social area and the raised expectations as a result of the recent rhetoric associated with the Internal Market and the Treaty on European Union, the European Union's history of a fragmented Social Policy, with an emphasis on employment, remains.

History and development of European Union Social Policy

It is possible to identify a number of phases in the development of the Social Policy of the European Union.

First phase: 1957 to mid-1970s

The period between the Treaty of Rome and the mid-1970s was characterised by little activity in the social area. The origins of Social Policy were in the European Coal and Steel Community and the concerns of the EURATOM Treaty as well as the European Economic Community. The main economic objective of the ECSC Treaty was to achieve integration in the areas of coal and steel to regenerate the economies of France, Germany, the Benelux states and Italy. To help alleviate the consequences of actions to rationalise and restructure in these industrial sectors, a number of limited social provisions were included in the Treaty, primarily to achieve the following.

1. Ensure no distortion to competition in the coal and steel industries as a result of an ability to charge low prices because of lower social costs in any one state.

2. Make more effective use of the labour force through assistance targeted on those who lost their jobs in these two sectors. Provisions were made to make payments to redundant workers, for retraining, or to employers, to encourage them to offer employment to redundant mine or steel workers.

The EURATOM Treaty's concerns centred on basic health and safety at work. The European Economic Community's concerns were to promote economic development.

In bringing these concerns together in the Treaty of Rome, there was no single separate chapter in the Treaty dealing with social issues nor any attempt to create a common social policy. Instead the articles relating to social concerns were scattered throughout the Treaty. A collection of the scattered articles into a single Social Chapter was not possible when the Treaty on European Union was agreed. The same political reluctance to bring social issues higher on the European Union's agenda is evident in the mid-1990s as it was in the First Phase of EU Social Policy.

While social cohesion was included as a commitment alongside economic cohesion, there was no indication of how this commitment was to be met. The assumption was that improved living and working conditions would naturally occur over time. Progressive harmonisation of national social policies would result without the need for specific European Union intervention. Any benefits that resulted from greater economic integration within the European Union would be left to the Member States to distribute.

European Union Social Policy in its earliest period revolved around two broad components.

1. Issues related to technical matters, such as measures to facilitate the movement of labour, industrial relations and technical aspects of social security.

2. A more abstract idea of social improvement across the European Union that should result from the operation of the market. Measures to stop national governments hindering the movement of people fell into this category.

These actions were to be backed by the European Social Fund (ESF). It was established to help with the movement of workers, but the actions it was able to take were curtailed by its levels of funding and also by the fact that it was an addition to the actions of the nation governments. It was not a mechanism by which the social welfare benefits of the EU could be distributed to the individual citizens of the EU. This was a role clearly left to the national governments.

Free movement of workers

Of the areas of concern in the Treaty of Rome, the most important for the EU to play an active role in was ensuring that free movement of labour was possible. The rationale was an economic one. Labour is a factor of production, and to have one of the factors of production not fully utilised would have undermined the economic progress being made. Concentration during this early period was therefore on the conditions for the free movement of workers. The supranational level of the EU was responsible for the dissemination of information on job availability, providing the basis on which professional qualifications could be recognised, and social security eligibility transferred, from one state to another.

Equality of pay

The social costs of increased competitiveness were addressed particularly in Article 119, which contained the commitment to the introduction of equal pay for equal work for men and women. Article 119 had been added to the Treaty of Rome at the insistence of the French government. In 1957 wage rates in manufacturing for French female workers were close to their male counterparts'. French standards of social legislation were higher than in many other states of the then EU6. In the textile sector, where many female employees had gained the right to equal pay, there was particular concern that the freeing of the market would result in competition from other Member States where female rates were lower than in France. This would give an unfair advantage to those states and result in the possibility of unemployment among French workers.

Over time the commitment to equality of pay has been an area where the EU claims to have made a great deal of progress. Certainly the existence of the Treaty articles has provided campaigning groups with a legal basis for their work. However, the actual position seems to have changed very little since 1957. There is still a differential between the wage rates of men and women across the EU. The position is better in some states than in others, but across the EU as a whole a plateau of 'achievement' seems to have been reached where wage rates for female workers remain at about 80 per cent of their male counterparts'.

The European Social Fund (ESF)

The main policy instrument of Social Policy, the European Social Fund (ESF), was established by the Treaty of Rome and became operational in 1960. It was one of the two means by which Italian concerns about being the least developed industrially in the EU6 were quietened, the other being the European Investment Bank. Unlike the EIB, the ESF received its funding from the EU budget and was able to allocate the funds on a grant basis rather than a loan.

The legal basis of the Fund was Articles 123 to 128 of the Treaty of Rome, which gave the ESF limited and constrained objectives. It was established at a time when there was a shortage of labour in the EU6, but with pockets of poverty and economic decline. Primarily it was to make the employment of workers easier by increasing their geographical and occupational mobility and, as a result, to leave them in a position to improve their standards of living.

Through the ESF, specific groups were to be compensated for difficulties that might arise as a result of economic changes in the operation of the common market. In its original form the Social Fund could intervene only at the request of the Member States, to reimburse 50 per cent of the expenditure for a particular scheme. Contributions were made by each Member State using a special scale which put the lightest burden on to Italy. In the event only a minor proportion of the early Fund (10 million ECUs of 320 millions) was used to assist worker mobility. The labour shortages across the EU meant that there was little need to encourage movement of workers. The greater part of the Fund was spent on vocational training or retraining schemes.

A major criticism of this early Social Fund was that the Member States that were most effective at making the applications were the ones that received the most benefits, and not those in most need. Between 1960 and 1975 assistance was available to help with the rehabilitation of 1.8 million workers in the EU. The Fund was mainly concerned to help workers in older long-established industry who were being made redundant. Consequently Germany received 43.2 per cent of all assistance from this early Fund, and not Italy!

From as early in its operation as 1963 it was apparent that radical reform of the ESF was necessary, but no major review was undertaken until 1971. The automatic granting of financial assistance from the Fund had become an issue of concern. In the reforms the Commission was authorised to select projects for assistance on the basis of criteria set by the EU. The Fund's financing was switched from the allowances allocated by the Member States to receipt of money from the EU's own resources. Financial assistance could be claimed, not just by the public institutions within the Member States, but also by private institutions and associations. More money was put into the Social Fund during this period, so that from 250 million ECUs in 1975 it was increased to 1500 million by 1982.

These revisions of the Fund in the early 1970s meant that intervention of two types could be carried through.

1. Temporary measures. Employment schemes could be directed to workers leaving agriculture, textiles, and the clothing industries. Migrant workers were helped by schemes that would cover them from the preparation for migration through to the return. Specific assistance was also given to vocational training of women over 25 and young people under 25.

2. Permanent actions. Action could be taken aimed at remedying difficult situations in specific industries in certain regions. By 1976, 73 per cent of the Fund was used for just such a purpose.

Second phase: early 1970s to mid-1980s

From the early 1970s social issues generally began to acquire a more prominent place on the agenda of the EU. The Paris Summit of 1972 marked a beginning of a more active period of social concerns. Following the calls by the Council of Ministers in Paris, the First Social Action Programme was adopted in 1974. Despite the growing number of social pressures on the EU from the First Enlargement in 1973, the 1973 Oil Crisis and its effect on levels of employment, this Action Programme was limited in the issues with which it dealt. The original 1973 proposals of the Commission had been more far-reaching, but these were not accepted in their entirety by the Council of Ministers.

Three objectives were set to be achieved in the EU by this Action Programme:

1.   protection of workers' rights in recession-hit Europe, particularly for those made redundant or whose firms ceased to exist

2.   equal treatment for men and women in work

3.   strengthening of the social dialogue between workers and employers.

Further steps were also taken to protect the health and safety of workers. Overall, these health and safety measures were the most significant in the period to the mid-1980s.

However, the major step forward and development of an effective Social Policy did not materialise. The economic pressures being exerted on the Union in the mid-1970s caused the Member States to fall back on national responses to economic difficulties rather than to advance the possibility of EU action.[6] The Social Fund was readjusted during the 1970s and early 1980s on a number of occasions to take account of rising unemployment and the enlargement of the EU. The level of funding available during this phase, however, remained small. By 1983 it was clear that another major reform was necessary.

Third phase: Single Market to Social Charter

The period of the mid and late 1980s was marked by what appeared to be a new dynamism in the social area which had slowed by the end of the decade. The introduction of phrases such as 'people's Europe' and 'the social dimension' into the vocabulary of the EU and a switch in emphasis from the purely economic in the description of Social Cohesion brought a raising of expectations. A new political commitment was made to social policy following the launch of the Single Market Programme to ensure that any adverse social effects of economic integration could be counterbalanced.

The aim of the Single Market Programme was to ensure that economic activity throughout the EU was not distorted by the presence of man-made barriers to trade. This removed the possibility of protection for national industry, introduced keener competition and the creation of an even more difficult situation for a number of regions and certain industrial sectors within the European Union.

It was clear that some groups would be disadvantaged, who either already had specific problems that would be worsened by the increased economic integration or would suffer as a consequence of it. These groups included the long-term unemployed, the growing group of under-unemployed under-25s, less qualified workers, women, part-time workers and those in the 'black' economy.

Concerns were raised about the issue of 'social dumping'. There were fears that the opening of the borders would enable states with lower standards of social protection to undercut those with higher, and encourage firms to change location. The potential would therefore exist to distort competition. The danger would be that the advantage to the state with lower protection would not remain for very long. An overall downward pressure would then be exerted on all social conditions, wages, levels of social protection and social benefits throughout the EU.

By the mid-1990s these concerns about the problem of social dumping had not materialised. While some companies had been involved in relocating within the EU, there had not been the massive movement envisaged. The main reason has been the inflexible regulation of employment in some of the lower wage areas of the EU. For example, in Spain, the protection of workers, begun in the Franco era, made it very difficult to cut the workforce when necessary. More than 40 per cent of Spanish workers, as a result, were employed on temporary contracts.

The decision by Maytag's Hoover unit to close its plant in Dijon and relocate to Glasgow in 1993 was a highly publicised example of what was regarded as social dumping. 600 jobs were lost in France and 400 created in Scotland. The main reason for the move was the lower non-wage labour costs to be found in the UK. The burden on employers of contributions to social security schemes for their employees was higher in France than in the UK. A number of German companies had also relocated within the EU to take advantage of lower costs, but by the mid-1990s German companies were beginning to look to Pacific Rim locations, where the labour force was building expertise in high value-added engineering. Other EU companies had relocated to locations in the Central and Eastern European states, e.g. Renault to Slovenia.

The accession of Spain and Portugal to the European Union in 1986 had emphasised the need to establish what the EU's response should be on social concerns. Particularly, how most effectively to meet the costs of achieving social and economic cohesion, and improve the living and working conditions of all the Member States of the EU.

However, the EU priority remained to encourage the free movement of people. Furthermore, the Cockfield White Paper, outlining the measures necessary to achieve the Single Market, did not contain any proposals related to social concerns. It was left to the Single European Act (SEA) to establish EU competence in two areas of action.

1. Dialogue between employers and workers was given a legal basis in the SEA as one of the pillars on which the Single Market was to be built.

2. Working conditions, especially the problems of hygiene, safety and health in the workplace, were to be harmonised while improvements were being made.

The Single European Act left unanswered a number of questions. Its primary concern was to ensure that measures necessary for the Single Market programme would be put into place. The provisions of the SEA therefore extended the use of qualified majority voting (QMV) procedures to include EU legislation on health and safety at work. But a number of areas remained exempt from the use of QMV. For example, unanimity was still required for measures where social security benefits were involved.

The role of the Social Charter in the Single Market

The lack of substance to social action associated with the Single Market programme led to the adoption of the Community Charter of the Fundamental Social Rights of Workers (Social Charter) in 1989. The Social Charter was drafted as a response to the danger of the development of a European economy where some groups were disadvantaged. It was followed by the Second Social Action Programme, which outlined a limited number of pieces of legislation. The background against which it was developed was one of controversy. It was called

'a mirage, a pious aspiration, a propaganda pipe dream, a balloon which has been stuck by twelve pins'[7]

'a tool for progress and enhancement...an instrument for ensuring that the search for competitiveness and greater economic efficiency is...accompanied by equal advances in the social sphere'.[8]

The Belgian Presidency of the second half of 1987 first launched the idea of the Social Charter. The aim was to create a Community-wide programme of social, primarily employment, rights. It was to counterbalance the British presidency of 1986 which had tried to redirect EU Policy in the direction of deregulation of the labour market in order to make for greater labour market flexibility. The Belgian proposal was that essential employment rights should not be undermined by heightened competitive pressures associated with the Single Market. These employment rights were to be guaranteed across the European Union.

The Social Charter was a non-binding solemn declaration of political intent. This distinction, that the Social Charter was a political commitment and not a legal obligation, was underlined by Vasso Papandreou, Commissioner for Social Affairs, in 1989. This was to allay national governments' fears that, because of the clear linkage between social rights and the internal market programme in the Preamble to the Charter, an attempt might have been made to pass measures under the qualified majority voting procedure adopted to speed the Single Market measures.

The Social Charter was built around 12 areas of action:

- protection of the rights of workers who move within the EU

- fair remuneration for employment

- the improvement and approximation of conditions of employment

- social security

- freedom of association and collective bargaining

- vocational training

- equal treatment for men and women

- information, consultation and participation arrangements

- health and safety at work

- young people

- retired people

- disabled people.

None of these were new or radical. The Charter did not contain a prescriptive list of legislation. It drew on other declarations, not just pronouncements from within the EU, but also the Universal Declaration of Human Rights, the International Conventions on Civil and Political Rights and on Economic and Social Rights, the European Convention on Human Rights, and others. Much of what was said in the Social Charter was already accepted in the Member States and it was drafted in such broad terms that, despite some concerns, only the UK government refused to sign.

In order to obtain agreement from all the Member States, some of the Charter's force was lost. The original draft of the Charter had called for a minimum employment age of 16: the draft adopted was vague on this point:

'...subject to derogation limited to certain light work, the minimum employment age must not be lower than the school leaving age, and in any case not lower than 15 years' (Art 20, Social Charter).

This was a compromise, in order to overcome concern expressed by the Portuguese government. The school leaving age in Portugal was 14 in 1989.

Opposition to the Social Charter did not come just from Margaret Thatcher and her often quoted accusation that the Social Charter was 'socialism creeping in through the back door'.

1. The UK government argued that far less social legislation would allow the market to operate freely.

2. The Belgian government felt that the Social Charter did not go far enough.

3. All the Member States were concerned to ensure that their industry remained competitive and was not hindered by any of the Charter's provisions. The more advanced industrial states feared competition from the Southern states with lower wage rates. The Southern states feared a movement of the most enterprising sections of their population to the Northern.

4. Within the partners of the social dialogue there were also different views. The organisation of European Trade Unions (ETUC) was in favour of the introduction of legally binding measures across the European Union that would protect part-time workers and other groups who would be disadvantaged by the effects of the Single Market. The European Employers Federation (UNICE), on the other hand, favoured no regulations, arguing that the labour cost variations are a mechanism of economic competition and not a distortion of it.

Despite these concerns, all the Member States adopted the Second Social Action Programme to implement the Social Charter. The initiatives presented in the Social Action Programme were subject to the application of three principles:

1.   the principle of subsidiarity

2.   the principle of respect for the diversity of national systems, cultures and practices

3.   the preservation of competitiveness of undertakings without threatening either the economic or the social dimension of policies.

Eventually 47 proposals were made, of which only 21 were Directives. Some of these Directives were amendments to ones already adopted. Most of the Directives were introduced under Article 118a SEA. Agreement on Directives relating directly to health and safety was quick, such as the Directive on the minimum health and safety requirements to encourage improved medical assistance on board vessels.[9]

Other Directives proved more controversial. Among these were the Directives on Working Time, the Protection of Pregnant Women at Work, the Protection of the Young at Work and the establishment of European Works Councils. By 1994 all but four of the proposals of the Second Social Action Programme had been presented and the majority adopted. As the lack of agreement on the Directive establishing European Works Councils had continued, the decision was made to re-table the proposal using the terms of the Social Protocol. Two proposals to give protection to workers in non-standard employment and a Directive to protect workers posted overseas were rescheduled as part of the Third Social Action programme in 1995.

Table 15.2 gives the progress made by the individual Member States in implementing all legislation relating to employment and social policy by mid-1994. The table includes all the legislation on employment and social policy since 1968. As can be seen, the number of actual pieces of social legislation is small in comparison to the total of more than 1200 EU legislative acts. Table 15.2 also shows that the UK government, despite its opposition to the social legislation, has ensured that the majority of the measures have been transferred into UK national laws.

Table 15.2 Progress in implementing Directives applicable to employment and social policy

Member States	Directives applicable on 31 December 1993	Directives for which measures have been notified	Percentage adopted
Belgium	37	28	76
Denmark	37	32	86
Germany	38	27	71
Greece	36	24	67
Spain	37	25	68
France	37	29	78
Ireland	37	32	86
Italy	37	21	57
Luxembourg	37	22	59
Netherlands	37	26	70
Portugal	36	33	92
UK	37	34	92

Directives included in the table: 68/360, 75/117, 75/129, 76/207, 77/187, 77/576, 78/610, 79/007, 79/640, 80/987, 80/1107, 82/130, 82/605, 83/477, 86/188, 86/378, 86/613, 88/035, 88/364, 88/642, 89/391, 89/622, 89/654, 89/655, 89/656, 90/239, 90/269, 90/270, 90/394, 90/659, 90/679, 91/269, 91/322, 91/382, 91/383, 91/533, 92/041, 92/057
Source : As Table 14.3, p. 58

Revisions of the Social Fund

Changes were made to the funding level and administration of the Social Fund during the mid to late 1980s. The most important pressure for these changes had come following the third enlargement of the EU. Along with the programme to complete the Single Market, the inclusion of Spain and Portugal increased the problem of regional disparities and social disadvantage within the EU. More funds were put into the Social Fund. In 1986, for example, 2500 million ECUs were added to the Fund. The priority for action was to concentrate on programmes to assist young people who were experiencing rising levels of unemployment and the depressed regions in the EU. 45 per cent of funding was directed to the poorest regions of Greece, Portugal and Ireland, and also the Italian Mezzogiorno and parts of Spain.

The major reform of the Structural Funds carried out in 1989 introduced a more coordinated approach to the use of the EU's Structural Funds.[10] The ESF was to act through the Community Support Frameworks and the Operational Programmes in specific regions and for specific initiatives across the Member States (see chapter 13). Specific European Union-wide objectives were set for additional assistance from the Social Fund.

Measures based on regions

These came under the regional priorities – Objectives 1, 2 and 5b – and were incorporated into the plans and operations of the other Funds. The primary objective of social funding for the regions was to promote stable employment and develop new employment opportunities for the unemployed, people threatened by unemployment and people in small and medium enterprises.

Measures based on people:

1. Objective 3: Combating long-term unemployment by means of the occupational integration of people over the age of 25 who have been unemployed for longer than 12 months.

2. Facilitating the occupational integration of persons under 25 from the age at which compulsory full-time education ends.

Certain guidelines for action were established. Criteria for support were based on the transnational nature of the programme, training for technology and for those with special difficulties in the labour market, e.g. the handicapped, women and migrant workers. In addition, a number of Community 'own initiatives' were financed.

The effectiveness of the Fund in the late 1980s and early 1990s is difficult to judge. Definitions of registered unemployed, unemployed receiving benefit and seeking work vary from state to state. The national governments do not disaggregate figures on unemployed over 25 from the totals. The European Social Fund regulation was revised in 1993 and these criticisms were taken into account in the review of Objectives 3 and 4 designation. The primary objective of the Social Fund is to stimulate the labour market. It therefore does not deal with issues such as poverty, handicap and support for the elderly in a direct way.

At the beginning of the 1990s, EU Social Policy covered a wide range of issues, but in an increasingly fragmented manner. Legislation was possible in some circumstances, e.g. health and safety. There was a significant increase in the levels of funding available for EU social programmes, but the amounts remained small. The application of the principle of subsidiarity, still imperfectly defined in the early 1990s, had reduced the EU role to that of adviser and coordinator on initiatives and programmes.

The Social Charter was not legally binding, it was a declaration of intent to act, but not all states agreed with it other than in very general terms. There was considerable controversy about Directives such as the Protection of Pregnant Women at Work and the Working Time Directive. The problem of unemployment was worsening and it was difficult to reach agreement on regulation or deregulation of the labour market as the best way forward to create jobs. None of these difficulties was resolved by the ratification of the Treaty on European Union in November 1993, as the Social Protocol allowed for further fragmentation of actions in the social area.

The Social Protocol – a tool to undermine European Union Social Policy?

The Social Charter had been seen as the basis for the amendments to the social provisions of the Treaty of Rome which would be made in Maastricht in 1991. The intention was that the terms of the Social Charter, giving a uniform framework for the protection of the individual and collective groups, would be included in a *Social Chapter* of the Treaty on Political Union. The failure of the UK government to sign the Social Chapter marked the beginning of the controversy between the UK government and the rest of the Member States, which led instead to the signing of the *Protocol on Social Policy*.

The argument of the UK government was that the level of protection being proposed, through regulation of the labour market, would remove necessary flexibility from the labour market. In turn, this would impose such costs on companies that increased levels of unemployment would result. The view put forward by the Commission, and accepted by the other states, was that while flexibility in the labour market is necessary to job creation, there is still a possibility of support for individuals in the labour market through regulation. Furthermore, the acceptance of an increased interventionist approach to protect individuals and groups within the labour market, and those excluded from it, was crucial to the creation of the social dimension of the EU and achieving the objective of social cohesion.

The resulting complex dual legal situation will exist at least until the Intergovernmental Conference of 1996. On the one hand, some social actions will still take their legal basis from the EEC Treaty (retitled the European Community Treaty) of the TEU. The UK is still bound by these social articles, which are those of the Treaty of Rome and the Single European Act. Other areas will be subject to action under the terms of the *Agreement on Social Policy,* following the UK decision to opt out of the proposed Social Chapter. All the states, including the UK, have agreed that the institutions and procedures of the European Union may be used when legislation is proposed under the Social Protocol.

Areas to be covered by the Social Protocol include:

● activities to improve the working environment, which includes health and safety measures

● activities relating to working conditions, including working time, and holidays

● information and consultation of workers

● actions to promote equal opportunities and the integration of people excluded from the labour market.

There are a number of areas of overlap between what is covered by the Social Protocol and what is in the social articles of the TEU. This can only result in future controversy and dilution of the action of the European Union on social issues. Legislation under discussion following the Social Protocol until 1994 was legislation that had been proposed before 1991 in the Second Social Action Programme. There was therefore little opportunity to test the legality of the new procedures until the mid-1990s.

Early in 1994 the problem was returned to once again. The Commission began work on the Third Social Action Programme, which was launched in 1995. The Programme was prepared on the assumption, by the Commission, that all the Member States would agree to its measures. The Commission had been given the responsibility to work in this way, as part of the Social Agreement. Unless the terms of the Social Protocol were invoked, the Commission was to try to ensure that all states adopted social legislation.

The decision about the use of the Social Protocol was to be based on the responses to the following agreed questions.

1.   What is the nature of the proposal?

2.   What is the attitude of the social partners to the proposal?

3.   Is there any need to move forward on the social dimension at the same time as other policy areas of the EU? (If the answer to this question is 'yes', then it has to be debated by all the Member States.)

4.   Is the proposal acceptable to all states?

The implications of the dual procedures for the future of Social Policy

Social Policy has developed in a fragmented manner throughout the history of the European Union. The introduction of the 'opt-out' for the UK has further undermined attempts to develop a more coherent policy and weakened the progress on social cohesion. It has left a number of political difficulties for the European Union which the 1996 revision of the Treaty may not be able to resolve. It has deepened the feeling that the UK government is out of step with the rest of the European Union, including the three new Member States.

Effectiveness of Social Policy

Issues covered by EU Social Policy

As the preceding brief review of the history of European Union Social Policy has shown, the progress the EU has made on social issues is not uniform. A wide range of issues has been covered under the umbrella of Social Policy, but not to the same depth in all areas. The free movement of workers remains as the priority concern of Social Policy action within the EU (this is dealt with in more detail in chapter 5). The rest of this chapter concentrates on the emphasis in EU Social Policy on employment policy, equal opportunities and social protection.

Promotion of employment

A commitment was made in the Treaty on European Union to introduce measures that would ensure a high level of employment within the EU. There was no quantification of the level that was to be the objective; nor, in committing the European Union to action, was there any intention to remove the responsibility from the Member States to create jobs. Rather, the task of the EU was seen as that of a catalyst for ideas and the takers of action to ensure the progress of economic integration was not interrupted.

'The Community shall have as its task, by establishing a common market and an economic and monetary union and by implementing common policies or activities...to promote throughout the Community...a high level of employment.' (TEU Art 2)

Table 15.3 Number of unemployed as % of the civilian labour force (July 1994)

	1983–1991	1992	1993	1994	1995
Denmark	9.2	11.2	12.2	11.0	10.5
Germany	7.3	7.7	8.9	10.0	10.0
Belgium	11.0	10.3	11.9	12.8	12.7
Greece	7.6	8.7	9.8	10.7	11.0
Spain	19.0	18.4	22.7	24.5	24.4
France	9.7	10.4	11.7	12.3	12.2
Italy	11.2	11.6	10.4	11.7	11.9
Luxembourg	1.5	1.6	2.1	2.7	2.5
Netherlands	9.5	6.7	8.1	9.8	9.5
Portugal	6.7	4.2	5.5	6.4	6.9
UK	9.4	10.0	10.3	9.6	8.9
Ireland	16.0	16.3	16.6	15.7	15.4
EU	10.2	10.3	11.3	12.0	11.9
Canada	9.5	11.3	11.2	10.8	10.2
USA	6.7	7.4	6.8	6.3	5.8
Japan	2.5	2.2	2.5	2.9	2.8

Source : Europe, 25 July 1994, 3

As Table 15.3 shows, levels of unemployment vary considerably across the EU, from an average of more than 20 per cent in Spain to between 2 and 3 per cent in Luxembourg. The scale of the problem and the increasingly national responses by the Member States threatened to undermine attempts to create a coherent framework for European Union Social Policy.

Scale of the problem

In the mid-1990s the European Union had 7 per cent of the working-age population of the world. It produced 30 per cent of the global output and had a per capita GDP 10 times the average of the whole of Africa and 2–3 times that of Central and Eastern Europe. Yet the level of unemployment exceeded that of either the USA or Japan. Of the working-age population of the European Union in 1992, only 60 per cent were in employment. This contrasted with 70 per cent in the USA and the EFTA states and 75 per cent in Japan.[11]

In the mid-1990s the US record of employment creation reached a level three times that of the EU. In order to match these levels the EU had to initiate a programme to create 20 million jobs by the end of the century. Five million new jobs were needed merely to maintain the level of employment as it was. Many of the jobs created in the USA were low-paid and low-productive, so there was no desire within the European Union to follow the model presented by the USA. Nevertheless, the US record was impressive in contrast to the 18 million unemployed within the EU.

The causes of unemployment within the Union

A number of causes were identified to explain the high levels of unemployment within the EU of the mid-1990s. In the White Paper on Growth, Competitiveness and Employment presented by the Commission President, Jacques Delors, in November 1993, three main trends were identified. The most probable explanation was that it was a result of the combination of all the characteristics associated with these trends:

1. cyclical unemployment

2. structural unemployment

3. technological unemployment.

The White Paper on a Medium-Term Strategy for Growth, Competitiveness and Employment, December 1993

The primary purpose of this action plan was to introduce measures to reinforce the competitiveness of the European economy. There was a clear connection between the rate of output growth within the EU, which had been falling since the latter part of the 1980s, and the rate at which the EU was able to create employment. The major concerns were to ensure that the EU labour market was able to adapt to the rapid changes in production systems, organisations of work and modes of consumption. At the same time account had to be taken of the increasing participation rates that had come to be characteristic of the labour market in the 1980s.

The action plan did not contain any details of legislation to be produced by the EU. It was an outline of policies to be followed in the Member States to promote employment and the actions that could be taken by the Union to supplement the actions of the Member States. The focus of attention was on the need to bring flexibility into the labour market, and at the same time the need to leave in place a body of social rights.

The Action Plan was based on four prerequisites.

1.   A healthy economy. The Commission Action Plan called for stable and coherent monetary and economic policies to be introduced within the EU. The ideas presented required the objectives of low inflation, controlled public expenditure and exchange rate stability to be in place to provide the environment in which investment would be encouraged and growth would occur.

2.   An open economy. This raised the profile and importance of the completion of the GATT negotiation, so that world trade was stimulated, with the pattern of regulations in place that would ensure a degree of control over unfair competition. The conclusion of the various agreements with Central and Eastern European states was also seen as a contributor to this general spirit of openness.

3.   Social cohesion. All the citizens of the EU had to feel that there was some benefit for them. So the objective was to improve the position of those outside the labour market as well as those in employment.

4.   More decentralised economies, with the needs of the small and medium enterprises taken into account and the promotion of new technology.

As this action plan was not introducing legislation, but working within the structures existing in the Member States, a number of suggested courses of action were proposed that would be supported by EU action, but left the choice of measure to the Member States' governments. The recommended measures to stimulate employment included:

1.   improving education and skills training

2.   deregulation of the labour market to introduce greater flexibility

3.   better use of public funds by an active policy to inform job seekers of the opportunities available to them

4.   specific measures to encourage young people leaving school without qualifications to follow skills training courses

5.   targeted reductions in the indirect costs of labour

6.   fiscal measures relating to the environment which could be one means of offsetting a drop in social contributions

7.   developing employment in connection with meeting the new requirements to protect the quality of the environment.

Specific European Union actions

The following six areas for EU action were identified.

1.   Ensuring that any outstanding Single Market legislation was incorporated as speedily as possible into national legislation. Combined with this was the need for rules on state aid and competition to be applied rigorously.

2. The completion of the Trans-European networks. These are transport and telecommunication networks which are seen as an important complement to the Single Market for a number of reasons.

3. Increased EU support for new information and communication technologies.

4. The funding of energy, transport and environment networks and infrastructures for information. This was identified from a number of sources – 5 billion ECUs from the 'networks budget', the Structural Funds, the Cohesion Fund, the appropriations for research and technology developments, the European Investment Bank and the European Investment Fund. As part of these developments the role of the private investor was also seen as being of crucial importance.

5. The Fourth Research Framework Programme for 1994–1998.

6. The Social Dialogue.

The White Paper on Growth of 1993 and the Consultative Green Paper on Social Policy Options contained complementary proposals. In order to turn these proposals into action, the White Paper on Social Policy produced in July 1994 outlined a number of priorities where EU action was needed. The measures proposed in the Third Social Action Programme, in 1995, were based on these priorities.

1. More effective use of the European Social Fund to help with job creation programmes.

2. Action to increase productivity.

3. Promotion of an active society, where no group felt it was excluded.

4. Equal treatment of men and women, especially the completion of outstanding legislation.

5. Assistance to promote mobility of the work force.

6. Increased democratisation of the decision-making process, so that the Social Partners had a greater input.

None of these measures was a radical departure from what had been done in the past. An evaluation of the likely success of the Third Social Action Programme is possible by looking at some aspects of the earlier progress of social action in these targeted areas.

The role of the European Social Fund

The European Social Fund remains the main financial instrument through which support may be given to the nation state to help with schemes to overcome the problems of unemployment. Between 1988 and 1989 the Fund targeted the long-term unemployed over the age of 25 through Objective 3 actions, and the young unemployed through Objective 4. This targeting was only marginally successful. Of the long-term unemployed over the age of 25, only 16 per cent actually received assistance from the ESF in 1991.[12]

It proved to be difficult to target this group because of the way in which measures within the Member States focused on the unemployed, without identifying this group specifically. The objectives set for the Community Support Frameworks (see chapter 13) and the accompanying Operational Programmes had been ill-defined, and as a consequence the take-up rate of allocated funds was low between 1989 and 1993. Assistance to workers in the coal and steel sectors was more effective than for any other groups.

In the review of the Structural Funds regulations in 1993, the priorities for action had been redefined. A new Objective 3, which combined assistance for the integration of the young into the labour market with support for the long-term unemployed, was designated. The new Objective 4 designation was given to actions to assist with measures to combat unemployment as a result of industrial change and restructuring. 13 948 billion ECUs were allocated for these Objectives to cover the period from 1994 to 1999. 80 per cent of these funds were to be used in the Objective 3 actions and 20 per cent in the Objective 4.

These Objectives are horizontal and not tied to a specific region. The only regions of the EU that may not benefit from them are the Objective 1 regions, which already benefit from higher levels of support.

The allocation of funding for each Member State was based on the following criteria:

1. unemployment rates

2. numbers of long-term unemployed

3. national and regional prosperity.

Table 15.4 Allocation of funds to Member States (millions of ECUs)

	1994–1999	1989–1993
Belgium	465	400
Germany	1942	1200
Denmark	301	200
Spain	1843	1200
France	3203	1800
Italy	1715	1200
Luxembourg	23	15
Netherlands	1079	500
United Kingdom	3377	2100
Total	13 948	8 615

Source: Europe, 20 January 1994, 8

The overall levels of funding have been increased, and each Member State will therefore receive more financing. The two main beneficiaries, as Table 15.4 shows, will be the UK and France. However, the overall levels remain small in comparison to the scale of the problem, and the amounts being spent within the Member States themselves. Part of the effectiveness of the funding was undermined by continued problems of monitoring, assessment, and the flow of information back to the Commission about what was being done. Careful monitoring of the use of the Funds is therefore needed if more effective use is to be made of the money in the future.

The 'social dialogue' – the European Union's framework for industrial relations

In the White Papers on Growth, Competitiveness and Employment (Commission, 1993) and Social Policy (Commission, 1994) the importance of the creation of an effective framework for industrial relations was emphasised. The idea of dialogue between the representatives of the workers, the employers, the national governments and the EU as a means of developing effective EU Social Policy is not new. It was a primary concern of the founder states of the European Union. The rationale for such a dialogue about working conditions and wages at EU level was that as positive relations were established, there would be a resulting improvement in working conditions and social security benefits throughout the EU.

It has, however, proved to be a contentious issue for the EU for a variety of reasons. The barriers to the participation of the workers and the employers (the so-called 'Social Partners' in the 'social dialogue') in the decision-making process are difficult to overcome because of

- the national context of the dialogue

- the apparent lack of an institutional framework for the dialogue to take place

- influences that have ensured that the question of industrial relations remains at the company sectoral level.

The national context of the dialogue

Within the Member States the dialogue between the partners in industry takes place in a predominantly national context, based on one of two approaches. In France, Greece, Italy and the Netherlands, dialogue is regulated by the government. Labour laws or more or less compulsory negotiations exist. In the UK, Denmark and Germany, the approach is more voluntarist, taking place at the sectoral level and in response to collective bargaining. A midway approach is adopted in Belgium, Spain, Portugal and Luxembourg, where the state does not act as controller, but as arbiter to ensure that consensus is reached more rapidly.

The apparent lack of influence of the European Union institutional framework for the dialogue

The Treaty of the ECSC and the Treaty of Rome established certain institutions within which the various representatives of the partners involved in the social dialogue could meet. The ECSC Consultative Committee and the EEC Economic and Social Committee (ECOSOC) were part of the formal structure, the Economic and Social Committee being the largest of the bodies.

The ECOSOC is based in Brussels and has representatives from the professions, farmers, small and medium firms and numerous interest groups, e.g. consumer groups. However, despite being an official institution of the EU, the ECOSOC remains a largely consultative body with relatively little impact on the decision-making process in the EU. The function of the 220 member body remains largely advisory.

Influences that have ensured that the question of industrial relations remains at the company sectoral level

- There has been a movement away from direct government involvement in the pay bargaining and conditions setting process. This has come as much from the ideological stance being adopted by the Member States as from the most recent economic crisis in Western Europe. The increasing number of unemployed has resulted in a fall in the influence of the trade unions, especially in Denmark, the UK, France and the Netherlands and to some extent in Germany.

- Within industry itself a major restructuring has been taking place since the 1970s. The introduction of new technology has altered working practices in many industries. The massive swing into the service sector, where the trade unions have traditionally not been well represented, has further undermined the possibility of dialogue.

- The role of the multinational and multilocational companies has grown. Industry in Europe does not operate just in a European context, but also in an international context.

- There has been an increasing tendency of the workforce to change jobs during their working life. These job changes carry an increased need for training, which in some instances is met within the industry or the particular company.

- There has also been a growth in the number of small businesses across the Union.

The overall result has been that the attempts to improve the framework of industrial relations have had limited impact. There were two main reasons for this lack of activity.

1.   The legal basis of the dialogue came from the Single European Act. However, the SEA authorisation was to *encourage* dialogue, without the power of action in an area other than working conditions.

2.   The fact that there was only a commitment to allow the representatives of the numerous national partners in the social dialogue to *represent*, and not take a more active role.

Despite the commitment to increasing the opportunities for the social partners to take an active part in the decision-making process of the EU, more recent events have added to, not lowered, the barriers.

Social dialogue in the 1990s

The TEU made a number of significant changes to the dialogue between the social partners. The social partners were given the right to be consulted by the Commission on both the general principle of EU Social Policy and the content of actions. The rationale for EU action in employer–employee relations was emphasised for a number of reasons.

1.   The Single Market could lead to a further fragmentation of the diverse patterns of industrial relations that already exist within the Member States.

2.   The Commission view is that the removal of the barriers to trade will create more problems in worker employer relations and therefore EU intervention is necessary.

3.   The problem of social dumping could be avoided if workers had more information and were consulted about the actions that companies intended to take.

However, opposition to the social dialogue remains in a number of areas.

1.   From UNICE (the Union of Industrial and Employers Confederations of Europe), the employers' representatives in the dialogue, which remains a reluctant partner.

2.   There is concern that institutionalisation of the social dialogue may see excessively rigid solutions imposed on companies, a particular concern given the high levels of unemployment within the Union of the mid-1990s.

3.   From the UK national government, whose insistence on the 'social opt-out' undermined the legal framework of the dialogue.

The European Works Council Directive – the test case for the new framework of industrial relations

All these problems were apparent in the progress of the first Directive to use the procedures attached to the Social Protocol in 1994 – the Directive on European Works Councils (EWC). This proposed the creation of works councils in companies with more than 1000 employees in the EU, but excluding the UK. It was to apply to companies whose operation included subsidiaries of more than 150 employees in at least two Member States. The intention was that the Councils should meet at least once a year to consult and receive information about the company's activities. As such it was a very minimal action, but it became the subject of a great deal of controversy.

The Directive was originally introduced under the social articles of the Treaty; as such it required a vote of unanimity for adoption by the Council of Ministers. The UK government refused to withdraw its opposition to the principle of the Directive and the decision was taken at the end of 1993 to resubmit the proposal under the terms of the Social Protocol.

The Social Protocol gives the opportunity for double consultation of the social partners:

1.   on the principle underlying the proposal

2.   on the content of the eventual legislation.

If agreement is possible between the employers and the employees on the proposed legislation, during the first period of consultation, then it is adopted as legislation immediately (see Figure 15.1). If agreement is not possible, the Commission is required to act as arbiter in the negotiations and recommend a second phase of consultation. If agreement is still not possible, the Commission must decide on the form of action to take.

In the case of the EWC Directive agreement was impossible, and the Commission was asked to table legislation in April 1994. Some minor amendments were made and the Directive came into force in October 1994. A large number of UK multinationals with operations in Europe were also affected by the legislation. They included Boots, Marks and Spencers, Blue Circle Industries and British Aerospace.

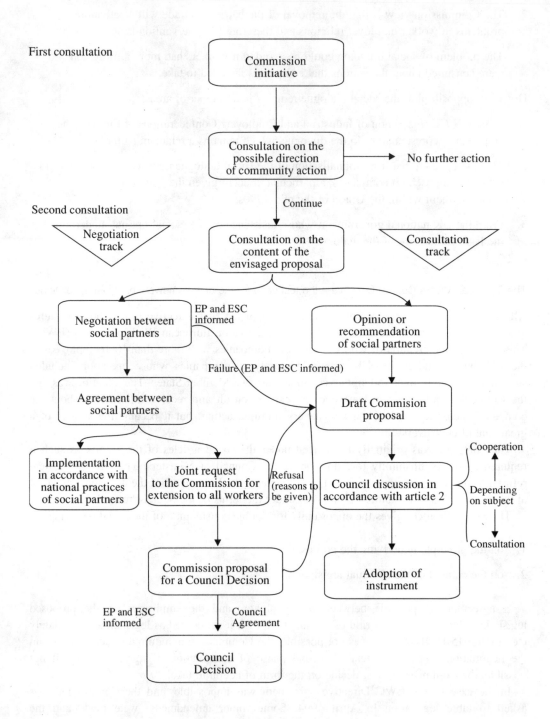

Figure 15.1 Operational chart showing the implementation of the Agreement on Social Policy
Source : *European Report*, 23 December 1993, 11

The progress of the EWC Directive demonstrated the lack of effectiveness of EU Social Policy, and provides some lessons for the future in two ways:

1. it highlighted the difficulty that continues to exist in reconciling the Social Partners

2. it underlined the lack of success of the 'social opt-out' for the UK, since a large number of UK companies were affected by the legislation.

In launching the White Paper on Social Policy in July 1994, Padraig Flynn, then the Social Affairs Commissioner, committed the EU to greater use of the procedures of the Social Protocol for the measures included in the 1995 Third Social Action Programme.

Equal pay and equal opportunities

Since the 1970s the number of women in the labour force or actively seeking work has grown. There are, however, a number of concerns about the barriers (lack of opportunity and the concentration of women in low-paid jobs) that leave women workers within the European Union at a disadvantage in the labour market. The unemployment rates among female workers are higher than among males. Female workers form the larger proportion of the long-term unemployed. During the late 1980s and early 1990s, unemployment among female workers in the EU increased by more than 7 million, in contrast to about 1 million for male workers.

This has a number of repercussions for the objectives of social cohesion. Within the European Union an increasing number of families are headed by a single parent, usually a woman. Many of these women are in part-time employment or have no paid employment at all, and as a consequence the families are existing on low incomes with the accompanying problems of deprivation and poor quality of life.

The structural changes taking place in industry have opened the opportunities for female workers. A number of issues need to be resolved before women are able to participate fully in the opportunities that the new technologies and restructuring of industry offer. The introduction of measures that will enable women to actively seek work carries major consequences for the public spending of the national governments and is a source of national political controversy. Women tend to be more dependent on public transport services and child care facilities, and these issues have to be taken into account by governments that are working to ensure that women have the opportunity to seek paid employment.

In the 1993 Green Paper on Social Policy options, the Commission advocated the adoption of 'a combined labour market policy and social policy to develop the rights and opportunities of women'.[13] This was not a new European Union objective. The aspirations of equal pay and opportunities were clearly outlined in Article 119 of the Treaty of Rome, and backed by Article 100:

'...to undertake actions for the purpose of achieving equality between man and woman as regards access to employment and vocational training and regards conditions including pay'.

The European Union sees the actions taken to date in establishing the foundations of equal pay and opportunities as one area where social policy has been successful.

However, progress in this area has in fact been slow. The first ten years of the Union's history saw little action on the question of equal pay and opportunities. It was not until the mid-1970s that action was begun, with three pieces of European Union legislation. A directive on equal pay[14] was adopted on 10 February 1975 and came into force in February 1976. The Directive was wide ranging since it also covered the elimination of all discrimination on the grounds of sex (except where job classification was used), the right of any worker to seek legal redress if discriminated against and protection against dismissal if legal proceedings were taken. The principle that equal pay for men and women was to be progressively implemented and extended into the area of social security was added by a Directive in 1978.[15] The groups to be included in this Directive were the entire working population, including the self-employed, the retired and the disabled. A Directive on equal access to employment was adopted in 1976 for implementation by 1978.[16]

In the ten years to 1985, the presence of the European Union legislation acted as a spur to the Member States to introduce or reinforce existing legislation. A comparison of the wage rates of Member States in 1972 and 1988 showed some convergence of wage rates in Greece and the Netherlands. On the other hand, wage rates in Denmark, France and Luxembourg did not show a similar move. Overall, the pattern that emerged was that wage rates for women in all states were roughly equivalent to 80 per cent of the male rates. In the mid-1990s the same picture was true. However, as the economic difficulties of the 1990s affected female workers more than males, the gap in some cases widened, as Table 15.5 shows.

Table 15.5 Wage rates for manual workers in selected EU states (1994)

Country	Male (%)	Female (%)
UK	100	54.2
Belgium	100	64.6
Denmark	100	84.5
France	100	66.6
Greece	100	69.8
Italy	100	69.2
Luxembourg	100	54.9
Netherlands	100	65.5
Portugal	100	70.7
Spain	100	62.3

Figures not available for Ireland or Germany
Source: Europe, 4/5 July 1994, 13

Implementation of the equal pay and opportunities legislation had been a priority concern in the Third Action Programme on Equal Opportunities, which covered the period from 1991 until the end of 1995. A mid-term evaluation of the effectiveness of the Third Action Programme was carried out in mid-1994. Its findings became the basis of the Fourth Action Programme on Equal Opportunities, which was begun in 1996. As the lack of progress of the implementation of the equal pay legislation by the national governments continued to be a problem, the measures of the Fourth Action Programme were supported by the introduction in 1996 of annual 'equality reports'. This annual reporting procedure was devised as a means of monitoring the policies being introduced by the Member States to ensure that the objectives of equal pay and opportunities were being met.

It is important for the objectives of economic and social cohesion for legislation on equal pay to be effectively implemented. It is politically unacceptable for any group within the EU to be subject to different conditions. The Internal Market has raised the importance of the issue on economic grounds. The industrial sectors where female workers are concentrated are under most threat in the restructuring of industry, accompanying the completion of the integrated market. The Internal Market offered many opportunities for growth, but 80 per cent of women work in employment with little protection and uncertain status which could be jeopardised by the effects of increased economic integration.

The fall in the number of young people in the labour force as the birth rate falls across Europe is highlighting the need to encourage women into the workforce. A number of obstacles have to be overcome if more women are to be encouraged to participate actively in the labour force. So far, the Commission has been concerned to ensure that a legal basis is established to guarantee equal pay. But there are growing pressures from the European Parliament and a number of women's groups in the Community for practical changes in working conditions to ensure that it will be easier for women to work.

Instruments at the disposal of the EU to assist the entry and protection of women in the labour force

Child care provision

Probably the biggest single obstacle to women being able to work is the level of available child care provision. A commitment was made in the Social Charter to ensure that women had the opportunity to work. When the Third Action Programme on Equal Opportunities was introduced in 1991, it did not detail any legislation on child care provision, but did call on the Member States to ensure that women had the opportunity to enter the labour force. The Council published a Recommendation on Child Care in 1992.[17] As a follow-up to this recommendation, a Network on Child Care Provision was established by the European Union to collect data and report on the provisions being made in the Member States.

The lack of interest in the provision of child care in some of the states of the EU was demonstrated by the progress on the Directive on Parental Leave for Child Care which was proposed in the Second Social Action programme. It was impossible to obtain unanimity for this Directive and in the 1995 Social Action Programme it was reintroduced under the Social Protocol Procedures.

In order to encourage women to return to work, the Community launched the NOW initiative (New Opportunities for Women) in 1990. This initiative, aimed at promoting vocational training and employment for women, was jointly financed from the Member States and the EU. Structural Fund support of £85 million was given between 1990 and 1993. (The UK government was not in favour of this initiative, since it referred specifically to women and appeared to be inconsistent with the stance of equal opportunities for all.) Although a number of European Union own initiatives were discontinued in the 1993 reform of the Structural Funds, the NOW initiative was considered to have been a success. Support for an extension of the NOW programme, EMPLOYMENT NOW, was given as part of the 1995 Third Social Action Programme.

For the EU, in its attempts to provide a framework in which jobs can be created, the large numbers of low-paid and unemployed female workers is a major concern. Legislation exists to ensure that equal pay and opportunities should occur. A number of Member States, which might not otherwise have done so, have as a result introduced national legislation. However, the reasons for inequality within the labour market are complex. The disparities between male and female workers within the EU are greater than those in other parts of the developed world. They are economically divisive as they entail a poor use of the human resource, socially divisive as the consequence of unemployment or low wage rates is poverty for a large number of people in Europe.

The implementation of the objectives of equal work and opportunities is limited in its success by a number of issues. As these objectives carry the potential of large-scale investment by the national governments, the actions proposed for implementation from 1995 were constrained.

Towards a Europe of solidarity

In the publication of the communication on the role for the EU in combating social exclusion in December 1992,[18] the Commission clearly identified the way in which an increasing number of groups in European society were being marginalised. These were groups excluded from the 'normal exchanges, practices and rights of modern society'.[19]

These rights included adequate housing, education, health and access to services. Poverty was identified as the underlying cause of these problems, and was clearly related to exclusion from the labour market or concentration within the low-paid sector. Within the EU there were more than 52 million people living below the recognised poverty line in their own home state.[20] Estimates suggested that of this group, more than 3 million were homeless.

The problems for these groups, who feel that they are increasingly being pushed out of society, appear in a number of different forms. The problems were not new ones for the 1990s, but had been growing in scale from the early 1980s. The numbers of long-term unemployed within the EU were high and levels of indebtedness had increased. Homelessness had become a problem in all areas, not just the major urban centres. There was also a rise in the levels of violent reaction to the problem of poverty. Levels of child abuse had increased, tensions were high within the urban centres and in some places had led to riots. Racial discrimination was showing itself in violent attacks on minority groups.

These problems became a priority for the EU in the 1995 Social Action Programme, when they appeared likely to undermine the process of integration and slow the development of social cohesion.

A clear legal basis for EU action had been established in the TEU.

'The Community shall have as its task...to promote...a high level of employment and of social protection' and '...economic and social cohesion and solidarity among Member States.' (Art 2, TEU)

'...the strengthening of economic and social cohesion...' (Art 3, TEU)

The Agreement on Social Policy contained a specific reference to '...the combating of social exclusion...' (Art 1, Social Protocol)

The competence of the EU to act in this area had therefore been increased to cover a range of issues. These included inadequate rights in housing, education, health and access to services. However, the action possible at European Union level was constrained in a number of ways. The expectation of EU action to create the wider social dimension, which had been heightened as a result of the TEU, remained to a great extent unfulfilled. The levels of financial assistance available to overcome the problem of social exclusion were limited. Strengthening economic and social cohesion appears in the list of actions in Article 3 TEU to which the principle of subsidiarity is to apply. This therefore means that there are limits to the actions that may be taken by the EU. The responsibility for combating social exclusion remains mainly with the Member States and their regional and local authorities.

Actions the European Union may take

The causes of poverty are complex and need an approach based on coordinated action from the general and structural policies of the European Union. While the objectives of these policies are not to combat social exclusion, by the nature of the policy objectives the underlying causes of poverty are tackled.

The work of the ESF

The primary objective of the European Social Fund is to ensure the functioning of the labour market. However, by targeting for priority action the long-term unemployed, the young, and such vulnerable groups in the labour market as women workers and migrants, the ESF is able to play a role in eradicating social exclusion.

'Own Initiatives'

There have been a number of specific Community initiatives dealing with the problem of promoting better use of the human resource. These include NOW, and its development EMPLOYMENT NOW, HORIZON and EUROFORM (see chapter 13). In the review of the Structural Fund regulations in 1993, a new framework was established for the Community initiatives. Promoting the human resource became one of three strands identified for specific and continued Union support.

The contribution of the ERDF and the EAGGF

Regional policy in its effects is essentially a social policy. Developing a region and removing the disparities in income levels has a direct impact on poverty. It is through earned income that the majority of people in the Union receive their means of support. The ERDF has therefore made a valuable contribution to eradicating the problems of social exclusion. The EAGGF has helped with restructuring in the rural areas.

Other contributing policies

A number of policies have had an indirect effect on combating social exclusion. These include:

1. the Single Market

2. Union action on
    - employment
    - working conditions
    - social protection
    - free movement of labour and migration
    - equality of treatment for men and women.

Poverty Action Programmes

The underlying cause of social exclusion is poverty. The EU has taken action against poverty through a series of Poverty Action Programmes. Since 1975 there have been a total of four. The medium-term Action Programme for 1994–1999 is building on the lessons that have emerged from the earlier ones in a number of ways.

The effectiveness of the Third Poverty Programme (Poverty III), 1989–1994

1. The Court of Auditors concluded in its 1994 Report that the value of this programme came from the fact that it encouraged the Member States that had not made any anti-poverty provision to produce a clear policy commitment to do so.[21] This was true of Portugal and Greece.

2. Programmes that had been supported were aimed at tackling all facets of social exclusion. Poverty III had a budget allocated to it of 55 million ECUs and targeted a smaller range of projects than the earlier Programmes had done.

Effectiveness of Union action to overcome social exclusion

The effectiveness of the actions the EU had taken to overcome social exclusion by the mid-1990s was difficult to evaluate. The Poverty III measures had been effectively monitored, but that was not true of all the measures. A large number of measures duplicated the work of other initiatives. Monitoring of the projects was problematic and the effectiveness of some of these programmes had been undermined because the Commission did not set clear objectives before the programmes began that could be measured. It was difficult to assess how much value for money was obtained from the EU investment.

Social exclusion and Poverty Action Programme 1994–1999

The major difference between this programme and the earlier ones was the increased level of funding. The total expected budget for the programme was 112 million ECUs to cover the period from 1995 to 1999. The levels of funding, however, remained grossly inadequate for the tasks involved. The overall picture of lack of coherent action with limited funding remained in this area of European Union Social Policy despite the high profile the issue was given in the 1995 Social Action Programme.

Conclusions

The Treaty on European Union made a number of commitments:

> 'The Union shall set itself the following objectives to promote economic and social progress which is balanced and sustainable...through the strengthening of economic and social cohesion.' (Art B, TEU)

> 'The Community shall have as its task...a high level of employment and of social protection, the raising of the standard of living and quality of life, and economic and social cohesion and solidarity among the Member States.' (Art 2)

The EU therefore has set ambitious goals that carry the possibility of far-reaching activity in the social area. The rhetoric of these Treaty Articles raises numerous expectations about what the European Union can achieve. The actions and policies of the European Union must ensure that all the citizens feel that they are benefiting from their state's membership of the EU.

The main areas of concern for the Social Policy of the European Union fall into a number of broad categories. They are measures related to employment, health and safety in the workplace, equal pay and opportunities, industrial relations and labour mobility. These categories of action cover a wide range of concerns, but they do not match the expectations of the scope of action the EU is competent to fulfil. The main argument of this chapter has been that instead of adding to the creation of the social dimension, the European Union of the 1990s is creating a Social Policy that is more fragmented, and therefore less able to meet the worsening European social problems. Instead of creating social cohesion and solidarity, the European Union is in danger of allowing the divisions in society to worsen.

A number of political developments have contributed to increasing the likelihood of tension between the national governments and the European Union. By agreeing to the 'opt-out' from the Social Chapter for the UK, the possibility has been introduced of the 14 signatories moving forward on social legislation without the UK. The presence of the Social Protocol as well as the social articles of the TEU has introduced a series of complications to the passage of legislation and increased the difficulties for the ECJ in its interpretation of the legislation. It creates a situation of weakened commitment to social legislation, as one of the largest states of the Union and one of the more assiduous in its implementation of social legislation is no longer to be party to all of the social deliberations.

The primary socioeconomic concern for all the states of the EU in the mid-1990s was the rising levels of unemployment and the resulting difficulties for the whole of Europe to maintain its economic prosperity. The debate, at both the national and the supranational levels, about the most appropriate actions to take, centred around the need to introduce greater labour market flexibility. The view put forward was that wage differentials should be allowed to widen and that social benefits should be reduced and more specifically targeted. However, there was concern that levels of social protection for workers should be maintained. This was considered important by the European Commission to ensure that the objective of social cohesion was not undermined through differences in the social protection policies of the national governments. The controversy over this issue divided the opinions of the Member States, and divided the views of the Commission and the European Parliament from the Member States of the EU.

The result was that when the Third Social Action Programme was introduced in 1995 none of its measures were either new or radical. Many had already been agreed. Much of European Union Social Policy is still based on rhetoric. In respecting the principles of national diversity and subsidiarity in the area of social action, the possibility remains of fragmentation and lack of coherence in the development of EU Social Policy. It is clear that the biggest single obstacle to the development of European Union Social Policy is the lack of political commitment to it in the Member States. The main concern of the European Union is economic integration. It is not the intention of the Member States to establish the framework to create a general EU Social Policy, rather the focus continues to be on agreeing on the basic principles of national social policies and measures to ensure that the Single Market operation is not distorted.

References

1. **Commission of the EC** (1994) *Commission Report on Social Protection in Europe* (1993), COM (93) 531, final.
2. *Communiqué of the Hanover Summit*, 27/28 June 1988.
3. **Commission of the EC** (1993) *White Paper on the Medium Term Strategy for Growth, Competitiveness and Employment*, COM (93) 700, final.
4. **Commission of the EC** (1993) *Green Paper on European Social Policy Options – Options for the Union*, COM (93) 551.
5. **Commission of the EC** (1994) White Paper on European Social Policy – a Way Forward for the Union.
6. **Wise M and Gibb R** (1993) *Single Market to Social Europe*, Longman, London, p. 134.
7. *The Independent*, 21 August 1991, 5.
8. **Papandreou V** (1990) *Social Europe*, Vol. 1, p. 8.
9. **Council Directive** EEC 29/92.
10. **Council Regulation** EEC 4255/88 establishing the Social Fund.
11. **Commission of the EC** (1993) *Employment in Europe*, COM (93) 314, p. 10.
12. *Official Journal of the EC* (1993) Court of Auditors Annual Report Concerning the Financial Year 1992, O.J. C 309, Vol. 36, 16 November, 131.
13. COM (93) 551, p. 25.
14. **Council Directive** EEC 45/75.
15. **Council Directive** EEC 6/79.
16. **Council Directive** EEC 39/76.
17. **Council Directive** EEC 92/241.
18. **Commission of the EC** (1992) *Towards a Europe of Solidarity*, COM (92) 542.
19. **Commission of the EC** (1993) *Social Exclusion and Poverty*, Background Report ISEC/B34/93, p. 1.
20. **Commission of the EC** (1994) *White Paper on Social Policy*, p. 37.
21. As Ref. 12, p. 141.

Further reading

Commission of the EC (1993) *Second Report on the Application of the Community Charter of the Fundamental Social Rights of Workers*.

Commission of the EC (1993) *Community Wide Framework for Employment*, COM (93) 238.

Commission of the EC (1994) 11th Annual Report on the Application of Community Law, COM (94) 500, final.

Grahl J and Teague P (1992) Integration theory and European labour markets, *British Journal of Industrial Relations*, Vol. 30.

Gold M (ed.) (1993) *The Social Dimension*, Macmillan, London.

House of Lords (1993) Select Committee on the EC, 7th Report, *Growth, Competitiveness and Employment in the EC*.

Majone G (1993) The European Community between Social Policy and Social Regulation, *Journal of Common Market Studies*, Vol. 31.

Rubery J (1992) Pay, gender and the social dimension to Europe, *British Journal of Industrial Management*, Vol. 30.

CHAPTER 16

The European Union and the world trading system

Introduction

The Common Commercial Policy (CCP) deals with the EU's international trading links with a range of countries and major organisations. Its most significant triumphs have been the unifying of many of the non-tariff barriers, and the creation of the Common External Tariff (CET), which the EU calls the Common Customs Tariff (CCT). This policy area has made particular progress since the completion of the Single Market, and the conclusion of the Uruguay Round of the General Agreement on Tariffs and Trade (GATT).

While the issue of trade policy is normally discussed at an economic level, it also has a substantial political dimension. The Common Commercial Policy has been a powerful tool to promote integration within the EU. There is also no doubt that the EU is a formidable force to be dealt with in international economic relations: far more so than the individual states would be on their own. Finally, the Common Commercial Policy has been a major component in the promotion of development, particularly to countries that are part of the Lomé Convention.

This chapter is concerned with global trade issues and leaves discussion of relations with the emerging economies of Central and Eastern Europe and with the developing nations to chapters 17 and 18. This chapter suggests that the EU's record on trade liberalisation is perhaps no better or worse than many others. The case of agriculture is used to illustrate many of the difficulties associated with the EU's position in world trade. This area shows the EU and a number of other major traders to have adopted poor trade practices in the past. However, the completion of the Uruguay Round offers a possible way forward to more constructive relations. If the EU is to contribute fully towards the liberalisation of world trade it must: .

1. stay fully within the GATT framework

2. make further progress in key areas such as agriculture.

Without the EU playing its full part in the liberalisation of world trade, there is a danger that the GATT Uruguay Round of multilateral trade agreements signed in April 1994 will not achieve its full potential. This may lead to a slower growth rate in the global economy. However, along with the progress on multilateral trade, it is important that the bilateral disputes between the world's major trading blocs be resolved.

The rationale for a Common Commercial Policy

The rationale of the Common Commercial Policy is based on the view that the EU is far stronger negotiating collectively than in a fragmented way. Article 110 of the Treaty stated that:

'By establishing a customs union between themselves Member States aim to contribute in the common interest, to the harmonious development of world trade, the progressive abolition of restrictions on international trade and the lowering of customs barriers.'

'The common commercial policy shall take into account the favourable effect which abolition of customs duties between Member States may have on the increase in the competitive strength of undertakings in those states.'

This suggests that the EU is committed to trade liberalisation, but only to the extent that it improves the position of the economies within the EU.

Article 113 (1) as amended by the Treaty on European Union gives the principles by which the policy should be conducted:

'The Common Commercial Policy shall be based on uniform principles particularly with regard to changes in tariff rates, the conclusion of tariff and trade agreements, the achievement of uniformity in measures of liberalisation, export policy and measures to protect trade such as those to be taken in the event of dumping and subsidies.'

The fact that the EU has managed to complete the Single Market means that the EU has moved beyond the point where trade policy is just concerned with the maintenance of the CET. As the borders between the Member States were removed, it became more difficult to isolate a range of trade instruments, because their effects spilt over the borders. The common tariff has been supplemented with common trade instruments over a range of areas. However, Article 115 permits Member States to take action to overcome economic difficulties on an individual basis, if there is difficulty in gaining a short-term collective solution. Also, the Member States retain some policy instruments that have an impact on trade such as the export credits, aid and development policies, and most crucially the exchange rate.

The decision-making process

The European Commission has a unique role in the CCP. It is responsible for generating the policy initiates, and plays a crucial role in negotiating in international forums such as the GATT. The Commission is also responsible for investigating and implementing actions against states that indulge in what are considered to be unfair trade practices. The Council of Ministers is responsible for making the key policy decisions with regard to trade policy, but qualified majority voting applies, which can speed up the process.

Article 113 also clarified the role of the Council of Ministers:

1. The Commission shall submit proposals to the Council for implementing the Common Commercial Policy.

2. Where agreements with one or more States or international organisations need to be negotiated, the Commission shall make recommendations to the Council which shall authorise the Commission to open negotiations.

3. The Commission shall conduct these negotiations in consultations with a special committee appointed by the Council to assist the Commission in this task and within the framework of such directives as the Council may issue to it.

The actual policy process is of course considerably more complex than would appear from the above. Trade issues bring to the fore a series of special interests, which operate to influence the consultation at both the national and the EU level. Added to this, Member States can threaten unilateral action if their voice is not heard. An example of this occurred in 1993, when the French government attempted to repudiate the Blair House Agreement (concluded in New York in November 1992) because it felt that its agricultural sector was not being adequately defended.

Protectionism and the global economy

For the market economist, the ideal state of affairs is where free trade exists, i.e. where there are no man-made obstacles to the trade between nations. This is because free trade allows individuals to exploit their comparative advantage, and therefore specialise in what they do best. It leaves the consumer with a wider choice of goods at competitive prices. Within nation states, arguments to restrict trade between one area and another would be regarded as illogical. However, states see it as being in their interest to restrict international trade, in the hope that they will gain at the expense of others.

In good times, the pressures to protect an economy may not be great, because as industries decline there are alternative sources of employment. Displacement by imported goods appears to be less of a problem. However, even when things are going well, sectional interests may be able to launch an effective campaign for exceptional treatment based on pleas that the national interest could be served by protecting a particular industry. The immobility of labour may lead to substantial pockets of high unemployment, for example. It is also frequently argued that temporary protection is required for certain industries when they are trying to become established or facing a period of change.

At times of high unemployment, cheap imports are often regarded as the cause of the national malaise, and so wider restrictions may be placed on trade. Import protection has political benefits including the following:

1. governments can use protectionism as a way of deflecting resentment away from the management of domestic economies

2. it appears to offer immediate and tangible benefits, in terms of identifiable jobs that can be saved

3. the costs of helping the groups that benefit cannot easily be identified, as they are apart from the national budget

4. it appears to avoid the need for structural adjustment

5. domestic interest groups can gain a significant reward from the restriction of imports, by being able to charge higher prices.

The threat of protecting domestic industry can offer a useful bargaining counter in international relations. In trade negotiations, it is helpful to be able to negotiate on the basis of being able to offer concessions. Protectionist measures may also be a way of encouraging foreign investment in a market. For example, many Japanese companies established themselves in the UK prior to the completion of the Single Market, in order to avoid possible discrimination. They were able to rely on the UK government to champion their cause in the EU policy process.

It is the consumers who have to pay higher prices for the goods they buy, but because the effects are diffuse and difficult to calculate, they are not normally aware of this. Protectionism is effectively a tax on imports, which punishes exporters into that economy and penalises the consumer. There may be short-term economic benefits from protecting vulnerable industry, while it adjusts to international competition. Eventually economies have to face up to the structural adjustments needed to promote competitiveness, or face an eventual decline. If no adjustment takes place, the industry will find that it is restricted to providing for the domestic market only. At the same time as prices are higher than those operating externally, there is likely to be a decline in the relative quality of the products. In addition, there is a risk of retaliation by states that feel they have been treated unreasonably.

The cost of retaliation is unlikely to be born by the protected industries, but it may lead other industries affected by it to call for help. If protection develops on a worldwide basis, the multilateral trade system is likely to break down, and all countries will lose. This was the case in the 1920s and 1930s, when the worldwide recession was made considerably worse by countries attempting to maintain exports at the same time as reducing their dependence on imports. Eventually trade relations deteriorated to the point where the multilateral system of trade collapsed, and bilateral trade became the norm, i.e. each country offering access to its markets only to countries that gave specific trade concessions in return: for example British coal being traded for Argentinian beef.

Tariff barriers

Tariffs are taxes on imported goods, which are used to

1. protect markets by making imported goods more expensive than those produced domestically

2. provide a source of revenue to governments.

The importance of tariffs has continued to decline. This trend has been reinforced by the series of GATT Rounds that took place after World War II. The average tariff level on imports of manufactures fell from over 40 per cent in the developed economies in the late 1940s to around 6.3 per cent in the early 1990s. However, this covers a wide range of duties from 50 per cent to zero. Tariff levels in the 1990s were significantly below those of the 19th century, which was regarded as the golden age of free trade. In the early stages of economic development, many countries have tended to impose high levels of import duty. However, they have also been reluctant to give up the protection that their domestic industry enjoys, even if their economic growth has taken off. But they may be forced to liberalise, as any economy that relies significantly on exports will find that pressure mounts for it to open up its markets.

While the use of tariffs was frowned on in the past, they are now regarded as being more transparent in terms of world trade. The Uruguay GATT Round saw an attempt to revive their use as an alternative to non-tariff barriers. Tariffication was the replacement of tariffs for other kinds of restrictions, which meant that the extent of constraints on trade became clearer. If the hurdle is clear, then strategies can be adopted to overcome it.

Non-tariff barriers

In the past it was assumed that tariff barriers were the most important obstacle to free trade. However, as the world trading system has developed, non-tariff barriers have seemed to offer the greatest threat to the global trading system. Reducing tariff barriers was a relatively easy task in the period of rapid economic growth up to the mid-1970s. From then onwards, as growth slowed down, the extent of non-tariff barriers became apparent, and it was clear that they were a considerable obstacle to the development of the world trading system.

The extent to which non-tariff barriers hamper trade is difficult to measure, because many of them are not apparent until there are complaints about them. They are, however, difficult to circumvent because, unlike tariffs, they cannot be overcome by a simple, if inconvenient, price reduction. Usually non-tariff barriers are the result of government action, although in some cases business can be directly involved. Some of the barriers are of long standing, and were not designed specifically to hamper trade, for example technical regulations. Governments regulate so much of national economies that they have direct control over a wide range of standards and trading practices, and this makes them a target for business and consumer groups. Groups are able to appeal to governments to regulate in their favour on the grounds of nationalism, tradition, or safety standards. These claims to be acting in the defence of national interests frequently disguise the protectionist nature of the proposals.

Table 16.1 Imports affected by non-tariff barriers

	1966		1986	
	%	Value ($ million)	%	Value ($ million)
All countries	25.3	29 510	48.0	355 532
European Union	20.8	14 695	54.1	169 153
Japan	31.4	3648	43.5	57 525
USA	36.4	9379	45.0	103 069

Source : OECD (1993), *Obstacles to Trade and Competition*, p. 24

The growing threat that non-tariff barriers posed the world trading system at the time of the launch of the Uruguay Round of GATT is illustrated in Table 16.1 which shows that trade liberalisation had not progressed as far as might have been expected. Indeed, it reflects what appeared to be a deteriorating situation.

Quotas

Quotas place a limit on the extent of imports into an economy. The use of quotas to restrict imports from developing countries has been a feature of EU trade. An example of this is the restrictions placed on the import of textiles and clothing, under the Multifibre Arrangement (MFA), which came into existence in 1974. It is also estimated that barriers to textiles and clothing cost the developing countries in the region of $50 billion per year in lost trade.

There is also a cost to the countries imposing the quotas. The UK was estimated to be losing £980 million per year at 1988 prices.[1] The measures saved 33 000 UK jobs, but at a price of an additional 5 per cent on the prices of clothing. This amounted to a cost of £29 000 per job saved, which was between 3 and 4 times the average earnings in the textiles and clothing industry. It must be reasonable to assume that the costs were similar for other EU countries.

Voluntary export restraints (VERs)

In the period from the 1970s onwards, there was a substantial growth in the use of VERs. These are voluntary only in the sense that they are the subject of negotiation, and they are monitored at the border of the exporting country. These are agreements negotiated, normally between governments, but with the involvement of industrial groups. They are agreements to limit exports into a market, often on the basis of specific market conditions. For example a VER might be agreed as a percentage of a market, such as cars. If the car market goes into decline, the exports into the market are reduced. The cost of the VER is born by the consumer, because prices are higher. However, the exporter will gain from the higher prices. If tariffs are used, the importing state gains from the restriction, because it keeps the tariff income. Figure 16.1 illustrates the impact of VERs. We see that if only home supplies are available, the price will be P_3 and the quantity demanded will be OQ_3. If, however world supplies are allowed into the market, prices will fall to P_1 and the quantity demanded will expand to OQ_5. The supply available to home suppliers will then contract to OQ_1. This may not be satisfactory, because it means the industry has to contract, creating political pressures. In order for the industry to retain a larger share of the market OQ_2, a VER is imposed. Prices then rise to P_2, and foreign supplies have to be content with only Q_2Q_4 of the market. Consumers will lose to

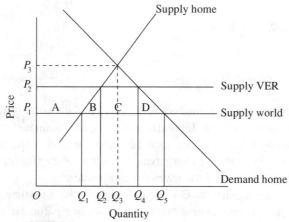

Figure 16.1 The impact of VERS

the extent of ABCD. Area A will be a transfer from home consumers to home producers, who will receive higher prices for their product. Area B is a dead weight loss, because less efficient producers are supplying the market. Area D is a loss, because home consumers will now consume less. However, Area C is the most significant loss because this is the gain to overseas suppliers who now receive a higher price at the expense of the consumers.

An example of a VER is the accord between the EU and Japan that restricted the importation of cars into the EU market. This agreement came into place after a number of problems arose concerning the free movement of cars within the EU. In some of the Member States, such as Italy, Japanese cars had been virtually excluded and enjoyed less than 2 per cent of the market in the early 1990s, while in Germany they entered almost without restriction. The UK had an agreement to restrict imports to 11 per cent of the market. In order to remove these internal market restrictions, the EU negotiated an agreement with Japan which replaced the national VERs with one that covered the EU as a whole. The intention was to move towards open trading only after 1999. It was then envisaged that the Japanese share of the market would have risen to over 16 per cent. A significant part of this would be taken by Japanese cars being produced within the EU. The actual numbers of imports in any one year would depend on the state of the total market. So, for example, the Japanese were allowed to increase imports in 1994 by 0.4 per cent of the market. This gave the Japanese the potential to have 8.4 per cent of a market estimated to have a demand for 11.97 million cars.

Table 16.2 The cost of the EU–Japanese Accord on the importation of cars, 1993–1999 (£ billion)

Losses by consumers	
1. Losses due to higher prices of imports	9.0
2. Losses due to higher priced European cars	12.8
3. Welfare losses due to reduced consumption of imports (offset by gain in consumer surplus)	1.6
Total consumer loss	23.4
Offset by	
4. Increased dealer margins on imports	1.1
5. Increase in producers' surplus	12.8
6. Import duty gained	0.7
Total offset	14.6
Net economic loss 1993–1999 (at 1989 prices)	8.8

Source: National Consumer Council (1993), *International Trade; the Consumer Agenda*, p. 89

The National Consumer Council commissioned a survey of the costs of the agreement, and came up with the estimates given in Table 16.2. What these estimates indicate is that the consumer would be paying £743 more for each Japanese car than if the restrictions did not exist. Purchasers of European cars are also paying more than they should, because domestic producers can charge more because of the restricted competition.

The above restrictions are against the GATT rules, not only because they are not temporary, but also because they discriminate against the exports from one particular country. The quota on Japanese cars remained in existence beyond the GATT Uruguay Round settlement.

Anti-dumping measures

Dumping is defined as the exporting of goods into a market at a lower price than is being charged for those goods in the home market. (In the absence of such a comparison, the GATT permits reference to prices in a third country.) It is thought to be harmful if it damages the industry of the country receiving the goods. Dumping may be state-inspired in order to correct balance of payments problems. This was a frequent charge against the former socialist economies, which sold goods cheaply in order to earn hard currency. In these cases, the state provides a subsidy to the exporters. Although subsidies were common in the case of the former socialist economies, the pricing mechanism was so chaotic that the extent of them was often not clear. In capitalist economies, the greatest problem tends to be state aids which are designed for modernisation and restructuring of industry. These can give unfair trading advantages. So, for example, the Airbus consortium has frequently been regarded by the USA as having had an unfair amount of help to establish itself (see chapter 12).

Firms have often been thought to have indulged in predatory pricing in order to squeeze out potential competitors. Also, prices have been reduced, in order to get rid of surplus production. If dumping results in damage to the industry of the country concerned, it is legitimate to defend domestic industry by imposing a tariff, or some other form of trade restriction. This should be no more than that required to compensate for the excessive cheapness of imports. What should not happen is that goods are declared to be dumped because they are produced by foreign industry that is more efficient than its competitors.

Consumer groups within the EU have long suspected that the EU Commission has tended to take the side of European industry to the extent that anti-dumping measures are used as a form of protectionism. In total the EU had 160 anti-dumping actions in force in 1993, which were generally in place for a five year period. The UK's National Consumer Council estimated that in 1992, the anti-dumping measures on electrical goods cost the EU consumer £1293 million.[2] This can be confirmed when the prices of electrical goods are compared in the USA and Britain. In 1993, a Sony compact disc player cost £170 in the UK as against £109 in the USA, and a Panasonic Video Cassette recorder cost £350 in the UK as against £138 in the USA. While there are a number of reasons for some differences, including exchange rate movements, clearly EU consumers were paying higher prices than they should.[3]

Regional trade blocs

The world trading system should operate, as does any sensible domestic economy, on a multilateral basis, i.e. where individuals make their purchases on the basis of where goods are available at the best price, or on the best terms and conditions. In reality this has not come about, and the movement of world trade patterns has been towards multilateralism within more restricted areas. The creation of trade blocs came to the fore as an issue in the 1980s, with the feeling that the completion of the EU's Single Market might create a 'fortress Europe'. While the creation of trading blocs is not a new phenomenon, they have tended to proliferate. These regional attempts at multilateralism can take a number of forms, ranging from the preferential trading agreements to full-scale economic union.

Table 16.3 Value of world merchandise trade by region in 1993 (in $ billion)

	Exports (fob)[1]	Imports (cif)[1]
World	3580	3690
North America	610	743
Latin America	157	181
Western Europe	1561	1595
EU	1326	1360
EFTA	210	195
Eastern Europe and the CIS	88	83
Africa	88	93
Middle East	121	116
Asia	955	877
Japan	361	241
China	92	104
Asian Tigers[2]	354	373

[1]   The difference between free on board (fob) and carriage and insurance and freight (cif)
    reflects the costs associated with transporting the goods
[2]   Chinese Taipei, Hong Kong, Republic of Korea, Malaysia, Singapore and Thailand
Source : GATT (1994), *GATT Activities 1993,* p. 13

The value of world merchandise trade by region in 1992 is given in Table 16.3. In addition to this, GATT estimated the value of commercial services to be $960 billion.

The most important global trade block is the EU. The continued enlargement of the EU with the deepening of integration and the pooling of economic sovereignty of its Member States has reduced the diversity of trade practices. This has helped to create greater certainty in the business environment for business operating across borders. A wider range of markets became available, and firms were able to gain economies of scale. States have become tied to one another as their economies have become increasingly interdependent. The EU has removed the tariffs between the Member States, and has removed them for manufactures against the European Free Trade Area (EFTA) states. The process of integration was taken further by the EFTA states, minus Switzerland, joining the European Economic Area (EEA), and later by Austria, Finland and Sweden expressing a willingness to join an enlarged EU.

The growth in the number of regional trade groupings that have attempted to repeat the success of the EU has been a feature of international trade organisation in the late twentieth century. The EU is dominated by its larger economies, in particular Germany, with France, Italy and the UK being of major importance. This kind of balancing between major states is not evident on the global scene. The EU's two major rivals, the USA and Japan, dominate their respective regions, but their power is not fully counterbalanced by rival states.

While many of the organisations have been of regional importance, they have had only a limited impact on the global economy. No organisation actually matches the global importance of the EU, although in the future there may be potential rivals. The relative importance of the various trade blocs is indicated in Table 16.4.

Table 16.4 Trade blocs' share of world exports in 1991 (%)

EU	35.8
EFTA	6.9
CUSTA[1]	15.7
ASEAN[2]	4.6
LAFTA[3]	3.2
ANCERTA[4]	1.5
Andean Pact	1.1

[1] Canada–USA Free Trade Area
[2] Association of South East Asian Nations
[3] Latin America Free Trade Area
[4] Australia–New Zealand Closer Economic Relations Trade Agreement
Source: United Nations (1993), *World Economic Survey 1993*, UN, New York, p. 82

The regional grouping with the greatest potential to rival the Single Market of the EU (although it is not as ambitious) is the North American Free Trade Area (NAFTA), which has as its members Canada, Mexico and the USA. This built on the Canada–USA Free Trade Agreement (CUSTA), which came into effect in 1989. While NAFTA came into effect on 1 January 1994, it was designed to have its full impact on trade and investment of the three members over a 15 year period. However, there was to be no general provision for the free movement of labour. There have been rivals in the Far East, but few look to have coherence, which leaves Japan as the major economic superpower in the region, with a number of smaller rivals. If there is a sustained threat to the trade interests, the Asia Pacific Economic Co-operation, which met in 1993, may lead to further developments.

The growth of trade blocs and interdependence both within them and between them has led to a wider range of issues being discussed. These include the environment, the provision of services, taxation and competition policy. The elimination of tariffs within the EU was followed by the move to complete the Single Market. This involved the removal of a range of non-tariff barriers against goods and services, a development mirrored by the widening of trade issues covered by GATT's Uruguay Round.

The movement towards the creation of major trading blocs led to the generation of rival scenarios. On the one hand, there was the belief that the two blocs would, with their widening influence, help to promote trade liberalisation. Indeed it would be logical for neighbouring states to trade with each other. The other view was that protectionist interests would develop within the rival areas, and would resist liberalisation. Indeed there was the thought that this development might lead to a coherent Pacific area, dominated by Japan. The prospect of an aggressive series of trade conflicts within an increasingly tripolar world was one of the factors contributing to the desire to resolve the Uruguay Round of the GATT Round. While there are benefits from strengthening regional trading, as in the Single Market, it would be unfortunate if these were at the expense of the global multilateral system. The regionalism versus multilateralism debate centres around the strategies that geographically proximate states might adopt towards third countries. States might choose to follow a policy of liberalisation, or adopt an aggressive stance that strengthened their joint position against third states.

The GATT

The GATT was an American-led initiative set up on 30 October 1947, which came into force on 1 January 1948. It was an attempt to avoid the trade restrictions that did so much to damage the multinational system during the inter-war period. It aimed to encourage trade liberalisation by establishing a code for the conduct of world trade. It was based on the view that economic welfare can best be promoted by the exploitation of comparative advantage; i.e. free trade allows specialisation, and the countries that are best at producing particular products should specialise in them. The GATT was meant only as a temporary treaty, but developed into a permanent organisation with a secretariat of 450 based in Geneva. In 1993 it had an annual operating budget of $129 million.

The original intention was for the GATT to develop into the International Trade Organisation (ITO), a third pillar in international trade relations, along with the World Bank and the International Monetary Fund (IMF). The membership has grown from 23 to 125 in 1994, when the Uruguay Round was completed. The growth in membership numbers was particularly rapid with the general proliferation of new states after the fall of Communism in the late 1980s.

The GATT provides a structure for agreeing the rules of world trade. The task of the organisation is to monitor the implementation of these rules, and to encourage further liberalisation by providing a framework and forum for trade negotiations. GATT members handle about 90 per cent of international trade.

The GATT is multilateral in character, i.e. it encompasses the trade relations between all member states either directly or indirectly at the same time. At the centre of the agreement is what is described as the *most favoured nation clause*. Article 1 of the GATT requires that 'any advantage, favour, privilege or immunity' granted to a GATT member must immediately and unconditionally be made available to all other members. The GATT did not therefore get rid of tariffs, but had the merit that any tariff reduction negotiated between two member states would automatically be available to all other members. Countries that employed high tariffs were able to maintain them. Also, the rules did not prevent some other forms of discrimination. First, because members are still free to set different tariffs for different products, it is possible to favour some countries' products against others. For example, it is possible to set a high tariff against cars that is universally applied but has a specific discriminatory effect against car producers. Second, the rules of GATT permit the existence of customs unions and free trade areas. In this respect, the original drafters of the GATT did not envisage the formation of anything as substantial as the EU, and its potential for trade domination.

The hope was that trade blocs would contribute towards an increased freedom, because of the impact of economic integration. Customs unions were expected to be formed quickly to avoid the practice of claiming that discriminatory practices were part of the formation of a union, when they were really only designed to avoid the GATT rules. The tariff structure was supposed to be no more restrictive than that which was in place prior to the formation of the union. In order that the true effects of member states' actions are clear, the principle of transparency should apply. That is, the purpose or consequences of any government action that affects trade should be apparent.

Trade negotiations

There have been eight completed rounds of trade negotiations since the Uruguay Round was ratified following a general agreement in December 1993. These are as follows:

1947	Geneva
1949	Annecy (France)
1950–51	Torquay (UK)
1956	Geneva
1960–62	Dillon (Geneva)
1964–67	Kennedy (Geneva)
1973–79	Tokyo (launched in Tokyo, completed in Geneva)
1986–93	Uruguay (Launched in Punta del Este, Uruguay, on 20 September 1986, completed in Geneva in December 1993, signed in Marrakesh, Morocco, on 15 April 1994)

The Tokyo Round reduced tariffs by about 38 per cent, but the impact was small because tariffs were already at a low level. Tariff reductions were not as generous for goods from developing countries such as textiles and shoes. The Tokyo Round resulted in some agreement with regard to agricultural trade, accepting the highly protectionist mechanism of the CAP. Also, a series of codes was adopted which was designed to improve the position with regard to non-tariff barriers covering customs valuation, technical barriers to trade, government purchasing, subsidies and countervailing duties, and measures to combat dumping. The signing of these codes was not compulsory for GATT members. It was also possible to exclude parts of the codes, for example a high proportion of developed economies opted to exclude open tendering for telecommunications from the code concerned with government purchasing. This was done in order to protect domestic producers. The effectiveness of these codes was therefore marginal, given that there is a limited incentive for members to reform their ways as long as others keep barriers in place.

The GATT in practice

Although most of the developed world belongs to the GATT, its rules are frequently circumvented. When the EU came into existence in 1958, it was never formally recognised by the GATT under Article 24, which concerned customs unions. The meeting where it was discussed was abandoned without coming to any conclusion. The EU then proceeded over the years to build up a range of preferences in contradiction to the spirit of the GATT, for example the Lomé Convention.

A number of trade disputes arise in the course of any year. A good many of these reflect the skill of the economically powerful interests within states to create support for their claims. Most disputes are settled by negotiation directly between the states. The GATT provides a forum for the discussions on either a formal or an informal basis. Members can ask for a disputes panel to be appointed to report on a breach of the rules by another member, but there is no method of enforcement, so the results of the findings can be ignored. (This process was improved as a result of the completion of the Uruguay Round.)

An example of the kind of dispute that the GATT has tried to defuse was that between the USA and the EU in 1986. When the EU expanded, it started to bring Portugal and Spain into the CAP, which excluded the USA from one of its most important markets. Under the GATT, the USA was entitled to seek compensation in other areas of trade, although it is difficult to compensate the US farm producers directly. An agreement was reached that stopped the dispute from degenerating into an all-out trade war.

The Uruguay Round

A new round of trade negotiations was started in September 1986 as a result of negotiations at Punta del Este in Uruguay. These talks were the result of a two year process to get the members of the organisation to accept that a new round of negotiations was required. The talks were due to be completed by the end of 1990, but did not move to a conclusion until December 1993. However, the new agreements were not due to be implemented until 1995.

With a pattern of generally slower economic growth emerging, from the 1970s there had been a drift toward more protectionism, which if it continued would have significantly damaged world trade. In its original form, the GATT was a rich countries' club; today about two-thirds of the membership come from the developing world, with an ever-increasing number of former socialist economies becoming members. There was an increasing danger that interests would start to polarise, which would close down trading opportunities to the detriment of rich and poor countries. The purpose of the negotiations was to:

1. further liberalise world trade

2. strengthen the GATT and improve the multilateral trading system

3. increase the responsiveness of the GATT to changing trends in the international economy

4. encourage cooperative action to link trade policies with policies that encourage faster economic growth.

Once the Uruguay Round of trade negotiations commenced, the principle of standstill and rollback was agreed. This meant that members agreed that no new restrictions contrary to the GATT will be introduced, and existing trade practices that are contrary will be phased out as per an agreed timetable.

The outcome of the Uruguay Round

The GATT settlement came after a very lengthy series of negotiations. It produced a document containing 500 pages of legal text. In addition to this, there were individual national concessions on the access to markets of goods and services that occupied 20 000 pages. The agreement was ratified on 15 April 1994 in Marrakesh. It established a World Trade Organisation (WTO), and the GATT was to lose its nominally temporary status. The expectation is that the WTO will be a higher profile organisation than the GATT, with initiatives to promote cooperation in trade. This could be via the Trade Policy Review

Mechanism, which was negotiated as part of the Round. The WTO will also cooperate closely with other key international bodies such as the International Monetary Fund (IMF) and the World Bank.

Tariffs

These were reduced on industrial goods for developed countries, and even more for some developing countries. The actual impact of the reductions will be limited for the trade between the advanced economies, except for 'sensitive' products, because tariff levels are already low. Most significant was the move away from non-tariff barriers to tariffs in the advanced economies. The adoption of tariffication was designed to make trade barriers more transparent, and to offer a greater degree of certainty for exporters from the developing economies.

It is likely that by the year 2000 tariffs on manufactured goods will not be a significant barrier to world trade. Table 16.5 indicates the likely outcome for trade by developed economies once the trade round has been put fully into operation.

Table 16.5 Tariff reductions on industrial products by developed countries from selected groups of countries (percentages and $ billion)

Imports from	Import value	Before	After	Percentage reduction
developed countries	736.9	6.3	3.9	38
developing countries (other than the least developed countries)	167.6	6.8	4.3	37
least developed countries	3.9	6.8	5.1	25

Source: *The Gatt* (1994), The Uruguay Round Deal – an Outline of the New Multilateral Trading System, 15

Agriculture

For the first time, agriculture was brought fully within the framework of multilateral trade rules. The Blair House Agreement between the USA and the EU was broadly upheld. The tariffs on tropical products was reduced by 40 per cent, and the rice markets of Japan and South Korea were to be opened up. The move towards tariffication had implications for the CAP. It meant replacing the system of variable levies, which offered almost 100 per cent protection against imports (this issue is dealt with later in the section dealing with agricultural trade).

Services

This sector had not been subject to meaningful trade rules prior to this round. However, there was an agreement on fair trade principles, with special provision for sectors such as telecommunications and air transport. A new treaty was negotiated called the General

Agreement on Trade in Services (GATS). A Council for Trade in Services was to be set up to monitor the agreement. The rationale for GATS was the very substantial growth in trade in services among developed economies. While the developing economies saw a growth in their comparative advantage in manufactures, trade in services offered significant trading opportunities for a number of the advanced economies.

An important development within the GATS was the adoption of most favoured nation status, although this could be phased in, so that the liberalisation of trade in services would take some time. There was a difference between the Single Market in services within the EU and the GATS. The Single Market operated on the general principle of mutual recognition and minimal harmonisation. The GATS was more restrictive, and gave significant opportunity to limit the extent of liberalisation, especially for less developed economies.

Intellectual property

This was covered by the Agreement On Trade Related Aspects Of Intellectual Property Rights (TRIPS). It was hoped that this would provide a minimum level of protection for patents, copyright and trade marks. This was an area where standards of protection had been poor, for example the widespread copying of designs, computer software and music.

Textiles

From 1974 onwards there had been restrictions on the import of textiles into many of the advanced economies under the Multi-Fibre Arrangement. These were to be dismantled over a period of 10 years after 1995. There was to be enhanced treatment for small-scale textile producers.

Anti-dumping and subsidies

The definition of subsidies was made clearer, as were the rules with regard to anti-dumping duties. The aim was to prevent the inflation of dumping margins, which were the basis of imposing levies. Duties were to lapse after five years, unless positive action was taken to renew them. There were three categories of subsidies.

1. *Prohibited subsidies* : these included export subsidies and subsidies tthat depended on the domestic goods rather than imported ones being used.

2. *Actionable subsidies* : these might cause damage to another trading partner, and could be dealt with under the WTO disputes procedure.

3. *Non-actionable subsidies* : these include subsidies that cover up to 75 per cent of industrial research or regional assistance, and subsidies that cover 20 per cent of environmental measures.

Technical barriers

The voluntary codes which were signed by 40 members were to be replaced by rules that applied to all members of the GATT. Members were required to use international standards when they were relevant. They were also expected to participate in the 28 international standards-setting organisations. In practice this supplemented the process that had been taking place with the globalisation of world industry. The growth of multinational enterprises, selling their products into many different markets, had the effect of reinforcing the process of setting standards. The better rules were introduced to ensure that these were not used as a trade barrier.

Public procurement

Attempts were made to improve the bidding for state contracts.

GATT rules

These were modernised to take account of the changed patterns of global trade. The disputes mechanism was to be speeded up. This was perhaps the most important element of the GATT, so that while there will probably always be trade restrictions, trade rules offer some method of assuring that they do not get out of hand.

The benefits of trade liberalisation

The estimates of the benefits of trade liberalisation are likely to be highly speculative. Generally they are made to present the strongest possible argument for the opening up of global markets, but many of the aspirations are subject to the realities of how the trade cycle is operating. Also, much depends on the promises that states make turning into realities. An estimate by the OECD, made prior to the details of the agreement being finalised, suggested annual gains of $274 billion by 2002. Following the completion of the trade round, it was suggested that the gains from liberalisation might be even higher. Table 16.6 represents the estimates made by the GATT, and indicates attempts to quantify the dynamic effects from increased competition, as well as the static effects from lower tariffs.

The benefits from trade liberalisation should come from the following sources.

1. *The consumer*, because domestic markets will be more open to competitive goods from abroad.

2. *The taxpayer*, because subsidies to inefficient industry will be cut.

3. *The producer*, because of the gains from larger markets, more vigorous competition, the encouraging of structural adjustment, and the stability of the trading environment.

4. *Creating employment*, because the increased GDP will increase demand and create jobs. This will more than offset the job losses in the protected industries. For example, it was estimated that the Uruguay Round would create 400 000 new jobs in the UK over time.

Table 16.6 The winners from the Uruguay Round

Country/Region	Increased annual income in 2005 ($US billion)
European Union (12 States)	163.5
United States	122.4
Developing and transition countries	116.1
EFTA	33.5
Japan	26.7
China	18.7
Canada	12.4
Taiwan	10.2
World	510.0

Source : *Financial Times*, 11 November 1994, p. 7, quoting GATT sources

The most important benefit, however, was that the trading system did not collapse. The GATT process kept trade liberalisation on the agenda when the world economy was going through a very difficult period. It assisted business confidence, and meant that the system could move forward when better times appeared. So while the gains may amount to around 0.5 per cent of GDP calculated on a static basis after the year 2000, the dynamic gains from trade may be well in excess of this.

Implications for the EU

The objective of the Uruguay Round was not to achieve free trade. It was a move towards greater trade liberalisation. The MacSharry Reforms were protected for a number of years by the Uruguay Round, because of a peace clause that protected the CAP from challenges under the GATT. This did not, however, stop criticism of the CAP. The EU retained a 14 per cent tariff against the import of semiconductor components imported from outside the EU. The personal computer manufacturers protested, for example Olivetti claimed that it added ECU 20 million to its costs.

The EU gained in other areas. It had already been cooperating with the International Standards Organisation (ISO) since 1991 over the issue of standards, so that its own standards bodies generated standards that were compatible with those set internationally. The aim was to ensure that time was saved, and that the EU gained a competitive advantage. This compares with the USA, where typically standards have often been set without reference to those elsewhere. An example of this is the use of the imperial weight and measures system some 20 years after much of the rest of the world had gone metric. However, the standards NAFTA adopts will be international ones.

The World Trade Organisation (WTO)

The establishment of the WTO will provide the institutional structure for the operation of world trade agreements, and will provide a framework for the various trade agreements to work within. The secretariat is based on the existing GATT secretariat, with members contributing according to their share of world trade in goods and services (GATT was based on goods). Although the EU conducted much of the negotiations on behalf of the EU members, the individual members will pay their own subscriptions, and speak and act for themselves on budgetary and administrative questions. The cost of the WTO is expected to be an additional $65 million, which makes it one-third of the size of the IMF.

The WTO created a Disputes Settlement Body (DSB) to manage disputes across the organisation. This is to consult with those in dispute, and if a solution is not found the dispute can be referred to a body of experts. This will report to the DSB, and if it is adopted, any adverse findings must be responded to.

What still needs to be done?

It would be easy to be complacent about the success of the GATT following the resolution of the Uruguay Round. Certainly the world trading system looked a great deal more secure, but trade issues have a habit of simply erupting without prior warning. Simply implementing the agreements is a difficult task, especially given the fudged nature of the final settlements. Also, a number of issues were simply laid on the table to be resolved at a later date.

The GATT did not address the issue of environmental protection, and the ability of some nations to win a competitive advantage through operating lower environmental conditions. With the increased globalisation of the economy, the need to be concerned about monopoly and restrictive practices should be addressed, as should the unequal treatment given to foreign as against domestic firms. Finally, the issue of variable social conditions was not considered, although there would seem little economic justification for preventing firms moving to locations where they can gain a cost advantage.

International trading relations

The EU has not been successful in eliminating bilateral deals between the Member States and non-member states. This is despite the fact that Article 113 transfers the competence to engage in tariff and trade negotiations to the EU, and that all imports are subject to a common external tariff. Individual states have their national export insurance schemes, credit arrangements and aid programmes, which allow scope for national action. In markets such as the Middle East and Africa, the competition to secure export business can be intense and involve very active rivalry between the Member States' governments, each pursuing independent commercial policies. This is particularly the case where national champions are involved in competition for large contracts, such as those in the defence industry. In addition, the variable way that aspects of the services sector are regulated within the EU means that the Member States directly control this part of the Commercial Policy.

The need to take a common approach further became particularly apparent after the completion of the Single Market. Borders could no longer be relied on to keep goods from crossing into states where they were not welcome, because the removal of barriers meant that individual trade deals would impact on other Member States. In February 1994, the EU announced that it was to abolish 6417 national quotas, and replace them with a limited number of Community ones (seven were a defence against China's huge low-cost labour force). Many of these quotas had been in place for 30 years. This decision did not affect arrangements that were in place for textiles, agriculture, iron and steel, which were the subject of separate arrangements.

The EU retained its anti-dumping defences, so in 1993, for example, an anti-dumping duty of 34.4 per cent was applied to Chinese bicycles. Between 1989 and 1991, the number of Chinese bicycles sold into the EU rose from 693 000 to 2.1 million. It was claimed that damage was being done to EU manufacturers because prices had been pushed down and their market share had diminished from 33 to 27 per cent.

The EU likes to see itself as making a positive contribution to world trading relations. The import elasticity of demand of economies is one measure of the degree of openness (i.e. the extent to which a 1 per cent increase in GDP increases the demand for imports). Between 1982 and 1991 the elasticity of imports to GDP for the USA was 2.67, for the EU it was 2.21 and for Japan it was only 1.33. This was not a problem associated with high tariffs. The weighted average tariff on industrial goods after the Tokyo Round had been implemented in 1988 was 4.8 per cent for the EU, 4.4 per cent for the USA, and 2.6 per cent for Japan. Advanced economies tend to organise their tariff regimes in a way that favours the importation of raw materials, and of items they do not produce. The extent of tariff protection is often significantly higher against manufactures, and of course agriculture.

European Union–USA

The USA has been one of the more liberal trading economies in the post-war period. Generally trade relations with the EU have been good, although there were periodic bouts of tension, as with the case of agriculture. A great many of the USA's trade disputes have tended to be with Japan, but have implications for the EU. The USA developed a major problem from the 1980s onward with huge domestic budget deficits and external trade deficits. In 1993, the trade deficit was $115 billion, of which $59 billion was with Japan. However, the USA had a trade surplus with the EU of ECU 6.5 billion. This was a shared difficulty, and indicated that the EU and the USA had an opportunity to move together to resolve the problem.

Although less than 5 per cent of the world's exports and imports of merchandise passes between Europe and the USA, trade issues between the two tend to be an important force for change in the GATT. Because the USA is the world's largest trading nation, with 14 per cent of all imports and 12 per cent of exports, any trade distortions concerning the USA market have an adverse effect on others. In particular there have been continued concerns about high tariffs against agricultural products, textiles and the use of bilateral trade pressure to open markets. Two agreements caused particular concern to the EU in the early 1990s. The first was an attempt to ensure a 20 per cent share of the Japanese microprocessor market for US producers; the second was to obtain a doubling of US car components in the period 1990 to 1994. Clearly, if parts of a market are reserved for one state, they are not available to others. The USA also increased the use of anti-dumping measures in the early 1990s, and threatened the use of Super 301 trade law. This gives the USA government the right to take unilateral actions in retaliation against discriminatory trade practices.

Periodic bouts of tension have arisen between the EU and the USA. In part this is because of the inability of EU policy-makers to agree among themselves, so causing frustration in the

USA, which can put together more coherent policies. Agriculture has been a particular point of stress, as has the issue of public procurement. The EU and the USA have both been guilty of discrimination in the area of public procurement. The USA has adopted 'buy America' campaigns, and denied access to foreign firms for contracts at a sub-federal level. The EU has adopted legislation that permitted a 3 per cent price advantage, and allowed bids that were predominantly from non-EU sources to be discarded. In 1993 and 1994, in an attempt to break the EU's solidarity, the USA endeavoured to enter into a bilateral deal with Germany. This was investigated by the Commission, and was the subject of protests from the other Member States.

There were a number of outstanding issues between the USA and the EU following the GATT settlement in 1993. Of some importance was that concerning the wish to restrict the access of US television programmes and films to the EU. The USA has about 50 per cent of the EU market for television programmes, and earns about 80 per cent of the revenue from films. While US films may be regarded as not to every taste, it is difficult to justify protectionism in this industry.

European Union–Japan

In a global sense, the Japanese market, with its 125 million inhabitants, is important for its size and growth potential. Japanese goods have generally had a good reputation for quality and reliability, and Japan's manufacturing capability has been the envy of the world. This has turned the Japanese economy into a powerful export machine.

Trade relations with Japan have been characterised by a sense of continuing frustration over many years. The Japanese balance of payments has shown a consistent surplus on the current account. In contrast, the EU has had a series of deficits, so that in 1993 the EU had a trade deficit with Japan of ECU 26 billion (£19.5 billion). For this reason a range of trade restrictions are applied against Japan, for example the VER on cars discussed above.

The EU and the USA tried to counteract the problem of Japanese trade surpluses by a series of bilateral and multilateral negotiations. The concern for smaller nations was that the USA and the EU would do separate deals with the Japanese, when there was a need for a consistent global approach. The USA, with a very long-standing overall trade deficit, tended to be the more resolute in its dealings with Japan. The EU has said that it would prefer a trilateral approach to dealing with Japan. This reflects a fear of the USA doing separate deals, rather than demonstrating a common strategic approach. In both cases, however, the increasing trend towards Japanese investment in their economies has been a useful way of deflecting anger over trading practices.

The placing of restrictions on access to the EU's Single Market by the use of VERs and anti-dumping duties has always been regarded as unsatisfactory, because the consumer loses out. The EU would prefer the trade-creating option of gaining better access for its goods into Japan. The EU, and indeed other trade partners, has had problems gaining access to the Japanese markets. Macroeconomic initiatives to stimulate demand within the Japanese economy have frequently been promised, but failed. In part this was because of a lack of enthusiasm by Japanese governments, which fear the inflationary effects of excessive demand within their economy more than retaliation from frustrated foreigners.

Apart from prohibitively high tariffs in some areas such as rice, the range of non-tariff barriers, which are both bureaucratic and cultural, makes access difficult. For example, at the time of the GATT settlement, foreign insurance companies had only 2 per cent of the Japanese market, whereas elsewhere they enjoyed between 12 and 30 per cent. The same situation applied in the market for motor vehicle parts. Customs clearance is time-consuming. Very often the technical standards demanded are difficult to meet. Alcohol taxes are set in a way that favours local producers, and there is less respect for intellectual property rights. Also, the distribution system is complex and foreign goods often do not find their way onto the shelves.

While it might appear that the Japanese have every reason to take note of requests to liberalise trade, the fact that their manufacturers have invested heavily abroad makes them less vulnerable to trade sanctions. Also, Japanese penetration of alternative markets in Asia offers alternative destinations for their products. In addition, the collapse of the communist threat leaves them less politically dependent on the West than in the past. The one thing that might cause some change over time is the appreciation of the yen. If surpluses continue, then inevitably the currency will rise in value, which in turn will either choke off exports or cause serious action to be taken to liberalise imports. The danger is that the surpluses become so persistent that a strategy of increasingly managed trade between Japan and its major trading partners becomes fully institutionalised.

While the EU has complained about unfair trade practices, at times it has been less willing to target sectoral objectives in the way that the USA has done, i.e. requiring the reservation of a specific portion of the Japanese market in a particular sector. Part of the reason for this, given the diversity of national interests within the EU, could well be the lack of agreement as to what sectors might be appropriate. Instead the EU has pushed for better access generally, and has displayed a willingness to supplement Member States' efforts to sell into this market. An example of this is the 'Gateway to Japan' initiative launched in February 1994. This campaign had a budget of ECU 7.1 million, and aimed to set up seminars, organise trade missions, and give follow-up help to companies. There were to be two phases. The first covered 1994–1995, and was aimed to support companies in sectors such as machine tools, furniture and medical equipment. The second phase was to run from 1995 to 1996, and cover sectors such as maritime equipment, waste management and construction equipment.

EU agriculture in the world economy

Trade in agricultural products is the most controversial aspect of EU trade policy. In chapter 8 it is pointed out that the reasons for the EU defending its agricultural interests are complex, and the problems associated with overproduction have come about because of the difficulty in reaching agreement about reform. This policy area spills over into international trade politics, because the EU has not been a major food exporter in the past. From the 1970s onwards it became a significant seller into international markets, selling off its surplus production at prices that undercut traditional food exporters.

Agricultural trade

Most countries or trading blocs have their own agricultural policies, which aim to respond to their particular production conditions. They wish to have a degree of border protection, in order to offer stable market conditions for their own farmers. Border controls also help to maintain the health of their plants and animal stock, by keeping out diseases from abroad. However, it is neither practical nor desirable, in the context of the world trading system, to isolate agriculture. If economies wish to trade in manufactured goods, for example, markets for agricultural products also need to be kept open. The basis of trade is that each economy should specialise in what it does best. Anything that prevents this not only reduces economic welfare, but also is likely to lead to retaliation from those who feel deprived of a legitimate market opportunity.

Agricultural goods are widely traded, and are an important supplement to a number of countries' national production. Some countries lack the resources to grow their own food, and have to specialise in services, manufacturing or the extraction of minerals. In other cases there are periodic harvest shortfalls, which have to be made good by occasional imports. A system of global trade in agriculture evolved in the nineteenth century, which led to specialist producers with important sectors of their economies devoted to production for sale to the countries that needed to import food. As agricultural productivity increased, the position of these specialist producers became threatened. Between 1971 and 1992, agriculture's share of world trade was reduced from 15 per cent to 9.4 per cent, reflecting the trend towards greater national self-sufficiency and the growing importance of trade in manufactured goods.

The EU's role in agricultural trade

The artificial stimulus given to agricultural production within the Union is controversial, because the EU is not a natural surplus producer. A significant proportion of the surplus production can be attributed to the stimulus of high support prices and Union preference. As surpluses are unlikely to be consumed within the Union, they are dumped on to world markets. Countries that enjoy a comparative advantage in food production believe the EU surpluses destabilise their traditional markets. Consequently there is a constant risk of trade and price wars breaking out. This in turn, may put greater pressure on the budget of the CAP, as the cost of subsidising exports rises due to intense price competition in third markets.

International currency movements can compound the problems of price competition on global markets. For the EU a rise in the value of the ECU can add significantly to the cost of disposing of surplus production on to the world market. It has been estimated by the Commission that every 10 per cent depreciation of the dollar relative to the ECU would add between ECU 7 and 10 billion to the EU budget.

It is something of a paradox that despite all the criticism of its surpluses, the EU is a net food importer. The only states showing an overall surplus in agricultural trade are Denmark, Ireland and France. This is not an indication that the EU is a virtuous international trader in terms of agricultural products, or that it allows farm products to be freely imported. The need to import tropical and seasonal foods accounts for the situation shown in Table 16.7.

The global problem

Surplus production of specific agricultural commodities is not just an EU problem: the increase in agricultural productivity is a feature of almost all economies. World output of wheat was 538 million tonnes in 1989, but by 1993 it was expected to have risen to 575

Table 16.7 External trade balance of the EU in agricultural products (1988–1990, million ECU)

Belgium	−1424
Denmark	1086
Germany	−6461
Greece	−143
Spain	−2732
France	193
Ireland	569
Italy	−5321
Luxembourg	−1424
Netherlands	−1235
Portugal	−1163
UK	−4212
EU12	−20 842

Source : Commission of the EC, *The Agricultural Situation in the Community: 1992 Report*, 1993, p. T/20

million tonnes. Coarse grain production was 847 million tonnes in 1992, up 47 million tonnes on the previous year. However, demand for these products was roughly stable.[4] The same trend has been visible in many other sectors of the industry.

The OECD states have advanced economies, but their activities in protecting their own agricultural markets and dumping surpluses on to world markets, cause damage to producers in the developing world. Normally, cheap imports are beneficial to an economy. However, agricultural production for the domestic markets of a number of developing states is discouraged, because imports are cheap. This means that they must pay for the imports, and lose the opportunity to earn valuable foreign exchange. If subsidies could be removed, it is estimated that the world price of agricultural products might rise by as much as 20 per cent for most commodities, but that it might rise by as much as 50 per cent in the case of dairy products. In the developing world, domestic production would be encouraged by these higher prices, so assisting with development and reducing the dependency on aid.[5]

As Table 16.8 illustrates, the situation is one where incentives have been offered on a global basis, so that each state or trading bloc that wished to support agricultural products frequently found itself the victim of an ever-increasing competition of subsidies. Subsidies for agriculture within the OECD states amounted to ECU 273.3 billion in 1992, which was an increase of 7 per cent on the previous year.[6] Although some states such as New Zealand adopted more market-oriented strategies and reduced their levels of support to farmers, this was more than compensated for by others. Table 16.8 illustrates the changes over the period 1988–1992.

Global surpluses have impacted on world markets, leading to a battle of subsidies that dragged in all producers. Any reduction in surpluses and subsidies should be of benefit to economies, especially in an era when serious attempts are being made to control state expenditure. A loss of income from tariffs is likely if markets are liberalised, but governments would save money on the actual support costs. The average citizen would certainly gain from the elimination of support, as the CAP costs ECU 328 per man, woman and child per annum. Few industries would warrant the extent of support indicated in Table 16.9. Taking away

Table 16.8 International farm subsidies

	Transfers (total ECU billion)		Contribution per person (ECU)	Average amount per farmer (ECU)
	1988	1993	1993	1993
USA	56.0	74.7	290	29 600
Japan	59.8	61.0	485	19 800
EU	102.4	115.7	328	13 100

Note : The above includes transfers from the taxpayer and the consumer, minus any budget revenues received from agriculture
Source : OECD (1994) *Agricultural Policies, Markets and Trade – Monitoring and Outlook 1994*, p. 124–25

support and protection would not make the industry disappear. However, it is difficult to believe that these resources could not be put to better use.

Table 16.9 Agricultural support (PSE) (% of production value)

	1988	1989	1990	1991	1992	1993
Australia	10	10	13	14	12	9
EU	46	41	46	49	47	48
Japan	74	70	66	67	71	70
USA	34	29	27	27	28	23
OECD	46	41	44	44	44	42

Note : Producer Subsidy Equivalent (PSE) is a measure of the value of payments made to the farmer as a result of agricultural policy. These payments include market support, direct payments and other support.
Source : OECD 1991 and 1994, *Agricultural Policies, Markets and Trade – Monitoring and Outlook 1991 and 1994*, p. 115 and Summary and Conclusions

The remarkable feature of agriculture in the world markets is that the GATT had little influence on the way that agricultural policies were developed. The GATT rules for agriculture were strongly influenced by the requirements of the USA in the early 1950s, and were designed to accommodate national policies that were already in place. In practical terms therefore, agriculture was excluded from the GATT. However, from the 1980s onwards, the USA and other traditional food exporters found that they were being challenged in world markets by dumped EU surplus production. Not unnaturally, they reacted against this in order to preserve their market share.

There was a realisation that unless an effective international agreement was in place, global markets would be subject to almost permanent price wars, as producers tried to rid themselves of surpluses. Hence the inclusion of agriculture in the Uruguay Round of trade talks launched in 1986. The aim was to liberalise trade in agriculture, and improve access to markets. The EU agreed to the inclusion of negotiations about farm price support, but the main promoters of liberalisation were the USA and the 14 members of the Cairns Group of exporters of agricultural products, which included Australia, Canada, Hungary and Uruguay.

The issue of access to EU markets had been raised within the GATT on a number of occasions, as the Union became closed to outside producers by the use of the variable levy. In the Uruguay Round of the GATT, the level of support for the agricultural sector became a central issue, and threatened to bring the whole process of trade liberalisation to a halt. The USA wished to see an agreement to cut EU export subsidies by 90 per cent, with a cut of 75 per cent in domestic support and border protection. Initially the EU offered only 30 per cent cuts on a very conditional basis.

A number of the members of the EU made great efforts to avoid addressing the agricultural issues raised by the GATT. The 1988 CAP Reforms offered virtually nothing in improved international trading terms. It was only in the early 1990s, when the Uruguay Round looked in danger of running out of time and collapse was imminent, that substantial progress was made. In particular, there was a realisation that issues in the GATT Round were linked: for the developed world to make progress in liberalising trade in manufactured goods and services, it also needed to make progress in the agriculture negotiations.

USA–EU trade disputes

Agriculture trade reform started to make serious progress when it became clear that there were pressing reasons for reform of the EU's domestic policy, and because of the EU's wish to avoid costly trade disputes with the USA. Without agreement on agriculture, progress on the 14 other areas of the GATT Round might have been sacrificed. The dispute that the GATT issues centred on was that of oilseeds used predominantly for cheap animal feed.

A 1962 Agreement between the EU and the USA to keep the EU oil seeds market open for US producers was put under threat by EU subsidies. The market was never closed, but the EU encouraged domestic production by subsidies, with the result that in 1986–1987 the EU produced between 7 and 8 million tonnes, but by the early 1990s this had risen to 13 million tonnes. This is an example of the CAP in operation. Oilseed production was encouraged because the EU was a net importer of the commodity, and it wished to divert land from producing crops that were already in surplus.

Oil seeds were important to the USA, as they accounted for about one-fifth of its agricultural exports. The USA was responsible for half the world production, and three-quarters of the world exports (mainly soya beans). The EU was the main market, accounting for half the world's imports, but US producers felt that they could not compete with just world market prices against subsidised EU production. Table 16.10 illustrates the problem of static sales into the EU market, which had an impact on the USA and also Brazil and Argentina.

The US government took the case to the GATT disputes panel, and won favourable judgements in January 1990 and again in March 1992. However, the EU was intransigent, leading to the USA threatening to take sanctions by imposing 200 per cent duties on $300 million worth of EU agricultural exports. This led to the threat of escalation on the part of the EU, which would have held back the whole of the Uruguay Round.[7]

The dispute appeared to have been ended by a compromise, and a general peace clause being adopted with the USA, which was contained within the Blair House Agreement of

Table 16.10 EU imports of soya beans and soya cake (1000 tonnes)

From	1985	1987	1989	1991
USA	9644	12 576	9768	11 731
Brazil and Argentina	11 044	10 481	8005	10 122

Source: Commission of the EU (1993), *The Agricultural Situation in the Community: 1992 Report*, p. 58

November 1992. The EU agreed to restrict its oilseed output to being grown on 5.128 million hectares as against 6.293 million hectares in the past. The area of land for 'set-aside' was to be 10 per cent, which was less than the amount applied to the MacSharry Reforms earlier in 1992. Production was assumed to drop overall to 9.7 million tonnes, with oilseed for industrial use being restricted to 1 million tonnes. Overall there was an assurance that subsidised EU farm exports were to be cut by 21 per cent in volume over six years, with internal support cut back by 20 per cent. In return the USA offered to monitor the exports of cheap cereals substitutes, which would assist with the process of rebalancing for which the French and German governments were pressing.[8] That is, increasing the price of oilseed products should encourage an increased use of EU-produced cereals as animal food.

The EU also asserted that its reduction in cereal prices would be of benefit, in that it would cut the EU's grain exports from 30 million tonnes in 1991 to 15 million tonnes in 1996,[9] although this would inevitably be at the expense of some of the oilseed imports, because feed grains would be relatively cheaper and therefore would be used as a substitute.

The Blair House Agreement became a source of major controversy within France in 1993. This led to the threat by the French to repudiate the Agreement, on the basis that the deal was signed by the Commission, not the EU.[10] In the course of 1993, attempts to resolve the problem within the framework of the GATT nearly brought the Uruguay Round to a halt.

The GATT settlement of December 1993 confirmed the reduction in subsidies to farmers. With the inclusion of agriculture within the GATT, and a Peace Clause between the EU and the USA which offered a nine year period free of challenges, the way looked clear for a period of stability. The agreement aimed to promote a more market-oriented approach to world trade in agriculture, which meant getting rid of many of the subsidies. There was a requirement that tariffs be cut by an average of 36 per cent. Also, where other measures existed, for example the EU's variable levy, the value of these had also to be converted into tariffs. These were then to be subject to the same tariff cuts. Most of the elements of the Blair House accord stayed in place, but many of the cuts in subsidies were delayed until the end of the six year process.

It meant that the amount of subsidised wheat would be reduced by 50 000 tonnes per year, and that agricultural exporters such as Australia, New Zealand and Argentina which were part of the Cairns group would gain significantly. Australia estimated that it would gain over $1 billion in agriculture exports as a result of the settlement. In particular it was thought that the markets of third countries, such as Russia and China, would be more accessible. The major doubt about the outcome was that the MacSharry reforms, the Blair House Agreement and the GATT settlement might be incompatible. This would not be truly apparent until after the

Uruguay Round came into effect after 1995.

Trade tactics and agriculture

The GATT settlement concerned many longer term issues, but in the short term there were still trade problems created by the CAP. While there were promises to improve market access into the EU for production from Central and Eastern Europe in 1993, the EU was still selling very cheap grain and meat into the former Soviet Union. There were claims that wheat was being dumped at $90 per tonne into the Baltic ports, which represented no more than half the cost of production. A similar situation applied to beef, where deliveries fell dramatically from traditional suppliers like Hungary, which saw their exports fall to a tenth of the 1980s level.[11]

One of the most controversial aspects of access to the EU market in the 1990s arose from the completion of the Single Market. The market for bananas was worth $2.7 billion in 1993, but was compartmentalised prior to the completion of the Single Market. The internal borders allowed exclusive access for fruit from the Caribbean to enter the UK and French markets under the Lomé Convention, so that prices remained higher than in Germany, for example. Where there was free access to the market, prices were lower, and the more efficient Latin American producers were able to predominate. Once the internal barriers within the EU came down on 1 January 1993, the importation of bananas became a problem. The EU removed the internal barriers to trade, but permitted entry on the basis of quotas, which reduced the Latin American share to 2 million tonnes of the 3.6 million tonne market. As this was less than the 2.3 million tonnes that they had enjoyed in the recent past, they protested to the GATT. The result was that the GATT panel found in favour of the Latin American producers. Attempts were then made to resolve the issue, with states such as Germany being in favour of removing quotas altogether. Overall, however, the EU had a problem, because it wished to assist the Lomé states by the use of trade.

The EU has major problems with the external aspects of agricultural trade, which can be fully resolved only by all parties moving closer to the free market price. The MacSharry reforms will cost more than was originally anticipated, and will reduce production by less than had been hoped. Despite this, the Uruguay Round's resolution should have provided at least a period, perhaps up to nine years, when the EU's agriculture was not under constant attack. This of course depends on the EU delivering on its promises.

Conclusions

The success of the development of the Common Commercial Policy owes much to the campaign to complete the Single Market, and the attempt to create a united front to the EU's global competitors. While the EU must share some of the responsibility for the restrictions that hamper the full liberalisation of trade, it is clear that it has also done a great deal to open up the European market. This has been achieved by removing the many different national practices that not only held back intra-EU trade, but also retarded the trading ambitions of non-members. The success of the Uruguay Round negotiations showed that a great deal could be done by presenting a common front externally, although there have been times when national Member State enmities have made the EU appear less than coherent.

The case of agriculture trade illustrated the difficulties of accommodating the tensions within the EU, where there are differences in the desired final outcome. The one thing that assured agreement was that the cost of failure would have been very high indeed, given the loss of potential growth in the world economy. Even if some Member States were unconvinced by the outcome of negotiations in this sector, the gains in trade of industrial products should offset the losses in one sector. The challenge for the EU is to ensure that it plays its part in ensuring that the GATT is fully implemented.

References

1. **Silberston Z A** (1989) *The Future of the MFA – Implications for the UK Economy*, HMSO, London.
2. **National Consumer Council** (1993) *International Trade: the Consumer Agenda*, p. 97.
3. *Sunday Times*, 14 November 1993, 1.5.
4. *Farmers Weekly*, 5 February 1993, 25.
5. *The Economist*, Agricultural survey, 12 December 1993, 7.
6. **OECD** (1993) *Agricultural Policies, Markets and Trade – Monitoring and Outlook 1993*, OECD, Paris, p. 160.
7. *Financial Times*, 5 November 1992, 3.
8. *Financial Times*, 21 November 1992, 1.
9. *Financial Times*, 5 November 1992, 3.
10. *The Economist*, 11 September 1993, 35–36.
11. *Financial Times*, 22 June 1993, 6.

Further reading

Board of Trade (1994) *The Uruguay Round of Multilateral Trade Negotiations 1986–94*, Cm 2579, HMSO, London.
Bulmer S and Scott A (eds) (1994) *Economic and Political Integration in Europe*, Blackwell, Oxford.
Commission of the EC (1993) *Europe in a Changing World*.
European Economy (1993) The European Community as a world trade partner, No. 52.
GATT (1993) *Trade Policy Review – European Communities*, Vols 1 and 2.
House of Lords (1994) *The Implications for Agriculture of the Europe Agreements*, Select Committee on the European Communities, 10th Report, Session 1993–94, HL Paper 57-1.
Hine R (guest ed.) (1992) *Journal of Common Market Studies*, June, Vol. XXX, No. 2.

CHAPTER 17

Trade and development

Introduction

As the process of economic integration has led to increased wealth, expectations have risen that the EU will take greater responsibility for assisting developing countries. The role that the EU performs both overlaps and is in addition to that of the Member States, many of which have responsibilities that date back to when they were colonial powers. This chapter offers a critique on the special responsibility the EU has for the development of the African, Caribbean and Pacific (ACP) states, which are signatories of the Lomé Convention.

The ACP states have been dependent on the EU members for a very long time, and receive help both on a bilateral basis from the Member States and on a multilateral basis from the EU. There is a certain disenchantment with the overall process, however. The EU does not have sufficient resources to help all deserving cases, and the aid policies of the Member States are not well coordinated with one another, or with the EU as a whole.[1] At the same time, few of the ACP states seem capable of breaking out of the cycle of poverty. Given the emergence of other priorities, such as the need to assist with the transformation of the Central and Eastern European economies, there is a danger that these states do not receive the priority that they deserve. A possible solution is that the EU use its trade policy more fully to assist these states.

The launch of the Single Market campaign caused concern to a number of states that depend on trade with the EU. These concerns lessened about access to markets with the completion of the Uruguay Round of trade negotiations (see chapter 16). The Single Market should eventually lead to an increased demand for imports as growth in the European economy accelerates. However, if the EU producers become more competitive, it may be difficult for third world manufacturers to compete in Europe. The liberalisation of trade will really help only those that are best able to respond to the changes. There are for example, costs to be met of adopting new technical standards, and general quality standards are far higher in Europe. The likely consequence is that there will be an increased demand for primary products, which will assist certain states in terms of their balance of payments, but will not help to achieve more balanced development.

This chapter argues that the EU needs to enhance its development policy. Much of the liberalisation of trade does not assist the countries with the greatest development needs. This is because of restrictions on the importation of 'sensitive' products, which relate to the problem sectors of the EU economy, including agriculture. In addition, there is the issue of rules of origin. Where there are lower trade barriers there are opportunities for abuse, if imports into the EU are simply diverted via them into the EU's markets. Bearing this in mind, liberalisation needs to be taken further, and at the same time increased direct aid might assist the process of change. However, money is only a partial help: it needs to be spent wisely. The danger for the EU is that a long-term dependency is maintained, which may be regarded as neo-colonialism.

The EU's Development Policy

The EU's policy on development is set out in Articles 130u to 130y of the Treaty on European Union. Article 130u states the following.

1. Community Policy in the sphere of development cooperation, which shall be complementary to the policies pursued by the Member States, shall foster:

   - the sustainable economic and social development of the developing countries, and more particularly the most disadvantaged among them
   - the smooth and gradual integration of the developing countries into the world economy
   - the campaign against poverty in developing countries.

2. Community Policy in this area shall contribute to the general objectives of developing and consolidating democracy and the rule of law, and that of respecting human rights and the fundamental freedoms.

Article 130x states that

The Community and the Member States shall co-ordinate on development and co-operation and shall consult each other on their aid programmes, including international organisations and during international conferences. They may undertake joint action. Member States shall contribute if necessary to the implementation of Community aid programmes.

The above clearly place the EU's role as that of a coordinator and facilitator of the EU development policy. The EU's resources are finite, and therefore any assistance that can be given at this level is limited. Whilst this is regrettable, in many cases the Member States have historic ties with developing countries, particularly with former colonies. This gives those states a special responsibility to assist with the development of certain states. Where the EU has a special advantage over the Member States is that it can negotiate access to the European market. This is a powerful development tool, which could be used more effectively.

The hierarchy of privilege

The EU has a variety of trade relationships with states. These form a hierarchy of privileged access to its markets. The privileges offered are typically lower tariffs, higher quotas or other relaxations of trade restrictions. The least favoured countries are those that are normally subject to the rules of the GATT, although some countries have yet to join the organisation.

Table 17.1 The hierarchy of privilege in 1990 (% of EU Imports)

Intra-EU trade	59.0
EFTA	9.6
ACP	1.8
Eastern Europe	2.7
Mediterranean countries	3.8
Developing countries	8.2
Industrial countries	14.9
Total	100.0

Source: *European Economy* (1993), No. 52, 23

The order of privilege tends to change over time. In the early 1990s (Table 17.1) the order of privilege was as follows.

1. The EFTA states, all of which are part of a free trade area with the EU, and apart from Switzerland belong to the European Economic Area (EEA). The CAP is not covered by this agreement.

2. African, Caribbean and Pacific states (ACP). These 70 states are members of the Lomé Convention. Many of these were former colonies of the EU members. These enjoy duty-free access to the EU market for all but agricultural products that are part of the CAP. Safeguards are provided by rules of origin (i.e. it is not possible to deflect goods via these states into the EU in order to take advantage of the absence of tariffs and quotas).

3. The Super General System of Preference (GSP) states. These are some of the poorest states of Central and South America. These arrangements were similar to those offered to the Lomé members, but they were temporary.

4. Mediterranean and Eastern European states. The number of agreements with these states has tended to grow, as the EU has consolidated its relations with its Southern neighbours, and because of the collapse and fragmentation of the Communist states. Access is limited for 'sensitive' goods, for example textiles and iron and steel.

5. The Less Developed Countries, which gain from the General System of Preference (GSP). This allows access to EU markets but there are limits to access for 'sensitive' products.

Concessions are awarded on the basis of a mixture of criteria, ranging from the development needs of states to the need to offer political help (Russia's gaining GSP status is an example of this). The ACP states gained their preference partly on the basis of historical ties.

The definition of 'sensitive' in this case refers to the products of the problem industries within the EU. Extra quantities of 'sensitive' products entering the EU may make it difficult for the EU to organise the restructuring of these industries. It might reasonably be suggested that rather than being sensitive they are simply industries where the EU is not competitive. However, this would not be an acceptable definition to the interest groups within the EU trying to maintain jobs or investment in the sector.

The extent to which particular states are able to take advantage of the concessions on offer will vary. So, for example, the ACP states are not well placed to send manufactured products into the EU, simply because they lack the production base. It could also be the case that where a country is able to make advances into a market, it finds that this situation is unwelcome. The extent to which developing countries depend on exporting primary products is illustrated in Table 17.2.

Table 17.2 Composition of developing countries' exports to the EU in 1989 (%)

Fuels	25
Agriculture and food	7
Other primary	20
Textiles	15
Manufactures	33

Source: As Table 17.1, 78

It should be noted that this situation is an improvement on the position 10 years earlier, but that was because primary exports were even more dominated by fuels as a consequence of high oil prices at that time.

The preferences that the EU offers tend to be against other exporters into the EU market, rather than the EU itself. Only in an area like sugar are the ACP states at an advantage against the EU. In this case the ACP states can sell 1.3 million tonnes into the high-priced EU market instead of the low-priced world market, despite the fact that the EU is a surplus producer, and sells its excess production onto the world market.

An example of EU policy being trade-diverting was the case of the importation of bananas. As a result of the completion of the Single Market, the EU moved to a common quota for imported bananas. Prior to this, Britain, for example, had agreements to buy bananas from the Caribbean which, although they were expensive, offered a high-value market for countries such as the Windward Islands. In contrast, Germany imported bananas at a lower world market price, mainly from South America. Once the Single Market was complete, it was no longer feasible to retain the national quotas, because they could simply be circumvented due to the absence of border controls. The national quotas were replaced by an EU quota of just over 2 million tonnes. For bananas imported as part of the quota, the tariff was ECU 100 per tonne. However, those outside the quota carried a tariff of ECU 850 per tonne. The largest part of the quota went to the Caribbean producers, and so the South American producers felt that they had been cheated of a valuable market. Within the EU, Germany felt that the trade diversion had been at its expense. The ACP states' advantageous quota for bananas into the EU was at the expense of Latin American countries, which were the most efficient producers. The dispute could have been resolved by giving much higher quotas to the South Americans, in the context of a larger overall quota. However, in any price war within Europe, the Caribbean producers would lose.

A criticism of the policy is therefore that it may be trade-diverting rather than trade-creating. If lower tariffs or fewer restrictions mean that the EU imports more from developing countries as a result of its policy of preference, then the policy may be justifiable.

However, this will depend on the extent to which the preferred countries can actually take advantage of the more liberal trade regime. If the policy disadvantages other, less preferred developing countries, it might reasonably be seen largely as a political gesture.

EU–ACP cooperation

The historical links between the ACP and the EU states date back to the early origins of the EU, when the Yaoundi Convention was agreed between the original six members and their former colonies. When Britain joined the EU in 1973, further provision had to be made for a wider group of states. The first of the Lomé Conventions was signed in 1975, with what were then 46 ACP states. This was renewed in 1980 and 1985, and the Fourth Lomé Convention came into effect in 1990. This time it was due to last for ten years to the end of 1999, but with funding to be renewed after five years. There were 70 members by this time. (47 African, 15 Caribbean and 8 Pacific). The arrangement was meant to combine elements of both trade and aid.

The value of the trade concessions offered by Lomé has diminished over time, as the EU has offered concessions to other groups such as the Central and Eastern European States. Also, as successive enlargements have taken place, the benefits have been further eroded. However, new EU members do offer a wider range of markets to which the Lomé States have access, and the potential for more generous aid donors. Because of growth elsewhere, the ACP states' proportion of developing countries' exports to the EU declined from 17.3 per cent in 1980 to 10.6 per cent in 1990.

The EU can still impose constraints on trade from the ACP countries, although it generally avoids doing so for manufactured goods. Rules of origin can be applied, which means that goods that enter the EU must have a significant local content from the exporting country. This stipulation is to avoid trade being deflected via the countries with the best access to EU markets. The tighter the rules of origin, the less risk there is of simple assembly operations being set up as a way of defeating EU trade restrictions. However, few advanced manufactured products originate from just one country. Rules of origin must therefore offer a balance between local content and the possibility that manufactures are the result of just 'screwdriver' operations. If local content rules are set too high, they will tend to discourage the early steps towards industrialisation, which may be based on elementary tasks.

Some estimates put the loss of trading privileges by the ACP states, as a result of the Uruguay Round, as high as $90 million.[2] To counteract the problem of trade concessions being given to other states, there is a need for more assistance to be given to the developing countries. In a world of more liberal trade they will not be able to compete fully unless they are able to generate growth internally, or they are offered:

● more aid to promote trade diversity

● a greater relaxation of the rules of origin

● improved technical assistance

● improved arrangements to stabilise commodity prices.

Aid and the ACP

About half the world's overseas aid is provided by the EU and the Member States, either directly or via organisations such as the World Bank, the International Monetary Fund and the United Nations. However, only 17 per cent comes from the European Development Fund (EDF) or from the EU budget.[3] The justification for the EU's having an aid policy in addition to other providers is that

- there is a moral duty to assist poorer countries

- all Member States participate, even those that were not colonial powers

- the aid can be spread more evenly

- expertise and resources can be better coordinated

- multilateral aid from the EU may be less politically tied.

Aid given under the Lomé Convention is organised under the EDF, which is not part of the EU budget. It is financed by direct contributions from the Member States' budgets, so for example 16.7 per cent of the EDF comes from the UK.[4] For the period 1990 to 1995, the allocation of EU aid was as follows in Table 17.3.

Table 17.3 Aid funding to the Lomé Convention countries 1990–1995 (ECU millions)

Grants	7995
Risk capital	825
Stabex[1]	1500
Sysmin[2]	480
Total EDF	10 800
EIB loans	1200

[1]   Stabex is a system of compensating for the fall in commodity prices
[2]   Sysmin is similar to Stabex, but applies to mineral prices
Source: Commission of the EU

The problem with this aid is that the amounts are not adequate to promote real diversity in the economies concerned. There are also concerns that, in the past, many of the projects have had more political than economic significance. While the existence of Stabex and Sysmin may assist with the balance of payments problems associated with fluctuations in commodity prices, it does not reduce that dependence. Indeed the price support, though welcome at a time of crisis, may encourage the maintenance of a sector that benefits the developed world rather than the underdeveloped nations.

The actual administration of the aid has been criticised in the past. Often the process is slow, and the take-up rates are inadequate, with funding taking far too long to spend. In 1993, funds that related back to Lomé II were still being spent, while Lomé IV was hardly under way.[5] Monitoring and controls on spending have been defective, leading to suspected abuse. This brought criticism from the Court of Auditors. In a 1994 report, it complained that there was an estimated loss of tens of millions of ECUs associated with import programmes. These were funded by the EDF for the benefit of the ACP states, and yet their impact was substantially reduced due to poor management.[6]

In addition to EU aid, there are national aid programmes. The poorest EU states contribute little, while the major donors tend to tie aid, i.e., the aid must be spent with the donor (Table 17.4). While aid-giving is often unpopular within donor states, it can be made to appear a more attractive proposition if it furthers national commercial interests.

Table 17.4 Aid from EU members 1989–1990

	Aid (% GDP)	% (untied aid)
France	0.78	40.2
Germany	0.41	39.4
Italy	0.36	5.8
UK	0.29	13.9
Netherlands	0.94	33.0
Denmark	0.93	43.1
Belgium	0.46	26.0
Ireland	0.16	32.1
EU	0.50	–

Source: House of Lords (1993), Select Committee on the European Communities, *EC Aid and Trade Policy*, Session 1992–93, 27th Report, HL Paper 123, p. 54

Overall aid and trade arrangements with the developing world are less generous than might be expected, given the needs of these states. Many of the actions of the EU and the Member States seem to indicate a reluctance to permit development plans that do not meet the full approval of the donors. Tied aid means that purchases are often at an inflated price, because there is not adequate competition to supply the goods or services. The wrong priorities are often targeted, and the decision-making process is often complex and slow. EU aid has the advantage that it is less constrained by conditions, although political conditions related to human rights are important to the EU. In 1993, six countries had their aid curtailed because of human rights problems (Haiti, Liberia, Zaire, Sudan, Togo and Equatorial Guinea).

Conclusions

It is easy to see how EU aid and trade policies could still be viewed as neo-colonialist. This is a difficult accusation to refute, given the long tradition of European involvement in many third world countries. However, there are few clear alternatives on the part of the developing countries, especially those of the ACP. European trade and aid must be accepted on the terms offered, or there is a risk that nothing will be available. Public opinion in the Member States is often cynical about the value of concessions, unless some benefits can be demonstrated. There is a case for more aid being given via the EU instead of by the Member States. This will not happen, however, unless the EU can demonstrate that it is able to administer funds effectively.

References

1. **European Parliament** (1993) *Report Of The Committee on Development and Cooperation on Increased Coordination of the Development Aid Provided by Member States and the EEC,* A3-0293/93.
2. *Europe,* 19 February 1994, 11.
3. **House of Lords** (1993) *EC Development Aid,* Select Committee on the European Communities, Session 1992–93, HL Paper 86, p. 7.
4. Ibid., p. 6.
5. *The Courier* (1994) No. 145, May–June, 6–12.
6. *Europe,* 6 April 1994, 11.

Further reading

Commission of the EU (1993) *Europe in a Changing World.*

European Economy (1993) The European Community as a world trade partner, No. 52.

House of Lords (1993) *EC Aid and Trade Policy,* Select Committee on the European Communities, Session 1992–93, HL Paper 123.

Ravenhill J (1985) *Collective Clientelism: the Lomé Convention and North South Relations.*

Robson P (ed.) (1990) Europe and the developing countries, *Journal of Common Market Studies,* special issue.

The Courier (a bimonthly publication of the EU which covers a wide range of ACP issues).

CHAPTER 18

Expanding the EU eastwards

Introduction

Over the period from the EU's creation in 1958 to the mid-1990s, the number of Member States has more than doubled. The EU6 were a homogeneous group of developed industrialised countries, characterised by a high level of economic growth. In retrospect, the process of integrating these states proved to be relatively easy, despite often heated arguments and the existence of areas of economic backwardness, such as Southern Italy. The first expansion in 1973 was to the north and west, and brought membership for the UK, Denmark and Ireland. Although these countries were welcomed for their democratic traditions, this was not a comfortable process for the EU. A number of acrimonious disputes followed before Britain, in particular, was prepared to accept membership as a permanent feature of the political and economic landscape. The second phase of expansion brought EU membership for three Mediterranean states: Greece in 1981, and Spain and Portugal in 1986. These semi-industrial countries had emerged from a period of right-wing dictatorship only in the 1970s. The three Mediterranean states all experienced rapid rates of economic growth in the 1960s and early 1970s, and Spain and Portugal did well in the 1980s. Despite this, they remain relatively poor compared to the other Member States, and their membership made the EU substantially more heterogeneous. The total number of Member States grew to 15 with the enlargement in 1995. The addition of Austria, Finland and Sweden increases diversity, with the EU's borders stretching further both to the north and east

Many of the issues that emerged as part of the 1995 enlargement have been dealt with already in this book. This chapter, as a consequence, deals with the pressing issue of further enlargement, taking particular account of the issues raised by the incorporation of Central and Eastern European states (CEEs) into the EU (Bulgaria, the Czech Republic, Hungary, Poland, Romania and the Slovak Republic). It examines the desirability of an Eastern expansion, as a response to the new Europe that emerged after the end of the Soviet Union's dominance of the region. It suggests that the EU was slow to respond to the changes that took place because they were so unexpected. The EU adopted a protectionist response because of the pressures of a recession and the vested interest within a number of states, which feared the arrival of new competitors.

The EU's strategy has only gradually emerged. It involves making progress in integrating the economic and political systems of the CEEs, including foreign and security policy via the

Europe Agreements. The process of absorbing the new states into the EU will be a question for the Intergovernmental Conference in 1996, but these Agreements may be inadequate in their present form. Finally, the implications of EU enlargement to include Cyprus, Malta and Turkey are discussed.

Who qualifies for membership?

Article O of the Treaty on European Union set out the basic principle that:

> 'Any European State with a system of government founded on the principle of democracy may apply to join the Union.'

This did not, however, give a clear definition of what is meant by 'European'. It is generally accepted that the criteria for being European are a mixture of historical, geographical, cultural and religious features, but there are no firm rules.

The rules that set out which states are likely to be accepted as members are not part of the Treaty, but are well understood. For example, at the 1994 Corfu European Council, the Commission was requested to make specific proposals for the further implementation of the Europe Agreements. This was in order that the CEEs should be able to assume the obligations of membership by satisfying the economic and political requirements of membership.

The conditions for these states becoming EU members were

- a stability of institutions guaranteeing the rule of law, human rights and the respect of minorities

- the existence of a functioning market economy

- a capacity to cope with the competitive pressures and market forces within the Union

- the ability to take on the obligations of membership, including adherence to the aims of political, economic and monetary union.

In addition there was an overall condition that offered the prospect of the EU choosing members according to the political and economic circumstances at the time. This was that the '...Union's capacity to absorb new members, while maintaining the momentum of European integration is also an important consideration in the general interest of both the Union and the candidate countries'.[1] This final point is a catch-all, which offers the EU the possibility of veto even if the main criteria appear to have been achieved.

The rationale for expanding the EU

In an ideal world, any new member of the European Union should be

1. rich, and able to make a net contribution to the EC budget

2. democratic, in the sense of having a tradition of competitive political parties and pluralism

3.   capitalist, and operate a market economy with a system of private ownership

4.   without problem sector industries that require restructuring and demand significant resources.

The enlargement that encompassed Austria, Finland and Sweden might have met these ideals in the 1980s. However, in the 1990s, the effects of recession in Sweden, and the added complication of the decline in Finland's trade with the Soviet Union, meant that two countries had a GDP per head lower than the EU average.

The prospects for absorbing further states becomes more difficult the further East and South the EU goes. The CEEs do not meet the above criteria. There are, however, strong political reasons why there might be a mutual wish on the part of the EU and a number of the CEEs that they become members of an enlarged European Union. For the EU, an Eastern expansion may be justified on the following political grounds.

1.   It may help to preserve liberal democracy in what were totalitarian states dominated by the former Soviet Union.

2.   It will strengthen European unity.

3.   Central and Eastern Europe is a complex political area, especially since the decline of the Soviet Union. Adding new members to the EU would contribute to the security of the region, and help to ensure that these states do not fall under Russian dominance once again.

4.   It will enhance the EU's standing in world diplomacy.

The economic reasons for expanding the EU eastwards are not a question of high ideals, but concern the trade-off between benefits and costs. They are:

1.   the increase in the size of the Single Market, which will increase trading opportunities

2.   the assistance membership will give the development of CEEs

3.   the further consolidation of the EU as the world's most important trading bloc

4.   the linkage to important trading partners to the east and south of the EU.

On the negative side, there are a number of problems related to further expansion. The new members will:

1.   bring new sets of national interests, which without reform of the EU's institutions will dilute or even stop completely the process of policy-making (see chapter 2 for some of the institutional problems of enlarging to 15 members)

2.   make it more difficult to implement policies on a common or uniform basis

3.   make demands on the EU budget

4.   raise awkward and sensitive issues, for example the rights of minority groups in certain states.

The above points cast doubt on the desirability of expanding at all, but it is difficult to refuse entry to a range of states because of a wish to keep the EU as an exclusive club. However, there may be good grounds for refusing membership to Turkey on the grounds of its human rights record, and its continued occupation of Northern Cyprus. These are also useful reasons to avoid stressing important underlying reasons for denying early entry, such as the size of Turkey, the fear that open borders would bring a flood of unwanted migrants, and general doubts about the state's overall Europeanness.

There is also an issue about attracting a host of small states as Europe becomes more fragmented. There is no stated minimum size of EU member: Luxembourg, with a population of 377 000, was one of the founding members of the EU. However, if the EU attracted a large number of other small states, there might be a problem. Not only will it be difficult to accommodate states as diverse as Estonia and Malta within the decision-making process, but they may lack the resources to chair meetings of the Council of Ministers.[2] This suggests that the EU might have to develop alternative strategies to cope with these kinds of states, such as unhindered access to the Single Market and a less formal participation in the decision process (this is likely to be a solution that sovereign states find difficult to accept).

Preparing for membership

The process of preparing for membership comprises a number of stages.

1. Prior to an application for membership, the applicant state should be preparing to accept the responsibilities of membership, such as harmonising key legislation and adapting to the market economy. This process can take a number of years.

2. Applications for membership have to be addressed to the Council of Ministers, preferably after there are indications that the application will be supported.

3. The Commission is asked to investigate and give its opinion on the suitability of a state for membership.

4. A process of detailed negotiation may then start. This inevitably means that demands are made by all parties. This is a good point for some of the poorer states to try to win extra resources, for example (see chapter 13).

5. Once the terms of entry have been agreed, the Council of Ministers must unanimously agree to the terms, and the European Parliament must also give its assent.

6. The applicant states must then decide if they are prepared to accept the terms offered. The method of choice depends on their national constitutions.

7. New Member States are normally given a period of time in which they can adapt fully to the EU, and accept the *aquis communautaire*. This is the body of rules and regulations on which the EU is based. Even prior to the adoption of the TEU there were 12 000 pages of the *aquis communautaire*, which means that the EU laws may take some time to come to full effect in the new Member States. The terms of any transition period are set out in the Treaty of Accession between the EU and the new member.

EU relations with Central and Eastern Europe

This section examines the developing relations between the EU and the prospective candidate states of Central and Eastern Europe. It analyses their economic situation in the post-communist period, and the viability of their membership of the EU.

As long as the region to the east of Germany was controlled by the Soviet Union, it was possible to analyse the relationships between that group of states in terms of the operation of the Council of Mutual Economic Assistance (CMEA) and the military organisation the Warsaw Pact. Direct relationships between CMEA and the EU hardly developed at all, because of a reluctance of the CMEA to recognise the EU. Instead there was a series of bilateral relationships between the EU Member States. The states of Central and Eastern Europe were generally at the bottom of the hierarchy of EU trade preferences. Exports from the West were restricted in the area of high-technology products, because of the fear that they might have a military as well as a civilian application. However, the main barrier to trade was an absence of demand from the East, because of a lack of hard currency. Eastern bloc products did not sell well, largely because they were of poor quality compared to those available elsewhere in the global economy.

After 1989, the collapse of communism and the fragmentation of the region caused a more complex series of relationships. CMEA was formally abandoned at its 46th Session in June 1991. The whole edifice had completely lost its substance. It was no longer acceptable to trade via the use of barter, or with soft non-convertible currencies. All states started to demand the settlement of debt in hard currency, which made the previous trading arrangements no longer valid. It also made it difficult to calculate the true worth of past trade debts. By necessity all the CEEs started to look to the West.

The EU was not prepared for the speed of change in Central and Eastern Europe. By the early 1990s, the whole of Europe appeared to subscribe to a common ideology. Attempts were made to put into place trade and aid arrangements which would help to prevent a return to the confrontational relationships of the past. While in theory all European states are, under the right conditions, eligible to join the EU, the Member States did not generally favour the vision of a united Europe spreading to the Urals and beyond. It became clear that the line for EU membership would be drawn at the border of the successor of the Soviet Union, the Commonwealth of Independent States (CIS). The Central European states are considered potential applicants, along with the Baltic States of Estonia, Latvia and Lithuania. The reasons for this are a mixture of practical considerations and a feeling of responsibility for having abandoned some of these countries to their fate. In the case of the Central European states, there was a feeling that their role as a buffer between East and West had been imposed on them, while the Baltic States had been invaded by the Soviet Union.

Prior to the Soviet occupation in the 1940s, the Central European states had progressed to positions where their industries could compete effectively with those in the West. The years of occupation, however, saw the relative efficiency of these economies decline, and following the Soviet withdrawal they were left with economies that would require considerable restructuring and modernisation.

The problems had been brought about by a system of economic management designed to reduce dependence on the capitalist economies of the West. Because trade in Central and Eastern Europe was largely internal to CMEA, little thought was given to quality issues or labour productivity. The maintenance of full employment was considered to be of far greater importance. A lack of democratic control led to environmental standards being ignored, and the infrastructure was designed to comply with the views of the central planners rather than the economic imperatives. While it is reasonable to argue that there were many good aspects to the system, it created an industrial structure that was unable to compete with its profit-oriented counterparts in the West.

It has been suggested that this poor economic performance was in part due to attempts to limit the availability of high-technology goods to the CMEA countries. The reasons for this were predominantly military, in that there was a fear that equipment might be used to make munitions as well as having peaceful uses. An elaborate system of export controls was put into place, directed by Cocom. This was based in Paris, and had been established in 1947 at the height of the cold war. It was finally disbanded in 1994.[3] While there were exports that needed to be monitored, there was not a great deal of evidence to suggest that Western technology was used to any great effect in the CMEA countries. This was not due to a lack of availability, but to the general inefficiency of the system.

Regional cooperation in Central Europe

While there was a natural tendency for the Central European States to look westward in their relationships, as a response to their imposed separation of the past, this was not an easy option in practice. The collapse of the Soviet Union and a number of traditional markets did not mean that there could easily be a switch in direction. Not only were many of the goods that were being produced of a lower standard than might be acceptable in the West, but they lacked the political strength to negotiate a really favourable trade deal. Also, there was a need to give reassurances on human rights, political stability and pluralistic democracy to attract investors from the West.

The idea of economic and political cooperation in the process of transformation between the former Soviet satellites developed quickly. In January 1990, the Czechoslovak President Valclav Havel visited Warsaw and Budapest to urge his neighbouring states to coordinate a return to Europe. This led to the Visegrad Joint Declaration of 15 February 1991. This agreed to cooperate in areas of security, introducing market-based reforms, and in a number of linked areas such as ecology, energy, telecommunications and issues such as national minorities. It was proposed that the cooperation should be taken further with the establishment of a Central European Free Trade Area (CEFTA). This covered both industrial goods and agriculture. The CEFTA idea had more to do with a common wish to prepare for EU membership than a wish of these states to cooperate and create a rival organisation to the EU.

Foreign direct investment (FDI)

Foreign direct investment can have a significant role in the process of transition to an advanced industrial economy. This is because of its importance in increasing output, encouraging better working practices and technology transfer. The existence of a well educated labour force whose wage rates were comparatively low increased the flow of foreign capital into the CEEs. A number of foreign firms wished to take advantage of new markets in the East, as well as to supply the West from a geographically close source.

Table 18.1 Growth of foreign direct investment in Poland, Hungary and Czech and Slovak Republics (CSR) in $ US

	1989	1990	1991	1992	Total
Poland	100	252	328	1320	2000
CSR	256	180	664	1000	2100
Hungary	550	910	1540	1300	4300
Total	906	1342	2532	3620	8400

Source : OECD (1994), *Economic Survey: the Czech and Slovak Republics*, p. 36

Table 18.1 shows that Hungary did particularly well in attracting investment, because it had already started the transition to a market economy when the borders to the West were opened. It was also politically stable, with few problems associated with ethnic minorities within its borders.

Investment might have been higher had there been an immediate agreement to permit free access for all the products from this region into the EU. Better communications would also have helped. Sustained growth in the West and greater political stability in the CEEs are important for the future. However, while these conditions help to promote a better climate for investment, additional assistance to guarantee investments would also help.

Problems of adopting the market economy

The optimistic adoption of the new free-market style of economic management in CEEs did not lead to the sustained economic growth that had been hoped for. In macroeconomic terms, these were cash-rich societies, where the excess of spending power had frequently led to shortages in the shops under the communist regimes. Where attempts were made to reduce inflation, the process was painful. However, the consequences were far worse for the economies that simply let inflation get out of hand, as happened in Russia. In a microeconomic sense, some of the decline reflected the disappearance of some industries that had been producing goods which were now not needed. An example of this was the reduction in arms manufacturing. In other cases, investment ceased because projects had now to show a return. In the past, investments decisions were often politically motivated, or resources were wasted, because of the absence of proper accountancy procedures.

The major problem was a loss of markets in the East, and the task of restructuring the economies was far greater than had been expected. It is easy to construct arguments for the closure of inefficient industry, but it is more difficult to encourage the growth of new firms.

While Table 18.2 suggests that the Central European states declined, but were able to at least stabilise their economic situation towards the mid-1990s, the task for Russia was far greater. This was due to a complex set of reasons associated with the nature of the problems that Russia and the rest of the CIS states faced. These included chronic problems of political instability, and the fact that they had no real experience of the market economy. The Soviet Union was formally dissolved on 21 December 1991. This meant that new arrangements had to be put into place. Food aid was an important early element of assistance to the

Table 18.2 Change in real GDP in Central and Eastern Europe (% change over previous years)

	1990	1991	1992	1993
Bulgaria	−9.1	−11.8	−7.7	−4.6
Czech Republic	−1.6	−14.7	7.1	0.0
Hungary	−3.3	−10.0	−5.0	−1.0
Poland	−11.6	−9.0	1.0	3.0
Russia	−4.0	−17.0	−19.0	−11.0
Slovak Republic	−3.5	−15.0	8.3	−7.0

Source : Financial Times, 24 February 1994, 24, based on OECD figures

Commonwealth of Independent States, with Russia being a major beneficiary. Technical assistance under the EU's Tacis programme followed, but was more difficult to organise than had been expected, so that despite money being allocated it was not paid out. This was because of problems with the viability of the early schemes, in a time when the region was facing economic turmoil. Some of the problems appeared to have been resolved by 1993. A multiannual programme was put into place covering the period 1 January 1993 to 31 December 1995. This indicated that the EU had started to take a longer term perspective on its technical assistance programme for the 13 states involved.

Trade negotiations between the individual CIS states and the EU started with an agreement with Russia, and also took place with the Ukraine. These fall short of the kind of partnership agreements given to the Central European and Baltic states, but hold the prospect of the completion of a free-trade zone by 1998.

The Europe Agreements

The Europe Agreements were designed to assist the economies in transition of Central Europe as they moved forward to a point where they were able to compete effectively with those of Western Europe, and at the same time maintain their newly found liberal democracy. Table 18.3 gives a profile of these states.

The Europe Agreements were originally signed between the EU and Poland, Hungary and the Czech and Slovak Republics. The trade aspects of the Agreements started to come into effect as of 1 March 1992 with Poland, Hungary and Czechoslovakia. They were formally signed at the Foreign Affairs Council of 4 October 1993, and came fully into effect in February 1994. On 1 January 1993, Czechoslovakia had become two states, the Czech Republic and the Slovak Republic, which meant that new Agreements were negotiated. In addition, Bulgaria and Romania also signed Agreements which came into force in May and December 1993 respectively. In February 1994, the EU agreed to give the Baltic states of Estonia, Latvia and Lithuania a free-trade agreement, which meant that they enjoyed unrestricted access for manufactures into the EU from 1 January 1995. Estonia offered immediate access to EU goods in return, while the other two states had six years to adjust. The three states also created their own free-trade area, and hoped to negotiate Europe Agreements after 1995. Slovenia and Albania may also be signatories of Europe Agreements.

Table 18.3 The economies in transition

	Land area (km^2)	Population (millions) 1992	GNP per capita (US$) 1991	Unemployment (%) 1993[2]	Inflation rate (%) 1993[2]
Bulgaria	110 994	9.0	1840	17.0	60.0
Czech Republic	78 864	10.3	2450[1]	4.5	17.0
Slovak Republic	49 035	5.3	2450[1]	17.0	30.0
Hungary	93 032	10.3	2690	13.0	23.0
Poland	312 683	38.4	1830	17.0	38.0
Romania	237 500	22.8	1340	10.8	370.0

[1] This is a combined figure for Czechoslovakia: the GNP per head is expected to be lower for the Slovak Republic

[2] Estimates

Source: House of Lords (1994), *The Implications for Agriculture of the Europe Agreements*, Select Committee on the European Communities, 10th Report, Session 1993–94, HL Paper 57-1, p. 43

The Europe Agreements were different to many of the past EU agreements in that they had a political as well as an economic dimension. They contained:

1. a commitment to pluralistic democracy based on the rule of law and the market economy

2. a recognition that the Central Europe states wished to become members of the EU (this was to be taken up by the EU at the Copenhagen Summit).

Established as part of the Agreements was an Association Council, which involved meetings at a ministerial level, and a Parliamentary Association for the Parliaments. The Association Council met for the first time in March 1994. The Agreements came in two stages, which were not related to the free movement of goods. The hope was that a free-trade area would be established between the two areas by 2002.

The Agreements covered five main elements:

1. free movement of goods over a ten year period

2. movement of workers, establishment and supply of services

3. payments and the approximation of laws

4. economic cooperation

5. financial cooperation.

The movement towards a free-trade area complied with Article XXIV of the GATT. This permits the construction of customs unions and free-trade areas as long as they do not raise barriers against third countries. However, the EU did not offer the Association states as much as it might have under these agreements. Restrictions were placed on the export of 'sensitive' products in key areas such as agriculture, textiles, and iron and steel. These three sectors were important to the Association states. In 1990 they amounted to 41.1 per cent of Poland's exports to the EU, 33.5 per cent for Czechoslovakia and 47.5 per cent for Hungary. Unrestricted access would have little effect on the EU in the short to medium term, as Central and Eastern European trade is less than 3 per cent of total. However, the potential benefits for the Association states of open access to EU markets would have been considerable. The dependence of these states on EU markets is illustrated by the fact that in 1991 80.7 per cent of their exports to the developed world went to the EU, with 12.3 per cent going to EFTA, leaving only 7 per cent for the rest of the developed world.

Despite the EU's trade surplus, special industrial interests were able to mobilise the EU policy-makers against imports from the CEEs. This was to reduce access of goods in which the CEEs had a comparative advantage, because these were areas where the EU had a substantial problem of over-capacity. Cuts in EU steel capacity, for example, were particularly difficult to negotiate in the mid-1990s without placing restrictions on non-EU producers. Where CEEs did appear to be making progress, for example in structural steel supplies, EU producers demanded further protection and lodged an anti-dumping complaint. EU producers claimed that Hungarian and Czech producers had increased their market share almost three-fold from 1993 to 1994. They were accused of gaining nearly 9 per cent of the market by undercutting prices by as much as 50 per cent.[4]

Restrictions were maintained on the free movement of workers, which was not a feature of the Agreements. Migrants were subjected to the normal national restrictions on entry into EU states. Payments were not restricted, which was important from the point of view of future investment, as there were no restrictions on the repatriation of profits. There was to be a harmonisation of commercial laws to those of the EU, which would permit easier absorption into the Union.

The 1993 European Council in Copenhagen recognised some of the shortcomings of the Europe Agreements, and took action to speed up the process of liberalisation. Initially, it was apparent in the early 1990s that the new situation in Central Europe was not as welcome as might have been expected given the post-cold war rhetoric. However, it became clear that the foreign policy interests of the EU and the Association states were very similar, and that there was a need for greater cooperation. The EU actively considered building on the relations with the Association states by

1. restricting the extent of EU subsidies to agriculture exports into their domestic markets, so permitting the development of the CEE agricultural industry

2. reforming the aid programmes by placing greater emphasis on infrastructure projects, in line with the methods used for the EU's Structural Funds

3. trying to persuade the Association states to adopt EU competition rules with regard to issues such as state aid, in order to avoid EU anti-dumping actions.

Aid programmes to Eastern and Central Europe

Financial help to the region has come from a variety of Western sources. These include:

1. EU Member States' bilateral aid schemes

2. loans via the EU's European Investment Bank (EIB)

3. the European Bank for Reconstruction and Development (EBRD)

4. the PHARE programme (Pologne, Hongrie: Assistance à la Reconstruction Economique)

5. The Tacis Programme for the former Soviet Union.

The existence of schemes sponsored by the Member States was to be expected, given the differing priorities of the EU members. It also reflects the wish to gain a commercial advantage in the medium term from the development. While the EIB was involved in mobilising capital, as an EU organisation it could borrow and lend money at attractive interest rates. The main commercial development loans were directed via the EBRD. In its early years the Bank was the subject of criticism, based on the fitting out of its lavish London headquarters and the high levels of expenses paid to senior officials. The Bank was reorganised, and apart from offering advice was able to increase lending. Total loans were only $120 million in 1992, but had risen to $560 million by the end of 1993. They were expected to rise to $750 million by the end of 1994.[5] While business in commercial loans was difficult to organise in the period of economic decline, the Bank's operation started to look more viable once the economies started to stabilise.

The PHARE Programme is the main instrument for economic and technical assistance to the CEEs. It was originally designed for Poland and Hungary, but took on a wider role as the number of Central European states abandoning communism increased. The PHARE programme is administered by the EU, but is a joint initiative by the Group of 24 western industrialised countries. The PHARE budget was ECU 500 million in 1990, and was in excess of ECU 1 billion in 1993. The EU has provided about two-thirds of the PHARE funding. An education and student mobility programme called TEMPUS is also part of the scheme.

The aim of PHARE over the period 1993–1997 was to lay the foundations of the market economy, by encouraging structural adjustment and economic reform in the CEEs. This required:

● a balance between technical assistance and support for investment

● support for institution building

● the use of funds to support CEEs' own national sectoral and regional programmes

● cooperation with the EIB and EBRD.

The PHARE programme is organised on a multiannual basis, and it is hoped that as time goes on, more funds will be channelled via institutions in the partner countries. In this way the model would resemble that which the EU uses for Structural Funds.[6]

The idea of a more substantial aid package, something along the lines of the Marshall Aid scheme which the USA launched to assist post-war recovery, was discussed. The problem with such a scheme was its enormous cost. To make an impact, such a scheme would involve a huge transfer of resources from the developed market economies, which was not feasible at a time of recession in the West.

The Tacis Programme granted ECU 450 million in 1992, and was generally criticised for not using its full resources. One of the reasons for this was the problems caused by the collapse of the Soviet Union.

The aid programmes have not been as well organised as they might have been. The insistence that much of the aid was tied to technical assistance has been criticised on the grounds that the funding tends to find its way back to many of the original contributors. All the Member States lobby hard to ensure that their nationals get a share of the available work. Other criticisms include:

- slowness to set schemes up

- the EU being slow to pay its bills

- officials being high-handed when dealing with applicants

- consultants being overpaid.[7]

While a number of these accusations may have been true, EU aid has helped to fund a range of good projects, such as assistance with privatisation schemes and the establishment of business advice centres. However, it appears that much of the early success has been in the Central European states rather than the former Soviet Union.

Central Europe: the next enlargement?

An important development that arose from the Copenhagen European Council of June 1993 was the agreement that the Europe Agreement states could become members of an enlarged EU as soon as they were able to fulfil the relevant obligations. Generally, even the strongest economies of Central Europe (the Czech Republic, Hungary, Poland and the Slovak Republic) do not compare well with the poorest states of the EU (Table 18.4).

Table 18.4 A comparison between the EU Cohesion States and Central European States

	Income per capita EU12 = 100 (1991)
Spain	80.5
Ireland	69.0
Portugal	57.1
Greece	52.2
EU4	71.6
Czechoslovakia	45.7
Hungary	40.5
Poland	36.4

Source : European Economy (1993), No. 53, 113

Despite these disadvantages, Poland and Hungary applied for membership in April 1994. Although these countries have great future potential, they will bring further problems for the

EU. A particular issue is likely to be agriculture, where the EU currently restricts access to its markets. If membership becomes a reality, the budget costs of the CAP could rise sharply, unless the EU succeeds in bringing about further reforms. The importance of the agricultural sector to these economies can be seen from Table 18.5.

Table 18.5 Agriculture and the Central European states

	Contribution to employment (%)	Contribution to GDP (%)
Bulgaria (1992)	22.0	35.0
Czech and Slovak Republics (1992)	12.0	7.0
Hungary (1992)	13.5	13.6
Poland (1992)	25.0	8.0
Romania (1991)	27.5	–
EU Average (1991)	6.3	3.0

Source: *Europe*, 18 June 1994, 13

In addition to the problem of agriculture, there is a fear that, unless the restructuring of industry is a success, these states will find they are not able to compete, and will be swamped by the more efficient EU producers.

Table 18.6 The budgetary costs of Central European enlargement (in ECU million, based on 1989 output levels)

	Contribution	Receipts from Structural Funds	Receipts from CAP	Net contribution
Bulgaria	263	1205	516	–1458
Czech and Slovak Republics	617	1360	446	–1189
Hungary	341	1255	544	–1458
Poland	817	4600	1409	–5192
Romania	396	3190	809	–3603
Total				–12 900

Source: CEPR (1992), *Is Bigger Better? The Economics of EC Enlargement*, p. 72

Apart from the problems related to specific sectors, there is an overall budgetary cost of enlargement. Estimates of this vary, because it is not clear what the position of EU policy will be post-enlargement, or indeed the state of the Central European economies at that time. Clearly, the more assistance the EU is able to offer now, the lower will be the potential costs in the future, if these states do achieve their membership goal. Table 18.6 sets out one view of what the position might be, and shows that these states would represent a considerable burden on the EU if they were to join. This suggests that there may be thoughts about how to limit the burden if expansion to the East comes close to being a reality.

The GATT settlement of 1994, and the MacSharry reforms, will help to move EU prices closer to those of the world market. This should mean that there will be less need to support prices. But the EU budgetary costs of CAP reform are high, because of the income support given to farmers to compensate them for the fall in prices. There should not be a need to compensate CEEs for the higher prices they never had, if they become EU members. However, if some farmers in the Member States of the EU had income support and others did not, it would be unacceptable. This means that there would be a need to move the costs of the support from the EU to the budgets of the Member States.

The Structural Fund element of the budget might also need to be cut back. A possible area of saving might be the Cohesion Fund. This was designed as a side payment for accepting the Maastricht Agreement on the TEU. As such, it may not be available to the CEEs. However, there will still be a need to fund adequately the completion of the Trans-European Network, and to maintain progress in the improvement of the environment.

In addition, the need is to take further the progress towards reducing the role of the state sector, and liberalising the economies of the CEEs. Currencies will also need to become fully convertible, so that there can be full participation in the Exchange Rate Mechanism (ERM) of the European Monetary System (EMS).

Southern European states

Three Southern European states applied for membership of the EU within a short space of time: Turkey in 1987 and Cyprus and Malta in 1990.

Malta

Malta would have the least problem in adapting to membership. Its cultural heritage and consistent respect for human rights establishes its credentials as a European state. The Commission's Opinion on the Maltese application published in June 1993 stated, however, that the Maltese people must demonstrate their commitment to the EU by the introduction of measures to overhaul Malta's economic, financial and budgetary structures.

The clearest concern is the size of the state, and the problem of guaranteeing that it would receive appropriate treatment in the decision-making process. Also, with a population of 352 000, there are questions as to Malta's ability to discharge its responsibilities as a member of the EU, for example by hosting the meetings of the European Council.

Cyprus

Cyprus has a population of nearly 700 000, which means that if it did belong to the EU it would have similar problems to those of Malta. In addition, the occupation of the North of the island by Turkey has created a situation that needs to be resolved before membership proceeds. It is the Greek part of the island that has sued for membership.

The Commission's Opinion on the Cypriot application, published in June 1993, concluded that the European identity of Cyprus was unquestionable. But Cyprus would have to find a political solution to its ethnic division before EU membership could be agreed. It was felt that the division of the island undermined the development of pluralistic democracy and fundamental freedoms and human rights throughout the island.

A number of economic problems are associated with the North of Cyprus. However, rapid economic development has taken place in the South of the island, which would be enhanced as a result of EU membership. The leadership of the North of Cyprus objected to the conditions under which the Southern Cypriot government applied to join the EC. In the Commission Opinion of 1993, it was suggested that membership negotiations could begin as soon as the island was reunited.

Turkey

Turkey is the most problematic applicant state, with a population of 57 million and a great deal of its land mass in Asia. While Turkey had an important military function in the cold war as part of NATO, this role diminished with the decline of the Soviet Union. The Commission's Opinion in 1989 was that political and economic problems would not be overcome in the medium term. But as a way of strengthening the move towards democracy, the Association Agreement with Turkey was intensified. Particular problems to be overcome include high rates of inflation, weak political structures, an income level only about 10 per cent of the EU average, and a rapidly growing population. Many of the working population would like to migrate to higher paid employment in the EU. There are problems about the antagonism of Greece, exacerbated by the occupation of Cyprus. The 1994 Corfu Council of Ministers made EU membership an even more distant prospect. It was decided that the Greek part of Cyprus would be considered for membership, along with Malta, after Austria and the Nordic states had been dealt with. Prior to this it had been assumed that a federal solution to the Cyprus problem was a prerequisite to membership. This means that it is likely that both Greece and Greek Cyprus will be able to veto any Turkish application for EU membership.

The fact that EU membership is a distant prospect has meant that there has been an attempt to integrate Turkey into aspects of the EU without membership. In March 1993, a joint EC–Turkish steering committee was created, which aimed to establish the customs union. The customs union would have consequences for the highly protected Turkish home market.

There will still be restrictions on agricultural products, but it was hoped that by 1996

1. tariffs would be eliminated between Turkey and the EU

2. Turkey would have adopted the Common Customs Tariff for goods from third countries.

As Turkey is the only country that will be a member of the customs union without full membership of the EC, the Turkish government requested that EU funds be available to compensate for a loss of revenue in the order of £2 billion per annum. It is hoped that as the trade barriers are removed, Turkey will be more attractive to foreign investors.

Conclusions

In the mid to late 1980s, the deepening of the integration process was the EU priority, with the completion of the Single Market and the creation of a social dimension. The situation in the mid-1990s was very different, with the collapse of communism in the East, and the debate about widening the membership of the EU was at the forefront. The natural boundary of the EU ceased to be the wall that divided Germany, and the potential limits to the size of the Union were removed. The potential population of an enlarged EU could be as high as 450 million. Capital cities such as Prague and Budapest are closer to the natural heart of Europe than Madrid and Athens. EU membership for the CEEs therefore looks to be a real possibility. In 1994 the EU was taking about 50 per cent of all CEE exports, and access had improved significantly, with the exception of agricultural products. Part of the problem was that CEEs were able to make only limited use of the opportunities offered. Trade liberalisation is not, however, an exercise in altruism. The benefits for the EU consumer from a more liberal trade policy are considerable.

The changed political barriers within Europe also reduced the significance of neutrality, which enabled states such as Austria, Finland and Sweden to consider membership. (Ireland had been the first neutral state to achieve membership in 1973.)

Within the EU, each enlargement has brought questions about the extent to which adding further members will interfere with the process of integration. Is the relationship between widening the EU and deepening it concerned with a trade-off: for example, does more widening lead to less deepening? Or is it possible to achieve both at the same time? Certainly an EU with 20 or 30 members will look and operate very differently to the original EU of only six members in 1958.

A number of forces will tend to create pressures on the integration process. Not all states in Europe can withstand the competition caused by a Single Market, and certainly it is difficult to see full participation in an Economic and Monetary Union until well into the 21st century. Accompanying this is a need to consider how major policy areas such as Regional Policy and the Common Agricultural Policy might be reformed. Issues such as the creation of transport and energy networks are of immediate importance. With respect to foreign and security policies, the problem is create a feeling of greater security in the East that reinforces the efforts of the Western European Union, the North Atlantic Treaty Organisation (NATO) and the Partnership for Peace. Finally, there are issues concerning justice and home affairs. The opening of borders across Europe means that greater cooperation concerning drugs and organised crime is particularly important.

References

1. *Europe*, 21 July 1994, Europe documents, 2.
2. **House of Lords** (1992) *Enlargement of the Community*, Select Committee on the European Communities, 1st Report, Session 1992–93, HL Paper 5, p. 22.
3. *Financial Times*, 31 March 1994, 4.
4. *Financial Times*, 2 August 1994, 5.
5. *European Economy*, No. 52, 1993, 32.
6. **Commission**, (1993) Background Report, *Towards a Closer Association with the Countries of Central and Eastern Europe*, 17 February, ISEC/B6/93.
7. *The Economist*, 10 April 1993, 21.

Further reading

Anderson K (1993) *Implications of EU Expansion for European Agricultural Policies, Trade and Welfare*, CEPR Discussion Paper 829.

CEPR (1992) *Is Bigger Better? The Economics of EC Enlargement*.

Commission of EC (1993) *Europe in a Changing World*.

Commission (1993) The European Community as a world trade partner, *European Economy*, No. 52.

Commission (1993) Stable money – sound finances, *European Economy*, No. 53.

Economic Commission for Europe (1993) *Economic Bulletin for Europe*, Vol. 44.

Hopkinson N (1994) *Enlarging the European Union in Northern, Central and Eastern Europe*, Wilton Park Paper 8, HMSO, London.

House of Lords (1993) *EC Aid and Trade Policy*, Select Committee on the European Communities, 27th Report, Session 1992–93, HL Paper 123.

House of Lords (1994) *The Implications for Agriculture of the Europe Agreements*, Select Committee on the European Communities. 10th Report, Session 1993–94, HL paper 57 I&II.

Oxford Review of Economic Policy (1992) Macroeconomics of Transition in Eastern Europe, Vol. 8, No. 1, Spring.

OECD (1994) *Integrating Emerging Market Economies into the International Trading System*.

OECD (1992) *Reforming the Economies of Central and Eastern Europe*.

Panic M (1992) *Managing Reforms in the East European Countries*, Economic Commission for Europe, Discussion Papers, Vol. 1, 1991, United Nations.

Portes R (1994) Integrating the Central and East European Countries into the International Monetary System, CEPR Occasional Paper No. 14.

Portes R (ed.) (1993) *Economic Transformation in Central Europe, a Progress Report*, CEPR.

Redmond J (1993) *The Next Mediterranean Enlargement*, Dartmouth, Aldershot.

Rollo J and Smith A (1993) The Political Economy of Eastern European Trade: Why so Sensitive?, *Economic Policy: a European Forum*, No. 16, April.

Rosati D K (1992) *The Politics of Economic Reform in Central and Eastern Europe*, Occasional Paper No. 6.

INDEX